Juvenile Delinquency:
An Introduction

Consulting Editor: *Leonard Savitz,* *Temple University*

JUVENILE DELINQUENCY:
AN INTRODUCTION

Stephen Schafer

Northeastern University

Richard D. Knudten

Valparaiso University

340963

Random House *New York*

To The Women in Our Lives

Irene and Lili Schafer

Ruth, Mary and Susan Knudten

■ *Preface*

The problem of juvenile delinquency is not new to our generation, but it has now reached major proportions, due to the large numbers of juveniles in our society, the ready availability of manufactured goods, the social emphasis upon acquisitiveness, and disparities in human existence, among other factors.

Historically, regardless of age juvenile offenders were processed and punished in the same manner as adults. The English experiment in 1847 in holding separate hearings for juveniles and the creation of the juvenile court in Chicago in 1899, however, opened an era of a new approach to the juvenile and to the problem of delinquency. Although this involved a change of emphasis from mere punishment to a new concern for the solicitous care of the adolescent offender, the juvenile was spared the formality and inflexibility of adult criminal court procedures, except in serious cases, and was subject to the jurisdiction of the juvenile court judge, who was legally empowered to act as a father on behalf of the child. The juvenile court judge was authorized to make available the best treatment facilities and resources to the juvenile in cases of delinquency, neglect, and dependency. Relying heavily upon the social sciences for diagnosis and treatment and emphasizing a thorough investigation into the juvenile's environmental relationships, the judge and his agents attempted to pass beyond a concept of social control through punishment in the desire to rehabilitate the youth at an age when he is most flexible.

Now, after more than seventy years of implementation, the philosophy and practices of the juvenile court are currently under review. Questions pertaining to the rights of juveniles, the best methods for treatment of adolescents and youthful offenders, and the most effective means for social control have gained prominence as the number of youths involved in delinquency has reached a new high. Even the overdependence upon the use of juvenile court procedures to effect urban social control is now being questioned. Related to these issues, however, are such additional factors as the inadequacy of modern urban education, changes in familial roles, increased skill demands for employment, and the unavailability of significant social roles for many juveniles. As the issues mount and social concern increases, the debate over these problems continues. Some people hold the superficial view that delinquency can be controlled simply by listing the names of juveniles in the newspapers when they commit an offense or come to the attention of the police; others argue that such action merely hardens the juvenile's negative attitude and causes him to commit other violations to get his name in the papers. A few juvenile court judges even correlate delinquency with smoking, beer drinking, and wearing long hair, and naively believe that they can prevent delinquency by merely prohibiting such behavior. Others emphasize weekend lockups or community work projects as means of rehabilitation. Whereas no single solution exists to the problem of juvenile delinquency, almost all nations have had to grapple with it in relation to their national values and cultural goals. They have achieved varying degrees of success.

Juvenile delinquency is actually a problem of multiple variables. Delinquency follows no monolithic pattern but ranges widely from single truancy to sex offenses and possible homicides. Although several of the more serious juvenile offenses may be waived to the adult criminal court for disposition, they are exceptions. Most cases, if even brought to its attention, remain within the juvenile court's jurisdiction. Although many citizens criticize the increase in delinquency and conclude that it is due to the court's permissive probation practices, the release of juveniles under supervision within the community has been far more effective than commonly assumed. Whatever form the argument takes, the two basic positions were postulated many decades ago by Cesare Beccaria, who argued that crime must be punished in relationship to the degree of pleasure that the offense gives, and Cesare Lombroso, who maintained that the individual's problem and action must be evaluated carefully in order to effect a meaningful rehabilitation. Although there are no easy answers to the problem of juvenile delinquency, new research and experimentation offer much promise.

In this context, *Juvenile Delinquency: An Introduction* offers an intercultural examination of the delinquencies and offenses, adjudication and treatment of youth. In its eight parts, the volume examines the context of delinquency, the causes of delinquent conduct, variations in delinquency, sociocultural influences in delinquency, law enforcement and delinquency control, delinquency and the juvenile court, the treatment of juvenile delinquent and youthful offenders, and delinquency prevention and treatment in the context of social change. This work is intended to acquaint the student with the universality, as well as the diversity, of the delinquency problem. The volume attempts to blend the knowledge of generations with the challenges of the present, while describing the scope of the delinquency problem.

The authors must acknowledge the assistance of Leonard Savitz,

Theodore Caris, Arthur Strimling, and Elaine Rosenberg; our wives, Lili Schafer and Mary Knudten; and William Kuehn of Northeastern University and Natalie Rayder of Valparaiso University. But many others deserve credit. Cheryl Buser, Barbara Gerken, Linda Crowell, Judy Ernst, Trudy Heinecke, and Beverly McCollum, among others, receive our special thanks. We must also acknowledge the contributions of the administrations and library staffs of Northeastern University and Valparaiso University, and the cooperation of our students.

STEPHEN SCHAFER
RICHARD D. KNUDTEN

■ *Contents*

▪ *Introduction*

Hardly any aspect of the crime problem causes as much confusion or disagreement at does juvenile delinquency. Since the middle of the nineteenth century, when protests against the cruel character of criminal justice prompted a world-wide movement for the separate and distinct treatment of children and adolescents by juvenile courts, authors, scholars, and representatives of the mass media have tried to bring order and understanding to this complex problem. Despite a century of attention, however, no world-wide consensus on the concept and definition of delinquency, its causes, or the most effective treatment policies, programs, or methods has emerged.[1]

Juvenile delinquency is only one aspect of the total crime problem. As each aspect represents a primary threat to the general social order and stirs sensationalism and public excitement, all facets of the crime problem continue to receive universal attention. Parents' emotional involvement with their own children aggravates their special concern about the delinquent offenses of other youths, which they often visualize as the potential conduct of their own offspring. Sensationalizing delinquency and crime also suits those who believe that the delinquent of today will be the criminal of tomorrow. Well-meaning adults thus contribute their "home remedies" for the control and solution of the problem of deviance. The contradictory, inconsistent, and often mutually exclusive opinions of parents, teachers, psychiatrists, social workers, ministers, sociologists, and judges yield an excess of approaches to the delinquency problem.[2] These perspectives often attribute all "undesirable" conduct—including disobedience, resistance to discipline, disrespect, incorrigibility, smoking without permission, hawking stolen merchandise, and scavenging cigarette butts— to single causes, but it is difficult to discover the real link between delinquent conduct and the often presumed causal factors in the youth's past history.[3] Meanwhile the contributions of experts have frequently been overshadowed. Therefore antecedents and causes, mischief and crime become confused. The United Nations proposal in 1960 to define juvenile delinquency in more specific terms was undoubtedly motivated by this conceptual defect.[4]

The layman, whether through ignorance or choice, tends to minimize the principles of "care, protection, and prevention" that govern contempo- rary approaches to delinquency and to perceive delinquent behavior as necessarily dangerous to society. Unaccustomed to the idea of providing help or treatment for those who disrupt society, he prefers to punish them instead. The layman's perception of delinquency is, as a result, seriously distorted, partly also thanks to the exaggeration and repeated misrepre- sentations common in contemporary mass media. Unaware that only a fractional minority of the juvenile population is *technically delinquent* and that the overwhelming majority of those who are referred to juvenile courts need society's care and protection more than its hatred and condemnation, the layman unknowingly aggravates an already difficult situation: His basic misunderstanding of delinquency encourages an official and public at- titude of fear that often bears no relation to reality.[5] The layman, while urging that energetic measures be taken against juvenile delinquency, for- gets that his own adolescent conduct probably included behavior that could be labeled "delinquent" today.

More perceptive students of delinquency generally recognize their own previous delinquent conduct. Stephen Schafer discovered in a class- room experiment (conducted over a four-year period) in which students answered research questions that no more than three of fifty college stu- dents in an average juvenile-delinquency class denied having participated in some form of delinquent activity; only one had ever been brought before the juvenile court. Although the great majority of these university students admitted to such delinquencies as shoplifting, petty theft, "souvenir col- lecting from restaurants and hotels," truancy, disobedience to parental or scholastic authority, and early drinking, few had ever been arrested or brought to the attention of the court.[6]

A comparison by Austin L. Porterfield of the delinquent behavior of 337 Texas college students and of 2,000 delinquent boys brought before the Fort Worth juvenile court confirmed these findings. Although 43 per- cent of the college students admitted to truancy, none had ever been brought before a juvenile court. By contrast, 43 percent of the delinquent boys had been convicted for truancy. Although 50 percent of the college students admitted to offenses against property for which none had been arrested, approximately 27 percent of the delinquent group had been booked for theft.[7]

Fred J. Murphy, Mary M. Shirley, and Helen Witmer report similar findings and suggest that court statistics are wholly inadequate to measure the volume of illegal youthful conduct in the community.[8] Youthful mis- conduct, in fact, is so frequent that even a moderate increase in arrests for delinquency could create the semblance of a "delinquency wave" without the slightest change in adolescent behavior. James F. Short and Ivan F. Nye also found little difference in quantity between the delinquent activities of high-school boys in general and those sent to training schools.[9]

The serious disparities between the official reports of delinquency rates and the personally admitted volume of delinquent conduct raises serious doubts about the accuracy of current delinquency statistics. Admittedly, all known delinquencies are not recorded in the Federal Bureau of Investigation's *Uniform Crime Reports* or other compendiums of delinquency data. Disparities have even been found between the data gathered by professional researchers and by peer investigators.[10] The potential value of self-report instruments is clear. Although the greatest value of these techniques may be to offer insight into the number of "delinquents" in a community rather than into the number of "delinquent acts," they ultimately depend upon respondents' willingness to provide clear and accurate answers. Because respondents tend to give socially acceptable answers, the validity of the self-report varies with the attitude of the respondent.[11]

The discovery of many former undetected delinquents who have become successful citizens in later life raises the troublesome, but pertinent, question, "At what point and why did our present respectable friends decide to mend their ways?"[12] Not all professional students of delinquency are prepared to answer this question. Different professional groups offer different interpretations of youthful antisocial behavior.

■ *The Legalistic Approach*

Proponents of the legal approach to juvenile misconduct customarily prefer that offenses and penalties be described in specific terms. Lawyer and judge are inclined to demand that, first, a specific charge be lodged against the defendant; second, the charge be expressed in specific legal terms; third, the offense be proved conclusively; and fourth, protection against false, misleading, irrelevant, or prejudicial evidence be given to the accused during trial.[13] Questions of causation are of little relevance to legalists. The act and not the actor is the main subject of concern.

Despite the separation of delinquency from adult crime and the establishment of a distinct system of juvenile justice, which can be credited to the commendable efforts of lawyers at the end of the nineteenth century, the legalistic attitude toward juvenile delinquency remains too formal. Reflecting its historical background, it is tied closely to the principle of *nullum crimen sine lege* ("no crime without the law"). Although most, if not all, practicing lawyers tend to view delinquency almost exclusively as a legal category of crimes committed by juveniles, their attitudes differ markedly from the deeper understanding of the problem apparent among legal philosophers.

■ *The Social-Welfare Approach*

The broader approaches common to social work and psychology offer a sharp contrast to the rigid and restricted legalistic attitude. The law's preoccupation with individuals who have violated specific and official legal norms is modified in this approach by a humanistic concern with the "whole individual," and illegal acts are viewed merely as symptoms of underlying personal or social maladjustment. Delinquency, part of the general problem of social welfare, can largely be solved, adherents of this approach believe, by the child's readjustment to the social situation, rather than by reorganization of the social fabric.

Although plans and programs vary, social-welfare agencies aid individuals and groups to "promote their well-being in harmony with the needs of their families and the community."[14] When directed more specifically to the problem of delinquency, however, "social work," as Walter A. Friedlander has suggested, "assists young people in their efforts to abide by the rules of social conduct," including "the development of social attitudes and modes of behavior which are not necessarily embodied in legal provisions."[15] As social welfare emphasizes the service, or helping, approach, it encourages the widest possible examination of each aspect of a child's development in the search for indicators of future deviant behavior. The overeager social worker may, as a result, observe "delinquency" even when the danger of crime *is not and never has been really present.*

■ *The Psychological Approach*

The psychological approach is basically similar to that of social welfare, for it, too, interprets the concept of delinquency from a broad perspective. Although it does not neglect the role of social forces, it focuses primarily on the development of the individual personality. On the assumption that an unhealthy or defective physical and emotional developmental pattern results in psychic disturbances that in turn produce antisocial or criminal behavior,[16] the psychological approach supposes an intrapsychic struggle, occurring as early as the latency period and stimulating the development of a delinquent personality.[17] The emotional disorders of childhood may lead to delinquent behavior like mild disobedience and recalcitrance or even more serious delinquent acts.[18] Although differing schools of psychological thought emphasize particular facets of the total approach, all agree that the theory of individual maladjustment caused by personality disorders offers the best explanation of delinquency. The entire development of individual personality, beginning in earliest childhood, must be examined in detail if personality disorders are to be diagnosed and treated effectively.

■ *The Sociological Approach*

Sociology offers a unique approach to and insight into the problem of delinquency, as it attempts to reconcile many other approaches. As the individual delinquent is viewed within the context of his cultural group, sociologists insist that delinquent conduct can be understood only in terms of the social relationships surrounding it. Delinquency and crime cannot therefore be divorced from the normative organization, the youth's relationships to the organization and to the other members of his group, and the structure of his society. This approach provides the perspective from which the authors of this book view the problem of juvenile delinquency.

NOTES

1. U.N. Department of Economic and Social Affairs, *New Forms of Juvenile Delinquency: Their Origin, Prevention and Treatment* (New York: 1960), p. 51. See also Tadeusz Grygier, "A Concept of Juvenile Delinquency: An Obituary Notice" (unpublished paper; Montreal: August–September 1965).

2. Sophia M. Robison, *Juvenile Delinquency: Its Nature and Control* (New York: 1960), p. 3.

3. U.N. Department of Economic and Social Affairs, *op. cit.*, p. 35.

4. *Ibid.*, p. 64.

5. *Ibid.*, p. 62. Similar findings are reported in the Child Welfare Department of New South Wales, Australia, *Annual Report* (1959).

6. Stephen Schafer, "An Attempt to Find Unreported Delinquency" (unpublished study; Boston: 1966).

7. Austin L. Porterfield, *Youth in Trouble* (Austin, Tex.: 1946).

8. Fred J. Murphy, Mary M. Shirley, and Helen Witmer, "The Incidence of Hidden Criminality," *American Journal of Orthopsychiatry*, 16 (October 1946), 686–696. See also Thorsten Sellin and Marvin E. Wolfgang, *The Measurement of Delinquency* (New York: 1964), pp. 55 ff.

9. James F. Short, Jr., and Ivan F. Nye, "Extent of Unrecorded Juvenile Delinquency: Tentative Conclusion," *Journal of Criminal Law, Criminology and Police Science*, 29 (November–December 1958), 296–302.

10. Robert H. Hardt and George E. Bodine, *Development of Self-Report Instruments in Delinquency Research* (Syracuse: 1965), pp. 1–12.

11. *Ibid.*, p. 19.

12. Robison, *op. cit.*, p. 7.

13. Paul W. Tappan, *Juvenile Delinquency* (New York: 1949), p. 4.

14. Walter A. Friedlander, *Introduction to Social Welfare* (2nd ed.; Englewood Cliffs, N.J.: 1961), p. 4.

15. *Ibid.,* p. 419.

16. David Abrahamsen, *The Psychology of Crime* (New York: 1960), p. 56. See also Kate Friedlander, *The Psycho-Analytical Approach to Juvenile Delinquency* (New York: 1947).

17. Theresa Benedek, "Personality Development," in Franz Alexander and Helen Ross, eds., *Dynamic Psychiatry* (Chicago: 1957), p. 94.

18. Margaret W. Gerard, "Emotional Disorders of Childhood," in Franz Alexander and Helen Ross, *Dynamic Psychiatry* (Chicago: 1957), p. 197. The role of parents in the transmission of delinquent values is examined in Beatrice Simcox Reiner and Irving Kaufman, *Character Disorders in Parents of Delinquents* (New York: 1959).

Part One

THE CONTEXT OF DELINQUENCY

Chapter 1

■ *The Nature of Delinquency*

Although crime and delinquency are basically similar concepts, they differ with respect to the age of those who can be regarded as lawbreakers, the range of behavior that is defined as lawbreaking, the treatment reserved for lawbreakers, the method of defining illegal conduct, and the type of behavior prohibited and the reasons for the proscriptions. As most crimes are also delinquencies in that they are acts of which society disapproves, crime must be understood before delinquency can be comprehended. Not every delinquency, however, is a crime. And some crimes, like statutory rape or the corruption of the morals of a minor, cannot be delinquencies.

According to criminal law, a crime is conduct or an action that is defined and codified in law as a crime. Although this definition of crime reverts to itself, all criminal codes continue to define types of behavior as criminal according to the various individual criminal laws. Functionally, criminal law exists in order to determine what kind of action will be labeled "murder," "shoplifting," and so on. Criminal law, therefore, determines norms or action (*norma agendi*) and also authorizes the executives of the state to apply penal sanctions, that is, punishment, in order to enforce observance of these norms.

The formal legal definition of crime upholds the principle that no crime exists unless it is so defined by the law (*nullum crimen sine lege*). The principle operates as a civil guarantee, allowing punishment only for conduct that has been defined is criminal *prior* to its occurrence.[1] Although this principle developed at the time of the French Revolution in response to the previous arbitrary processes of criminal justice, it led to the formation of rather inflexible legal procedures, which ultimately hindered the court in dealing with unforeseen new forms of behavior that, though basically similar to previously defined criminal actions, were sufficiently different to cause uncertainty over whether or not existing law could be applied to them. Theft, for example, was originally defined as the stealing of another person's "thing" or property. When the "stealing" of electric current

3

by disconnecting the meter first occurred, however, the question arose whether or not electric current could be regarded as a "thing" and therefore as an object of theft. Attempts to make allowances for such unforeseen developments led to the use of analogy[2] to bridge the gap between the law and possible future "criminal" actions. As judgment by analogy extends the power of the judge, eases the principle of *nullum crimen sine lege*, and permits some legal uncertainty and the judicial misuse of power, it has remained controversial and generally unaccepted.

Crime, then, as defined in criminal law, involves disturbance of some legally protected interest. The disturbance of any interest not under the protection of criminal law by definition cannot be a crime.[3] As private property is in most societies protected by the criminal code, theft is usually a crime. Because private loans are, by contrast, protected only by civil law, debt is not a crime. Nonpayment of debt was, however, a crime under English common law; this definition was discarded in the United States, possibly because of pressures brought to bear by former indentured servants. Accordingly, which specific interests are sheltered depends upon the legislators who draw up and pass criminal law. Although certain behavior may be despised by public opinion, condemned by the church, or disapproved by society as a whole, nevertheless it will be regarded as a crime, that is, a criminal offense, only if the legislators so define it.

Legislators' values and attitudes toward the necessity and usefulness of particular types of behavior determine their responses to conduct which they ultimately define as criminal. (Pressures brought to bear by constituents help to shape these values and attitudes.) If particular behavior is a threat to vital interests, they will normally attempt to protect these interests through the enactment of prohibitive legislation or severe sanctions. Consequently, the increase in crimes against property during periods of economic depression may lead them to impose heavier penalties for economic violations. They may also find it essential in wartime to restrict free trade temporarily and to define trade violations as crimes in order to deprive the enemy of essential goods and to ensure supplies for their own country. Ultimately, however, legislators' philosophical postures, rather than their perceptions of immediate dangers inherent in certain activities, tend to determine their attitudes toward particular forms of conduct. Their religious predispositions, for example, may determine whether or not they find it necessary to restrict some religious practices. Although a legislator may personally object to charging people with treason during peacetime, he may support restriction of the freedom of speech during periods of war and support criminal penalties for those who, he feels, endanger his country's safety by presenting certain points of view publicly. The views of his constituents will generally play an important part in these types of decisions.

Because social norms develop from folkways, mores, tradition, and necessity, the specific content of criminal law is constantly changing. Crime can therefore be regarded only in relative terms, for its definition is never unalterable. Although criminal law is necessary to safeguard order, the contemporary definition of order depends upon the existing lawmaking process and the interests that control society. Crime is therefore no longer regarded as the manifestation of the devil's power against the divine order.[4] Instead, it is realistically interpreted as a form of opposition by human beings to a dominant social order structured and operated by other human beings.

Criminal law represents the interests of the ruling social powers who codify their advantage in order to maintain power. Using their legitimating powers in an essentially coercive manner, they legalize one set of human aspirations, meanwhile attempting to thwart the aspirations and goals of those who might challenge their interests. They believe that acceptance of their goals by individuals and groups is in the best interests of society; they regard those who define their own goals in opposition to those of the dominant group as potential criminals and as threats to social stability. The structure of socially approved goal fulfillment is not rigid and static, however, but flexible and dynamic. Not only do the character and content of human aspirations change, but the political structure of society and the ethos of the era may change as well. Legislation, the supreme expression of organized society and its dominant elements, continually redefines what is acceptable or unacceptable. As lawbreaking depends upon lawmaking, the specific nature of crime is always changing too.

Because the views of the ruling interests should and ought to coincide with the general beliefs of the groups that they rule, some degree of positive correlation between general group goals and legislation exists under normal circumstances. "Legislation," William Graham Sumner once remarked, "must be consistent with the mores."[5] Sometimes, however, public attitudes and legislation do not coincide, as can be seen, for example, in much of the present antidiscrimination laws. In such instances the law may act as an instrument of group education (helpful or harmful, depending upon one's point of view) as it attempts to create new attitudes, aspirations, and avenues of achievement and to change or eliminate older ones. In both post-Reconstruction southern segregationist and modern national antidiscriminatory laws, certain people's goals have been restricted, whereas those of others have been encouraged.[6] In each instance, the law has served as a vital factor in the socialization and education process.[7] Criminal law, as Rudolf Jhering recognized, is a good indicator of the value that a society places on its norms, just as prices indicate the value of economic assets. Both fluctuate.[8]

Many types of human behavior that were once approved have now been rejected and declared criminal, whereas other actions that were once unacceptable and regarded as criminal are currently accepted as legitimate. The slaughter of deer, for example, was once a capital crime in ancient China, Britain, and other lands; the killing of a newborn child, on the other hand, was customary under certain conditions among the Eskimos and Fiji Islanders. Deer hunting, however, has since become a favorite form of recreation, and the infliction of harm on children has been redefined as a serious criminal offense everywhere.

Those in control of society are not always able to bring about changes in human behavior in exactly the same manner. Once acceptable behavior, for example, may be made criminal simply through the creation of a new law. If previously prohibited conduct is no longer to be regarded as a criminal offense, however, a change can be accomplished without the formal elimination of existing legislation through the tacit consent of ruling interests not to enforce the law. The well-known "blue laws" of the United States, particularly those in New England, illustrate this point. Although previously prohibited conduct may not have been specifically repealed from the criminal code, public opinion, in effect, nullifies earlier definitions of illegitimacy.[9]

Such group decisions to legitimate previously unacceptable behavior are not exclusively or predominantly motivated by monetary considerations. Although dominant groups may periodically misuse or twist the legislative process to achieve their own goals, generally they define normative or criminal behavior and conduct in terms of existing social values, especially in a democratic society, in which the legislative, enforcement, and judicial processes are subject to various kinds of political review. On the other hand, in societies in which ruling political interests are unchallenged by other political and social forces, criminal law may beome a tool by which the government guarantees its own stability. In such an instance the law may actually define the value and thus create crime, rather than simply defining what is criminal according to existing values. In the post-Revolution foundation of Soviet criminal law, for example, it was assumed that crime is a special feature of social relations, which are affected by the continuing struggle between the social classes.[10] Subsequent changes in Soviet society, however, stimulated many redefinitions of criminal law. As a result the criterion of "social danger," defined according to the political needs of the day, replaced the more rigid and puritanical Marxist interpretations of the Revolution and determined the direction and content of existing Soviet criminal law at any particular time. As the current Soviet concept of "social danger" and therefore of crime is politically determined, constantly modified and officially interpreted according to the ideals of the regime, the power of the dominant political group determines what conduct is permitted, prohibited, or punished according to its ideology.

■ Public Knowledge of the Law

Criminal law consists of norms of behavior, established by legislative definitions and omissions and representing the legitimate ways in which human beings can fulfill their aspirations. Norms, however, have meaning only if the public is familiar with them and understands their implications. Although common sense suggests that no one should be obliged to conform to unknown norms, in the application of the criminal law ignorance of the law is generally no excuse. Evidence suggests, however, that the presumed popular knowledge of the criminal law is merely a social fiction.

Modern society is characterized by a multitude of rules and regulations presenting the appearance of an intricate network of legal pitfalls. As most people are involved daily in various types of legal relationships and are constantly subjected to various orders and prohibitions, they may stumble unwittingly into crime at any moment. Yet, although all the vast number of rules that order their lives are unknown to them, only a small percentage of the people in any society commit crimes. Criminal law, which the ordinary citizen understands only superficially, represents, however, only one system of rules that may govern human conduct. Although it is a formal and written body of social rules, the criminal code may be neutralized by other normative systems supported by a network of inter-relationships.

The mere formal publication of legal codes, in an effort to prevent unfamiliarity with the law, does little to acquaint people with their contents. Although most people, especially children, never see any official regulations or statute books, the majority of them do not commit serious crimes or break the law at all. As other social norms offer explicit directions on these matters, it is generally unnecessary to inform people that murder and theft are legally forbidden. On the other hand, some people, though well aware of the requirements and prohibitions of informal norms and formal laws, do commit crimes. Herbert Spencer recognized, for example, that some people who would never violate the social code prescribing the color of the ties to be worn at formal gatherings might not be adverse to occasional smuggling.[11] Similarly, a modern executive who regards it as *de rigueur* to dress properly may willingly engage in the kind of illegal price-fixing maneuvers that resulted in the conviction of several high Westinghouse and General Electric executives a few years ago.

Although one person may comply meticulously with religious or social rules, he still may not obey all the provisions of the criminal law. Conversely, another person may not subscribe to religious values and doctrines or to the formal principles of an ordered society but may still avoid crime. But, whereas some citizens who are familiar with the criminal code become "clients" of the police, others who know nothing about its contents and never commit infractions knowingly may become its victims. By what process do law-abiding citizens learn society's laws? How do they become aware of the many orders and prohibitions that, when violated, may lead to punitive sanctions?

■ The Problem of Free Will

Any answers to the preceding questions are incomplete without previous recognition of the philosophical and social implications of the concept of free will.[12] The problem of the extent to which the exercise of human will is determined by external forces is, however, generally insoluble. Immanuel Kant, for example, noted that a thousand years of work had been expended in vain on its solution;[13] modern philosophy is still no closer to an answer. Yet any attempt to explain the causes for crime and delinquency and to assess personal and social responsibility must inevitably include consideration of the problem of human will and the law of causality.[14]

In John E. Coogan's criticism of criminologists for neglecting this problem he not only encouraged discussion but also defended the concept of freedom of the will.[15] Paul W. Tappan, however, has observed that meaningful discussion is highly limited by lack of consensus on the definition and connotations of the term "free will," which has remained subject to different interpretations.[16] Unsurprisingly, therefore, criminological literature has, with a few exceptions, avoided the more fundamental problem. The debate on *determinism* and *indeterminism*, however, has to date produced only the conclusion that the extreme determinist explanation of causality is as invalid when applied to the human will as is the extreme indeterminist metaphysical position. Both are grandiose hypotheses without empirical support. The strictly *determinist* point of view that behavior is merely the automatic result of external forces disallows the existence of free will. Strict *indeterminism* maintains that will is causally unrelated to reality and can therefore be only an illusion. Yet one of the main characteristics of the will is that it can both influence and be influenced by external forces.

Only *moderate determinism* and *moderate indeterminism* offer adequate explanations of the problem of free will. Although both are mixtures of deterministic and indeterministic elements, the distinction, not always recognized by the proponents of either view, rests on the different ratios of the two elements. This distinction is less often found in the differential explanations of human will and more often in their results. Both points of view assume, however, that the problem of free will cannot be solved by a dualistic doctrine that recognizes two independent and unrelated worlds: the world of empirical reality (*mundus sensibilis*) and the world of intellect (*mundus intelligibilis*). In the actual universe, empirical and intellectual forces interact causally, and human will cannot be confined to either realm.

The general problem of free will includes dimensions of culture, ideas, values, and individual personality, and each individual will have a different amount of free will. Before a decision is made, the functioning will of the socioethical personality (the personality subject to social and ethical norms) weighs the values involved and makes an appropriate choice. The choice is thus determined not by a conflict of causal forces but rather by this weighing of values. Although the individual personality is formed around innate or inherited characteristics, it generally emerges from the culture in which the individual is a participant. The human will can consider alternatives and arrive at decisions only to the extent that it is rooted in a particular culture. In this sense human free will poses no *metaphysical* mystery, and its possessor should be regarded as an intelligent and reasoning being within the limitations posed by his culture. His personality, derived from both inherited predispositions and traditional culture, represents an unequal fusion of both. Normal social interaction thus may affect the socioethical personality, but human will influences its eventual impact. The law of causation, which asserts that every event has a cause, remains the primary factor, however, despite some freedom of the will, which is ultimately limited to the residual area unclaimed by the surrounding culture or inherent qualities.

Although its limitations cannot be ignored, free will must still be considered an integral part of the problems of crime and delinquency. Both are affected by the structure of positive and negative norms and sanctions in the existing social order. Although it is absurd to require that individuals who are not entirely able to know, understand, or adjust their own wills adhere to these norms, most societies do just that. It is not unreasonable, however, to expect compliance by individuals who understand the norms but fail or refuse to fulfill their demands.

Social norms that influence and limit an individual's will are always defended and justified by the social power that establishes them. But the duty of society to inform its members of these rules and make compliance possible is frequently overlooked. Although socioethical responsibility, not necessarily identical with legal responsibility, can be assumed only for those who *are* able to exercise some degree of "freedom" of the will, the limits of socioethical responsibility are reflected in the limits of legal responsibility and in the type of treatment meted out to norm violators. The assumption of the existence of limited free will and of a socioethical personality that guides and directs it helps to explain why people show different levels of awareness of the contents of criminal law and why some people conform to normative behavior and others do not.

■ *The Socioethical Personality and Crime*

Literate societies, in which particular norms have been incorporated into civil and criminal codes, have also developed additional social norms, coexistence, bodies of social and ethical orders, obligations, and prohibitions that transcend the limits of legal rules and also govern social behavior. These *cultural norms*[17] are presumably acquired by individuals through socialization. It is hoped that they will become the foundation of the future personality. All participants in a culture are expected to learn these norms in the course of their personality development. By the time they have reached adulthood they thus should respect human life, corporeal integrity, individual reputation, private property, and personal and social freedom, without ever having seen the criminal code.

Socioethical rules, particularly in large urban and industrial states, are not as homogeneous or as precise as is criminal law. Not only do they vary in different subcultures, but they are also influenced by social class, occupational and religious commitment, political preference, ethnic and racial ascription, economic capacity, geographic region, and community character. Although each community possesses its own subculture and rules, outstanding personalities may wield disproportionate influence on the norms for sizable segments of the population. Any dominant culture is, however, continually changing, as evident, for example, in the changing attitudes toward birth control and use of contraception in the United States during the last 100 years. Such change should not be surprising, for socioethical norms differ from society to society and from time to time. Although some religions of ancient Cyprus and Lydia recognized prostitution as an established and legitimate institution, for example, practically all societies today try to suppress or to regulate it. Although the citizen of the Western world possesses the political right to read any newspaper he wishes, a citizen of a country under Soviet influence or rule may have political difficulties if he attempts to fulfill a desire to read *The New York Times* or the London *Observer*.

The norms of any one society are not identical with its criminal law but are more diverse.[18] "The actual ethical law, the code of positive morality, of a country," M. J. Sethna has written, "is a huge mirror in which is reflected the image of its culture."[19] Metaphysical and natural legal theorists prefer to conclude that law and morals correspond, even though they may not be identical in meaning or content, for essentially this reason. Although both are laws of behavior and generally are mutually supportive, they nevertheless do not necessarily correspond and are rarely identical in application.

In any case, criminal law cannot avoid consideration of moral standards and socioethical values. Morality and law as set forth in the Ten Commandments, one of the earliest civilized criminal codes, were held to be identical in source and content. Similarly, all early laws, insofar as their various elements can be identified, were mixtures of religious, moral, ethical, and social rules. The moral point of view embodied in Roman law, for example, made possible the integration of different legal departments, such as criminal law and constitutional law, within the body of civil law. Since the time of the earliest legal formulations, it has thus been largely impossible to distinguish fully between the socioethical code and the criminal law. Should the formal concepts of crime and delinquency ever be detached from the concept of moral and socioethical standards, consistent legislators could, as explained in Karl Binding's norm theory,[20] easily be led to the conclusion that all crimes should receive uniform punishments.

Social norms and criminal law are vague and precise respectively in their descriptions of expected and acceptable behavior. The punishment of murder, theft, larceny, shoplifting, robbery, or any other criminal offense is precisely defined in criminal law, but socioethical norms are more general and demand only that citizens do not kill one another and do not take what belongs to one another. As such norms operate within a broader frame of reference than does formal criminal law, general statements are assumed to be sufficient to acquaint the personality with specific demands of the criminal code, so that he may act as his own internal tribunal in deciding what he may or may not legitimately do. Socioethical norms therefore serve as a signaling apparatus that warns the individual when he is about to commit a crime.

Criminal law also penalizes behavior that has little to do with conduct condemned by the moral or socioethical code. Laws dealing with asocial and amoral behavior that are inapplicable to and unaffected by the internal signaling apparatus are also designed to coordinate social duties and activities.[21] Ordinances defining parking regulations, for example, impose social duties in support of the administrative, rather than the ethical, order. The administrative importance of the law is all that matters in thousands of similar cases; the moral code is almost irrelevant. The content of such laws which regulate asocial behavior can be learned only by careful reading of the text of the relevant regulations, by observing the rules of etiquette, and generally by following the daily practices of the majority in a society.

The criminal code may also include "immoral" laws that are thrust upon the socioethical personality by the threat of enforcement. Neither morally conceived nor administratively necessary, they may reflect the crude interests of dominant political groups acting in their own immoral or amoral interests. As these laws exist largely to facilitate the interests of a dominant political power and are not based upon prevalent moral standards or social norms, the normal socializing process does not and cannot familiarize the person with their contents. Such laws frequently contradict moral and socioethical standards, and the latter therefore offer little or no assistance to the human will in resolving tensions between social norms and legal demands upon the socialized socioethical personality. Consequently, fear or respect for the power behind the law, rather than harmony between the ethical and criminal codes, stimulates observance of the criminal code.

The fact that criminal laws have periodically been proclaimed in the name of morality suggests that these laws must have moral or pseudomoral sanction in order to obtain maximum legitimacy. The coercion of the Middle Ages or the mass murders of the Nazi regime, all legitimated by distorted criminal codes that have presumed inherent moral superiority, offer examples of the intrinsic dangers to the establishment of legal rules without the validation of ethics and tradition. In these instances, internalized and traditional socioethical rules have been replaced by formal definitions propagated by the state. Legitimate behavior has been dependent upon such definition; conduct has been governed by legal directives.

The recent tendency to define crime merely as *antisocial* behavior is related to legislative definition of crime.[22] As the criterion of what is anti-social leads easily to justification of some criminal laws on the grounds of political utility, this trend may be socially realistic but dangerous. Although criminal law defined in these terms may still help to protect society, the abandonment or deemphasis of the ethical element can result only in weak and inadequate definitions of crime and delinquency and the added threat of arbitrary laws. Although its antisocial character is an essential criterion of crime, crime must nevertheless always be subject to socioethical examination and evaluation.

■ Criminometrics: The Measurement of Responsibility[23]

If a socioethical personality is the basic factor in decision making by the human will, it seems necessary to assume that the will resists criminal or delinquent decisions and socially disapproved behavior. The normal process of socialization encourages early internalization of values that are regarded by the society, the dominant political power, or both as non-criminal and nondelinquent in nature. It also supports the development of behavior patterns consistent with these values. During socialization, however, the will is continually exposed to the temptations of crime and delinquency, which may corrupt the personality. The handling of large sums of money by a bank cashier, for example, undoubtedly exerts pressure toward embezzlement. Shoplifting or theft may tempt penniless parents who fear that their children may otherwise starve. The desire for quick riches may act as an incentive for robbery or check forgery. The fear of losing a partner's affection to a rival may lead to consideration of murder. Pathological processes that may be manifested in physical defects, menopause, schizophrenic delusions, or any of thousands of desires and fears press people toward crime in spite of previous socialization against participation in criminal acts. A vast array of external and internal factors of varying intensity are always tempting the will toward criminal conduct and neutralization of socioethical personality restraints.

A deterministic view of free will necessarily maintains that such factors alone cause decisions to participate in crime and that the individual is not accountable for his act, for he is unable to decide otherwise. The indeterministic view, in contrast, places responsibility upon the person, arguing that the choice of legitimate or illegitimate conduct is his alone. Realistically, however, the individual's responsibility for his criminal or delinquent behavior depends upon the resolution of the conflict between socioethical resistance and pressures favoring criminal conduct.

The actual degree of individual responsibility for any antisocial behavior is best illustrated by a formula expressing the relationship between socioethical resistance (SER) and pressures favoring criminal participation (CP). CP exerted against SER results in the individual's limited socioethical responsibility factor (LSER). The relationship can be stated

$$\frac{SER}{CP} = LSER.$$

Normally, socioethical resistance and criminal pressures are of comparable strength, thus canceling one another and leaving what may be called the *criminometric average*.[24] If the criminometric average is weighted in favor of socioethical resistance, crime normally will not occur. A bank cashier or a store clerk, for example, is presumed to possess socioethical resistance sufficient to withstand the typical desire to steal bank assets or store receipts. On the other hand, the criminometric average may be weighted in favor of criminal pressures. Although the pressures may be such that most members in a society could resist them easily, a particular individual may confront them with more limited socioethical resistance, which may be inadequate to withstand them. Although shortcomings in the socialization process or some psychophysical defect may explain a chronic tendency to criminal or delinquent action, temporary conditions or transitory psychophysical disturbances may also cause chronic deviance patterns. The extent of socialization varies widely from individual to individual, time to time, and even place to place. The degrees of resistance and pressure affect one another in various ways. Although higher than usual socioethical resistance is generally expected of a person who occupies a responsible position or high status, for example, his special situation may actually foster increased pressure toward crime.

The use of the criminometric model to determine degrees of criminal responsibility cannot be as precise and accurate as a mathematical formula. The dimensions of delinquency and crime cannot be measured simply in mathematical terms. Moral, socioethical, or criminal responsibility cannot be measured as pounds of fish or yards of cloth are measured. Nevertheless, although our tentative criminometric equation lacks scientific precision, it serves its intended function as a guide to understanding the problem of assigning responsibility for crime.

■ Delinquency as an Extension of the Concept of Crime

The term *delinquency* is basically similar to the term *criminality*. Both express relationships between the existing lawmaking power structure and the lawbreaking of some members of society. Although the main distinction is largely quantitative rather than qualitative, the term *delinquency* (an offense commonly committed by a juvenile between the ages of seven and sixteen to eighteen) is used as a convenience to indicate an extension of the concept of criminality and a group of individuals differentiated by age from ordinary criminals.[25] Without an adjustment in the definition of criminality, the illegal acts committed by juveniles and adults would be considered equivalent. The delinquency concept, however, permits a distinction between levels of responsibility. As a result, a murder committed by a fifteen-year-old boy may be regarded as a form of juvenile delinquency, whereas the same act by a forty-year-old man is held to be a criminal act. Similarly, shoplifting by a forty-year-old man is defined as criminal conduct, whereas the same activity by a fifteen-year-old boy is called "delinquent behavior." The two terms also involve radical distinctions in preliminary investigation procedures, court proceedings, and penal consequences. Although these differences logically result from the recognition of the age differences of those who violate laws, to this point they do not reflect any difference in the specific violations. Murder, whether committed by juvenile or adult, still results in the death of another; but the juvenile murderer may be sent to a foster home and the adult sentenced to life imprisonment or death.

The relations among pressures toward criminality, socioethical resistance, and the ability of the socioethical personality to distinguish between right and wrong differ among individuals for a variety of reasons. Not only do human beings fail to act identically, but the circumstances in which they live are generally somewhat dissimilar. Age differences alone, for example, result in markedly different socioethical personality achievement, socioethical resistance, and exposure to criminal pressures. Because adults are believed to possess more thoroughly socialized and mature personalities, greater socioethical resistance, and less vulnerability to criminal pressures, their crimes automatically bring different consequences to them. The complete concept of juvenile delinquency, as distinguished from criminality, however, depends upon age differentials and an *additional aspect of criminality*, called *crime plus*. The *plus* refers to additional dangers that may lead juveniles into criminality. For example, if an adult does not report to his job, he may be fired; if a juvenile does not attend school, he may be taken to juvenile court. *Crime plus* suggests the fundamental necessity for society to protect and care for juveniles, who are more in danger of succumbing to pressures toward crime. Although the mature adult is presumed to possess a developed socioethical personality and consequently a reasonable degree of socioethical resistance to ordinary pressures toward crime, the development of the socioethical personality and the maturation of socioethical resistance are necessarily incomplete in the juvenile. Because he represents an incompletely developed physical, physiological, and psychological organism, his apperception of moral standards and socioethical values has not necessarily reached the level of maturity necessary to resist even ordinary crime pressures.

The inability of most juveniles to attain an adequate level of socioethical development is largely the result of biological factors, among other causes. Even under the most favorable circumstances, a large majority of juveniles is unable to equal adult socioethical personality strength and resistance. Criminal pressures, however, are not subject to biological factors and fail to distinguish between juveniles and adults. They continue to operate regardless of the fact that many of the individuals affected by them, that is, juveniles, have not yet acquired the socioethical strength necessary to resist them. As a result, juveniles, largely because of their ages, are continually in danger of succumbing to criminal pressures that they are psychologically and biologically unprepared to meet. Although a juvenile may be subject to less than average criminal pressure, it may still outweigh his socioethical resistance. Although he is supposed to avoid violating norms, he cannot elude crime by himself if the pressures toward crime outweigh his resistance. The term "delinquency" therefore implies not only a specific age group but also responses to the variable challenges and influences that impinge upon resistance capabilities within that group. For this reason, the period of the juvenile's life before he commits a delinquent act is sometimes called "predelinquency" or "potential delinquency." These appellations, however, seem inappropriate, for they actually refer to delinquency itself.[26] The vast literature on crime and delinquency generally assumes that "precriminal" delinquency covers practically anything that may happen in a child's or juvenile's life, a concept that ultimately "contributes to the inflation of the problem."[27] Such an indefinite extension of the term, without any restriction to a workable framework, may easily lead to a totalitarian control of every facet of a child's life.

Theoretically, it can be predicted that a juvenile will commit a crime if he is subjected to criminal pressures with which his socioethical resistance is insufficient to cope. Although this principle appears vague, any attempt to define causal relationships further may lead to error. Any full-scale attempt to assess the pressures favoring crime and the juvenile's potential response to them may result in mistaken speculation and unwarranted intervention. Noninvestigation, on the other hand, may result in permitting license to substitute for excessive restraint. Error is possible in either direction.[28]

If the juvenile has already entered the *crime zone* (an area that includes all punishable criminal offenses) his violation stimulates a form of legal intervention that is designed to prevent further crimes and to enlist care and protection for him. Conversely, if he has entered only the *danger zone* (for example, by becoming a truant), which is itself an area of delinquency, society intervenes in order to prevent the possibility of crime and to redirect the juvenile toward normative goals. Under current law, the state may intervene in juvenile affairs even if a formal criminal offense has not been committed. Contrary to the general prohibitions surrounding the prosecution of adult offenders, the state may intervene in the interest of the juvenile's welfare in order to defend him against his own presumed inability to resist criminal pressures. "The State," Sethna has explained, "extends its paternal care for the juvenile concerned"[29] instead of, or in addition to, the concern and protection of parents. The 1967 Gault decision has clouded this distinction, however.

■ *The Unitary Nature of Crime and Delinquency*

Delinquency cannot be understood without an understanding of crime because of their unitary nature. Both delinquency and crime are forms of deviation from the values stipulated by the society and its ruling elements. Although this fact does not mean that useful classifications according to the age of the lawbreaker and the seriousness of the crime must be discarded, it does suggest that these classifications do not reflect real distinctions. Distinctions between crime and delinquency or murder and shoplifting are important for preventive and corrective planning. The unitary basis of delinquency and crime, however, suggests that most people have committed, and possibly continue to commit, delinquent or criminal acts during much of their lifetimes. Which of these acts will be "officially" defined as delinquent or criminal and to what degree this behavior will be punished ultimately depend not only upon the age of the offender but also upon the prevailing system of social values. The juvenile delinquent and the adult criminal, whether murderer or shoplifter, both deviate from standards established by society.

Because society's dominant forces attach greater value to human life than to consumer goods, murder is punishable by death or imprisonment, whereas shoplifting is punishable by imprisonment or fine. As the juvenile is presumed to be less responsible and more "salvageable," he is treated differently from the adult who commits the same crime. Although the *delinquency zone* is broader than the *crime zone*, crime and delinquency still remain forms of behavior that deviate from established social norms. The distinction is not in specific behavior, but in the values attached to the individuals, juvenile or adult, who thus endanger social values.

NOTES

1. This guarantee is valueless when applied only in legal and formal terms. In the so-called "socialist" states the criminal law takes on "socialist contents," representing the program or views of the ruling Communist Party. As will be seen when we distinguish between crime and delinquency, *nullum crimen sine lege* is applied only as a general principle in cases of delinquency and not to the behavior of each individual delinquent. This application is, however, part of the well-reasoned structured informality of the law for handling juvenile delinquency.

2. An analogy can be defined as an extension of the originally intended sense of the legal rule. It can be regarded as an interpretation of the law. In the socialist countries, however, where the law is adjusted to "socialist contents," the analogy concept does not apply.

3. As we shall demonstrate, however, it can be regarded as a delinquent act.

4. Benedict Carpzov, *Practica Nova Imperialis Saxonica Rerum Criminalium* (Frankfurt am Main: 1635). See also George B. Vold, *Theoretical Criminology* (New York: 1958).

5. William Graham Sumner, *Folkways* (Boston: 1940), p. 55. The problems inherent in this assumption are discussed in Stephen Schafer, "Anomie, Power Structure and Crime in Disorganized and Overorganized Societies," (unpublished paper; presented at the Fifth International Criminological Congress in Montreal: August-September 1965).

6. C. Vann Woodward, *The Strange Career of Jim Crow* (New York: 1955).

7. "Legislation" is used here in its broadest sense, as a comprehensive term for the lawmaking authorities and the processes by which laws are made. This question, in its detailed aspects, properly belongs to constitutional law or general sociology. Edwin H. Sutherland correctly warns that "criminal law is not merely a collection of written prescriptions . . . both the techniques used by the court in interpreting and applying the statutes and the body of ideals held by the court are a part of the law in action, as truly as are the written statutes." Sutherland and Donald R. Cressey, *Principles of Criminology* (6th ed.; New York: 1960), p. 5.

8. Rudolf Jhering, *Der Zweck im Recht* (Berlin: 1877).

9. This practice is called *desuetudo*; in a certain sense it may be regarded as the contrary of *nullum crimen sine lege*, which is strongly formalistic.

10. A. A. Gertsenzon, *Sudjebnaja Statvistike* (Moscow: 1948). See also T. C. N. Gibbens and R. H. Ahrenfeldt, *Cultural Factors in Delinquency* (London: 1966).

11. Herbert Spencer, *Essais de morale de science et d'esthétique* (4th ed.; Paris: 1898).

12. Gyula Moór, *A Szabad Akarat Problémája* (Budapest: 1943), pp. 3ff.

13. Immanuel Kant, *Critique of Pure Reason*, trans. by Norman Kemp Smith (London: 1952).

14. A regrettable and major defect of the work of many modern criminologists is their tendency to ignore the problem of free will; as a result, some of their views on crime and delinquency appear to be contradictory.

15. John E. Coogan, "The Myth Mind in an Engineer's World," *Federal Probation*, 16 (March 1952), 26–30. See the replies to this article—Ruth Shonle Cavan in *Federal Probation*, 16 (June 1952) 24–31; Lowell J. Carr in *Federal Probation*, 16 (September 1952) 36–39; Harry Elmer Barnes in *Federal Probation*, 16 (September 1952) 39; Negley K. Teeters in *Federal Probation*, 16 (September 1952) 40–42. See also Coogan, "Free Will and the Academic Criminologist," *Federal Probation*, 20 (March 1956), 26–30.

16. Paul W. Tappan, *Crime, Justice and Correction* (New York: 1960), p. 264.

17. See M. E. Mayer, *Rechtsnormen und Kulturnormen* (Berlin: 1903).

18. Socioethical norms should not be confused with the conventional rules of society, however deeply they are rooted in that society's beliefs. For example, failure to use the proper clothing on a ceremonial occasion does not result in punishment.

19. M. J. Sethna, *Jurisprudence* (Bombay: 1959), p. 80.

20. According to Karl Binding, when there is disobedience to a norm that has been established without reference to morality, there is no necessary relationship between the gravity of the criminal offense and its punishment. When criminal law is established without reference to moral standards, norms become merely orders without explanations. Under these circumstances, the reason for the punishment is the disobedience itself. See Karl Binding, *Normen* (3rd ed.; Berlin: 1916).

21. Concepts of crime that have not taken this point into account may lead to the hypothesis that all behavior prohibited by criminal law is immoral *ipso facto*. Such thinking results in the presumption that socioethical norms are defined exclusively by the criminal law and thus negates the possibility of independent socioethical norms.

22. See Hermann Mannheim, *Criminal Justice and Social Reconstruction* (London: 1946); and Oliver Moles, Jr., *et al., A Selective Review of Research and Theories Concerning the Dynamics of Delinquency* (Ann Arbor: 1959).

23. *Criminometrics* is a tentative term put forward by the authors for the measurement of criminal responsibility.

24. The average amount of resistance is the resistance to criminal pressures that can generally be expected of a person with an average amount and type of socialization and personal circumstances. The average amount of criminal pressure is the volume and intensity of pressure toward crime that might be expected to result from the average social life and physical and psychic conditions of the individual.

25. Although many people argue that crime and delinquency are not qualitatively different and involve similar activities, and social and legal consequences, the authors base their distinction upon the legal definition of what constitutes crime and delinquency.

26. The idea that delinquency is a legal concept and not a clinical symptom leads to the conclusion that the term "predelinquent" must be eliminated. See J. V. Fornataro, "It's Time to Abolish the Notion of Pre-Delinquency," *The Canadian Journal of Corrections* (April 1965).

27. U.N. Department of Economic and Social Affairs, *New Forms of Juvenile Delinquency: Their Origin, Prevention and Treatment* (New York: 1960), p. 62.

28. Herbert A. Bloch and Frank T. Flynn, *Delinquency: The Juvenile Offender in America Today* (New York: 1956).

29. M. J. Sethna, *Society and the Criminal* (Bombay: 1952), p. 351. West German Juvenile Court Law of 1953 prescribes correctional treatment of juvenile offenders in cases in which juveniles are found to have criminal tendencies and are not expected to benefit from educational or disciplinary measures intended for less serious delinquents. See Bauman, "Der Begriff der 'Schädlichen Neigungen' nach Artikel 17 JGG," *Bewährungshilfe,* 14 (1967), 177–183.

Chapter 2

■ *The Extent of Delinquency*

■ *Age Limits of Delinquency*

The lower and upper age limits of juvenile responsibility determine the scope of delinquency. They can be defined only in terms of chronological age, determined according to national, geographical, cultural, psychological, physiological, and other considerations. Although extremely young children, usually under seven, are generally held incapable of criminal intention and are therefore outside the definition of "delinquency," youths who are not yet adults, usually between the ages of seven and eighteen, are also exempt from the harsh provision of the adult criminal code and are handled under the juvenile code. The greater the span between the two limits, the greater the population that will be defined as delinquent.

Age limits, however, are established at the ages at which juveniles are presumed to have acquired sufficient socialization to be responsible (lower limit) and functional appreciation of the normative order (upper limit). They have not been standardized throughout the world. Although no discernible international trend exists, northern countries tend to fix the earliest age of delinquency higher. The lower limit of responsibility is set at nine in Spain; ten in Bulgaria, Greece, and Uruguay; twelve in Switzerland and Hungary; fourteen in Germany and Denmark; fifteen in Finland. Although Great Britain, an exception, fixes the age of first responsibility at eight years, the Ingleby Report recommended in 1960 that it be advanced to twelve. The minimum age may be raised to thirteen or fourteen in Great Britain, however. The lower age of criminal responsibility is ten in Austria and Poland, whereas it is fifteen in Cuba. As age of juvenile maturity actually varies in connection with individual development, the lower limit of responsibility could be abolished without loss, leaving ultimate determination to a competent juvenile court. Although this change would make every child subject to possible court intervention in cases of potential or actual criminal involvement, it would also allow the flexibility necessary to deal with the child as a child.

Although it is generally presumed that a child under the minimum age limit cannot assume responsibility for his conduct, most American states and foreign countries provide for some intervention in the child's life at any age. The Standard Juvenile Court Act,[1] for example, recommends that the court preserve jurisdiction in any juvenile case that involves medical, psychiatric, psychological, physical, or educational neglect; abandonment; incorrigibility; or occupational, behavioral, conditional, environmental, or associational relationships that may injure or endanger the child or the welfare of others, regardless of the child's age. The Austrian Child Welfare Act of 1954 (Jugendwohlfahrtgesetz) provides for the possibility of intervention in cases involving physical or moral deprivation of children, whereas the Belgian Child Protection Act of 1912 (Loi sur la Protection de l'Enfance) permits court intervention in cases of bad conduct or lack of discipline. The 1922 Youth Welfare Act (Reichsgesetz für Jugendwohlfahrt) of Germany, as amended in 1953, provides for a form of protective supervision (Schutzaufsicht) against physical or moral neglect.

The Greek Criminal Code of 1950 allows a variety of interventions on behalf of those who are not yet considered responsible at the time of their crimes, whereas the Netherlands Civil Code of 1838 (Burgerlijk Werboek) provides supervision in cases in which children are found to be in physical or moral danger. The Norwegian Child Welfare Act of 1953 permits intervention if the health or physical and mental development of a child is seriously endangered or if he is unable to adjust to the demands of the law. The Act on the Public Care of Children allows action on behalf of Swedish children who are neglected or whose physical or mental health is in danger. The Civil Code of Switzerland (le Code Civil Suisse) also provides protection, education, and assistance for children whose physical and moral development is unsatisfactory. The Children and Young Persons Act of 1953 and its amendments allow a wide range of intervention in United Kingdom cases involving juvenile need for care and protection.

The upper age limit is no less variable than is the lower age limit. It is usually between sixteen and eighteen, the latter age recommended by the National Council on Crime and Delinquency and the U.S. Children's Bureau and followed by the Federal courts.[2] Although earlier maturation of youth has led some critics to propose that the upper limit be lowered, others argue that all minors (under twenty-one) should be included in juvenile provisions, as their behavior parallels that of younger delinquents in many ways. The contemporary American attitude, however, rejects this high limit in favor of the currently most common distinction between delinquency and crime at the age of eighteen.

Legal attempts to set limits lead to many illogical results. A violation one second before midnight on the eve of one's eighteenth birthday may be a *delinquency*; two seconds later the same act would be a *crime*. All people do not, however, develop mature, nondeviant personalities with the same chronological precision. Extreme variation in the rates of personality development suggests that the courts should determine the age of transition from juvenile to adult status in each individual case. Such a process would demand redefinition of our present concepts of juvenile and adult jurisdiction. As such redefinition is unlikely, especially in view of the recent Gault decision, arbitrary and often inconsistent upper age limitations will continue to confuse our statistical and behavioral understanding of juvenile delinquency.

■ The Magnitude of Juvenile Delinquency

The volume of juvenile arrests continues to increase more rapidly than does the juvenile population throughout most of the world. Seventeen of nineteen countries surveyed in a report of the U.N. Secretariat to the second Congress on the Prevention of Crime and the Treatment of Offenders evinced marked increases in delinquency. Only two countries showed decreases.[3] Western Australia experienced a 131 percent increase between 1948 and 1958. Delinquency in Austria rose almost 68 percent between 1951 and 1956, whereas the number of juvenile offenders increased 252.5 percent on Taiwan (Nationalist China) from 1952 to 1956. Belgium, however, reported a smaller increase, less than a 30 percent rise from 1939 to 1957. Although delinquency in East Germany grew by 96.3 percent from 1951 to 1957, the Federal Republic of Germany claimed a smaller increase, 39.2 percent during the same period.[4] Juvenile delinquency rose 61.7 percent in Finland between 1946 and 1957 and 40.1 percent in Greece from 1951 to 1956. Japanese delinquency expanded slightly more than 166 percent between 1936 and 1957,[5] but delinquent conduct in Sweden increased approximately 210 percent between 1950 and 1956. Philippine figures for 1957 showed a decrease over those for 1956; the trend was offset, however, by a 61.2 percent increase in 1958.

Switzerland reported an increase of 18.7 percent between 1957 and 1958, but delinquency of white children and juveniles in the Union of South Africa rose only 10.6 percent from 1954 to 1956. Delinquency in the United Kingdom during the period 1938–1958 rose 77 percent among males aged eight to fourteen and 86 percent among males fourteen to seventeen. Females, however, showed even higher rates—143.5 percent in the eight-to-fourteen age bracket and 126.3 percent in the fourteen-to-seventeen group. The Vietnam increase between 1955 and 1957 was 59 percent, but the present Vietnam war has rendered these data obsolete. The U.N. Secretariat revealed that the number of convicted juvenile offenders rose 142.7 percent in Yugoslavia between 1950 and 1956, and a continuing upward trend was apparent in Brazil, Ethiopia, Mexico, Nigeria, Pakistan, Venezuela, and a few other nations. Only in France and Italy did small and irregular volume declines occur. United States delinquency data also reveal an increase. The President's Commission on Law

Enforcement and Administration of Justice recognized, for example, that, if current trends continue, approximately 40 percent of all male children now living in the United States will be arrested for nontraffic offenses during their lifetimes.[6]

Juvenile offenses are many and varied. Although in the United States specific juvenile violations vary according to the particular state, delinquency statutes define, in order of frequency, such violations as

1. Violates any law or ordinance.
2. Habitually truant.
3. (Knowingly) associates with thieves, vicious or immoral persons.
4. Incorrigible.
5. Beyond control of parents or guardians.
6. Growing up in idleness or crime.
7. So deports self as to endanger self or others.
8. Absents self from home and without consent.
9. Immoral or indecent conduct.
10. (Habitually) uses vile, obscene or vulgar language.
11. (Knowingly) enters, visits house of ill repute.
12. Patronizes, visits policy shop or gaming places.
13. (Habitually) wanders about railroad yards or track.
14. Jumps train or enters train or engine without authority.
15. Patronizes saloon or dram house where intoxicating liquor is sold.
16. Wanders streets at night, not on lawful business.
17. Patronizes public pool room or bucket shop places.
18. Immoral conduct around school.
19. Engages in illegal occupation.
20. In occupation or situation dangerous or injurious to self or others.
21. Smokes cigarettes, or uses tobacco in any form.
22. In place for permitting which adult may be punished.
23. Frequents place whose existence violates the law.
24. Addicted to drugs.
25. Disorderly.
26. Begging.
27. Uses intoxicating liquor.
28. Makes indecent proposals.
29. Loiters, sleeps in alleys, vagrant.
30. Runs away from state or charity institution.
31. Operates motor vehicle dangerously while under the influence of liquor.
32. Found on premises occupied or used for illegal purposes.
33. Attempts to marry without consent in violation of law.
34. Given to sexual irregularities.[7]

Although juvenile delinquency has been rising in the United States, data on volume, arrest trends, and court activity are incomplete. The exact number of unarrested delinquents is, of course, never known, for such youths are quickly released upon apprehension, turned over to their parents, "chewed out" by victims or apprehending officers without detention, or never caught at all. As many juvenile cases are processed without formal records or eventual court action, data on the larger volume of delinquent activities are not available. The extensive discretionary power of the juvenile court allows its officers to make wide distinctions between official and unofficial cases that come to its attention. Although an *official* case usually involves the filing of a petition and an ensuing court hearing, many cases are simply adjusted unofficially by a referee, juvenile officer, probation officer, or other court officer.

The previously mentioned study for the President's Commission on Law Enforcement and Administration of Justice, published in 1967, revealed that one in every nine youths—one in every six male youths—will be referred to the juvenile court before his eighteenth birthday for some offense other than a traffic violation. Approximately 30 percent of all 1965 offenders were under the age of twenty-one; nearly 20 percent were under eighteen.[8] The one-to-seventeen-year-old group, comprising 13.2 percent of the population, accounted for half the arrests for nontraffic offenses in 1965. Offenders between eighteen and twenty-four, representing only 10.2 percent of the population, accounted for more than 26 percent of arrests for willful homicide, 44 percent of those for rape, 39 percent of those for robbery, and 26 percent of those for aggravated assault. Boys under eighteen were arrested five times as often as were girls in 1965; four times as many boys as girls were referred to juvenile courts.[9]

More recent American juvenile-arrest data reveal that 36.4 percent of all 1967 arrests occurred among juveniles and youths under twenty-one years of age. Juveniles under eighteen were responsible for nearly 50 percent of all offenses on the Federal Bureau of Investigation's index of crimes and 24.3 percent of the total 1967 criminal-arrest volume (see Table 2.1). Juveniles under fifteen were arrested for nearly 24 percent of all reported 1967 index crimes (see Table 2.2), including larceny (30 percent), burglary (26.1 percent), auto theft (16.8 percent), and robbery (11.5 percent). Juveniles under eighteen were arrested for more than 50 percent of all burglaries, larcenies, auto thefts, and acts of arson or vandalism during 1967. The peak ages of American male and female delinquency were fifteen and sixteen (see Table 2.1), and their offenses were concentrated in the categories of larceny, auto theft, burglary, vandalism, liquor violations, disorderly conduct, curfew violations, and runaways. The most feared crimes against the person (that is, criminal homicide, forcible rape, robbery, and aggravated assault) were clearly fewer in number. The number of arrests of males under eighteen (see Table 2.3) rose by more than 20 percent in such categories as forgery and counterfeiting (26.4 percent), fraud (22.1 percent), embezzlement (30.9 percent), possession of stolen property (25.3 percent), prostitution (37.4 percent) and narcotic drug

Table 2.1. Total Arrests by Age, 1967 (4,566 agencies, 1967 estimated population 145,927,000)

Offense Charged	Grand Total, All Ages	Under 15	Under 18	18 and Over	Age 10 and Under	11–12	13–14	15	16	17	18	19	20	21
Total	5,518,420	527,141	1,339,578	4,178,842	79,956	125,831	321,354	249,240	289,329	273,868	260,316	225,868	189,576	165,258
Percent distribution*	100.0	9.6	24.3	75.7	1.4	2.3	5.8	4.5	5.2	5.0	4.7	4.1	3.4	3.0
Criminal homicide:														
murder and nonnegligent manslaughter	9,145	137	830	8,315	12	25	100	141	222	330	354	389	375	377
manslaughter by negligence	3,022	30	246	2,776	4	4	22	26	76	114	157	172	186	136
Forcible rape	12,659	475	2,515	10,144	19	93	363	458	687	895	1,100	962	841	821
Robbery	59,789	6,885	18,889	40,900	625	1,754	4,506	3,394	4,205	4,405	4,804	4,606	3,812	3,383
Aggravated assault	107,192	6,559	18,359	88,833	824	1,665	4,070	3,299	4,127	4,374	4,804	4,543	3,948	4,079
Burglary—breaking or entering	239,461	62,510	128,169	111,292	10,210	16,440	35,860	23,204	22,898	19,557	17,658	13,497	9,941	8,086
Larceny and theft	447,299	134,216	246,057	201,242	22,324	38,537	73,355	40,764	39,100	31,977	26,526	19,401	14,631	11,358
Auto theft	118,233	19,902	73,080	45,153	390	2,066	17,446	19,302	19,904	13,972	9,670	6,773	4,774	3,443
Subtotal of above offenses	996,800	230,714	488,145	508,655	34,408	60,584	135,722	90,588	91,219	75,624	65,267	50,343	38,508	31,683
Percentage distribution*	100.0	23.1	49.0	51.0	3.5	6.1	13.6	9.1	9.2	7.6	6.5	5.1	3.9	3.2
Other assaults	229,928	14,837	37,849	192,079	2,118	3,832	8,887	6,332	8,016	8,664	9,878	9,353	8,742	8,947
Arson	8,058	3,768	5,236	2,822	1,461	1,061	1,246	587	478	403	328	222	167	145
Forgery and counterfeiting	33,462	806	3,918	29,544	60	177	569	678	1,031	1,403	1,910	2,004	1,951	1,790
Fraud	58,192	643	2,444	55,748	64	151	428	385	607	809	1,457	1,958	2,153	2,313
Embezzlement	6,073	53	256	5,817	2	11	40	38	72	93	144	200	210	217
Stolen property—buying, receiving, possessing	28,620	3,542	9,901	18,719	253	859	2,430	1,898	2,274	2,187	2,102	1,815	1,429	1,241
Vandalism	109,299	54,782	83,571	25,728	14,449	15,822	24,511	11,894	9,778	7,117	4,340	3,024	2,118	1,754
Weapons—carrying, possessing, etc.	71,684	3,738	12,967	58,717	297	756	2,685	2,461	3,134	3,634	4,226	3,583	3,208	3,185
Prostitution, commercialized vice	39,744	97	848	38,896	2	20	75	114	170	467	1,311	2,139	2,431	3,589
Sex offenses (except forcible rape and prostitution)	53,541	4,959	13,075	40,466	535	1,009	3,415	2,571	2,909	2,636	2,390	2,301	2,158	1,971
Narcotic drug laws	101,079	2,812	21,405	79,674	87	344	2,381	3,762	6,418	8,413	9,946	9,742	7,978	6,309
Gambling	84,772	343	2,143	82,629	13	33	297	361	591	848	1,200	1,143	1,249	1,655
Offenses against family and children	56,137	264	860	55,277	100	47	117	101	179	316	1,808	1,872	1,895	2,068
Driving under the influence	281,152	57	2,846	278,306	10	5	42	148	811	1,830	4,222	4,977	5,762	7,250
Liquor laws	209,741	4,924	63,587	146,154	55	345	4,524	9,271	20,112	29,280	36,735	31,809	22,766	5,379
Drunkenness	1,517,809	3,509	34,621	1,483,188	111	301	3,097	5,460	10,385	15,267	35,730	30,332	25,103	23,591
Disorderly conduct	550,469	38,078	110,004	440,465	1,356	3,459	33,263	19,127	24,450	28,349	37,302	31,356	28,432	30,423
Vagrancy	106,747	1,646	9,777	96,970	114	278	1,254	1,274	2,356	4,501	7,845	5,950	4,583	3,830
All other offenses (except traffic)	654,915	76,082	189,921	464,994	13,356	16,623	46,103	36,658	39,879	37,302	34,644	30,567	27,167	22,737
Suspicion	95,794	5,674	21,800	73,994	888	1,269	3,517	3,342	4,398	8,386	9,001	7,556	5,774	5,181
Curfew, loitering law violations	94,872	23,794	94,872	—	1,295	4,219	18,280	20,410	29,477	21,191	—	—	—	—
Runaways	129,532	52,019	129,532	—	4,860	8,864	38,295	31,780	30,585	15,148	—	—	—	—

*Because of rounding, the percentages may not add to total.

Source: Federal Bureau of Investigation, Uniform Crime Reports—1967 (Washington, D.C.: 1968), pp. 121–122.

Table 2.2. Total Arrests of Persons Under 15, 18, 21, and 25 Years of Age, 1967
(4,566 agencies, 1967 estimated population 145,927,000)

Offense Charged	Number of Persons Arrested					Percentage			
	Grand Total, All Ages	Under 15	Under 18	Under 21	Under 25	Under 15	Under 18	Under 21	Under 25
Total	5,518,420	527,141	1,339,578	2,015,338	2,613,887	9.6	24.3	36.5	47.4
Criminal homicide									
murder and nonnegligent manslaughter	9,145	137	830	1,948	3,415	1.5	9.1	21.3	37.3
manslaughter by negligence	3,022	30	246	761	1,295	1.0	8.1	25.2	42.9
Forcible rape	12,659	475	2,515	5,418	8,133	3.8	19.9	42.8	64.2
Robbery	59,789	6,885	18,889	32,305	43,776	11.5	31.6	54.0	73.2
Aggravated assault	107,192	6,559	18,359	31,654	47,520	6.1	17.1	29.5	44.3
Burglary—breaking or entering	239,461	62,510	128,169	169,265	196,538	26.1	53.5	70.7	82.1
Larceny and theft	447,299	134,216	246,057	306,615	344,807	30.0	55.0	68.5	77.1
Auto theft	118,233	19,902	73,080	94,297	104,860	16.8	61.8	79.8	88.7
Subtotal of above offenses	996,800	230,714	488,145	642,263	750,344	23.1	49.0	64.4	75.3
Other assaults	229,928	14,537	37,849	65,822	101,073	6.5	16.5	28.6	44.0
Arson	8,058	3,768	5,236	5,953	6,495	46.8	65.0	73.9	80.6
Forgery and counterfeiting	33,462	806	3,918	9,783	16,572	2.4	11.7	29.2	49.5
Fraud	58,192	643	2,444	8,012	18,534	1.1	4.2	13.8	31.8
Embezzlement	6,073	53	256	810	1,863	.9	4.2	13.3	30.7
Stolen property—buying, receiving, possessing	28,620	3,542	9,901	15,247	19,502	12.4	34.6	53.3	68.1
Vandalism	109,299	54,782	83,571	93,053	98,357	50.1	76.5	85.1	90.0
Weapons—carrying, possessing, etc.	71,684	3,738	12,967	23,984	36,111	5.2	18.1	33.5	50.4
Prostitution and commercialized vice	39,744	97	848	6,729	21,017	.2	2.1	16.9	52.9
Sex offenses (except forcible rape and prostitution)	53,541	4,959	13,075	19,924	27,391	9.3	24.4	37.2	51.2
Narcotic drug laws	101,079	2,812	21,405	49,071	69,565	2.8	21.2	48.5	68.8
Gambling	84,772	343	2,143	5,735	12,865	.4	2.5	6.8	15.2
Offenses against family and children	56,137	264	860	6,435	15,829	.5	1.5	11.5	28.2
Driving under the influence	281,152	57	2,846	17,807	48,975	*	1.0	6.3	17.4
Liquor laws	209,741	4,924	63,587	154,897	169,228	2.3	30.3	73.9	80.7
Drunkenness	1,517,809	3,509	34,621	109,655	225,654	.2	2.3	7.2	14.9
Disorderly conduct	550,469	38,078	110,004	201,169	282,074	6.9	20.0	36.5	51.2
Vagrancy	106,747	1,646	9,777	28,155	41,455	1.5	9.2	26.4	38.8
All other offenses (except traffic)	654,915	76,082	189,921	282,299	364,765	11.6	29.0	43.1	55.7
Suspicion	95,794	5,674	21,800	44,131	61,814	5.9	22.8	46.1	64.5
Curfew and loitering law violations	94,872	23,794	94,872	94,872	94,872	25.1	100.0	100.0	100.0
Runaways	129,532	52,019	129,532	129,532	129,532	40.2	100.0	100.0	100.0

*Less than .01 percent.

Source: Federal Bureau of Investigation, *Uniform Crime Reports—1967* (Washington, D.C.: 1968), p. 123.

Table 2.3. Total Arrest Trends by Sex, 1966–1967 (3,678 agencies, 1967 estimated population 129,384,000)

Offense Charged	MALES — Total 1966	1967	Percentage Change	MALES — Under 18 1966	1967	Percentage Change	FEMALES — Total 1966	1967	Percentage Change	FEMALES — Under 18 1966	1967	Percentage Change
Total	4,146,479	4,300,583	+3.7	895,705	982,919	+9.7	575,271	618,119	+7.4	188,037	214,652	+14.2
Criminal homicide												
murder and nonnegligent manslaughter	6,304	6,867	+8.9	669	681	+1.8	1,268	1,350	+6.5	62	71	+14.5
manslaughter by negligence	2,266	2,133	−5.9	176	186	+5.7	308	242	−21.4	14	20	+42.9
Forcible rape	11,114	11,399	+2.6	2,166	2,314	+6.8	—	—	—	—	—	—
Robbery	44,875	53,142	+18.4	14,174	16,954	+19.6	2,357	2,939	+24.7	665	904	+35.9
Aggravated assault	82,220	84,256	+2.5	13,972	14,801	+5.9	12,860	12,781	−.6	2,163	2,266	+4.8
Burglary—breaking or entering	185,304	207,412	+11.9	100,034	111,404	+11.4	7,535	8,874	+17.8	4,190	4,511	+7.7
Larceny and theft	293,632	309,072	+5.3	171,303	179,078	+4.5	89,157	100,018	+12.2	44,201	47,583	+7.7
Auto theft	98,142	103,231	+5.2	61,451	63,626	+3.5	4,162	4,619	+11.0	2,701	2,975	+10.1
Subtotal of above offenses	723,857	777,512	+7.4	363,945	389,044	+6.9	117,647	130,823	+11.2	53,996	58,330	+8.0
Other assaults	170,052	180,201	+6.0	25,698	28,787	+12.0	20,579	22,230	+8.0	4,830	5,596	+15.9
Arson	6,064	6,582	+8.5	4,294	4,389	+2.2	485	496	+2.3	235	203	−13.6
Forgery and counterfeiting	22,092	23,629	+7.0	2,240	2,831	+26.4	5,543	6,370	+14.9	603	679	+12.6
Fraud	38,249	38,502	+.7	1,480	1,807	+22.1	10,734	11,609	+8.2	312	426	+36.5
Embezzlement	4,645	4,546	−2.1	162	212	+30.9	1,027	1,113	+8.4	37	23	−37.8
Stolen property—buying, receiving, possessing	18,620	24,013	+29.0	6,845	8,574	+25.3	1,527	1,968	+28.9	469	540	+15.1
Vandalism	84,421	89,810	+6.4	65,768	69,805	+6.1	5,523	5,951	+7.7	3,779	3,931	+4.0
Weapons—carrying, possessing, etc.	51,639	60,619	+17.4	10,635	11,423	+7.4	3,665	4,359	+18.9	399	454	+13.8
Prostitution and commercialized vice	6,993	8,670	+24.0	179	246	+37.4	27,062	30,060	+11.1	450	564	+25.3
Sex offenses (except forcible rape and prostitution)	45,608	42,560	−6.7	9,611	8,886	−7.5	7,517	6,347	−15.6	3,423	2,901	−15.2
Narcotic drug laws	51,453	82,325	+60.0	7,304	16,706	+128.7	8,198	13,145	+60.3	1,181	3,179	+169.2
Gambling	88,674	74,242	−16.3	2,204	1,957	−11.2	7,940	7,086	−10.8	62	66	+6.5
Offenses against family and children	47,937	44,351	−7.5	469	538	+14.7	5,323	4,672	−12.2	222	211	−5.0
Driving under the influence	218,101	232,068	+6.4	1,982	2,302	+16.1	14,913	16,544	+10.9	77	103	+33.8
Liquor laws	157,961	161,652	+2.3	44,446	46,707	+5.1	20,593	21,542	+4.6	7,257	8,264	+13.9
Drunkenness	1,319,656	1,295,583	−1.8	24,900	27,753	+11.5	107,518	100,697	−6.3	2,814	3,238	+15.1
Disorderly conduct	437,749	427,919	−2.2	77,262	85,578	+10.8	64,725	67,865	+4.9	12,604	14,556	+15.5
Vagrancy	90,190	90,105	−.1	7,236	8,011	+10.7	9,364	9,737	+4.0	969	1,030	+6.3
All other offenses (except traffic)	446,791	504,468	+12.9	123,318	136,137	+10.4	73,017	82,221	+12.6	31,947	37,074	+16.0
Suspicion (not included in totals)	68,647	73,843	+7.6	15,739	17,155	+9.0	12,414	15,646	+26.0	2,198	2,365	+7.6
Curfew and loitering law violations	65,588	71,280	+8.7	65,588	71,280	+8.7	14,661	15,750	+7.4	14,661	15,750	+7.4
Runaways	50,139	59,946	+19.6	50,139	59,946	+19.6	47,710	57,534	+20.6	47,710	57,534	+20.6

Source: Federal Bureau of Investigation, *Uniform Crime Reports—1967* (Washington, D.C.: 1968), p. 125.

use (128.7 percent) between 1966 and 1967. Female juvenile arrests increased more than 20 percent in the areas of manslaughter by negligence (42.9 percent), robbery (35.9 percent), fraud (36.5 percent), prostitution and commercialized vice (25.3 percent), narcotic drug use (169.2 percent), driving under the influence of alcohol (33.8 percent), and runaways (20.6 percent).

Although the data reveal sharp percentage increases, a qualitative evaluation of arrest data from the Federal Bureau of Investigation's *Uniform Crime Reports—1967* reveals a less dramatic picture of juvenile delinquency in many cases. Although female juvenile murder arrests, for example, increased nearly fifteen percent from sixty-two to seventy-one, male juvenile homicide arrests grew by only 1.8 percent from 669 to 681. White juvenile arrests outnumbered Negro juvenile arrests nearly 2.5 to 1 in 1967 (see Table 2.4), but Negro youths were overrepresented in the arrest data in proportion to the Negro juvenile population. Nearly two-thirds of all juvenile robberies were committed by Negro youths. Negroes accounted for approximately half of all 1967 aggravated-assault, one-third of all burglary, one-third of all larceny, and one-third of all auto-theft arrests. Other nonwhite racial groups accounted for fewer than 25,000 of the 1967 juvenile arrests.

■ *The Visibility of Delinquency*

Nearly all data suggest that delinquency is increasing throughout the world, but statistical information on delinquency is even less valid than are data on adult crime. Not only is the definition of delinquency more flexible than is that of crime, but juvenile-arrest data-recording procedures are also less accurate. Juveniles, already more susceptible to pressures of conflicting values, have less legal protection as they respond to these adjustments. Delinquency data, therefore, must be especially carefully scrutinized in order to achieve a qualitative insight into their meaning.[10] Delinquent conduct does not truly reflect the actual state of juvenile delinquency.[11] A rash of broken windows, for example, may involve less social harm than does a series of burglaries. Those who prefer to quote figures without examining their true meanings may fall victim to their own fears. Posing as experts and using semirelated figures,[12] they lead the public to false conclusions and mistaken decisions. The inaccuracy of delinquency statistics makes the comparative study of international delinquency difficult, if not impossible.[13] Most figures are crude and of dubious scientific value. Delinquency categories vary according to the interests of the era. The increased availability and use of pornographic materials and marijuana have also increased the number of juveniles taken into custody by the police and caused increases in delinquency-arrest data.

The shortcomings of delinquency and crime data, however, are not

Table 2.4. Total Arrests by Race, 1967
(4,508 agencies, 1967 estimated population 135,203,000)

Offense Charged	Total	White	Negro	Indian	Chinese	Japanese	All Others*
Total	5,265,302	3,630,787	1,462,556	121,398	1,726	3,490	45,345
Criminal homicide:							
Murder and nonnegligent manslaughter	8,218	3,200	4,883	49	2	9	75
Manslaughter by negligence	2,852	2,202	629	15	2	8	26
Forcible rape	11,339	5,737	5,381	81	1	3	136
Robbery	51,672	19,459	31,398	360	6	18	431
Aggravated assault	86,367	42,578	42,367	671	36	26	689
Burglary—breaking or entering	224,699	147,478	73,001	1,609	65	185	2,361
Larceny and theft	425,988	288,406	130,008	2,774	295	481	4,024
Auto theft	109,814	73,389	33,998	996	43	94	1,294
Subtotal of above offenses	920,979	582,449	321,665	6,555	450	824	9,036
Other assaults	223,595	136,639	83,202	1,630	35	83	2,006
Forgery and counterfeiting	7,384	5,439	1,849	38	–	5	53
Arson	30,169	23,007	6,795	232	19	15	101
Fraud	56,278	45,155	10,564	245	13	23	278
Embezzlement	5,285	4,306	946	18	–	4	11
Stolen property—buying, receiving, possessing	24,045	14,638	9,007	180	7	8	205
Vandalism	102,543	81,791	19,486	431	19	37	779
Weapons—carrying, possessing, etc.	67,776	31,977	34,713	299	14	34	739
Prostitution and commercialized vice	33,456	12,315	20,706	131	8	38	258
Sex offenses (except forcible rape and prostitution)	49,767	36,613	12,221	239	27	79	588
Narcotic drug laws	81,454	57,146	22,848	187	40	137	1,090
Gambling	71,682	18,090	49,007	15	189	689	3,692
Offenses against family and children	55,210	37,354	17,157	449	11	4	235
Driving under the influence	272,664	219,095	48,259	3,783	78	229	1,220
Liquor laws	198,803	165,755	28,746	3,252	90	76	884
Drunkenness	1,489,528	1,071,249	326,152	84,575	152	384	7,016
Disorderly conduct	526,822	333,040	179,775	7,186	181	90	6,600
Vagrancy	100,805	73,665	24,433	1,653	33	80	941
Curfew and loitering law violations	632,082	456,079	161,501	7,772	297	338	6,095
All other offenses (except traffic)	94,451	50,445	43,531	376	14	6	79
Suspicion	93,675	70,951	19,955	901	43	216	1,609
Runaways	126,849	103,589	20,038	1,251	50	91	1,830

*Includes race unknown.

Source: Federal Bureau of Investigation, *Uniform Crime Reports—1967* (Washington, D.C.: 1968), p. 126.

new. A. Moreau de Jonnés, for example, noted the difficulties inherent in evaluating crime statistics as early as 1838.[14] Even Adolphe Quetelet urged the first session of the 1853 International Statistical Congress in Brussels to try to find a scientific data-gathering procedure.[15] A long list of publications has claimed to offer new statistical techniques and more useful analytical methods, but deficiencies in the data remain.[16] The complexity of the problem of causation cannot be resolved by a mere listing of quantitative data. National and regional delinquency and crime data usually serve official, rather than scientific, purposes. As statistics pertaining to crime and criminals are unreliable and filled with error, it is impossible to determine accurately the amount of delinquency and crime in any jurisdiction at any specific time.[17] Although the pre-World War II Mixed Committee of the International Statistical Institute and the International Penal and Penitentiary Commission has influenced many students of delinquency,[18] its "pessimistic school of thought" is not without opponents. The search for meaningful local and comparative data on crime and delinquency continues. Although the U.N. Economic and Social Council and an international group of experts were brought together in 1949 by the Secretary-General for the purpose of examining the problem of criminal statistics,[19] the ensuing years have not justified their optimism at that time and the problem of gathering meaningful data persists.

Although the publication of official or semiofficial delinquency figures is usually followed by ready interpretations by the general public and even a few "experts" or public officials, the data on which they base their conclusions are often incomplete and misleading. A judgment on the decrease or increase in delinquency cannot be made easily. Either deflation or inflation in reported delinquency figures may reflect only the quantitative variable of *visible* delinquency, which is meaningless without qualitative analysis of all delinquency variables. The vicissitudes of crime reporting, as Walter C. Reckless notes, make it difficult to obtain not only "a reliable index of the volume of crime"[20] but also accurate comparisons between times and places.

In the United States data on juvenile delinquency are recorded in the F.B.I.'s *Uniform Crime Reports* and the U.S. Children's Bureau's *Juvenile Court Statistics*. These periodic reports are not without major weaknesses, however, for they depend upon voluntary submission of data by victims, police administrators, probation personnel, and juvenile courts. *Uniform Crime Reports* list all the offenses known to the police; obviously these reports are incomplete, as those who commit crimes attempt to keep their acts secret. Also available statistics do not indicate the volume of known crime in particular age or sex categories because victims are usually unable to give adequate age or sex information on perpetrators of crimes. Only arrest statistics begin to reveal age and sex differentials in the criminal process. As fewer than 20 percent of the "index crimes" against property and 70 percent of those against persons currently result in arrests of the offenders, these data too may be somewhat misleading. Considering the many variables of age, sex, race, and environment, and the fact that many apprehended juveniles are quickly released without coming to the attention of the court, the *U.C.R.* data, although serving as an index to delinquent and criminal activity, do not provide fully reliable insights into the delinquency problem.

Similar shortcomings exist in the *Juvenile Court Statistics.* The number of reporting courts varies from year to year. The criteria for assigning children and adolescents to the juvenile court have continually changed with the passage of state and Federal legislation. Because the role of juvenile courts varies from community to community, statistics often reflect local biases. Juvenile violators charged with Federal offenses may not even be included in these statistics, for their activities are registered in reports of the Federal Bureau of Prisons or the administrative offices of the U.S. Courts.[21]

■ *Factors Affecting Availability and Reliability of Data*

Accuracy in delinquency data is often undermined by the emergence of *topical* (temporary, current, or short-term) delinquent conduct, variations in the volume of legally defined criminal offenses, dissimilar definitions of delinquent behavior, differing juvenile-court practices, inaccurate reporting, and limited visibility of "white collar" juvenile delinquency. A sudden shock to the general economy, war or revolution, political upheaval, or other disruptive social events may encourage the rise of topical delinquency. In wartime, for example, purchasing excessive quantities of gasoline is a crime; during peacetime, the same act is legal. Topical delinquency sometimes appears in the form of new kinds of criminal offense but more often in new quantitative or qualitative forms of old crimes. Although delinquency may seem to increase considerably when figures are compared with earlier data that apparently demonstrate stability, they may actually reflect an extraordinary social situation rather than a sudden change in the state of delinquency. If the topical crime or delinquency appears only as a new variant of an old type of delinquency, its separate character may go unrecognized, and it may simply be classified in an existing delinquency category. As a result, the rise in delinquency, statistically undifferentiated, is never understood or explained. The ensuing public misunderstanding further obscures the nature and meaning of the increase.

Because an economic depression or a war may also lead to the alteration of life patterns, such events may produce an identifiable, but unidentified, increase in the total delinquency volume. Black-marketeering, drug addiction, and prostitution, for example, may be stimulated by a temporary social change, but they often become entangled with a group of juvenile deviations that appear undifferentiated from conventional delinquency. Because revolution or political upheaval may lead to an unusual number of arrests and court cases, the figures should be adjusted to purge special cases from conventional delinquency data before any comparison is attempted.

Sudden catastrophes, wars, and revolutions, however, do not provide the only areas of confusion in delinquency statistics. Variations in procedural provisions,[22] proceedings,[23] administrative efficiency and policies,[24] enforcement of court dispositions or orders, and volume of legally defined crimes are largely responsible for the incomparability of delinquency variables and trends from one culture to another. As changing procedures and interpretations create *new law*, they undermine the common basis necessary for comparison of delinquency rates and accurate recognition of trends in juvenile conduct. But the issue is even more complex. Does new law, for example, *cause* the increase or decrease of delinquency statistics? Or does statistical evidence help to establish the need for new law? Since the adoption of the Ten Commandments, the codification and interpretation of new laws have produced great variations in legally defined crimes and have increasingly contributed to distortion of our understanding of the volume and character of delinquency and crime.

New law may appear in different forms and guises. It may appear as an extension or restriction of an already existing norm definition; then statistical dislocation occurs only in relation to the changed coverage of the "new" law. The new law may also involve revision of definitions of criminal and noncriminal behavior, which automatically causes a serious and broad statistical confusion. Not only is the new law a dislocating factor in itself, but its mere existence also generally encourages more emphatic police enforcement during the period immediately after enactment. As enforcement is often determined by concepts of social need and expressions of public attitudes, the interpretation and enforcement of delinquency law are largely matters of human sensitivity and judgment. The flexibility of available interpretations, therefore, makes a fully unified statistical frame of reference impossible.

Any effort to gain an accurate insight into delinquency is further confounded by the changing attitudes of parents, guardians, and school authorities and by varying public willingness to report delinquent conduct. Juvenile delinquency, consequently, may be extensively underreported or even overreported in any given period or location. Although adults inclined to leniency may overlook particular delinquent acts, those with authoritarian attitudes may quickly report such behavior and demand severe punishment to promote social conformity. Application of these attitudes, however, is not limited to juveniles. Publication of statistics on delinquency may also influence the mood of the public. People who believe that delinquency control can be accomplished only through strict punishment may use delinquency statistics to justify their belief. More lenient individuals, on the other hand, may interpret the same statistics as an indication that punitive procedures have essentially failed. These attitudes vary according to period, country, state, district, social situation, and even individual personality. Occasionally, deviant behavior that should be regulated by outside authority is simply overlooked by the "kindhearted." At other times harmless mischief is reported and results in juvenile-court intervention.

The participation of the general public in the struggle against delinquency appears to be growing. Inability to cope with destructive personalities or community forces causes parents to turn to juvenile courts or other public and private agencies for advice and assistance. Many of these cases are far removed from serious delinquent conduct and involve instead the broader social problems of the day. The "generation gap," for example, may prevent a parent from understanding a juvenile's actions and cause him to bring the problem to juvenile court. Although the voluntary efforts of parents to secure assistance from public and private agencies should not be discouraged, such actions may actually contribute to the misinterpretation of delinquency data. "Inconsistencies in identifying the delinquent," Sophia M. Robison has observed, "are major roadblocks to bringing order into delinquency statistics."[25]

Middle- and upper-class juvenile delinquency is less often detected and processed.[26] The United Nations report on new forms of juvenile delinquency noted that "while, in the past, juvenile delinquency was erroneously considered as being confined to juveniles from the lower-income brackets, at present more and more juveniles from the higher-income brackets are becoming delinquents."[27] Most *official* delinquents, however, still come from working-class homes.[28] (The terms "working class" and "lower class" are often erroneously used interchangeably.) Two principal factors may account for increased delinquency among higher-strata youth. The currently intensified causes, such as increased use of drugs and general student rebelliousness, instrumental in stimulating a delinquency increase, have not spared the higher classes. They, like the lower classes, have been influenced by the universal forces that cause delinquency in excess of the conventionally accepted pattern. The general tendency of parents to publicize the problems of children has also contributed. The middle and upper classes, however, are more effectively able to hide delinquency among their children thanks to their privileged positions. As their social and financial power is similar to that among adult white-collar criminals, they use their considerable influence to minimize the consequences to white-collar juvenile delinquents. Because lower-class parents, more limited in the intellectual and financial resources necessary to solve juvenile problems, have less to lose by unmasking their children's delinquency, they more frequently rely on the court's power to enforce conformity.

Delinquency should not affect, nor be affected by, parents' financial and social power, regardless of the consequences that delinquent behavior may have upon the youth's future. The special privileges of middle- and upper-class delinquents are unjust to those coming before the juvenile court. Not only are the privileged more able to avoid the court, but also the exact dimensions of delinquency are thus distorted, and the impression that middle- and upper-class people are more moral and law-abiding than are other citizens is strengthened.

Adult white-collar crimes and juvenile white-collar delinquency, although class-oriented, are quite dissimilar. Although financial and social power facilitates white-collar crime and allows adult violators to escape its consequences, parental power is most often used in instances of white-collar juvenile delinquency to protect youths from discovery and court-ordained treatment. Although social and economic power rests with the adult white-collar criminal, the white-collar delinquent depends upon the power of others: father, mother, or other family members or friends for protection. Statistics on white-collar juvenile delinquency are therefore especially incomplete and inadequate.

Although crime and delinquency statistics are quantitative tools,[29] they should be useful to explain, as well as to describe.[30] Such interpretive data are too frequently missing, however. Statistical tables and official and semiofficial data hardly offer the undistorted picture of the actual volume of local, national, or international delinquency ultimately necessary to preventive planning or treatment. Also is it possible that early detection and handling of delinquency do not give youths the chance to overcome their own delinquency and to resume conforming behavior without detection and treatment? Do the current stigmatization by the juvenile court and the current treatment process serve to encourage the very acts that they are designed to control? Statistical data are the chart and compass of the legislative navigator,[31] but available delinquency figures offer limited insight into the total delinquency problem. The fact that delinquency and crime statistics in the United States are probably the least reliable in the Western world makes the development of new means of measuring criminality imperative. One attempt to develop such means, by Thorsten Sellin and Marvin Wolfgang, began with the assumption that the function of an index is to describe changes in the amounts and types of delinquency, rather than the reasons for those changes. Consequently, an index of delinquency, they argued, should be based upon offenses that can be assumed to be reliably reported; known to the police; attributed to apprehend juveniles; and involving harm to the victim, theft, or damage or destruction of property. Such a method would help to reveal the types of delinquency committed instead of concealing them as many current legal labels now tend to do.[32]

■ New Forms of Delinquency

The second U.N. Congress on the Prevention of Crime and the Treatment of Offenders in 1960 made a respectable effort to clarify the problem of juvenile delinquency. It assumed, for example, that *new forms of juvenile delinquency* change the child- and juvenile-crime problem itself. Although the term *new forms* meant *new manifestations* of old delinquency rather than entirely new kinds of delinquency, even the old delinquencies were new in some countries. In others, however, their growing volume, gravity, and violence only made them appear to be new. The changes could be summarized in five general categories:

1. *Delinquent behavior against property.* Although juveniles primarily committed acts against property, increases were also noted in offenses against persons, including sex offenses and delinquencies related to drug and liquor use.

2. *Delinquencies involving violence.* The greater tendency to use violence appeared in offenses against persons and property. Increases were noted not only in homicides and physical injuries but also in burglary and breaking and entering. Gang activities and acts of serious damage and vandalism for revenge, fun, or rebellion were included in this category.

3. *Delinquent conduct among younger juvenile groups.* Some forms of delinquency especially showed increasing frequency among twelve-to-fourteen-year-olds.

4. *Delinquent acts by upper- and middle-class juveniles.* Stratification barriers were not a deterrent to delinquent conduct.

5. *Growth of associational and gang delinquency.* As not all youth associations are gangs, the United Nations subdivided this category into three tentative types:

    a. The *gang*, an exclusively juvenile association, not necessarily organized for delinquent goals but characterized by latent or visible rebellious or antisocial attitudes. A structural (organized) group that often operates within a particular geographical area, it emphasizes loyalty, recognition, and obedience by its members.

    b. *Loose groups of juveniles* are periodically formed temporarily or even accidentally. A group of adults, for example, may assemble such a group of juveniles for criminal purposes.

    c. *Juvenile riot mobs*, concentrations of juveniles at certain moments and places without prior planning or recognized leaders, in which property is damaged and people are harassed by a disorderly crowd.[33]

■ Origins of the New Juvenile Delinquency

Although juvenile delinquency is partly encouraged by poor living conditions, a higher standard of living alone, the United Nations report noted, does not necessarily reduce or prevent delinquency. Higher living standards, for example, have not led to decreases in the volume of juvenile delinquency in the United States, the United Kingdom, or Sweden. On the contrary, delinquency has increased in those countries as living standards have risen.[34] Although delinquency cannot be correlated with increased average family or national income, educational opportunities, housing potential, welfare, health services, and social security, new forms of delinquency tend to emerge and coexist with old forms as such increases occur. The increased incidence of car theft, for instance, reflects a higher standard of living and is not necessarily related to the unsatisfactory fulfillment of fundamental needs. Although car theft is practically unknown in many less-developed countries, thefts of food and clothing are common there,[35] whereas highly developed countries less frequently report simple thefts of food and clothing. Cigarette-butt collecting, for example, is a frequent delinquency in Boulac, an area of Cairo, and is inconsequential in Roxbury, a suburb of Boston, but sex crimes and traffic offenses, common in the Boston area, are unknown in Boulac.[36]

The improvement of material living conditions without parallel improvement in discipline, moral values, and social responsibility does little to control, prevent, or reduce the emergence of *new forms* of juvenile delinquency. On the other hand, poverty and unfavorable economic conditions are also decisive factors in the manifestation or formation of new delinquency forms. Although poverty appears to be closely related to acts of delinquency, it does not cause all such acts, as is clear from violations committed by juveniles from higher-income strata. Improvement in living conditions, however, can help to decrease and eliminate some forms of so-called "economic delinquency."

Although war ultimately encourages expressions of delinquency, it does not account for all new forms of delinquency either. Car theft, for example, did not originate during World War I; it started to flourish as a new form of delinquency before World War II, after two decades of peace. A general increase in juvenile delinquency, in fact, was apparent in the United States and Sweden before World War II. The delinquency rate in France, Belgium, and Denmark, countries more directly affected by the war, did not even approximate that in the United States or Sweden. Furthermore, France and Italy, which had suffered heavily from the war, reported slight decreases in delinquency in the years immediately following the conflict.

The growth of industrialization has also encouraged the development of new forms of juvenile delinquency. Although urban growth and industrial expansion do not in themselves cause delinquency, they often serve as *criminogenic factors*. The absence of economic, industrial, urban, and social coordination, for example, has allowed continued evolution of delinquency by default, for social integration has lagged behind the development of economic and industrial life. Crime and delinquency problems cannot therefore be separated from the total approach to economic, industrial, and urban development.[37] Although the influence of mass communications in stimulating juveniles in rural areas to imitate urban "models" is still hotly debated, many people do believe that the rise of rural delinquency is related to imitative behavior. As urban and rural life patterns become more similar, other urban delinquency forms are likely to spread to rural communities.

The decline of moral values and the disintegration of the family are also widely believed to be factors contributing to the present increase in delinquency. The family, as the fundamental unit of society, has long been challenged by the pressures of economic and social changes.[38] Because newly independent or highly developed countries suffer similar threats to family structure and unity, the family, especially in urban areas, cannot fulfill traditional functions. The need to redefine the functions of the family and the roles of family members is central to delinquency control.

Many believe that lower moral standards contribute to increasing juvenile delinquency. Growing materialism, contradictory value systems, distrust and insecurity, and general corruption are mentioned as symptoms of a declining moral level. Many juveniles and young adults evince attitudes of protest and rebellious distrust toward some prevailing principles and mores, whereas others actually participate in delinquent acts, in order to bear personal witness to a higher morality.

Youths, particularly those in highly developed countries, enjoy material and economic advantages never before available to their age group. Yet delinquency continues to increase. Economic opportunity is not uniform for all classes, however. The margin between poverty and an adequate standard of living, for example, has widened in the United States since World War II. Although juvenile or young-adult rebellion is not new, the fact that the majority of the population is under twenty-five years of age today has undoubtedly influenced the contemporary mood. Although the U.N. Congress concluded that the appearance of new forms of juvenile offense was a factor in increasing juvenile and youthful delinquency and crime, it recommended that further study of the new forms should continue, in order to ascertain whether or not the apparent increases are indeed real.[39]

NOTES

1. National Probation and Parole Association, *A Standard Juvenile Court Act* (rev. ed.; New York: 1949), pp. 16–17. Most American state statutes do include such provisions, but the standard act has not been universally adopted in the United States.
2. Manuel Lopez-Rey, "Present Approaches to the Problem of Juvenile Delinquency," *Federal Probation*, 23 (June 1959).
3. U.N. Department of Economic and Social Affairs, *New Forms of Juvenile Delinquency: Their Origin, Prevention and Treatment* (New York: 1960), pp. 24–32.

4. The steady increase in juvenile-delinquency rates in West Germany has caused continuing concern. Although delinquency usually starts at an early age, the delinquency pattern shows that the rate of activity among youths fourteen to twenty-one is nearly similar to that of adults twenty-one to thirty. Property, violent, traffic, and sex offenses are common among young offenders. See Walter Becker, "Probleme der Jugendkriminalität," *Die Polizei*, 57 (1966), 369–373.

5. About 234,956 juvenile delinquents were arrested in Japan in 1965, a decrease of 1.6 percent over 1964. The data reveal, however, an increase in the numbers of arrests of first offenders, delinquents living with both parents, middle-class delinquents, and boys in their early teens charged with theft. See Shuichi Miyaki, "Present Status of Juvenile Delinquency in Japan," *Acta Criminologiae et Medicinae Legalis Japonica*, 33 (1967), 8–14.

6. President's Commission on Law Enforcement and Administration of Justice, *The Challenge of Crime in a Free Society* (Washington, D.C.: 1967), p. v.

7. Walter A. Lunden, *Statistics on Delinquents and Delinquency* (Springfield, Ill.: 1964), p. 31.

8. President's Commission, *op. cit.*, p. 55.

9. *Ibid.*, p. 56.

10. Hugo Hoegel, *Die Grenzen der Kriminalstatistik*, Vol. 12 (Brno, Czech.: 1907).

11. Veli Verkko, "Kriminalstatistiken och den verkliga brottsligheten," *Nordisk Tidskrift for Strafferet*, 8 (Cophenhagen: April 1930).

12. D. Huff, *How to Lie with Statistics* (London: 1954). Available figures are related to delinquency but do not reveal the basic character of the problem.

13. Ronald H. Beattie, "Criminal Statistics in the United States—1960," *Journal of Criminal Law, Criminology and Police Science*, 51 (May–June 1960), 61.

14. A. Moreau de Jonnés, *Statistique de la Grande Bretagne et de l'Irlande*, 2 (Paris: 1838).

15. *Bulletin de la Commission Centrale de Statistique*, 6 (Brussels: 1855).

16. A reasoned bibliography of 203 works published between 1829 and 1933 can be found in Ernst Roesner, *Bibliographie zum Problem der Internationalen Kriminalstatistik* (Berlin: 1934). For descriptions of the recent American situation and comments, see, among others, Donald R. Cressey, "The State of Criminal Statistics," *National Probation and Parole Association Journal*, 3 (July 1957), 230–236; Daniel Glaser, "Administrative Use of Institutional Statistics," *National Probation and Parole Association Journal*, 3 (July 1957), 288–291; Ronald H. Beattie, "Criminal Statistics in the United States—1960," *Journal of Criminal Law, Criminology and Police Science*, 51 (May–June 1960), 49–65; and Joseph W. Eaton and Kenneth Polk, *Measuring Delinquency* (Pittsburgh: 1961).

17. Edwin H. Sutherland and Cressey, *Principles of Criminology* (6th ed.; New York: 1960), p. 25.

18. Mixed Committee of the International Statistical Institute and the International Penal and Penitentiary Commission, "Directives pour l'élaboration des statistiques criminelles dans les divers pays," in Ernest Delaquis, ed., *Recueil de documents en matière pénale et pénitentiaire*, 12 (Bern: March 1947), 254.

19. U.N. Economic and Social Council, *Report by the Secretariat on Criminal Statistics* (New York: March 2, 1959), p. 6; see also U.N. Economic and Social Council, *Resolutions* (Seventh Session; New York) and U.N. Economic and Social Council, *Official Records of the Economic and Social Council, Seventh Session, Supplement No. 8, Report of the Social Commission, Third Session* (New York).

20. Walter C. Reckless, *Criminal Behavior* (New York: 1940). Reckless' views became even more pessimistic in *The Crime Problem* (2nd ed.; New York: 1955), p. 19, where he stated, "The volume of crime in time and place cannot be assayed."

21. Sophia M. Robison, *Juvenile Delinquency: Its Nature and Control* (New York: 1960), pp. 14–18.

22. Roesner, "Die Internationale Kriminalstatistik in Ihrer Methodischen Entwicklung," *Allgemeines Statistiches Archiv*, 22 (Jena: 1932).

23. Wilhelm Sauer, *Kriminalsoziologie*, 1 (Berlin: 1933), 4.

24. Verkko, *op. cit.*, pp. 95–128.

25. Robison, *op. cit.*, p. 13.

26. Edmund W. Vaz, *Middle-Class Juvenile Delinquency* (New York: 1967) deals with the many phases of this problem.

27. U.N. Department of Economic and Social Affairs, *op. cit.*, p. 34. See also Gilbert Geis, *White Collar Crime* (New York: 1968).

28. President's Commission, *op. cit.*, pp. 56–65.

29. Paul Reiwald, *Vom Geist der Massen* (2nd ed.; Zurich: 1946), pp. 23–25.

30. Franz von Liszt, *Zur Vorbereitung des Strafgesetzentwurfs: Festschrift für den XXVI. Deutschen Juristentag* (Berlin: 1902), p. 61.

31. *Report of the Proceedings of the Fourth Session of the International Statistical Congress* (London: 1861), p. 217.

32. Thorsten Sellin and Marvin E. Wolfgang, *The Measurement of Delinquency* (New York: 1964), pp. 145–164.

33. U.N. Department of Economic and Social Affairs, *op. cit.*, pp. 33–35.

34. *Ibid.*, pp. 41–50.

35. *Ibid.*, *op. cit.*, p. 41.

36. S. Ewies, "A Comparative Study of Two Delinquent Areas: Roxbury and Boulac," *National Review of Criminal Science*, Vol. 3 (November 1959).

37. U.N. Department of Economic and Social Affairs, *op. cit.*, p. 44.

38. *Ibid.*, p. 49.

39. U.N. Department of Economic and Social Affairs, *Second United Nations Congress on the Prevention of Crime and the Treatment of Offenders* (New York: 1961), pp. 61–62. See also U.S. Children's Bureau, *New Perspectives for Research on Juvenile Delinquency* (Washington, D.C.); and Travis Hirschi and Hanan C. Selvin, *Delinquency Research* (New York: Free Press, 1967).

Chapter 3

■ *Development of the Problem of Delinquency*

■ *From Private Revenge to Social Defense*

From earliest times, crime has been recognized as a violation of social imperatives. Even the most primitive groups have recognized the necessity of social norms as a means of social control. Norms, however, have generally been products of human experience legitimized through socioreligious acceptance. Antisocial behavior has therefore occurred *before* the norms defining it as criminal have been defined. The social behavior has been the *prius* (prior element), the normative formulation the *posterius* (following element). What we consider delinquency and crime thus existed long before they were normatively defined as such. Delinquency, crime, and punishment in all human groups are by-products of social interaction.

Before the emergence of formal criminology five fundamental ideas governed, in rough succession, group attitudes toward delinquency and crime: private revenge, blood revenge, superstitious revenge, state revenge, and humanitarian reform. Although the exact period of the emergence and acceptance of each of these ideas cannot be delineated, each idea reflected popular reaction to the general crime problem.

The era of private revenge marked the early days of social development, when man lived in semi-isolation. Alone in his struggle for existence, he defended himself from attack and fought to control those who would cause him harm or injury. He faced his "crime problem" single-handed, as part of his struggle for self-preservation. His response to crime, still the basis of many present-day attitudes, was to use his power to neutralize or to conquer his opponent. Although the concepts of repression and prevention, as means of self-preservation, were known to him only in primitive and possibly subconscious form, they did effectively restrain violence and help him to consolidate personal supremacy. Not only did the threat of punishment prevent aggression; punishment itself also served as a weapon of vengeance. In redressing a grievance, the victim assumed the function of judge. Because early crime was a private matter, vengeance too was private.

The era of blood revenge brought little change in the interpretation of crime and punishment, although the focus of response shifted from the individual to the kinship group. Relatives of the victim now shared in the act of revenge. Although blood vengeance and blood feuds led to imposition of sanctions similar to those applied in private revenge, the victim now received more assistance in neutralizing attack or punishing his attacker. The new age thus marked the beginning of "organized" revenge. At first, the victim attempted to redress a grievance by an attack on the offender or his relatives with the help of his own friends and kin. The eventual consolidation of the primitive community, however, forced some changes in this procedure. If the injury affected the vital interests of the community (as did, for example, treason), the community itself took measures against the perpetrator. Gradually, a concept of "public crime" developed. If the crime involved members of a different tribe, revenge was taken by blood relatives of the victim. If the crime was committed by a member of the same tribe, however, the closer relatives of the victim assumed the obligation of retaliation as a substitute for private revenge. In either private or blood revenge, the victim's response to an earlier attack sowed the seeds for continuing conflict. Perpetual feuding between tribes and clans, a typical feature of the era, hindered the development of an integrated system of criminal law.

The era of superstitious revenge arose when religious beliefs became a strong social power, including belief in spiritual or divine vengeance. Although this new source of legitimation served to modify unlimited blood revenge, it also led to highly arbitrary and cruel punishments. Crime became confused with sin, a challenge to, or an act against, God. Both private and blood revenge were curbed by religious institutions. The practice of *asylum* (granting sanctuary and refuge to criminals), *treuga dei* (a temporary peace in the name of God), or even *talion* (legalized retaliation) helped to reduce personal arbitrariness and, to an extent, saved many people who would have perished through personal revenge.

The same conception of crime, however, also led to the practice of superstitious revenge to placate the gods or God. As most injurious acts were defined as insults or offenses against divinity and were believed capable of causing serious personal and public harm in the form of pestilence, flood, earthquake, or other widespread devastation, punishment was applied to appease anticipated divine fury. As the ecclesiastical class increasingly influenced the course of criminal justice, punishment was consistently applied as conciliation of the divinity. Under *talion*, revenge, redefined as a part of the divine order, was inflicted in proportion to the injury incurred. The Hebrew Ten Commandments, the Indian Manama

Dharma Sastra, the Egyptian Ten Books of Hermes Trismegistos, the Chinese Ta-Tsing-Len-Lee, and the Babylonian Code of Hammurabi (about 2250 B.C.), however, regulated the ruthlessness of even this revenge.

The period of state revenge, marked by state monopoly of retaliation, began with the system of *composition,* replacement of revenge by exaction of monetary or economic compensation. This process, which began in the Middle Ages, ended in the emergence of state-dominated criminal law. Composition represented an attempt to replace personal vengeance with reparations of money or goods. It originally appeared as a form of private settlement of individual wrongs. If the injuring party offered monetary or economic satisfaction and the injured party accepted it, revenge could be avoided.

The victim and his family were the sole beneficiaries of composition in its early stages. The amount of compensation varied according to the nature of the crime and age, rank, sex, and prestige of the injured party. Free men were deemed more valuable than slaves, adults were worth more than children, and men were valued more than women. Because some laws (*leges barbarorum*) stipulated the amounts of compensation, they stimulated the development of an intricate tariff system that ultimately led to "outlawry" (*Friedlosigkeit*), the status of one who defaulted on a composition agreement or requirement. The wrongdoer who was either reluctant or unable to pay the compensation was ostracized as an outlaw (*Friedlos*). Anyone could kill him without fear of prosecution.

At a later stage a portion of each composition was claimed by the community overlord or king. As rulers grew in power, they demanded shares of compensation as commissions for services rendered in reconciling the parties. As a result, the compensation was divided into two portions: that for the victim (*Wergeld, Busse, emenda, Lendis*) and that for the community or king (*Friedesgeld, fredus, gewedde*).[1] Through this process the offender could reestablish the broken peace. As the proportion demanded by the king or overlord increased, however, the victim's share decreased. At the time of the division of the Frankish Empire by the Treaty of Verdun, the practice of composition already produced diminished payments for victims of crimes, and eventually such payments died out completely. As the king or overlord claimed the entire compensation, private crimes became public crimes, and revenge became nationalized.

The development of Athenian law had redefined crime in Athens—one of the two leading powers of the ancient world—as a matter of state interest rather than of private vengeance. In the early stages of this development, the laws of Draco, Solon, and Cleisthenes had been based on despotic principles and had prescribed cruel punishments. Although Roman law made an early distinction between private crimes (*delicta privata*) and public crimes (*delicta publica*), the Law of XII Tabulares and the Corpus Juris Civilis frequently prescribed death, confiscation, or exile. Even crueler punishments, results of uncurbed tyranny, developed in later years. The institution of the *delators* (official informers), which allowed the conviction of innocent men, was perhaps the worst feature of this period. In the first decades after the Middle Ages in Europe, vagabonds, adventurers, and other new types of criminals compounded the crime problem. A philosophy of deterrence, rather than revenge, prevailed.

Criminal offenses in this period were vague and ill-defined. Not only was the definition of crime itself arbitrary, but barbarous punishments also varied according to the crimes, which were sometimes fictitious. Criminal justice even encompassed questions of individual conscience. The public had no protection against the corrupt practices of their rulers or against miscarriages of justice, and grotesque practices and punishments characterized the era. For example, in Thuringia the oldest relative of a murdered man was commissioned in 1470 to execute the convicted murderer; in some German cities the newest husband was given the right to carry out the executions in his locality, a strange honeymoon gift. The influence of canon law, however, led to modification of some of these practices. Ecclesiastical courts assumed responsibility for criminal justice in all cases involving breaches of Church rules or interests. Although Church representatives greatly influenced secular legislation, they were also bound by current moral practices. Ecclesiastical courts abstained from application of the cruelest punishments (*ecclesia non sitit sanquinem*), but they did share in the general practices of the age.

All parts of the human body could be subjected to punishment. Whatever was left of the body after mutilation could be subjected to branding, stocks, pillory, or other corporal measures. A few criminal codes published in Europe after the second half of the fifteenth century were, however, harbingers of the Constitutio Criminalis Carolina, the C.C.C., which was authorized by the Imperial Diet of Regensburg in 1532. Six possible methods of execution, including burning, beheading, quartering, hanging, drowning, and burying alive, were specified within strict limits. The C.C.C.'s procedural provisions represented an effort to provide a legal process and structure that would ultimately provide a sense of public security in place of legal arbitrariness. Many of its vague definitions, however, prompted alternative interpretations, including those of Benedict Carpzov, one of the judges in the seventeenth-century Leipzig witchcraft trials, who sentenced approximately 20,000 people to death during a period in which he read the Bible in its entirety some fifty-three times.[2]

The era of humanitarian reform in the West originated in the Enlightenment of the eighteenth century and put an end to some of the horrors of the previous periods. A seemingly minor judicial mistake on March 9, 1762, was centrally important in this development. Jean Calas, a sixty-two-year-old Huguenot merchant, was accused of murdering his son, who, the prosecution claimed, had been converted to the Roman Catholic faith: In fact, however, the boy had committed suicide. Although Calas repeatedly protested his innocence during a two-hour period of torture, the court sentenced him to death. Not only was he broken on the wheel, but his family was also arrested and his property confiscated. When Voltaire learned of this judicial murder from a Marseilles merchant, he and his friends challenged government officials and sought an annulment of the sentence or Calas's posthumous rehabilitation. Voltaire's success in this and other cases encouraged his continuing fight in his old age against the criminal practices of the *ancien régime*. When the Swiss Economic Society in Bern offered a prize for the best essay on a new criminal code in 1777, Voltaire doubled the honorarium from his private funds and presented his own reform ideas as a guide to contestants.[3] Voltaire and the contemporary encyclopedists thus prepared the way for the later success of the Italian Cesare Bonesana Marquis di Beccaria in his work *On Crimes and on Punishment*.[4]

Although Beccaria was raised in Parma by the Jesuits, like many progressives of his period he was early influenced by the works of Charles Baron de Montesquieu, Francis Bacon, and Jean Jacques Rousseau. Reasoning from the *social contract* hypothesized by Rousseau, Beccaria proposed to reorient criminal law—then alien in form to the concept of the natural rights of man—toward more humanistic goals. He was also influenced by Jeremy Bentham's Utilitarian stress on the greatest happiness for the greatest number and opposed the use of torture in carrying out the death penalty. Arguing for the limitation of punishment to the minimum necessary for the security of society, he stressed the importance of prevention of crime. He also suggested that punishment itself is a form of injustice if the violation could have been prevented and argued that the purpose of punishment is only to restrain offenders and to deter other people from future crimes. He assumed that freedom of the will would guarantee self-restraint among potential criminals, who would fear strict but just punishment.

Beccaria's arguments were put forward with great eloquence, which prompted Professor Hommel of Leipzig to remark that Beccaria wrote in the language of the angels. Although many opposed him, they could not impede his success.[5] His work was soon translated into many languages. Voltaire commented upon it; Czarina Catherine II of Russia offered him a post in her government; the Prince of Württemberg addressed a document of gratitude to him; and the French courts referred to his book as if it were law already in force. As "there were reasons," wrote Elio D. Monachesi, "for believing that the essay would have failed to impress or to have attracted but passing attention had it not appeared when it did,"[6] the general spirit of the age can also be said to have aided Beccaria's success. The greatest value of his work, however, was the foundation it offered for future changes in criminal legislation.

During this same period Bentham's own work was also significant.[7] "An eccentric personality, and an incredibly prolific writer, a thinker who had the colossal temerity to attempt to catalogue and to label all varieties of human behavior and the motivation giving rise to them,"[8] Bentham proposed that the general purpose of the law was to ensure the happiness of the community. Although Bentham focused primarily on the English legal system and seemed unaware of the general history of law, his ideas were

nevertheless widely influential. All acts that decrease happiness, he proposed, should be punished. Although his conception of crime appeared
to be coterminous with the concept of sin, he argued that penalties for
crime would represent deterrent *pain* greater than the *pleasure* derived
from its completion. Certain "groundless," "inefficacious," "unprofitable,"
and "needless" cases, he concluded, are "cases unmeet for punishment"
and beyond the scope of criminal justice.

An emphasis upon the individual marked the era of humanitarian
reform, the age most fertile in theories of criminal causation. The generally
accepted belief in autonomy of the individual so dominated evaluations of
the crime problem that legal defense of the individual dominated the content and direction of criminal law. Crime was viewed as action against
the interests or rights of the individual, but it was not interpreted as action
against community interests. The administration of justice, as of an abstract
legal phenomenon unrelated to human reality or to understanding of group
interrelationships, emphasized "equality for everybody." Although it represented a liberating victory, its limited concept of justice offered no real
solution to the problem of crime.

The criminal was believed to be a normal being who could choose
freely between good and evil. His free choice of evil accordingly merited
harsh punishment, in order to deter him from future violations. Only
at the end of the nineteenth century, when memories of the epochs of revenge had already faded and scientific criminology had begun to emerge,
was the theory of free will as sole determinant of criminal conduct questioned. Newer interpretations vacillated between the shaken pillars of
classical criminal law, based on individualism, and growing emphasis upon
the welfare of the group.

■ Absolute Theories of Crime and Punishment

As ideas of social defense and prevention of crime grew in strength, the
crime problem became increasingly differentiated between juveniles and
adults. This change was not accomplished quickly, however. There was a
major struggle between the proponents of absolute and of relative interpretations of crime and punishment. As absolute theorists assumed that violation of the law was violation of "justice" as well and that punishment was
therefore justified, they rejected the classification of crime into juvenile
delinquency and adult criminality. Relative theorists, on the other hand,
were more pragmatic and proposed the prevention of future illegal acts
through examination of causes and consequences of current legal violations.
Absolute theories focused upon retribution, treating punishment as an
end in itself. Although expressing the leitmotif of vengeance, the absolute
theories emphasized separate subthemes, according to the nature of the
crime and the goal of the law.

Theorists of *divine retribution,* for example, regarded the state as a moral empire (*sittliches Reich*), an "outer" order established by God on earth.[9] Human violation of this order therefore necessitates redemption of the offender through punishment. The state is authorized to exercise punishing power on behalf of God in order to bring about reconciliation.[10] Punishment as reparation for the wrong against the divinity reflects an ethical aspect (respect for divinity) associated with the interests of the state (fear of divinity). Because the state draws its power from a divine origin, it is obligated to ensure divine justice in a human world.

Theories of *moral retribution,* on the other hand, have been essentially based upon the philosophy of Immanuel Kant, who emphasized the "moral law within,"[11] one of his "two wonders of life." Crime was viewed as a moral wrong that merits sensory (physical) wrong, just as moral good merits sensory good.[12] The justification for punishment rests on the demand for moral balance, which is disturbed by human violation of the moral law.[13] Although punishment thus becomes a moral necessity in consequence of the disturbance of the moral order, the eventuality of future disturbance is not equal to a moral retribution in the present.

In theories of *curative retribution* a call for punishment is presumed to purge the criminal of his criminal tendencies,[14] and is thus a just and fair response to a wrong deed. One suffers, adherents of these theories have argued, only because one has committed a crime.[15] Retribution assuages the offender's guilt and permits him to atone for what he has done to others.

■ Relative Theories of Crime and Punishment

Although the various relative theorists have approached the concepts of justice and the utility of punishment from approximately the same perspective, they have differed in interpretation of the same phenomena. They have confused the absolute theoretical assumptions of the method and purpose of punishment, but they have also challenged the metaphysical arguments of the vengeance-oriented system of criminal justice and its collateral value system, which transcend human experience and empirical validation. The relative theories emphasize a pragmatic approach to penal measures, viewing them as salutary and effective procedures for prevention of future crime. Retribution cannot affect already-committed crimes, and measures should serve the interests of the future rather than of the past in any case. The theory of *general utilitarianism* had its origin in the period of Hugo Grotius, who early discussed the utility of punishment.[16] Bentham claimed that punishment offers more happiness to the community than pain to the offender.[17] Rudolf Jhering argued that the state is responsible for safeguarding society against future crimes.[18]

The *theories of social contract,* originating essentially in Aristotle's thinking and in Rousseau's philosophy,[19] presumed that whoever enters

society assigns to it his natural right to self-defense and authorizes the
state to apply punishment, even against himself if he violates the law.
Although the person establishes the contract as an individual with society,
he becomes an abstract part of the collective social order under the law.
Several of the classical criminological theorists shared this assumption.
Beccaria, for example, pointed to the criminal's fictitious agreement to his
own punishment and emphasized the state's unavoidable need to apply preventive measures to maintain social control.[20] Johann Gottlieb Fichte, however, approached the question in a slightly different manner. Whoever
breaches the social contract, Fichte concluded, becomes an outlaw and
may be expelled from society. Instead of driving him out of society, the
state, however, punishes him in the hope that he will not violate the contract again.[21]

Because *theories of self-defense,* also called *theories of subsistence*
or *theories of self-preservation,* stress the duty of the state to defend itself
and its members, they also presume that self-defense and self-preservation
justify attempts at prevention.[22] Many of the protection-prevention theories,
the largest group of relative theories, blend these two dimensions, in varying proportions, into theoretical unity. Although the idea of prevention is
only one among many elements in other relative theories, it is central to
this theoretical group. As the ultimate aim is prevention of further crime,
state intervention is necessary. And, because the theory of deterrence
assumes the necessity of severe punishment, punishment is believed to be
a natural ingredient of the prevention process.

The *psychological theory of prevention,* based on the philosophy of
Paul Johann Feuerbach, holds that violation of law is tantamount to violation of the function of the state.[23] The state is therefore obligated to apply
adequate pressures to restrict such violations. When all people are fully
aware that the consequences of crime are more intense than the pleasures
resulting from the crime itself, they will abstain, psychological theorists
presumed, from criminal conduct.

Although some future crimes can be prevented by *warning* potential
or actual offenders, warnings are not sufficient in all cases. Punishment,
prevention by warning, as the theorists assumed,[24] is used to alert potential violators of the consequences of crime. Punishment, or any warning
of the same nature, however, should be ultimately addressed to the moral
personality of the human being.[25] Although intervention by penal authorities is necessarily justified by the lack of sufficient force inherent in other
kinds of warnings, the pain of intervention (punishment) is insignificant
compared to the significance of its motivation.[26] As the education of citizens
and the propagation of moral principles are duties of the state, the state
must also assume ultimate responsibility for prevention of crime.[27] The
individual criminal lacks the necessary moral education, and special preventive correction is not only necessary but also justifiable.[28]

■ *Delinquency to the Nineteenth Century*

Before the nineteenth century all deviant conduct, including that of juveniles, was treated as crime. The general fury of the public and its passionate thirst for revenge were not affected by the criminal's age. The dispassionate and formalistic machinery of justice, even after the ages of vengeance had come to an end, did not distinguish between guilt and the guilty. As juvenile courts had not yet been developed, children and youths were tried in criminal courts. Criminal justice and the general public continued to view "guilty" children and young people as ordinary criminals. Neither sentencing policy nor punishment differed from that applied to adults. The first signs of special interest in children brought before the court appeared in the middle of the nineteenth century, when enthusiastic, but rather ineffectual, philanthropic societies and individuals began to interest themselves in protection of juveniles. As the modern concept of delinquency had not yet evolved, their accomplishments were limited and largely consisted of spreading sympathy for economic misery. Four main principles of common law exercised great influence about the processing of crimes committed by children or young people during this period.[29]

1. *The principle of equality before the law.* No exception or special provision could be made for the criminal because of his age. Children, young people, and adults received equal adjudication and punishment.

2. *The principle of criminal responsibility.* A child could not be exempted from liability for his criminal acts, each of which represented a conscious decision to commit a wrong.

3. *The principle of guilt or innocence.* Criminal procedure was limited to judgment of guilt and infliction of punishment. If the child was acquitted, the court was obligated to discharge him without taking further protective or rehabilitative action.

4. *The principle of punishment.* If the child was found guilty by the court, punishment was the only measure that the court could apply. All punishments, however, had to coincide with those imposed upon adults. As a result, children were hanged, transported to another location, or imprisoned, regardless of age and in accordance with legal requirements following upon the judgment of guilt. Although the system of common law was logical and coherent, it faced substantial reform in subsequent years.[30]

■ *The Change to Juvenile Courts*

An English law of 1847, amended in 1879, was the first to empower magistrates' courts to deal "summarily" with juvenile criminal cases. It resulted from the natural evolution of common (case) law and chancery (equity) jurisprudence pertaining to the rights and needs of children and adolescents. Whereas common law was based upon precedents established in previous court decisions, chancery jurisdiction was based on concern for the property of children. Common law helped to define the age of criminal responsibility (usually seven in the United States and Great Britain); chancery courts often moved to make children wards of the state, in accordance with the doctrine of *parens patriae*, which presumed that the ruler of the country was the ultimate father and protector of all his subjects. Consequently, the king stood *in loco parentis* (in place of the parents) in decisions affecting children.[31] The gradual development of specialized institutions for treatment of delinquent children in early eighteenth-century Rome, Germany, and England was based upon this presupposition.

The first juvenile institution of this type in the United States was the house of refuge that opened in 1825 in New York City, a forerunner of similar institutions in Boston and Philadelphia. The house of refuge was the model for the first state-supported and state-controlled institutions, founded after 1847, in which children were segregated from adults, though they still participated in a system of contract labor. The continuing evolution of related practices, however, led to a Massachusetts provision for a "visiting agent" to attend hearings on applications for commitment of children to reformatories. The agent was empowered to appear on their behalf and could seek placement of children in foster homes. This practice was later extended and formalized through such agencies as the Massachusetts Board of State Charities, created in 1863.[32] Similar provisions were soon adopted in New York, Rhode Island, and Indiana. An 1879 bill to reform the German prison system also included proposals for the special treatment of juvenile delinquents.[33]

The first formal juvenile court in the world was established in Cook County (Chicago), Illinois, in 1899, in an attempt to stop arrests of children by warrant, criminal indictments of children, and most other adult criminal-court features believed to be detrimental to the subsequent development of children.[34] The Illinois law, which arose from a desire to furnish juveniles with the care, custody, and discipline that should have been given them by their parents, provided for separate juvenile courtrooms, confidential records, and informal court procedures. Twenty-two other states developed similar legislation in the next decade. Legal modifications in Illinois in 1907 raised the upper age limit of boys to seventeen and of girls to eighteen and extended the court's jurisdiction to include any child who

> violates any law of this State; or is incorrigible, or knowingly associates with thieves, vicious or immoral persons; or without just cause and without consent of its parents, guardian or custodian absents itself from its home or place of abode, or is growing up in idleness or crime; or knowingly frequents a house of ill-repute; or knowingly

frequents any policy shop or place where any gaming device is operated; or frequents any saloon or any dram shop where intoxicating liquors are sold; or patronizes or visits any public poolroom or bucket shop; or wanders about the street in the nighttime without being on any lawful business or lawful occupation; or habitually wanders into any railroad yards or tracks or jumps or attempts to jump onto any moving train; or enters any car or engine without lawful authority; or uses vile, obscene, vulgar, profane or indecent language in any public place or about any school house; or is guilty of indecent or lascivious conduct. . . .[35]

The distinction between juvenile delinquency and adult crime was increasingly delineated in legal codes adopted in subsequent years, especially in 1907–1908, when Denver (Colorado), Canada, England, Germany, and Hungary all created independent juvenile courts. Characteristic features of the widely adopted juvenile-court system included sessions held in locations separate from those of adult criminal courts, separate selection of judges, and emphasis upon prevention of juvenile misconduct and upon treatment of nonadult offenders. The desire of judicial reformers to protect the rights of juveniles, however, was not fully realized in effective treatment programs and in time created conditions that were often diametrically opposite to what the reformers had intended.[36]

The introduction of the concept of delinquency and the formation of the juvenile court were more than mere philanthropy or gestures of sympathy and charity, however. As conceptual and legal tools, they offered a more realistic approach to understanding the crime problem.

Nowhere was this approach more apparent than at the international penitentiary congresses held during the middle years of the nineteenth century. The materials disseminated at Frankfurt (1846), Brussels (1847), Frankfurt (1857), Bern (1868), Cincinnati (1870), and London (after 1872) expanded the definitions of delinquency and crime beyond the narrow limits of earlier penology.[37] Questions of prevention and treatment assumed greater importance. Penology progressed from investigations of imprisonment to study of the causes of delinquency.[38] After World War II the International Penal and Penitentiary Commission (I.P.P.C.), which had organized the previously mentioned series of congresses, was incorporated into the U.N. Section on Social Defense, which assumed the leadership of the U.N. congresses on the prevention of crime and the treatment of offenders at Geneva (1955), London (1960), Stockholm (1965), and Japan (1970). A second important organization, the International Society of Criminology (*Societé Internationale de Criminologie*) developed in a similar way through unofficial gatherings of people interested in the crime problem. Its first congress was held in Rome (1938), and it sponsored later meetings in Paris (1950), London (1955), the Hague (1960), Montreal (1965), and Madrid (1970).

The move to convert penology from a *repressive* science to a *preventive* science was accelerated through these international conferences.[39] The application of preventive concepts to juvenile crime spread rapidly, largely in Europe in the middle years of the nineteenth century. Although most of the ensuing theories attempted to justify punishment, many thinkers did propose alternative theories and programs for prevention. Several were similar to present-day theoretical attempts and centered around the plethora of unsolved or unsolvable philosophical, religious, and legal problems. Although some theories differed only in nuances or terminology, all contributed greatly to the idea of prevention that led to the emergence of juvenile courts and to a change from repressive to preventive thinking about the problem of juvenile crime.

NOTES

1. See Frederick Pollock and Frederic Maitland, *The History of English Law,* 2 (2nd ed.; Cambridge, Eng.: 1898); and Heinrich Oppenheimer, *The Rationale of Punishment* (London: 1913).

2. Benedict Carpzov, *Practica Nova Imperialis Saxonica Rerum Criminalium* (Frankfurt am Main: 1635).

3. Voltaire, *Prix de la justice et de l'humanité* (Bern: 1777).

4. Cesare Bonesana Marquis di Beccaria, *Dei Delitti e Delle Pene* (Haarlem: 1764), first published anonymously.

5. *Note e Osservazioni.*

6. Elio D. Monachesi, "Cesare Beccaria," *Journal of Criminal Law, Criminology and Police Science,* 46 (November–December 1955), 439.

7. Jeremy Bentham, *An Introduction to the Principles of Morals and Legislation* (London: 1789).

8. Gilbert Geis, "Jeremy Bentham," *Journal of Criminal Law, Criminology and Police Science,* 46 (July–August 1955).

9. Friedrich Julius Stahl, *Die Philosophie des Rechts* (5th ed.; Tübingen: 1878).

10. *Ibid.* See also Victor Catherin, *Die Grundgriffe des Strafrechts* (Freiburg: 1901). This way of thinking is found even earlier in Carpzov, *op. cit.*

11. Immanuel Kant, *Kritik der Reinen Vernunft* (Leipzig: 1838). Adherents of these theoretical positions have not faithfully followed Kant's ideas.

12. Kant, *Metaphysische Anfangsgründe der Rechtslehre* (Königsberg: 1797).

13. Georg Wilhelm Friedrich Hegel, *Grundlinien der Philosophie des Rechts* (3rd ed.; Leipzig: 1930).

14. Josef Kohler, *Lehrbuch der Rechtsphilosophie* (3rd ed.; Berlin: 1923).

15. Fritz Berolzheimer, "Strafrechtsphilosophie und Strafrechtsreform," in *System der Rechts und Wirtschaftsphilosophie,* 5 (Munich: 1904–1907).

16. Hugo Grotius, *De Jure Belli ac Pacis* (1680).

17. Bentham, *Works: On the Principles of Morals and Legislation* (Edinburgh: 1838–1843).

18. Rudolf Jhering, *Der Zweck im Recht* (Leipzig: 1877–1883).

19. Jean Jacques Rousseau, *Du Contrat social* (1762).

20. Beccaria, *Delitti*.

21. Johann Gottlieb Fichte, *Grundlage des Naturrechts nach Principien der Wissenschaftslehre* (Jena: 1796–1797).

22. Christof Martin, *Lehrbuch des Deutschen Gemeinen Kriminal-Rechts* (1829); and Giovanni Romaghosi, *Gènesi di Diritto Pènale* (1791).

23. Paul Johann Anselm Feuerbach, *Antihobbes* (Erfurt: 1798); and Feuerbach, *Lehrbuch des Gemeinen in Deutschland Gültigen Peinlichen Rechts* (Geissen: 1803).

24. Anton Bauer, *Die Warnungstheorie* (1830).

25. *"an die sittliche Natur des Menschen gerichtet."*

26. Gaetano Filangieri, *La Sciènza della Legislazione* (Naples: 1780–1785).

27. Karl Christian Friedrich Krause, *Das System der Rechtsphilosophie* (Leipzig: 1874).

28. Heinrich Ahrens, *Cours de droit naturel: ou de philosophie du droit, fait d'après l'état actuel de cette science en Allemagne* (Brussels: 1828).

29. Home Office, *Report of the Committee on Children and Young Persons* (London: 1960).

30. *Ibid.*, p. 22.

31. Herbert A. Bloch and Frank T. Flynn, *Delinquency: The Juvenile Offender in America Today* (New York: 1956), p. 308.

32. *Ibid.*, p. 309.

33. Entwurf eines Gesetzes über die Vollstreckung von Freiheitsstrafen (March 19, 1879).

34. Gilbert Cosulich, *Juvenile Court Laws of the United States* (New York: 1939). Illinois established the first juvenile court, but prior to that, England held separate hearings as the first legal attempt to deal with the juvenile problem.

35. Laws of Illinois (Springfield: 1907), p. 70.

36. Richard D. Knudten, ed., *Criminological Controversies* (New York: 1968), pp. 265–305.

37. Negley K. Teeters, *Deliberations of the International Penal and Penitentiary Congresses, 1872–1950* (Philadelphia: 1949).

38. Franz von Liszt, *Die Aufgabe und die Methode der Strafrechtswissenschaft* (Berlin: 1900).

39. P. Couche, *Traité de la science pénitentiaire* (Grenoble: 1901).

Part Two

THE CAUSES OF DELINQUENT CONDUCT

Chapter 4

■ *Theories of Delinquency: Biological Explanations*

■ *Theories of Delinquency and of Crime*

Interest in crime grew rapidly after the birth of scientific criminology. Many theories were proposed by psychologists, psychiatrists, lawyers, philosophers, and sociologists in efforts to understand criminal behavior. As separate laws were formulated for delinquents, new theories of delinquency also emerged. Each theorist attempted to explain crime, and later delinquency, from the perspective of his discipline, often based on an incomplete analysis of the problem. As the presupposition that delinquency is merely a prelude to adult crime gained adherents, theorists increasingly focused upon juvenile conduct and juvenile laws. Because they believed that delinquency and crime are interrelated, they argued that one could not be comprehended without understanding the other. Other thinkers, however, placed less emphasis upon the relationship between delinquency and crime and regarded it as strictly a convenience in simplifying complex explanations of deviant behavior.

Even today the relationship between delinquency and crime has not been clearly established, although it is generally presumed. Consequently, any attempt to evaluate or even to order delinquency and crime theories historically immediately faces severe difficulties. Not only have the many views, opinions, criticisms, proposals, and suggestions about the causes of delinquency and crime been published in diverse sources, but they have also seldom been integrated. Although each theory has been presented as a new explanation in itself, it often depends to some extent upon previous theoretical formulations. Most explanations, however, imply recognition that delinquency and crime cannot be explained in terms of one single causal factor. As many of these theories lack inherent clarity, their full implications can be grasped only through tentative interpretation. Most theories fail to present new theoretical concepts or approaches but merely reiterate previous conceptions in more sophisticated or refined models.

■ Early Development of the Crime Problem

Until the nineteenth century, criminal behavior was thought to be either caused by an evil or supernatural power or the result of individual free choice. Explanations based on the scientific formulations of Cesare Lombroso, often called the "father of scientific criminology," dominate modern attempts to explain delinquency and crime. Lombroso (1836–1909), whose real name was Charles Levy, was a professor of medical jurisprudence at the University of Turin in the nineteenth century; he wielded a liberating influence on criminological thought.[1] While the discoveries of Charles Darwin were transforming scientific reasoning, Lombroso's thinking was transforming contemporary conceptualization of the crime problem. The classification of animal species and the recognition of evolution markedly influenced Lombroso's formulations. Attracted to study of the criminal personality, he focused upon the relationship between physical characteristics and crime. Although others followed his lead,[2] Lombroso's was the most prominent theoretical explanation of the crime problem.

With more ambition than objectivity, according to his critics, Lombroso reached his conclusions without critically evaluating his hypotheses. Although his views are no longer accepted, he is still recognized as an outstanding pioneer who directed explanations of crime to a more rational framework, and replaced speculation with more objective presuppositions. He was successful in countering the attacks of the more reactionary students of criminal law and thus sowed the seeds of modern criminology.[3] His theory of the delinquent man (l'uomo delinquente) was based on the assumption that he is an atavistic[4] being, a reversion to an earlier and more primitive type of human being unable to accommodate or assimilate to society because of his unrefined instincts, which cause antisocial conduct. Lombroso also assumed that criminality is predestined at birth (l'uomo delinquente nato),[5] in the sense that the criminal possesses animal resemblances that are throwbacks to a primitive type. Criminal instincts, he observed in a comparison of noncriminal soldiers with prisoners, are products of atavistic retardation, which is reflected in skull shape, forehead angle, nostril type, eyebrow projection, arm length, and other physical characteristics.

Lombroso's findings were challenged by critics who argued that most people evince one or more of the criminal characteristics (stigmata). Conversely there are attractive and handsome men entirely devoid of such characteristics who are nevertheless criminals.

Lombroso later modified his theory slightly and included people with inclinations toward epilepsy or delusions; he did not, however, modify his basic hypothesis and continued to maintain that the criminal is a degenerate product of biological mutations. He did take cognizance of economic conditions that might encourage crime, but his recognition of socioenvironmental factors always remained secondary to his basic assumption that the criminal represented a type of biological reversion.

Contrary to critics' claims, Lombroso never argued that *all* criminals are born criminals, however. Rather, he believed that only about one-third of the criminal population fell into his category of "undermen," a category intermediate between the human being and the animal.[6] Although he failed to define the exact boundaries of this category, Lombroso did attempt to explain the problem of crime in realistic terms.[7]

Enrico Ferri (1856–1929) and Raffaele Garofalo (1852–1934), two distinguished disciples of Lombroso, were more successful in propagating his ideas. With Lombroso identified as the "holy three of criminology," they led the attempt to investigate the biological and sociological facets of criminal causation. Although the separation between these two facets was not yet evident in their own works, they did help to launch the full-scale growth of scientific criminology. Lombroso's theoretical position, however, represented a sort of middle course between the somewhat totalitarian social defense of Garofalo and the humane social defense of Ferri.[8]

In his synthesis Ferri, a professor of criminal law in Rome, accepted the validity of the biological approach to criminal causation but emphasized sociological factors.[9] His use of the term *criminal neurosis*, which he defined as a result of somatic (physical) and social dispositions, represented an attempt to interweave physical, anthropological, and social factors into a consistent explanation of the causes of crime. He therefore rejected existing criminal law and emphasized instead the need for preventive measures, which he called "penal substitutes" (*restitutivi penali*), to neutralize the social causes of crime through sanctions applied consistently with criminological discoveries.[10]

Unlike Ferri, Garofalo, the public prosecutor of Venice, followed Lombroso's thought closely, while emphasizing an individualistic criminology.[11] Garofalo, who was known to his critics as the "sober anthropologist," tried to construct a theory of crime independent of the changing criminal law. Arguing that one cannot speak of criminality until the nature of crime has been exactly defined, he stressed a concept of "natural crime" (*delitto naturale*), which he defined as acts that offend the public's sense of compassion (*pietà*) and probity (*probità*). Because he believed that both physical and social factors influence what crimes are committed by an individual, Garofalo distinguished between natural crimes and "crimes without mark." Nevertheless he argued that the occasion enables the thief to steal rather than "makes the thief." He held that only those who commit natural crimes are born criminals, believing that such people are incapable of moral development because of some inherent deficiency. Although he was uncertain that a physical criminal type exists, he did believe that a physiognomic (facial) type exists. Because of his belief in innate moral degeneration as the main cause of crime, Garofalo focused upon the social danger posed by the criminal rather than by the criminal offense. He was thus the proponent of what might be called "totalitarian social defense," in a sense the forerunner of the current Soviet concept of "social danger," as the criterion for defining crime. Questioning the value of attempting to rehabilitate "immoral people," Garofalo advocated the physical elimination of those who cannot adapt themselves to social norms.[12]

The biological and sociological approaches differ markedly from Lombroso's hypothesis; they represent a challenge to the theory of the born criminal while arguing the importance of physical factors in criminal causation. The shortcomings of the Lombrosian theory, however, did not hinder the development of a scientific criminology that overshadowed his own work. The focus of scientific interest narrowed to concern with the sociological aspects of crime and delinquency and with the psychiatric, psychological, physiological, and anthropological characteristics of the delinquent and the criminal. *Criminal biology*, one of the two gradually emerging criminological perspectives, emphasized the criminal personality. *Criminal sociology* attached greater importance to social factors, viewing the personality as a member of society. Whereas criminal biology emphasized theories relating to physiological and psychological peculiarities of individuals, criminal sociology stressed cultural and structural conflict and group influences.[13] Neither science, however, was able to explain satisfactorily the causes of delinquency and crime from its single perspective, which led to the eventual development of a multifactor approach that attempted to reconcile the two positions. Consequently, any discussion of the causation of crime and delinquency automatically involves a whole series of other causal explanations. A tentative outline of the most important biological approaches (endogenous factors) to the problems of delinquency and crime include:

1. Somatological approach (physical factors)
   a. physiognomy and phrenology
   b. general inferiority
   c. somatotypes (body types)
   d. psychobiology
2. Psychological approach (mental factors)
   a. mental degeneration
   b. hereditary insanity
   c. intellectual inferiority
   d. general psychology and psychoanalysis

■ *The Biological Orientation*

The biological orientation is based on the assumption that criminals are radically different from normal human beings in organic structure, which largely determines their criminal actions. The criminal is therefore a biological phenomenon, a degenerate member of the human species, whose criminal behavior originates in his somatic or psychic deficiency. Consequently, any solution to the problem of crime rests with the human organism, which must overcome its own psychic or somatic limitations. Whereas "normal" people can be recognized by their conformity to law, the delinquent or criminal reveals his degeneracy in deviant conduct. As the violator's will is controlled by forces embodied in his person, conventional punishment is ineffective and must be replaced by curative measures. Although the biological approach has aroused extensive criticism since its inception, it has always received the serious consideration of criminological theorists. It actually appears, however, in two distinct versions. The *somatological approach* emphasizes the physical aspects of the human organism, and the *psychic approach* stresses the importance of mental factors.

The Somatological Approach

Adherents of this approach believe that somatic factors determine whether an individual is a conforming citizen or criminal. Because the physical characteristics of the criminal organism are products of heredity, they take on distinctive shapes or appear as discernible traits (*stigmata degenerationis*). The somatological approach offers a basis for categorizing criminal types,[14] emphasizing body measurement and statistical manipulation.[15] Because the focus is on physical rather than on social man, the somatic explanation of crime ignores moral, ethical, or philosophical considerations and minimizes social experience. Somatological explanations, however, may take many alternative forms.

Physiognomy and Phrenology

Perhaps the earliest version of the somatological approach, even earlier than that of Lombroso, was the attempt to explain crime in terms of physiognomy and phrenology. Crime was believed to be related either to the facial features (physiognomy) or to the exterior contours of the skull (phrenology). These characteristics were assumed to depict the true shape of the brain and to reveal potential criminal capacity hidden there. Johann Kaspar Lavater (1741–1801), one of the most prominent adherents of this school of thought,[16] focused attention on the criminal's face and skull and presented a thesis that received a favorable response even from Johann Wolfgang von Goethe.[17] The forehead, according to Lavater, reveals the individual's cultural abilities, the mouth and lips expose his tendencies, and the eyes disclose the psychological aspects of his personality. Franz J. Gall (1758–1828) included more than twenty-six characteristics of the skull in his attempt to prove a close connection between crime and the shape of the head.[18] He argued that certain psychological characters, propensities, and sentiments related to the exterior shape of the skull; unusual protuberances of the cranium; and the structure of the brain were related to specific criminal tendencies. With his collaborator, J. G. Spurzheim (1776–1832),[19] Gall also deserves recognition for drawing attention to the possible relationship between the criminal and his body build.

Despite the efforts of later followers, the phrenological approach was doomed. Before its demise, however, Charles Caldwell (1772–1853) listed thirty-five marks that might distinguish a criminal,[20] and Emile Laurent made a spectacular comparison between the physiognomies of the savage and of the criminal.[21] Their work was ultimately rejected, however, because phrenologists had failed to demonstrate that any single part of the skull or brain can be held solely responsible for any single variation in human behavior. Their thinking was also in opposition to one of the most cherished ideas of the period: that "man is the master of his own conduct and capable of making of himself what he will."[22]

General Inferiority

The most enthusiastic follower of Lombroso beyond the narrow physical bounds of physiognomy and phrenology was Hans Kurella, who related criminal conduct to the general physical inferiority of the violator.[23] Criminal acts, Kurella hypothesized, are inescapable expressions of the individual, regardless of social and environmental conditions. Although he strongly supported Lombroso's notion of the born criminal, arguing that crime is causally related to the criminal's physical characteristics, he closely identified inferiority with anomalies of the skull and believed that criminal nature is a form of personal degeneration that is marked morphologically by atavistic peculiarities.

Hamilton D. Wey stressed somatic factors in crime causation to the point that he suggested physical training to eliminate criminality and to counteract physical defects that cause crime.[24] Although another pioneer of the somatic approach, August Drähms, tried to collect data to prove that the physical organism is a cause of crime, he failed to compare his "samples" with other groups.[25] Frances Kellor also achieved questionable results in his investigation of the physical characteristics of white and Negro female criminals, using white female students as a control group.[26]

Charles Goring (1870–1919) was one of the few early constitutional (physical) theorists who were sophisticated enough in methodology to use satisfactory control groups in their experiments. Having made detailed bio-metric comparisons between 3,000 English convicts and a number of non-criminals on thirty-seven physical and six mental traits, Goring disagreed with Lombroso's ideas on constitutional criminal types. Although his com-parative study did produce sufficient evidence for an initial presumption of criminal inferiority in stature and body weight, he went beyond his data in further assuming the hereditary nature of criminality. He did, however, find that criminals were generally shorter and lighter in weight than were the members of his control group; criminals convicted of violent crimes were, by contrast, taller and stronger in relation to their weight. Despite Goring's in-ability to explain why these somatic differences should lead to crime, his work was pioneering in its own right and became one of the most instructive and significant contributions to post-Lombrosian criminal theory.[27]

The authors are aware that William Healy and Augusta F. Bronner, although they tended to presuppose multiple causation,[28] approached the crime problem from a psychological perspective. Holding the family con-stant, by studying it from the beginning to the end of its week, in a study of thousands of cases, they emphasized the infrequency with which delin-quent children have had delinquent siblings or parents with criminal records. Although in a later study they also compared 105 delinquent with 105 nondelinquent boys, they failed to offer at any time a positive statement on delinquency. But they do allude to certain somatic characteristics of delinquents.[29] Their contributions were thus less significant than the more spectacular discoveries of Ernest A. Hooton, who resurrected Lombroso's criminal anthropology and his idea of the constitutional criminal.[30] Com-paring 3,203 people whose honesty was believed to be beyond reproach with more than four times as many male criminals in ten states, Hooton attempted to demonstrate the general inferiority of criminals. He iden-tified criminality with somatological characteristics in his equation of criminal conduct with inherently inferior and degenerate human organ-isms, attributing criminal careers to lower constitutional development, but he used inadequate techniques in his study. Although Hooton alluded to the social circumstances of criminals (mainly to their occupations, educational backgrounds, and marital status), he did so only to demon-strate that social factors do *not* govern the fates of violators. Although he made slight allowances for the social environment of Negro criminals, he believed that these factors are significant only when compared to similar forces among white criminals. Because he believed that crime was a constitutional product, Hooton encouraged segregation of the criminal from society. His findings seemed plausible, but they were invalidated by the inadequate size of his sample and the inconsistency of his data. If Hooton, as George B. Vold has written, had been more careful, "he might even have been forced to abandon some of his extravagant con-clusions."[31] Hooton assumed but failed to prove the relationship between criminality and the various characteristics that he discussed; because he ignored methodological problems, his work is filled with mistaken assumptions and errors.[32]

Somatotypes

The development of the "body type" school of thought coincided with the emergence of the general-inferiority orientation. The somatologists were basically attempting to learn about internal constitution of the individual through examination of his external somatic traits. Although this approach thus emphasized the study of the individual physique, it was focused on more than simple physical characteristics. Assuming that criminal activity is inseparably connected with body build and function, theorists were interested in the *psychic* effects of body types.

The idea of a morphological (structural) criminal type was not new. As early as 1826, Léon Rostand described four human types: muscular, respiratory, cerebral, and digestive. Since then several similar classifications have been offered.[33] Lombroso's endogenous types, which seemed to distinguish between internally and externally produced criminal types, included

1. The *typical or born criminal*, whose criminal behavior cannot be suppressed by any external factor.

2. The *passionate criminal*, who acts without deliberation and commits crimes under the pressure of momentary emotions.

3. The *insane criminal*, who is involved in crime because of his mental illness.

4. The *professional or habitual criminal*, who acts criminally under the influence of environmental factors.

5. The *occasional, or "criminaloid," criminal*, who periodically commits crimes because of his inability to resist temptation.[34]

Emil Kraepelin (1856–1926), who developed one physical-classification theory, also established the foundation for further such investigations.[35] One of his followers, Ernst Kretschmer, became particularly well-known for his attempt to classify physical characteristics and temperamental differences.[36] Basing his conclusions upon medical observations, Kretschmer tried to account for the entire complex structure of the human being. Although he may have tailored his observations to produce the desired symptoms, his work was well-received.[37] His publication of his biopsychological constitutional typology prompted others to follow the same path.

Deducing his hypothesis from Kraepelin's basic distinction between two general mental types, Kretschmer classified the constitutional personalities as *cycloids* or *schizoids*, the latter being subdivided into *epileptoids* and *hysterics*. Kretschmer argued that the psychoses are merely exaggerations of the respective healthy types and that the aberrant cycloid is thus the basic manic-depressive or circular insane type, whereas the aberrant schizoid is the schizophrenic. Accordingly, he distinguished between the *cyclothyme* and *schizothyme* temperaments, both of which represent variations in physique and character:

1. The cyclothyme type is characterized physically by lack of sophistication, informality, spontaneity, and wavering of mood between gaiety and sorrow. Physically, it is a pyknic type, rotund of figure, generally soft-skinned with little muscle, and of medium or short height. Cyclothyme individuals are commonly the realists and humorists among poets, the descriptive and empirical scholars, and gifted organizers and conciliators. Although they are kindhearted, tractable, and sociable, they are also apt to be trivial, negligent, talkative, and sometimes rash.

2. The psychic constitution of the schizothyme type is characterized by strong reactions, vacillation between hypersensitivity and insensitivity, potential apathy, waywardness or tenacity, and general ambivalence. Physically, it is either asthenic (thin, narrowly built, flat) or athletic (wide, muscular, strong, tall). Schizothyme individuals are the logical systematizers and metaphysicists among scholars, the idealists and fanatics among leaders, and the romantic sentimentalists among poets. They are introspective and egotistical.

Kretschmer's supporters argued that criminals who commit less serious crimes are most often the cyclothyme type, whereas the schizothyme type commits the serious offenses. They noted not only that the latter is represented in 50–90 percent and the former in only 10–20 percent of the examined crimes, but the cyclothyme group is also more responsive to reform measures.[38]

Kretschmer's subdivision of the schizoids into epileptoid and hysteric types cannot be clearly defined in terms of physical characteristics. These "displastic," or mixed, body types are psychically depressed and evince tendencies toward explosiveness. As their criminality is rooted in emotions, their crimes generally involve violence. Their sexual development is functionally irregular, and Kretschmer believed that it might be a central factor in their sexual criminality. His model has not, however, been without its critics. "If the Kretschmerian mental and body types," Walter C. Reckless has written, "represent unwarranted sortings of individuals, the contention that the types have affinities is still more unwarranted."[39]

Kretschmer was, however, followed by others who attempted to classify people according to biopsychological types. Edward Spranger, for example, formulated six idealistic "life forms," including the theoretical, the economical, the aesthetic, the religious, the powerful, and the social.[40] Similarly Richard Müller-Freinfels presented a typology distinguishing two types of man: the one who lives an *intellectual life* (man of sense, man of deed, man of fantasy, man of abstraction) and the one who lives an *emotional life* (man of sympathy, man of aggression, man of eroticism).[41]

Later body-type theories were markedly superior to Kretschmer's formulations. William H. Sheldon, who studied relationships between body shape and criminal tendencies, was strongly impressed by Hooton's general somatobiological orientation.[42] In his study of 200 boys between the ages of fifteen and twenty-one at the Hayden Goodwill Institute in Boston, Sheldon distinguished three basic physical-psychological types: the endomorphic, the mesomorphic, and the ectomorphic. The *endomorphic* type maintains a predominantly vegetative function and is characterized by love of comfort and food, slow action, sociability, and calm behavior. The associated temperament is extroverted and convivial, the figure stout and soft. The *mesomorphic* type, on the other hand, has well-developed muscles, similar to those of Kretschmer's athletic schizothyme, and is characterized by aggressiveness, forcible action, and fighting behavior. The associated temperament is vigorous and active, the figure muscular and energetic. The *ectomorphic* type reveals a prominent skin development, similar to that of Kretschmer's asthenic type, and is characterized by introversion, love of privacy, self-restraint, insomnia, and coolness toward others. The temperament is predominantly intellectual, the figure generally tall and thin. Although the Hayden boys were "delinquent youths," Sheldon used the term "delinquency" in a manner different from conventional legal or sociological usage and closer to psychiatric ideas.[43] He defined crime in terms of "biological delinquency" or a similar concept, and introduced an index for differentiating various grades of delinquency.

Sheldon's typology has been strongly reinforced in recent years by further studies by Sheldon Glueck and Eleanor Glueck, in which they have repeatedly stressed the importance of physique in the explanation of delinquency.[44] Applying the typology to 500 "persistently" delinquent and 500 "true non-delinquent" boys in Boston public schools, they sought correlations between physique and sixty-seven individual traits and forty-two family conditions. Although reluctant to claim a direct relationship between crime and delinquency, the Gluecks closely associated delinquency with body characteristics. They agreed with Sheldon, however, that mesomorphs possess higher delinquency potential than do other body types, partly because they are characterized by energy, strength, insensitivity, aggression, and relative freedom from inhibitions, feelings of inadequacy, and emotional instability. Although some of the data support their arguments, their approach is now generally viewed as valuable but inconclusive. The total validity of the biopsychological approach remains in question.[45]

Psychobiology

The psychobiological approach places even greater emphasis upon psychic factors. It is based on belief in the unity of body and soul and hypothesizes that the body is the substructure upon which the psychological characteristics of the personality depend. Louis Vervaeck, who established in Belgium perhaps the first criminal biological diagnostic clinic in the world,[46] propounded a close connection between the human organism and its personality tendencies on a broad scale.[47] He found that body build, morphological traits, irregular somatic functioning, childhood diseases, intake of alcohol, functioning of ductless glands, and hereditary tendencies combine to stimulate the development of the biologically inferior individual. The overwhelming majority of recidivist criminals in his sample possessed these characteristics.

Adolf Lenz, who established an institute to collect data on criminal biology at the University of Graz, Austria, similarly adduced the influence of heredity and physical irregularities on the expressed antisocial tendencies of the personality.[48] Although he recognized the effects of environmental changes upon personality to a limited degree, he emphasized inherited somatic factors as the guide to understanding the deviant human being. Lenz believed that the criminal's predisposition to crime will manifest itself externally if his hereditary tendencies are in conflict with environmental forces (*Umweltlage*).

Karl Birnbaum, claiming to have disregarded all speculative, normative, or philosophical considerations, argued that men can be investigated exclusively through the methods of the natural sciences.[49] He proposed two main personality types marked by criminal pathological characteristics—the individual and the specific—and subdivided the former into five and the latter into two categories:

1. *Individual Types*
   a. *The general organic dementias,* including preseniles, senile dements, arteriosclerotic seniles, congenital syphilitics, paralytics, and postencephalitics.
   b. *Schizophrenics,* including passive-asocial and active criminal types, habitual criminals, and schizoid criminals.
   c. *Paranoiacs,* including degenerate types and mass criminals.
   d. *Epileptics,* including aggressive, brutish, degenerative, and traumatic types.
   e. *Alcoholics,* including episodic alcoholics, dipsomaniacs, and socially defective and intoxicated personalities.
2. *Specific Types*
   a. The *born feeble-minded,* including imbeciles and apathetic-asocials.
   b. *Psychopaths,* including fanatics, grumblers, hysterics, sexual psychopaths, and depressives.

Birnbaum used medical nomenclature, defining his criminal types in terms of illness, and thus interpreted deviations in social behavior as deviations in social health.[50]

Franz Exner, on the other hand, explained crime in terms of inherited predispositions whose expressions are prompted by unfavorable environmental factors.[51] Although some theorists categorize Exner with proponents of the multiple-causation approach, he was inclined toward the biological explanation of criminal causation. As the Gluecks generally concentrated on Sheldon's mesomorphic body type, Exner saw a relationship between Kretschmer's athletic type and criminal behavior. He also believed that mental illness and alcoholism, whether they appear in the family line or in the criminal himself, are important factors. As a result, he made special efforts to prove that the frequency of crime in a family determines the likelihood of further crime in that family and that the frequency of arrests determines the intervals between further arrests. To Exner, crime itself seemed a factor in crime. Following Exner's leadership Erwin Frey argued that, not only are early criminality and recidivism highly correlated, but that recidivists are also concentrated in the mentally defective and psychopathic population, and are largely from biologically weak families.[52]

The Psychological Approach

The psychic approach to the crime problem is not a clearly separate phase of the criminal-biological approach but is rather an extension of the somatological orientation. Many people who might be listed among the adherents of the somatic approach have periodically tried to explain crime in terms of psychic irregularities as well. The somatic orientation emphasizes the primary importance of physical characteristics in criminal causation, however, and attributes only secondary importance to psychic characteristics. The psychic approach, on the other hand, finds the essence of the crime problem in the psyche, apart from any physical traits. These psychic dimensions cover wide areas, however, including hereditary mental degeneration, mental illness, psychopathic disorders, and psychoanalytically discoverable psychological irregularities.

Mental Degeneration

Mental degeneration first became a focus of attention when the study of several family trees revealed a relationship between hereditary mental abnormalities and criminal families. Prosper Despine early described the characteristics of the Chrétien family in which several generations were associated with crime, and Aubry's study of the Keromgal family concluded that murder is contagious. In a similar study of hereditary family ties Richard Louis Dugdale (1841–1883) discovered that 106 descendants of Ada Juke, who died in 1740, had been born illegitimately. Of her descendants 142 were beggars and vagabonds, 181 prostitutes, 7 murderers, and 76 repeated offenders against property.[53] Henry Herbert Goddard studied the Kallikak family from Kansas; it had produced 143 idiots, 33 prostitutes, 24 alcoholics, 3 epileptics, and several other repeating criminals.[54] The Namm family, examined by A. H. Estabrook and C. B. Davenport,[55] also revealed criminal tendencies, which, despite inadequate statistical comparison and sociological analysis, were believed to be associated with mental disorders.[56] As all these studies were conducted without the benefit of acceptable investigation techniques, they offer little scientific insight into the problem of criminal causation. Authors from Aeschylus to Henrik Ibsen, for example, have described similar cases with no more— or less—scientific validity. According to Roman mythology, for example, Vulcan's deformity was caused by Jupiter's being drunk at the time of Vulcan's conception.

Hereditary Insanity

Some investigators have attempted to relate crime to hereditary insanity, a theory quite popular in past eras and still common in our own day. Although "insanity" is a legal and social term, most of these theorists have neglected to make a clear distinction between heredity and its effects upon the social milieu. Many of them approach crime and delinquency from the psychiatric dimension. Although Henry Maudsley (1835–1918), for example, suggested that crime is a product of degeneracy, he refuted the Lombrosian thesis that criminals bear the stigmata of degeneracy on their persons. He viewed criminality as a form of mental abnormality and supported the hypothesis that crime and mental illness are substitutes for each other. "Crime," Maudsley argued, "is a sort of outlet in which their unsound tendencies are discharged; they would go mad if they were not criminals, and they do not go mad because they are criminals."[57] Isaac Ray (1807–1881), on the other hand, originally supported the phrenological approach and even translated Gall's writings into English. Later, however, he became impressed by "an immense mass of cases related by men of unquestionable competence and veracity, where people are irresistibly impelled to the commission of criminal acts."[58] Although he eventually sought to relate medical science and the administration of justice, it was Auguste Forel who established a close relationship between crime and mental disorder, emphasizing a psychiatric explanation of the origins of crime.[59]

Gustav Aschaffenburg (1866–1944) was the most moderate pioneer of the psychiatric approach to the crime problem.[60] Despite his own commitment to a psychiatric approach, Aschaffenburg, who edited the respected periodical *Monatschrift für Kriminalpsychologie und Strafrechtsreform* (*Monthly Paper for Criminal Psychology and Reform of Criminal Law*) from 1904 to 1935, never failed to grant appropriate space to sociological study of crime and delinquency. His openness led his contemporaries to identify him with the leading group of European criminologists. Aschaffenburg, however, did divide criminal types into seven groups according to social factors:

1. Criminals by *chance (Zufallsverbrecher).*
2. Criminals by *affection (Affektsverbrecher).*
3. Criminals by *occasion (Gelegenheitsverbrecher).*
4. Criminals by *consideration (Vorbedachtsverbrecher).*
5. Criminals by *recidivism (Rückfallsverbrecher).*
6. Criminals by *habit (Gewohnheitsverbrecher).*
7. Criminals by *profession (Berufsverbrecher).*

Although this "elective" typology appears to be based on a mixture of biological and sociological factors, Aschaffenburg did maintain his predominantly psychiatric posture.

Intellectual Inferiority

Criminologists sometimes apply the systematic measurement of intelligence and mental aptitudes to explanations of crime and delinquency.[61] The first and best-known intelligence tests were created by Alfred Binet (1857–1911), who, with the assistance of his collaborator, Theodore Simon, produced the Binet-Simon Intelligence Tests in 1905. The "intelligence quotient," known simply as the I.Q., the "mental age" multiplied by 100 and divided by the chronological age, is the core of this approach. Assuming that the individual's knowledge should increase as he grows older, Binet hypothesized that the ratio should consequently also remain unchanged. As the norm was set at 100, an I.Q. under 100 would indicate a lower intelligence and one above 100 a higher intelligence. Binet and Simon believed that testing would reveal whether the person's innate ability had advanced to the level appropriate to his chronological age or whether he possessed intelligence deficiencies.

Some experiments were made on prison populations even before World War I.[62] A second testing effort, the psychological examination of American soldiers in World War I, produced especially controversial results.[63] Since then many attempts have been made to prove the criminological utility of intelligence-testing devices.[64] Yet no significant relationship between low intelligence and crime or delinquency has yet been discovered. Only a fraction of those who have low I.Q.s violate the criminal code, and many criminals and delinquents have high intelligence. The results of intelligence and achievement tests administered to 250 youths in a New York State Division of Youth Facilities remedial-reading and -mathematics program revealed that the average I.Q. of these boys was no different from that of the average of all American youth. No significant relationship between I.Q. and delinquency was discovered. The typical youth at the facility had average intelligence and capability but was four to five years behind in achievement and acquisition of basic learning skills.[65]

Various personality tests have also been used in conjunction with intelligence tests, with results that have been little better. The Rorschach "Ink-Blot" Test, designed by Herman Rorschach in 1911, has many supporters. As the subject finds "pictures" in neutral ink blots, he reveals his own attitudes and feelings to the trained questioner, who, in turn, analyzes, interprets, and scores his responses. Another test is the Minnesota Multiphasic Personality Inventory (M.M.P.I.), which consists of a large number of items in social, ethical, and health categories. The respondent's answers again reveal his attitudes and personality characteristics. The M.M.P.I. is more structured than is the Rorschach, and many investigators prefer the latter because they believe that its open structure affords greater diagnostic potential.

General Psychology and Psychoanalysis

The approach of general psychology and psychoanalysis to the crime problem is based upon the hypothesis that mental, emotional, and dynamic psychiatric characteristics are guides to the understanding of delinquency and crime. Of all orientations it seems to be the most popular. Yet as early as 1908 Hugo Hoegel doubted that it was possible to classify criminals on a psychological basis.[66] Although he was not the first or the last to question the validity of psychological approaches to the crime and delinquency problem, his doubts had especially serious ramifications. Psychological explanations are little worse than others, although they also suffer from the difficulty inherent in making concepts operational. Yet, though they produce no more definitive results than do other procedures, they are subject to more kinds of error than are others.

As early as 1884 A. Krauss proposed an extravagant and primitive criminal-psychological theory, in which he identified three main groups of criminals, each further divided into three subgroups:

1. *Energetic* criminals, including monsters, cholerics, and passionates.
2. *Evil* criminals, including demoniacs, intriguers, and crooks.
3. *Weakling* criminals, including mean people, sneaks, and revelers.

His highly fanciful typology differs little, however, from similar classifications, including that of the Greek Claudius Galen (A.D. 130–c. 200), who distinguished choleric, phlegmatic, sanguine, and melancholic criminal types.[67] Other early classification attempts were undertaken by Eyvind Olrik who distinguished between criminals according to their degrees of will power,[68] and Ottokar Tesar, who found "symptoms" that seemed to distinguish criminal types.[69] Tesar emphasized a historical approach, based on a developmental projection of the past. The criminal should be judged by his *symptomatic significance*, he argued, rather than by the injurious results of his delinquency or crime.

The French school founded by A. Lacassagne (1843–1924) and Adolphe Prins divided criminals into three main psychological groups:

1. *Instinctive criminals (criminels d'instinct)*, who commit crimes because of inherited or acquired penchants.
2. *Action criminals (criminels d'action)*, who commit crimes although they do not have penchants for crime.
3. *Mentally ill criminals (criminels de pensée)*, who commit crimes because of their mental illness.[70]

Although the French school emphasized the psychological features of delinquency and crime, it also revealed slight traces of an inherent social determinism as well. J. Maxwell described a similar typology:

1. *Habitual criminals*, with innate or acquired tendencies toward crime.
2. *Occasional criminals*, with physiological needs (like poverty, hunger, sexuality), emotional needs (like anger, hatred, revenge), or psychosocial needs (like reputation, religion, political conviction, superstition).[71]

M. Kaufmann was also unable to evade the influence of social considerations in his proposed listing of psychological types:

1. *Vagabond type*, involved in petty crimes.
2. *Energetic type*, involved in violent crimes.
3. *Intermediate type*, involved in occasional crime.[72]

Ferenc Finkey made a special effort to develop a purely psychological typology but failed to exclude social elements:

1. *Juvenile delinquents*, whose psychic status is not yet developed.
2. *Mentally abnormal criminals*, whose crimes originate in their mental illnesses.
3. *Tough, or passionate, criminals*, the most dangerous type, who lack human sentiment and are cruel.
4. *Persistent criminals*, who lack moral education and habitually commit crimes.
5. *Swindlers*, who habitually commit clever, intellectual crimes for gain.
6. *Violent criminals*, who habitually or frequently commit violent crimes.
7. *Emotional, or fanatical, criminals*, including political criminals.
8. *Criminals with antiethical and antisocial tendencies*, who only occasionally or rarely commit crimes.
9. *Criminals with vague antisocial tendencies*, whose crimes are products of the moment.
10. *Occasional criminals*, whose crimes may be excused on both ethical and social grounds.[73]

Erich Wulffen formulated an overdetailed typology, approximating the classification of the criminal code itself. The thief, the burglar, the sex offender, the murderer, and the embezzler are only a few of the many types he described.[74] On the other hand, Hans Gruhle distinguished five main psychological groups, including criminals by inclination, by weakness, by passion, by reputation or conviction, and by necessity. *Criminals by inclination* are characterized by their antisocial way of life. They defy the demands of law and order, more often violently. Gruhle distinguished active and passive criminals by inclination, the *active type* consisting of professional criminals (burglars, shoplifters, and so on), the *passive type* committing crimes only when the risks of arrest are acceptable. The passive type is no less inclined to crime, for he has no positive attitudes toward the social order, but he is less dangerous because his criminal activities are often subordinated to employment, marriage, or some other interest. The psychic structure of the criminal, Gruhle suggested, eventually determines the group to which he will belong.

Criminals of weakness cannot be regarded as antisocial personalities and in fact are often happier when they feel no "necessity" to commit crimes. Not only are their personalities amorphous and their lives unstable, but they also lack positive social attitudes, although they are not antisocial. Their behavior is determined or motivated by situational factors. Some alcoholics but mainly vagabonds and prostitutes belong to this group; often this type of criminal is mentally retarded.

Criminals by passion, or affective criminals, have strong personalities. Irritability, jealousy, vindictiveness, despair, and similar moods often mark their criminal behavior.

Criminals by reputation or conviction, on the other hand, believe that crime is their duty; they include assassins, fanatics, schizophrenics, and hysterics.

According to Gruhle, *criminals by necessity* are a theoretical type that does not exist in fact, for, he argues, a crime cannot be committed only and exclusively because of economic need. Although need is only a situation that opens the way for the activation of other criminal characteristics, Gruhle has defined a separate category because criminals of other types may also react criminally because of need. This category thus allows for diverse combinations of psychic factors in the causation of crime and delinquency.[75]

Raymond Corsini described seven groups of criminals:

1. *Accidental criminal,* who commits crimes "without intending to do so" (for example, the reckless driver).
2. *Situational criminal,* who "rationalizes the rightfulness of his behavior due to the peculiar structures and press of circumstances" (like the man who steals a loaf of bread to escape starvation).
3. *Irresponsible criminal,* who is not to be considered guilty (like the young child or the idiot).

4. *Neurotic criminal,* who commits a crime to fight a problem but "does not know what he is fighting, why he is fighting, nor even that he is fighting."

5. *Psychopathic criminal,* who commits crime impulsively.

6. *Mentally unbalanced criminal,* whose criminality is characterized by "the senselessness or lack of psychological necessity for the crime" (like the violent sex offender).

7. *Professional criminal,* who makes his living from crime (like Al Capone).[76]

Each one of these types, however, is only an example of the different psychological experiences involved in the various dimensions of crime and delinquency.

Another trend in the psychological approach to crime developed from the thinking of Sigmund Freud (1856–1939) and opened the way to understanding the psychodynamics of the criminal.[77] Just as Lombroso modified his hypothesis several times, Freud also modified his approach as he continued his work. Adherents and interpreters of Freud and enthusiastic followers of the psychodynamic approach have, however, introduced most of the criminologically significant modifications of Freud's original ideas. In fact, Freud himself had little to say about the specific problem of crime. Freud's "discovery" of the unconscious part of the psyche, his interpretation of the functioning of the human mind, and his dynamic explanation of personality development had immediate effects upon the study of criminal conduct. The functioning of the human mind, Freud concluded, is divided into three parts: the *id,* representing the biological or instinctual drives; the *superego,* embodying the socioethical or moral code; and the *ego* (the self), which mediates between the other two parts, integrating the demands of nature and of social reality in the personality. The human being is born as a complete id, and the superego and ego emerge as he grows and develops. Early childhood experiences and sexual factors, Freud maintained, have important formative influences upon the socialized dimension of mental functioning and on personality adjustment. Because certain desires and conflicts are unacceptable, the ego, through its defense mechanisms, represses them into the unconscious. Repressed materials may ultimately be expressed in the form of crime or delinquency.

In the Freudian therapeutic strategy, the contents of the unconscious are uncovered through the patient's free associations. As repressed materials are discharged into his consciousness, he is able to reeducate and restructure his personality. The therapist aids in this analytical quest by helping the patient to uncover and interpret this material. The patient can gain insight only when he is free of repressed materials; the therapist can misinterpret the patient's repressions and can even transmit his own "complexes" to the analysand. As the ultimate control of crime, according to psychoanalytic theorists, depends upon reeducation and restructuring of individual personality, psychoanalytically oriented penologists see the prison of the future as a special type of hospital, in which the delinquent or the criminal will receive adequate treatment in accordance with modern principles.[78]

Some of Freud's collaborators and disciples disagreed with several aspects of his theory and developed their own variations. Carl G. Jung (1875–1961), the founder of analytic psychology, differed with Freud's emphasis on the motivating force of sexual factors. He adopted the term *collective unconscious* to describe a social experience in psychological terms and also distinguished between introverted and extroverted personalities.[79] Alfred Adler (1870–1937), the founder of *individual psychology*, emphasized the human desire to belong to a group and to have status. The development of either a *will to power* or an *inferiority complex*, Adler concluded, may lead to criminal conduct. When an individual becomes aware of his shortcomings, he often overcompensates for them, which leads to excesses in behavior. Delinquency becomes a means by which he may draw attention to himself and compensate for his sensed inferiority.[80]

August Aichorn described and explained the problem of *wayward youth* and called for the "right" sort of parental affection, which he believed would help the juvenile to adjust to the controlled community.[81] Kate Friedlander, however, found only quantitative differences between criminals and noncriminals (indicating that everyone is a *potential* criminal) and posited the idea that delinquency, a product of childhood experiences, occurs when the child is unable to resist.[82] Kurt R. Eissler came nearer to a sociological understanding of the delinquency and crime problem, viewing delinquency as aggressive reaction to society's value system.[83] Although each of these theorists basically accepted a metaphysical conception of the unconscious, none neglected environmental factors. All, however, ultimately viewed the delinquent and the criminal primarily as individuals rather than as members of the group.[84]

NOTES

1. Harry Elmer Barnes and Negley K. Teeters, *New Horizons in Criminology* (3rd ed.; Englewood Cliffs, N.J.: 1959), p. 125.

2. Havelock Ellis, *The Criminal* (London: 1913).

3. Cesare Lombroso's works include *L'Uomo Delinquente* (Turin: 1876); *L'Amore nel Suicidio e nel Delitto* (Turin: 1881); *Il Delitto Politico* (Milan: 1890); *La Donna Delinquente* (Turin: 1893); *L'Anthropologie criminelle et ses récents progrès* (Paris: 1891); *Le Crime, causes et remèdes* (Paris: 1899); *Delitti Vecchi e Delitti Nuovi* (Turin: 1902).

4. A Latin word referring to ancestors.

5. The term "born criminal" was coined by Enrico Ferri in 1880.

6. W. P. J. Pompe, "L'Homme criminel," in *Une Nouvelle école de science criminelle: l'école d'Utrecht* (Paris: 1959), p. 62.

7. For a more detailed account of Lombroso's life and work, see Marvin E. Wolfgang, "Cesare Lombroso," in Hermann Mannheim, ed., *Pioneers in Criminology* (London: 1960), pp. 168–227.

8. Ferri, *Criminal Sociology*, trans. J. I. Kelly and John Lisle (Boston: 1917) from *Sociologia Criminale* (Turin: 1884).

9. When Ferri became attracted to apparently more socialistic views in his later life, his scientific commitment to criminology lessened. As he came to believe in the benefits of a socialist social structure, he increasingly blamed the existing capitalistic economic order for crime. At that time he was preparing the third edition of his *Sociologia Criminale* (the earlier editions were entitled *Nuovi Orizzonti del Diritto Penale*, or *The New Horizons of Criminal Law*). When the Mussolini regime asked him to prepare a new criminal code, he submitted the radical Ferri Project of 1921, which seems to have resulted from his positivist approach. For a more detailed account of Ferri's life and work, see Thorsten Sellin, "Enrico Ferri," *Journal of Criminal Law, Criminology and Police Science*, 48 (January-February, 1958).

10. Raffaele Garofalo, *Criminology*, trans. by R. W. Millar (Boston: 1914) from *Criminologia* (Naples: 1885).

11. For a more detailed account of Garofalo's life and work, see Francis A. Allen, "Raffaele Garofalo," *Journal of Criminal Law, Criminology and Police Science*, 45 (November–December, 1954).

12. Jean Pinatel, "La Vie et l'oeuvre de Cesare Lombroso," *Bulletin, Société Internationale de criminologie*, No. 2 (1959), p. 222.

13. George B. Vold, *Theoretical Criminology* (New York: 1958), pp. 41, 157.

14. These typologies have been distorted more than once in political efforts to prove the degeneracy of certain groups. It has been stated that attitudes toward the concept of the biological criminal personality will come to be of far-reaching importance in any totalitarian state, and under the Nazi regime it was predicted that it would "come to be a corner-stone in the German criminal law to come." Edmund Mezger, *Kriminalpolitik* (Berlin: 1934), 138.

15. Vold, *op. cit.*, p. 43

16. Johann Kaspar Lavater, *Physiognomische Fragmente zur Beföderung der Menschenkenntniss und Menschenlebe* (Leipzig: 1775).

17. Gustav Aschaffenburg, "Kriminalanthropologie und Kriminalbiologie," in Alexander Elster and Heinrich Lingemann, eds., *Handwörterbuch der Kriminologie* (Berlin: 1933), p. 833.

18. Franz J. Gall, *Introduction au cours de physiologie du cerveau* (Paris: 1809).

19. Gall and J. G. Spurzheim, *Recherches sur le système nerveux* (Paris: 1809).

20. Charles Caldwell, *Elements of Phrenology* (New York: 1824).

21. Émile Laurent, *Les Habitués des prisons de Paris d'anthropologie et de psychologie criminelles* (Lyons: 1890).

22. Vold, *op. cit.*, p. 49.

23. Hans Kurella, *Naturgeschichte des Verbrechers: Grundzüge der Kriminellen Anthropologie und Kriminalpsychologie* (Berlin: 1893); Kurella, *Die Grenzen der Zurechnungsfähigkeit und die Kriminalanthropologie* (Berlin: 1903); and Kurella, *Lombroso als Mensch und Forscher* (Wiesbaden: 1913).

24. Hamilton D. Wey, *Criminal Anthropology* (New York: 1890).

25. August Drähms, *The Criminal: His Personality and Environment* (New York: 1900).

26. Frances Kellor, *Experimental Sociology* (New York: 1901).

27. Charles Goring, *The English Convict: A Statistical Study* (London: 1913). See also Edwin D. Driver, "Charles Buckman Goring," in Hermann Mannheim, ed., *Pioneers in Criminology* (London: 1960), pp. 335–348.

28. William Healy and Augusta F. Bronner, *New Light on Delinquency and Its Treatment* (New Haven: 1936).

29. Healy and Bronner, *Delinquents and Criminals: Their Making and Unmaking* (New York: 1926), p. 99.

30. Ernest A. Hooton, *Crime and the Man* (Cambridge, Mass.: 1939); and Hooton, *The American Criminal: An Anthropological Study* (Cambridge, Mass.: 1939).

31. Vold, *op. cit.*, p. 63.

32. For an attack on traditional statistical methods of showing the causation of delinquency see Travis Hirschi and Hanan C. Selvin, "False Criteria of Causality in Delinquency Research," *Social Problems,* 13 (Winter 1966), 254–268.

33. See Olaf Kinberg, *Basic Problems of Criminology* (Copenhagen: 1935).

34. This list was compiled from several works by Lombroso, mainly *L'Uomo Delinquente* (5th ed.; Turin: 1896) and *Delitti Vecchi e Delitti Nuovi.*

35. Emil Kraepelin, *Psychiatrie* (Leipzig: 1883).

36. Ernst Kretschmer, trans. by W. J. H. Sprott (New York: 1925), from *Körperbau und Character* (Berlin: 1921). The German edition went through several published revisions.

37. Vold, *op. cit.*, p. 66.

38. See Viernstein, "Die Durchführung eines Stufensystems in den Bayerischen Strafanstalten," *Zeitschrift für Medizinalbeamte,* 12 (1923), 151.

39. Walter C. Reckless, *The Crime Problem* (3rd ed.; New York: 1961), p. 279.

40. Edward Spranger, *Lebensformen, Geisteswissenschaftliche Psychologie und Ethik der Persönlichkeit* (Berlin: 1914).

41. Richard Müller-Freinfels, *Philosophie der Individualität* (Berlin: 1921).

42. William H. Sheldon, *Psychology and the Promethean Will* (New York: 1936); Sheldon, *Varieties of Human Physique* (New York: 1940); Sheldon, *Delinquent Youth: An Introduction to Constitutional Psychiatry* (New York: 1949); and Sheldon, *Atlas of Man* (New York: 1954).

43. Vold, *op. cit.*, p. 72.

44. Sheldon Glueck and Eleanor Glueck, *Unraveling Juvenile Delinquency* (New York: 1950); and Glueck and Glueck, *Physique and Delinquency* (New York: 1956).

45. An examination of four case histories of physically disabled adolescent boys committed by a magistrate to an approved school in Singapore revealed that both parents of three of the four boys had died while the boys were very young, causing a period of emotional stress. Disability was a secondary factor and only aggravated the problem caused by these deaths. See Rosemary Mills, "Delinquent Disabled Boys," *Crime and Delinquency,* 13 (1967), 545–552.

46. Louis Vervaeck, *Syllabus du cours d'anthropologie criminelle donné a la prison de Forest* (Brussels: 1926).

47. Vervaeck, *Service d'anthropologie pénitentiaire* (1907).

48. Adolf Lenz, *Grundriss der Kriminalbiologie* (Berlin: 1926); Lenz, *Mörder, die Untersuchung der Persönlichkeit als Beitrag zur Kriminalbiologischen Kasuistik und Methodik* (Graz, Aus.: 1931); Lenz, "Die Bedeutung der Kriminalbiologie," *Archiv für Kriminalbiologie,* 88 (1931), 222–26; and Lenz, "Der Kriminalbiologische Untersuchungsbogen," *Mitteilungen der Kriminalbiologischen Gesellschaft,* 11 (1929).

49. Karl Birnbaum, *Kriminal-Psychopathologie und Psychobiologische Verbrecherkunde* (Berlin: 1931).

50. The task of modern criminal somatology, according to Lenz, is "not to forgive the criminal, but to evaluate him properly, often more strictly." Lenz, *Kriminal-biologische Untersuchungsbogen*, p. 139.

51. Franz Exner, *Kriminologie* (Berlin: 1949).

52. Erwin Frey, *Der Frühkriminelle Rückfallsverbrecher* (Basel: 1959).

53. Richard Louis Dugdale, *The Jukes: A Study in Crime, Pauperism, Disease and Heredity* (New York: 1895). A. H. Estabrook, *The Jukes in 1915* (Washington, D.C.: 1916) is a later examination of the Jukes family.

54. Henry Herbert Goddard, *The Kallikak Family: A Study in the Heredity of Feeble-Mindedness* (New York: 1913).

55. Estabrook and C. B. Davenport, *The Namm Family* (Lancaster, Eng.: 1912).

56. Stephen Schafer, *Sterilization and Castration in the Service of Penal Law* (Budapest: 1939), pp. 4–5, in Hungarian.

57. Henry Maudsley, *The Pathology of the Mind* (London: 1867); Maudsley, *Body and Mind* (London: 1870); Maudsley, *Body and Will* (London: 1883). See also Maudsley, "Insanity in Relation to Criminal Responsibility," *British Medical Journal* (September 28, 1895). For a more detailed account of Maudsley's life and work, see Peter D. Scott, "Henry Maudsley," *Journal of Criminal Law, Criminology and Police Science*, 46 (March–April, 1956), 753.

58. Isaac Ray, *Contributions to Mental Pathology* (Boston: 1873). For a more detailed account of Ray's life and work, see Wilfred Overholser, "Isaac Ray," *Journal of Criminal Law, Criminology and Police Science*, 45 (September–October, 1954), 249–263.

59. Auguste Forel and Albert Mahaim, *Crime et anomalies mentales constitutionelles, la plaie sociale des déséquilibrés à responsabilité diminuée* (Geneva: 1902).

60. Aschaffenburg, *Das Verbrechen und Seine Bekämpfung* (Heidelberg: 1903). For a more detailed account of Aschaffenburg's life and work, see Hans von Hentig, "Gustav Aschaffenburg," *Journal of Criminal Law, Criminology and Police Science*, 45 (July–August, 1954), 117–122.

61. For a brief historical account of mental testing, see Otto Klineberg, "Mental Test," *Encyclopedia of the Social Sciences* (New York: 1933); and Vold, *op cit.*, pp. 79–89.

62. Goddard, *Feeblemindedness: Its Causes and Consequences* (New York: 1914).

63. (Washington: 1921.)

64. See Carl Murchison, *Criminal Intelligence* (Worcester, Mass.: 1926); and Simon Fulchin, *Intelligence and Crime* (Chicago: 1939).

65. "I.Q. and Delinquency," *Youth Service News*, 18 (1967), 27–28. See also Starke R. Hathaway and Elio D. Monachesi, *Adolescent Personality and Behavior* (Minneapolis: 1963).

66. Hugo Hoegel, *Die Einteilung der Verbrecher in Klassen* (Leipzig: 1908).

67. A. Krauss, *Psychologie des Verbrechers* (Berlin: 1884).

68. Eyvind Olrik, "Über die Einteilung der Verbrecher," *Zeitschrift für die Gesamte Strafrechtswissenschaft*, 14, p. 73; and Olrik, "Die Strafgesetzgebung der Gegenwart in Rechtsvergleichender Darstellung," *Intern. Krimin. Vereiningung* (Berlin: 1894).

69. Ottokar Tesar, *Die Symptomatische Bedeutung des Verbrecherischen Verhaltens: Ein Beitrag zur Wertungslehre im Strafrecht* (Berlin: 1904).

70. A. Lacassagne, *Précis de médecine légale* (Paris: 1906); and Adolphe Prins, *La Défense sociale et les transformations du droit pénal* (Brussels: 1910).

71. J. Maxwell, *Le Criminel et la société* (Paris: 1909); Maxwell, *Le Concept social du crime et son évolution* (Paris: 1914).

72. M. Kaufmann, *Die Psychologie des Verbrechers* (Vienna: 1912).

73. Ferenc Finkey, *A Magyar Büntetöjog Tankönyve* (Budapest: 1914); and Finkey, *Adatok a Büntettesek Jellemcsoportjainak Megállapitásához* (Budapest: 1933).

74. Erich Wulffen, *Psychologie des Verbrechers* (Berlin: 1908); Wulffen, *Gauner und Verbrecher Typen* (Berlin: 1910); and Wulffen, *Der Sexualverbrecher* (Berlin: 1911).

75. Hans W. Gruhle, "Characterologie," in Alexander Elster and Heinrich Lingemann, eds., *Handwörterbuch der Kriminologie und der Anderen Strafrechtlichen Hilfswissenschaften* (Berlin: 1933), pp. 203–206.

76. Raymond Corsini, "Criminal Psychology, Criminal Types" in Vernon C. Branham and Samuel B. Kutash, eds., *Encyclopedia of Criminology* (New York: 1949), pp. 110–114.

77. Among the many well-known works of Sigmund Freud see *A General Introduction to Psychoanalysis* (New York: 1920); *Das Ich und das Es* (Vienna: 1923); *Hemmung, Symptom und Angst* (Vienna: 1926); and *An Outline of Psychoanalysis* (New York: 1949).

78. Gregory Zilboorg, "Psychoanalysis and Criminology," in Vernon C. Branham and Samuel B. Kutash, eds., *Encyclopedia of Criminology* (New York: 1949), p. 405. An acceleration of physical and sexual maturation in Japanese juvenile delinquents accompanies significant emotional and social immaturity. Nationwide investigations of Japanese juvenile delinquents show that 12 percent of those in reform and juvenile training schools are mentally deficient and that the percentage of psychopaths in these institutions fluctuates between 25 and 50. See Kokichi Higuchi, "Some Problems in Physical and Mental Characteristics of Juvenile Delinquents Today," *Acta Criminologiae et Medicinae Legalis Japonica*, 33, No. 1 (1967), 15–24.

79. See Carl G. Jung, *Modern Man in Search of a Soul* (London: 1933).

80. See Hertha Orgler, *Alfred Adler: The Man and His Work* (London: 1963).

81. August Aichorn, *Wayward Youth* (New York: 1935).

82. Kate Friedlander, *The Psychoanalytical Approach to Juvenile Delinquency* (New York: 1947).

83. Kurt R. Einsler, *Searchlights on Delinquency* (New York: 1949).

84. See Clara C. Cooper, *A Comparative Study of Delinquent and Nondelinquent* (Portsmouth, O.: 1960); and Hans J. Eysenck, *Crime and Personality* (Boston: 1964).

Chapter 5

■ *The Causes of Delinquency: Sociological Explanations*

The sociological view of delinquency assumes that a personality is structured by his relations with his environment. Rather than seeking biological explanations for the causes of crime, the sociologist views criminal behavior as a result of abnormalities of the offender's social existence or of society's attitude toward him. The criminal, who is *socially* different from those who conform to the law, is thus deviant in the socialized human group. His criminal activity, in contrast to normal, conforming behavior, is antisocial. Although the causes of his crime originate in exogenous factors, his criminality is stimulated by his defective relation with society. He is therefore unaffected by conventional punishment which must be replaced by measures aimed at reform. A solution to the crime and delinquency problem, sociological theorists argue, can be found only in evaluation of the offender's relations with his social environment.

Although sociological explanations have been widely criticized, they are most influential at the present time. Even the extremist adherents of the somatic or psychic approaches are now unable to ignore the causal impact of social factors in delinquency and crime. The sociological orientation can be divided into three separate categories:

1. *The Offensive Approach*

   This approach emphasizes the influence of organized society in development and prevention of crime.

   a. The delinquent or criminal reacts to society through his own free will, which provokes him to attack society, leading to consequent offensive action against him by society.

   b. Society is often unjust, provoking offensive actions against social wrongs.

2. *The Defensive Approach*

In this orientation delinquency and crime are viewed as products of social disorganization. Emphasis is on the need for a social defense against criminality because people learn to be criminals in a social context. As both society and the criminal are at fault, consequent defensive action should be taken against both. Among the theoretical formulations following this approach are:

    a. Life-trend theories.

    b. Ecological theories.

    c. The differential-association theory.

    d. The anomie theory.

    e. The containment theory.

3. *The Socialistic Approach*

This approach gives special attention to suprauniversalistic conceptions that demand unconditional obedience from members of society and requires that the violator of a given ideology should be suppressed. This approach is adapted to historical and contemporary ideological interests and includes:

    a. Economic-structure theories.

    b. Socialism.

    c. Suprauniversalistic theories.

■ *The Offensive Approach*

None of the sociological approaches to criminal causation is complete or all-inclusive. Even the explanation of the offensive approach is influenced by defensive elements. The offensive approach primarily reflects the predominant perspective from which the problem is conceived and interpreted. Although both it and the defensive perspective are interrelated at various points, each may be analyzed separately because of such distinct emphases as that of the offensive approach on the "attacking" attitude apparent in offenses by the criminal and on society's response.

Crime Initiated by the Criminal

Classical criminal law assumed that criminal initiative and irresponsibility led to deviant behavior. Such eighteenth-century philosophers as Voltaire, Jeremy Bentham, and Cesare Beccaria were among the first to propagate this point of view. They viewed crime as a product of the free will, an attitude that still finds strong expression in popular slogans and penal practice.

As man freely decides to commit his own acts, the criminal, who chooses negative acts, is ultimately responsible for his own criminal activity, according to this view. As the offender finds that one or more of his wants or wishes have not been realized satisfactorily, he eventually comes to believe that the structure of society is restricting him or is partly or wholly unjust. The criminal thinks only of his own interests and has no concern for injustices to the broader social group. He attacks society by violating standards that are in the way of his satisfaction. If he is hungry, he steals bread. If he wishes to live more luxuriously, he robs a bank. If he dislikes work, he forges a check in order to live at another's expense. If he hates someone, he kills him. The choice and decision are his. Delinquency and crime are expressed, through his free will, against social norms, regardless of society's influence, if any, in his decision-making process.

This formal retributive approach has dominated criminal theory for nearly 150 years. Today, even though most courts, legislatures, and penal systems continue to operate upon this principle, periodic reforms have softened its rigidity. Theoretical modification or extension of this principle has led to recent investigations of criminal causation and to the introduction of elementary prevention and treatment programs. The offensive approach to the crime problem, nevertheless, continues to dominate contemporary efforts to control delinquency and crime.

Crime in Response to Social Pressures

The emphasis upon social pressures, a second variant of the offensive approach, assumes that the criminal is not responsible for his crime because he cannot escape the pressures of society to commit it. Although society is charged with the responsibility of restraining individual will, its failure to provide adequate alternatives leads to criminal pressures and decisions. Criminal conduct is therefore an expression of environmental factors. Causation reflects little more than personal response to pressure. Proponents of this theoretical position assume that society, rather than the criminal, is at fault. Because society is organized, the concept of individual responsibility is replaced by an emphasis upon collective responsibility. Offensive action against the pressures of society itself, these theorists maintain, is justified as long as society blocks access to the goals of the criminal. The criminal, according to Léonce Manouvrier, is merely an expression of the social environment. Adolphe Quetelet (1796–1874) remarked, "Tout le monde [est] coupable du crime, excepté le criminel" ("Everyone is guilty of the crime, except the criminal"). A. Lacassagne (1843–1904), however, was less doctrinaire in his interpretation. Although he called the criminal a "microbe" and made vague allowance for his responsibility, he mainly blamed society for the emergence of the criminal personality. The criminal microbe breeds in the social environment. His action therefore reflects both individual and social sickness. Societies, Lacassagne observed bitterly, eventually create the criminals they deserve.

Although the theory of pressures toward criminality assumes a strong environmental influence in criminal causation, it differs from the Marxist theory of crime. Whereas Marxist theory holds the *economic* structure responsible for the origins of criminal conduct, the offensive-pressure theorists relate crime to existing *social* values. As the criminal lives in a society, only some of whose members are criminals, the society, or even the economy, cannot be regarded as completely disorganized. Although this view gained great popularity among those who believed entirely in the innocence of criminal offenders, it achieved its greatest triumph at the International Criminal-Anthropological Congress in 1889; there its adherents, led by Manouvrier, pressed Cesare Lombroso to recognize the value of sociological explanations of crime.

Donald R. Taft, a modern proponent of this view, has expressed the belief that "criminal behavior, like all behavior, is part and product of social relationships," and has proposed that the criminal should be viewed "as a product of past and current experiences."[1] Taft, however, did mention the social structure and the system of values and institutions derived from the past to which each man reacts, and suggested that they act upon the immediate situation to influence both law-abiding and criminal behavior. Frank E. Hartung, who has expressed a similar point of view, the "social-disorganization hypothesis," maintains that "the criminal is a normal human being, but he is living in a disorganized society which tends to disorganize its individual members."[2] W. I. Thomas (1863–1947) and Florian Znaniecki (1882–1957) supplied additional support for this thesis in their remarkable sociological study of the Polish peasant in his home country and after his immigration to the United States.[3]

■ *The Defensive Approach*

The offensive and defensive approaches to the crime problem are closely related, and it is difficult to establish a clear-cut line of demarcation between them. Present popular explanations of criminal causation, though containing elements of the offensive approach, are also influenced by the defensive hypotheses and their inherent pessimism about criminal rehabilitation and crime control. This approach does not entirely exclude biological, instinctive, and hereditary factors in the commission of crime.

Although the criminal's personal responsibility is not overlooked, the essential element of crime causation remains the interrelations between criminal and environment. The offender acquires criminal skills within his social environment, and his criminal acts are determined partly by cultural values and social procedures. Emphasizing the "social-psychological hypothesis," the defensive theorists view criminal conduct as a natural outgrowth of society. As the theory of the criminal's "functional state of readiness" to learn implies, in its most extreme sense, that crime is an integral part of any society, more emphasis upon defense against aspects of criminal causation is justified.[4]

A statement by Adolphe Prins, made before he joined Franz von Liszt and G. A. van Hamel in launching the more conciliatory multiple-causation approach, partially described the defensive orientation: "Criminality develops from the nature of humanity, it is not transcendent, but immanent."[5] Similarly, Emile Durkheim (1858–1917), who believed in the "normality" of crime, said that he could hardly imagine a society without it because the "fundamental conditions of social structure" necessarily implied its existence. Durkheim foresaw the modification of present forms of criminality only if society were to arrive at a stage of *collective sentiment*, in which crime would be recognized as a product of interacting social forces.[6] Even then, it would simply take other forms. Although the views of Prins and Durkheim seem to imply a deterministic view of criminal causation and to allow limited or no room for free will in decision making, most defensive theorists did not rely on social environment exclusively but also recognized that acquired or learned behavior develops from the interrelation and interaction of the criminal and his society.

Life-Trend Theories

In the life-trend theories criminality is explained in terms of biosociological behavior patterns, the criminal's way of life. Although at first this approach may be confused with multiple-causation theories, it actually offers an explanation of greater scope. The multiple-causation approach refers only to specific causes of crime; life-trend theories are concerned with the overall positive or negative character of the criminal's way of life. They therefore include all criminal components in a "dynamic structure-coherence"[7] to provide a complete profile of the criminal and an explanation for the criminal act.

The life-trend explanation is not a new discovery in the search for the causes of delinquency and crime. As early as 1840, H. A. Frégier distinguished between thieves who steal occasionally from necessity and those who steal professionally.[8] In the middle of the last century H. Mayhew also differentiated between casual criminals and those who commit crimes as part of their general way of life.[9] W. E. Wahlberg[10] used the terms "habitual" and "occasional" criminals (*Gewohnheitsverbrecher* and *Gelegenheitsverbrecher*) to characterize the general life patterns of individual criminals, and G. Moreau divided criminals into three classifications: professional, habitual, and occasional.[11]

Edmund Mezger based his life-trend theory on a conception of "culpability of life conduct" (*Lebensführungsschuld*), first in his paper on "crime as a whole" and later in his textbook on German criminal law.[12] As modern legislation provides not only for punishment but also for prevention, itself a form of penal intervention, Mezger argued that guilt must be found in the criminal but not in the crime. He affirmed belief in criminal character while supporting a parallel faith in the changeable nature of that character. He reconciled this contradiction, however, by suggesting that certain characteristics of the criminal personality cannot be changed, whereas other elements can. The criminal, Mezger argued, can to some extent modify (*etwas kann*) personality or character factors that would normally lead him into crime. If he does nothing to improve or to correct himself, however, he bears the guilt for his own shortcomings that have led him into crime. He has not only allowed himself to develop criminal characteristics, but he has also failed to counteract their influence in his behavior. He must accept the blame for his crimes because his present state has come about through his own fault (*sein So-Sein ein durch eigene Schuld So-Geworden-Sein ist*). If, on the other hand, certain characteristics cannot be changed by himself, he should not, Mezger argued, be blamed for their contribution to his crime.

Although Mezger paid little attention to the criminal's social circumstances, he expected the offender to change his own criminal personality and the circumstances in which he exists. The criminal, Mezger believed, is, within limits, less the product of society than a product of his own will. Although Mezger did not apply his "culpability of life conduct" hypothesis to construction of any criminal typology, he recognized that variable life patterns reflect the existence of a wide variety of factors that may influence culpability or the criminal's life conduct.[13]

Ernst Seelig, on the other hand, based his approach to the crime problem on distinctive "forms of life," although he could not escape consideration of the effects of the criminal's biopsychological "disposition." He was strongly impressed by Adolf Lenz' biological orientation, which influenced both his earlier typological attempts and his later work. His approach resulted from a "combined procedure" in which *heterogeneous momentums*, including patterns of behavior and forms of life, on one hand, and a characterological-psychobiological picture of the normative crime, on the other, offered insight into the causes of crime. Seelig therefore proposed the following criminal types:

1. *Criminals who live on crime* in an overtly antisocial way of life. Professional criminals, swindlers, vagabonds, thieves, and prostitutes are included in this classification.

2. *Frequent offenders*, usually against property, who nevertheless live socially acceptable lives most of the time. This type includes generally diligent workers like servants, headwaiters, upper-class ladies who drive dangerously, postmen, shop assistants, and others with low resistance to temptation.

3. *Aggressive violators* who habitually commit assaults, often including

the "bully," the "cutthroat," the alcoholic, and many kinds of murderers.

4. *Sexual criminals,* including some homosexuals.

5. *Crisis criminals,* who can resolve conflicts only through crime. Crises can include family troubles, difficulties in love, and other, similar events.

6. *Emotional criminals* in the strict sense. Not all criminals who commit crimes in states of affective excitement belong to this type. Only those whose repressed emotions have roots in biological factors fit this category. "Qualitative-specific" affective reactions and "blind rage" are typical. Murder without consideration of the meaning of the act is typical of this category.

7. *Debilitated criminals,* who show "primitive reactions." Frequently imbecilic, they cannot refrain from committing crimes because of internal disturbances.

8. *Ideological criminals,* who believe crime is a necessary duty to fulfill ideological goals.

9. *"Clinical-psychiatric" criminals,* who do not fall into the earlier "life-form and characterological personality structures," although they may be included with the mentally ill and the psychopathic deviants. Also included are the *etiological criminals,* classified as exogenous and endogenous delinquents; *prognostical criminals,* both reformable and incorrigible, and criminals identified by *body type,* closely identified with constitutional theories of criminal types.[14]

Another focus of the life-trend school is on categorization of criminals according to their tendencies to commit particular types of crime as legally defined. Using legal, psychological, social, and even constitutional explanations in a mixed approach to understanding delinquency and crime, theorists have sought to delineate the characteristics of the "normative type of criminal," in order to treat his interwoven personality problems in a penal setting. Although theorists have accepted penal practices as a reasonable consequence of the criminal act, normative theorists have claimed that penal practices ought to be a consequence of the criminal's "normative personality." They have thus attempted to find specific normative bases for sentencing. Punishment should be inflicted not necessarily upon the person who actually commits the murder but rather upon the person who can be considered a murderer type. A proved act of murder is not enough. The problem of guilt hinges on the question of whether or not the murderer belongs to the specific hypothetical criminal type. Although this life-trend approach is questionable, it had its origins in a challenge to the "objective" view of crime and called for more subjective understanding of crime and the criminal. A focus on the criminal and his crime replaced the former focus upon criminal law. It demanded recognition of the "criminal law of the criminal" (*Tater-Strafrecht*) in place of the "criminal law of crime" (*Tat-Strafrecht*).

No matter to what extent criminal justice took into consideration the personal circumstances of the criminal, however, criminal law remained the criminal law of crime. "The sentence on the man," Georg Dahm wrote, "is implemented through the sentence of the act. . . . To establish murder or high treason contains no sentence on the personality of the individual offender, and no standpoint on the question of to what extent the man matches with his act."[15] Normative theorists argued, not only that the single criminal act should be punished, but also that the total criminal personality of the offender as a "criminal being" should be scrutinized. Punishment should involve more than the retribution for the actual guilt of the offender.

Although typological theorists proposed the atonement of criminal guilt by the offender and treating him according to his normative type, in addition to punishment of the crime, an attitude which extended "double-tracked" (*Zweispurigkeit*) criminology to a "triple-tracked" (*Dreispurigkeit*) criminology, whether or not punishment was to be applied in accordance with the normative typological purpose remained unclear. The normative typologists suggested that there is little point in considering a case of murder, high treason, or theft unless the relationship between the crime and the criminal has been established. Crime cannot be understood merely as a symptom. If a murderer is not of a murderer type, it is wrong to punish him for the murder he has committed. Although the normative theorist may accept this position, however, the public view is, of course, in complete disagreement. The different criminal types must be identified not only in terms of their criminal characters but also in their relations to legal norms.

Eric Wolf pioneered the normative-typology approach.[16] The "political liberalism, religious naturalism and scientific positivism of the nineteenth century," he claimed, must be left behind, whereas "ethically indifferent positivistic individualism" and "phenomenological personalism" provide the foundation for future understanding. The concept of personalism, of course, includes a new way of thinking about the criminal personality. Wolf questioned, however, whether or not the criminal is really what he seems. He rejected the thesis that the criminal becomes a criminal through performing a criminal act. Although an external and apparent adjustment to law and order does not necessarily guarantee conformity, it fosters social attitudes favorable to conformity. The criminal, however, defies demands for conformity and commits specific crimes. Wolf therefore refused to speak in terms of "whoever" committed a murder, noting instead that a particular type of man, legally defined, commits murder. At a later date Wolf noted, "The crime appears in the totalitarian national socialistic state first of all as a disobedience and resistance."[17] Ultimately the deviation and the deviant type, he argued, should be viewed in this context.

A further step in the development of the normative orientation was taken by Dahm, who also put forth a totalitarian notion of crime.[18] His criminal typology was therefore based not only on the dimensions of the criminal personality and on the legal norms but also on an element of opposition to the government, "a doubled personality element," which compounded the difficulties in his attempt to classify crime. Crime and criminal, Dahm suggested, are not antithetical but represent an insoluble unity. The criminal should be viewed not as a conventional *criminological* being but as an *existential* being. The criminal's tendency to violate norms must be overcome by placing his entire activity on public view, through a National Socialist suprauniversalistic evaluation of the situation (primacy of ideology over individual or community interests). Although Dahm's conception of "public view" lacked concreteness, he believed that no two murderers are identical and in fact may even belong to different normative types. Yet the actual crime and the criminal type *are* interrelated. A "real" crime can be committed only by a criminal of the type associated with that kind of crime. Dahm is unclear, however, on whether or not social or biopsychological factors play any role in the development of normative criminal types, although he leaves the impression that at least some social factors must contribute to development of the "normative criminal."

Ecological Theories

Ecology, originally a branch of biology, focuses upon the special relations of organisms to their environment,[19] a study of habits and modes of life of living organisms in their surroundings. *Human ecology* includes sociological evaluation of relations between the social and institutional distribution and geographical environment of human beings.[20] Early ecological theorists attempted to relate the causes of crime and delinquency to the distribution of people and the characteristics of their surroundings. The Law of Imitation[21] proposed by Gabriel Tarde (1843–1904) was a forerunner of later studies;[22] application of the cartographic method to the crime problem and analysis of the physical environment can be traced back to A. M. Guerry in the first half of the nineteenth century.[23] Mayhew also found that rates of criminality appeared to be above the national average in the industrial centers of England and Wales, although they seemed lower than average near the borders of those countries.[24] Even Quetelet,[25] Lacassagne,[26] and Alexander von Oettingen[27] related crime to primitive ecological conditions. Although Georg von Mayr (1841–1925) also argued that "the conditions of accumulation of the population must have a special importance" in the consideration of criminality as an important sociopathological product,[28] the early contributors to criminal ecological theory generally tended to emphasize comparative study of rural and urban criminality.

In time, however, a more developed school of criminal ecology introduced ecological determinism, in order to examine geographical influences on social life and deviant behavior. Sophonisba P. Breckenridge and Edith Abbott, for example, examined "delinquent neighborhoods" in Chicago.[29] They directed their attention to such environmental factors as rivers, canals, large lodging houses, and railroad tracks, which seemed to be related to delinquent tendencies. Robert Park (1864–1944), Ernest Burgess, and Roderick D. McKenzie took a similar approach in an experimental socio-logical study in which they divided Chicago into concentric zones. At the core of the city is the main business area (central city).[30] Around this core as one moves toward the edges of the city are the zones of light manufac-turing (zone of transition), workingmen's homes, residential housing, in-dustrial development, apartment houses, and suburbs. Although their approach has been criticized, Park and his colleagues found different social characteristics in each zone and inspired a number of similar ecological studies, largely in Chicago. Clifford R. Shaw, for example, investigated the specific problem of delinquency and introduced the *delinquency area* hypothesis.[31] As he marked the location of each official delinquency on a Chicago map, Shaw found that the frequency declined as distance from the center of the city increased, a tendency that he explained in terms of the physical deterioration of the center and its concentration of social problems including adult crime, mental illness, suicide, and poverty. De-linquency rates, Shaw discovered, appeared constant in these "delinquency areas" despite changing ethnic composition of their populations.

Henry D. McKay subsequently joined Shaw[32] in further ecological investigations of delinquency in Birmingham (Ala.), Cleveland, Denver, Philadelphia, Richmond (Va.), and Seattle, where they found similar pat-terns. At a later date they restudied Chicago, in order to establish ade-quate ecological controls regarding delinquency rates "in relation to dif-ferential characteristics of local communities in American cities."[33] Calvin F. Schmid's research confirmed the existence of higher delinquency rates in the central business districts and diminishing deviance near the periph-ery of the Minneapolis–St. Paul area.[34] Although Stuart Lottier's Detroit findings supported Schmid's conclusions,[35] Bernard Lander disagreed with allegations of ecological determinism and rejected the *zonal hypothesis* of juvenile delinquency. Lander believed that the high levels of delinquency in certain areas of the city are caused by social disorganization and gen-eral anomie rather than by ecological factors.[36]

In their study of the *Polish Peasant in Europe and America* Thomas and Znaniecki revealed the relationships among ecology, second-genera-tion American birth, and culture conflict more fully. Concentrating on the connections among social organization, culture, and desirable mental and moral characteristics, they found that personality development is a product of the interaction of the individual and the group. As the individual strives to satisfy his needs within a social situation, he develops through social influences a set of organized attitudes that determine his character. But his "temperament," they believed, consists of the original and fundamental attitudes that mark the individual and are independent of any social in-fluence. Social rules serve to bring temperamental attitudes into a struc-ture of character attitudes that determine the organization of the individ-ual's life. In stable societies, the behavior and rules are more uniform. As the individual encounters unexpected situations, as in new cultural surroundings, however, familiar responses may no longer be adequate. Community disorganization is therefore maximized, and social sanctions are no longer able to maintain social integration and stability.

Thomas and Znaniecki found that the families of Polish peasants experienced such change as they moved from the solidarity of the Old World peasant community to the diversity of the New World. Confronted with new values, including even those related to diet and food, alcohol, tobacco, fashions, and the like, they entered into activities that conflicted with traditional family practices. Hedonistic attitudes undermined earlier attitudes and ultimately contributed to the increase in delinquency among Polish youth in the new country.[37] In partial support of the findings of Thomas and Znaniecki, Sheldon Glueck and Eleanor Glueck, in their well-known monograph *1,000 Juvenile Delinquents* (1934), reported that the native-born children of foreign-born parents display higher delinquency rates than do native-born children of native-born parents because of the culture conflict between foreign-born parents and native-born sons. After the enactment of United States immigration quotas in the early 1900s, however, such cultural differences became somewhat less a problem, at least until the migration of Puerto Ricans added a new dimension to the issue.[38]

Although ecological theorists observed apparent delinquency patterns, they failed to account for "unofficial" delinquency that never reaches the attention of the police or the courts. They also failed to differentiate between police and court statistics; among lower-, middle-, and upper-class delinquency; and among factors of social class and status. Their geographical zoning attempts were also not without flaw. Sociocultural borders do not necessarily follow political boundaries or concentric zones. Nor can ecology be fully divorced from problems of culture conflict. Consequently, Thorsten Sellin has in recent years argued the necessity for criminologists to extend their study of delinquency and crime to conflicts in norms of conduct confronting everyone in all life situations, in order to understand the dimensions of culture conflict and ecology. When divergent rules of conduct govern specific life settings, conflicts of norms arise, according to Sellin. As each person is a member of a number of social groups that have their own norms of conduct, tensions among the various group norms may also exist. Family, play, work, political, religious, or other group norms may sustain, weaken, or even contradict norms that have already been integrated into personality patterns. Therefore the more complex the culture, the greater the chance of normative conflict within any ecological setting.[39]

The Differential-Association Theory

Although Edwin H. Sutherland is usually credited with the formulation of the differential-association and learning theory, Tarde actually pioneered it in his Law of Imitation (*loi d'imitation*), which he perceived as the paramount factor in the learning process.[40] Although Tarde did not over-look the role of biological factors in human behavior, he believed that crime was essentially a social product. The Law of Imitation, he argued, arises because one man has contact with another. All behavioral and social processes, including crime and the creation of fashion and custom, can be explained by the Law of Imitation. Man imitates the behavior of other men: The less powerful imitate the more powerful, smaller communities imitate larger communities, and the lower classes imitate the higher classes. Crim-inal technique can also be understood, Tarde believed, in terms of the learning process.

Although Tarde was thus among the first to associate psychology with sociology, he ignored the question of who committed the first crime to set the imitative pattern in motion. He was also unable to say why the majority of people remain law-abiding, whereas only a minority imitate criminal behavior. Nevertheless his theory has stimulated several contemporary crim-inologists to offer similar explanations of the origins of crime and delin-quency.

Sutherland significantly refined Tarde's contribution in his own dif-ferential-association and learning theory, which stated that "criminal be-havior is learned in interaction with other persons in a process of commu-nication."[41] Both criminal techniques and specific motives are learned. Sutherland's theory, however, implies a limitation of learning, for he argues that a person becomes delinquent only because of an excess of definitions favorable to violation of the law over definitions unfavorable to violation of the law. When a person becomes criminal, he does so because of pre-vious contacts with criminal patterns. As he inevitably assimilates to the surrounding culture, he comes to reflect that culture in his behavior. Associations, however, may vary in frequency, duration, priority, and in-tensity and may therefore account for the wide variety of criminal and noncriminal conduct that is inevitably present in any society. Although the choices leading to associational participation are complex, individual involvement in associations is determined partly by existing kinds.

Sutherland's colleague Donald R. Cressey further observed, however, that the differential-association and learning theory is more than an empha-sis on "bad companions"; it also implies a *ratio* of associations to criminal or noncriminal patterns.[42] Cressey ultimately extended this theory even further, recasting it as a theory of different social organizations. He thus changed the theoretical focus from man as a member of the group to the structure of the group of which the man is a member.[43]

Although Walter C. Reckless' theoretical perspective markedly dif-fered from that of Sutherland, his *vulnerability components* and *categoric risk* are related to the theory of differential association. "Persons with vulnerability components," Reckless hypothesized, "break through and get into difficulty"; therefore "crime risks are essentially categoric risks that indicate the differential chances of persons in various subcategories for being arrested or admitted to prison."[44] Reckless further emphasized, however, that the study of "criminal risks" is not tantamount to study of criminal causation. One or more of the weaknesses of man, called "vulnerability components," reduce the capacity of the individual to conform to the laws and rules that regulate society. The social situation is thus decisive. Whereas one person may be able to conform in a favorable situation, he may face major difficulties in an unfavorable one. The situation plays on the individual's weaknesses or calls forth his strengths. Delinquency or crime, Reckless concluded, can result if his weaknesses dominate. Because of categoric risks some groups in society are more involved in crime than others. The categoric risk varies, however, with the varying *involvement of persons.*

Anomie Theory

Explanations of the crime problem in terms of anomie originated in the social-disorganization studies of Durkheim.[45] As he used the term, anomie meant absence of rules and norms, lawlessness, or weakened norms of any person or group, which may lead an individual to lose his ability to distinguish between right and wrong. As rules and norms ordinarily operate to regulate individual behavior and to maintain the group, they provide individual security while necessarily limiting individual aspirations and success. If the collective restraints on the individual break down, individual security is not only shaken, but the limits of individuality also become less certain. Because the accustomed or expected balance of cultural aspirations and social opportunities disappears, antisocial or deviant behavior, including suicide, may develop.

Although Durkheim's theory does not afford a suitable explanation of all crime and fails to clarify why some people in anomic situations do not become criminals and others do, Robert K. Merton, building on Durkheim's theory, relates crime and delinquency to the unequal achievement of success by all men.[46] When the culture places high value on success, the social structure, Merton argued, rigorously restricts or completely blocks access to approved channels for reaching such goals for a considerable part of the population. Large-scale delinquency and criminality then arise. Although Merton referred primarily to members of the lower classes who enjoy limited success potentials, such problems, he believed, are common to all social classes. The conflict between success aspirations and legal opportunity may lead members of *excluded* groups to strive for these goals illegally. The fact that certain goals cannot be achieved therefore aids in the development and helps to explain the origins of crime.

Although a large volume of deviant behavior can be explained by Merton's anomie theory, he left a number of questions unresolved. Are American success goals, for example, more demanding than those of other cultures, in Communist countries, for example? How can they be measured? A cursory examination reveals, for example, that the concept of anomie explains not only American crime but also crime in all societies. In socialist societies, the tension between success goals and social opportunities is similar to that observed in the United States. As the social structures of capitalist and socialist states differ, persistent anomie indicates that the explanation of variability in crime rests with other factors. Regardless of these limitations, however, the anomie theory was a noteworthy attempt at understanding the crime problem. Several recent theories of the causes of delinquency have grown out of this orientation. Lander's studies of Baltimore delinquents, for example, led him to the conclusion that anomic situations are more important determinants of delinquency than are economic factors.[47] Richard A. Cloward and Lloyd E. Ohlin contrasted status frustrations with available opportunities in their search for delinquent subcultures.[48] They pointed out not only the absence of opportunities for constructive aspirations but also the presence of destructive opportunities that encouraged delinquent aspirations. They identified illegitimate means that were used to reach legitimate goals and thus led to crime; they also noted the function of *illegal* role models (criminals) that encourage the development of *illegitimate* goals (to be a criminal). Although they assumed that the "first crime would encourage later crimes," Cloward and Ohlin failed to identify the source of the crime that initiated the process.

Albert K. Cohen theorized that delinquent gangs or groups tending toward becoming delinquent gangs develop a subculture as a solution to the problems of working-class boys. Participation offers such a youth status, reinforcement of his masculinity, security of belonging, and a base from which to fight middle-class society.[49] Although the stable corner boy accepts his life as it is and adjusts to its limitations, the delinquent working-class youth generally repudiates middle-class standards. The delinquent subculture thus legitimates aggression and inverts middle-class values to nonutilitarian, malicious, and negative conduct. Influenced by a short-term hedonism that places little importance on planned activity, long-range goals, or development of skills, the member of the delinquent subculture seeks immediate personal goals.[50] Whereas the delinquency of boys, Cohen suggests, takes the form of stealing or malicious mischief, female delinquency is associated with sexual adjustment to young males. Middle-class values related to ambition, individual responsibility, self-reliance, acquisition of skills, positive achievement, deferred gratification, rationality, etiquette, nonviolence, respect for property, and constructive leisure are rejected or minimized in the lower- or working-class culture.[51]

A process called "neutralization," explained by Gresham Sykes and David Matza, causes previously internalized norms, morals, and values to be silenced and therefore much delinquency results. The delinquent rationalizes his acts and shifts the blame to others. Although he may remain committed to the dominant system of norms, he is able to modify his responses, in order to justify violations. This process of "neutralization" takes the form of denial of responsibility (I am not responsible for what I did), denial of injury (stealing the car did not hurt anyone.), denial of the wrong (he deserved what he got), condemnation of the condemners (the arresting officer has his own shortcomings), or appeal to higher loyalties (I did it to protect a friend).[52]

Individuals, Matza has claimed in an extended statement on neutralization, drift functionally between various degrees of freedom and restraint. Consequently, they fall on a continuum between crime (freedom) and convention or law (restraint), responding to the demands of each in turn while postponing commitment and evading decisions. The majority of delinquents, he argued, are drifters who do not proceed into adult criminality. Although the delinquency subculture allows youths to be delinquent and to gain status through delinquent behavior, it also transmits many conventional norms. In fact, it is usually delicately balanced between crime and convention.[53] Nevertheless, drifting makes delinquent acts easier by weakening or removing the restraints of convention and law.

The ordinary subcultural delinquent, according to Matza, wills to commit or not to commit infractions. His will is activated as his conscience is freed and moral restraints are neutralized. Consequently the will undergirds drifting, which is in turn facilitated by neutralization.[54] This view was supported by David M. Downes, who found that delinquents in Great Britain are not driven by irrational forces and frustrations beyond their control but rather often act out of boredom, neutralized values, and indifference.[55]

As any young person is influenced by his peer or reference group, the juvenile delinquent must be approached both as an individual and as part of his group. If an individual offender is to be treated effectively, he must, as Pedro R. David has argued, be removed from his reference group, or an attempt must be made to influence the entire group.[56] Gerald Marwell, however, argues that delinquency is at least partially a response to the adolescent's lack of personal power. When he loses the last vestiges of agency power, wielded through parents, teachers, and institutions, he has no way of gaining personal power short of delinquent acts. Delinquency can therefore best be combated by decreasing through closer familial supervision the opportunities for illegitimate wielding of power.[57]

Following a different tack, Solomon Kobrin distinguishes between two kinds of delinquency areas: those in which criminal and conventional activities develop as separate and often opposing systems of values and those in which they are integrated. In the former instance, lack of local control permits delinquency to develop without restraint. Youths can participate simultaneously in both criminal and conventional value systems, which may account for role reversals in which delinquents become law-abiding citizens or juveniles with no police records become adult offenders. The conventional and the criminal value systems can be integrated on many different levels. When they are well integrated, adult violations tend to be systematic and organized. Participants in illegal acts share in the primary conventional orientation, and conventional members in turn tend to reinforce the criminal value system. Consequently, delinquency in such areas is somewhat controlled by the adult social structure.[58] As all delinquency areas, according to Kobrin, fall between these two polar types, changes in the character of a delinquency area may be explained as modifications in the integration of the criminal and conventional value systems. The basic character of community social life is determined by the explicit relationship between these two systems.

Containment Theory

The *containment theory,* also known as "Halt theory," of causation, involves the "internal and external containments of the ego, probably with greater weight assigned to the internal," which affect the individual's self-concept. First put forward by Reckless, it seems to owe much to Freudian psychology.[59] The self-concept, equivalent to Freud's notion of the ego, leads a person to evaluate his life as either "good" or "poor" if he is a "normal product" who has experienced a "normal range of childhood, adolescent, and adult development." Not everyone, however, experiences a normal developmental pattern. The good or poor self-concept, for example, "does not apply," Reckless believed, "to cases of compulsiveness, acting-out neurotics," or the "so-called psychopaths."

According to Reckless, all behavior develops as a result of conflict among "social pressures," "social pulls of a milieu," and the "inner pushes of the individual." *Social pressures* include family conflicts, minority-group status, lack of opportunities, and class and social inequities. *Social pulls* are exemplified by the desire for individual prestige, choice of "bad" companions, participation in delinquency subcultures or deviant groups, the enticements of advertising in the mass media, suggestion, and even propaganda. *Inner pushes,* on the other hand, include extreme restlessness and discontent, marked inner tension, hostility, aggressiveness, desire for aggrandizement, need for immediate gratification, extreme suggestibility, rebellion against authority, sibling rivalry, hypersensitivity, strong feelings of inadequacy or inferiority, guilt, mental conflict, anxiety, compulsion, phobia, organic impairment (for example, brain damage or epilepsy), and so on. These pressures, pulls, and pushes contend for domination of the structure of containment, which serves as a buffer or "Halt." It has several components, including moral front, institutional reinforcement, reasonable norms and expectations, and sense of acceptance, belonging, and identity. It also incorporates individual qualities: self-control, ego strength, well-developed superego, and high resistance to diversion. Whether or not crime or delinquency develops depends, according to this theory, upon the buffer influencing the individual.

The containment theory fails, however, to explain extreme character disorders, emotional disturbance, pathogenic damage, and group, family, tribe, or village parasitic activity. Although these exceptions weaken the theory. Reckless claims that it nevertheless offers the best explanation of delinquency and crime.

■ *The Socialistic Approach*

Although the offensive and defensive approaches to the crime problem have many points in common, the socialistic approach is quite different from other theories. It is the only orientation that seeks a solution to the problems of delinquency and crime exclusively and unconditionally in social structure, but in its early theoretical development it directed attention to the economic structure. It began with an assumption that poverty is a cause of crime, expanded to a critique of economic conditions under capitalism, and ended as the Communist theory of crime. Ideology, however, soon became more important than the immediate harm done to the community by criminal acts. The idea of a better, suprauniversalistic society was emphasized over the ordinary interests of the group. The flight from poverty became a fight for a better society focused on future justice. Anyone who attempted to frustrate the achievement of this future society would have to be restrained as a criminal.

Economic-Structure Theories

A milestone in the development of the socialistic orientation to the crime problem was reached in 1899, when the law faculty of the University of Amsterdam offered a prize for an essay on the influences of economic conditions on criminality. Both Joseph van Kan, who won the gold medal,[60] and Willem Adriaan Bonger, who received honorable mention,[61] produced memorable works, revealing their exhaustive knowledge of the various theoretical views of crime causation. Kan was, however, the pioneer, not merely because his work was published two years earlier than was Bonger's essay, but also because he systematically grouped and commented upon the contributions of earlier authors, whereas Bonger merely described their various views. But both believed in economic collectivism, and neither sympathized with any system of dictatorship. Bonger's suicide on the eve of the Nazi invasion of the Netherlands during World War II was convincing refutation of his critics' charge that he held suprauniversalistic ideas.

Although Kan and Bonger examined the works of previous writers on economic conditions and crime exhaustively, they did fail to mention the lecture in 1765 by Hommel, a professor at the University of Leipzig, in which he argued that poverty is the dominant cause of crime and that crime can be decreased only by radical improvement in the economic condition of the people.[62] J. M. C. Lucas was also overlooked.[63] Because Lucas saw a relationship between poverty and crime, he blamed society for the existence and rise of criminality. But, whereas many authors have argued the relationship among economic conditions, individual financial status, and crime, only those who have proposed radical readjustments in or complete realignment of society can be classed in the socialistic camp.

Theories of Socialism

Adherents of the socialist theories of crime can be grouped in two different factions. The first assumes that injustice in the capitalist economic structure and the consequent economic uncertainty of the people are the direct and central causes of most crimes. Consequently, they argue, structural changes in society should lead to decreases in the crime rate. The details of this group's position are unclear, however, for it attacks the economic structure without any accompanying political program to support its attack. The starting point of the second group is the same as that of the first: study of the capitalist economic system, which naturally produces a crime problem. The second group seeks a solution through political action. The conclusions of the two groups, however, coincide.

Although Karl Marx (1818–1883) and Friedrich Engels (1820–1895) did not discuss the problem of crime directly, they provided the theoretical and ideological framework for those who have regarded the economic structure as the prime cause of crime. Their social analysis has periodically been reinterpreted or misinterpreted in various places. The original Communist explanation of crime has since been modified and used to create a suprauniversalistic ideology of criminal law. Originally Marx proposed that all social phenomena, regardless of their political, religious, ethical, psychological, or material character, are products of economic conditions. He assumed that the life of man is guided not by his conscience but by his economic position, which determines the nature of his conscience. All social life is therefore subject to a strict law of causation: As all human beings are ruled by and dependent upon the economic structure of society, their personal and social lives constitute merely a superstructure (*Überbau*) upon the deterministic economic foundation.

Although Marxism cannot be discussed in detail in a volume on juvenile delinquency, the illusory logic and contradictory hypotheses of this view must be noted. A basic contradiction exists, for example, between the law of strict causation and Marxist sensual-existential empiricism. If man's social existence determines his mental development, then there is cause only for extreme fatalism in dealing with social problems. Crime, for example, cannot be prevented. Although Marx's theory of values points to a particular moral law, his general assumption that ethical views must be excluded in favor of evaluation only in terms of necessity challenges that theory of value. His conception of the role of man's will further contradicts his general fatalism. According to the Marxian hypothesis, science represents a variable function of economic conditions. Marxism, therefore, seems to reject the validity of objective scientific truths and to assert dogmatic ideological truth, which may ultimately hinder any attempts at research. Another tenet of Marxism, that speeding or retarding necessary and inevitable development is impossible, contradicts the belief in man's will and places insurmountable difficulties in the way of a scientific criminology.

Communist theorists have not been without criminological influence. Engels, for example, made a detailed comparison of the increase of crime in England with the depressed English economic conditions of 1844. The number of criminal offenses in England, he found, had increased sixfold between 1815 and 1842. Although he discovered a higher crime rate in agricultural areas than in industrial areas, he nevertheless concluded that the crime ratio depends on the economic position of the proletariat.[64] On the other hand, Turati, the first to delineate the Marxist theory of crime fully, proposed economic factors as the exclusive causes of crime. Although strongly opposed by Enrico Ferri, Turati believed that Lombroso's born-criminal hypothesis could not explain why only a small proportion of the population commits crimes, for biological factors ought to affect all men equally. Personal factors, Turati implied, account for less than 10 percent of crime, regardless of economic conditions.[65]

Bruno Battaglia also could not accept Lombroso's theory, but he did accept the existence of a type of anatomically and psychologically degenerated criminal, one who is unable to conform to the demands and conditions of society and who is out of moral harmony with others. As an adherent of the basic tenets of Marxist sociology, however, Battaglia believed that economic conditions are solely responsible for difficulties and degeneration in the family.[66] Antonio Marro argued, similarly, that poverty and low financial status among the proletariat account for the criminal's faulty central nervous system, which in turn leads to deviant behavior.[67]

Napoleone Colajanni also discussed Marxist criminology at considerable length. He criticized the Lombrosian thesis and the hypothesis of atavism and argued that economic questions rule all other social dimensions, including the moral order. Although he did not exclude consideration of biological factors, or other factors such as war, industrial development, family life, marriage, political institutions, vagrancy, and education, he concluded that only economic structure can be blamed, either directly or indirectly, for crime.[68] August Bebel came to similar Marxist conclusions.[69] Ferri, although he had originally supported the biological approach, redefined his point of view after 1894, accepting many aspects of socialist theory, especially the idea that, when working-class poverty disappears, the main cause of public degeneracy will also disappear.[70]

More recent Western data do not support claims of an exact relationship between poverty and crime. A study of the business index and delinquency cases in Allegheny County, Pennsylvania, from 1918 to 1934 revealed that court cases increased as business conditions advanced and decreased as business declined. Other studies by the U.S. Children's Bureau, tabulated in relationship to the employment index during 1940–1956, reveal similar patterns, although the rise of delinquency after 1952, the Bureau concluded, must be explained in terms of factors beyond simple employment and unemployment.[71] Walter A. Lunden concluded that delinquency cases that reach the courts have increased during years of relative prosperity in the United States and have decreased with declines in the business cycle. He noted, however, that variations in delinquency may be caused by other than economic conditions.[72]

Suprauniversalistic Theories

Suprauniversalistic theories of criminal causation found widespread expression first in the Soviet Union and in Fascist Italy; somewhat later most of the Marxist theoretical principles, adjusted and transposed, were adopted by Nazi Germany in order to strengthen its system. These principles preached the primacy of ideology over individual and community interests. Arguing that overemphasis upon safeguards of individual freedom merely overloads the criminal law and makes it unable to fulfill the defensive purposes of the ideology, suprauniversalists sought to establish a different principle of social responsibility within the legal and judicial process.[73]

The extreme Marxist view of the individual as the mere tool of antiindividualistic goals and dissolved in the sea of collectivism was itself based on collectivist political and economic ideas that may override the strict rule of the conventional moral or ethical code and traditional safeguards of community interests. The individual, in the authors' view the principal asset of society, was eliminated as pivot and replaced by suprauniversalistic ideas. The concept of crime consequently underwent change as deviations and violation of the social order were redefined. Overemphasis on social interests, however, led to the persecution and extermination of the Jews at Auschwitz, Belsen, Dachau, and Buchenwald for "crimes" against the Nazi social order.

Although the Soviet conception of crime was closely identified with Marxist socioeconomic theory, its practical application did not reflect the full implications of orthodox Marxism. Transitory political needs or party policies often caused modification or temporary suspension of original Marxist ideas. The central ingredient of the Soviet conception of crime was *social danger*. Although the term has been widely used by modern criminologists, in socialist criminology it has also been modified to serve an ideological purpose. Suprauniversalistic ideas have been readjusted to meet pragmatic needs of the day. The concepts of "law" and "justice" have therefore assumed different meanings in the socialist systems of criminal justice.[74]

Soviet criminology theorizes that "crimes, without exception, mean the breach of the rules of socialistic life and/or workshop discipline." Crimes are "relics of the past" or "the actions of the people's enemies, foreign agents and their accomplices, wreckers and saboteurs, spies and traitors, and manifest forms of the open battle waged by the capitalistic world" against the socialist state.[75]

Criminology in its traditional, "universal" sense is not acceptable in Communist countries. Instead crime is defined by subjective interpretation based on ideology.[76] The behavior of the people is assessed in the light of socialist efforts to build a new society. As in socialist societies man is believed capable of reforming his social attitudes in conformity to current prescribed interpretations of suprauniversalistic ideas, standards of behavior are frequently adjusted or altered. The practical definition of crime is therefore more often determined by political policies than by traditional understanding of the problem.

■ The Biosociological Synthesis

Early strivings toward a scientific criminology were marked by debate over the validity of the various approaches toward the study of crime. Many theorists modified their theories several times in the course of their lives. Lombroso, for example, changed his views four times; Freud reinterpreted his positions even more frequently. Ferri totally reversed himself in later life and came to support a theoretical frame of reference that he had opposed earlier. These debates and revisions within the biological and sociological orientations ultimately led to a third major orientation, the *multifactor approach,* which represented a compromise of the earlier traditions. This biosociological approach, also known as the *multiple-causation theory,* was an attempt to reconcile the warring schools of criminological thought. Its pioneers, the German Liszt,[77] the Belgian Prins, and the Dutch Hamel, founded the International Association of Penal Law (*Union Internationale du Droit Pénal,* or *Internationale Kriminalistische Vereinigung*) in 1888, in an effort to gather together students of both criminal law and criminology and spokesmen for both conservative and modern schools, in order to reach a compromise theoretical position. The Association was successful in its goal, and its members supported the conclusion that crime can originate only from multiple causes, including social-psychological and psychiatric factors. They held that both the criminal and his social environment must therefore be scrutinized thoroughly.

Liszt gave his entire life to the multifactor approach and served as its sharpest critic.[78] In his early years he believed that the criminal is an exclusively sociological phenomenon. Shortly thereafter, however, his interest turned to the criminal personality, which he believed to be influenced by social environment. As early as 1882 he felt it necessary to decide whether anthropological, psychological, or sociological factors promised the likeliest explanation of criminal causation. Consequently he was in the vanguard of those who proposed the merger of criminal somatology and criminal psychology to form criminal biology, mainly as an alternative to criminal sociology. Later he united both larger trends in one great comprehensive study of the crime problem, relying on what he called the *assembled science of criminal law (Gesamte Strafrechtswissenschaft)*, including penology, criminal politics, and criminal statistics. Liszt's first efforts, however, produced a psychological classification of crime into eight categories:

1. Crimes in which *consciousness of having injured* the rights of other people is completely absent or at least obscured; the psychic roots of crime rest in the criminal's recklessness, negligence, ignorance, or immoderate eagerness to act.

2. Crimes based on *attachment to other persons* by affection, devotion, love, or sympathy; one or more of these sentiments lead offenders to commit crimes in the other persons' interests.

3. Crimes of *self-preservation,* including desperate crimes arising from economic emergency, fear of punishment, shame, or other pressures.

4. Crimes originating in *sexual desire.*

5. Crimes of *passion,* involving reactions to real or imagined indignity, insult, or rejected love prompted by thirst for revenge, hatred, jealousy, anger, or envy.

6. Crimes motivated by *desire for glory.*

7. Crimes committed from *conviction,* including all political crimes.

8. Crimes of *greed or desire for gain,* including "businesslike" or professional crimes, hedonistic crimes, or crimes as breaks in the monotony of daily life.

Although others found little wrong with this typology, Liszt himself came to reject it. Psychic characteristics by themselves, he believed, rarely lead to crime. Both recklessness and passion may well occur without breaches of law. Sexual desires, strong convictions, desire for glory and outright greed may stimulate acts either of public utility or of social harm. Even the noblest person, on the other hand, may commit crimes. Crime involves so many factors that a typology of crime and criminals based on individual personality seemed largely meaningless. As a result, Liszt worked to find a consensus on measures of the characteristics of crime and criminals in relation to questions of law and order. He sought to understand the social values and sentiments of criminals and their variable attitudes toward the law. He then proposed a two-part classification of criminals:

1. Instantaneous criminals *(Augenblicksverbrecher)*.
2. State criminals *(Zustandsverbrecher)*.

The *criminal of the moment* is one who commits a crime as an episode (situation) in his life. Such crime, Liszt believed, does not result from the criminal's personality and involves comprehensive social factors that are only superficially taken into account. On the other hand, the crime of the *chronic criminal* is an expression of his way of life. Although his tendencies toward crime are stimulated by various sources, such activities are a permanent part of his way of life. The criminal's personality is motivated both biologically and sociologically to commit antisocial acts.

The insufficiency of this broad typology led Liszt to define criminal character further. He distinguished between corrigible and incorrigible offenders, and tried to develop even more refined classifications of the multiple types and causes of crime, but his efforts were largely futile. His greatest contribution was his presentation of the multiple-causation theory of crime. By recognizing the validity of both biological and social factors, he served as founder of the dualistic approach to criminology. Although Liszt's followers Prins and Hamel put forward similar theoretical propositions, the problems of delinquency and crime exceeded their knowledge at that time. Not only were they unable to explain why crime occurs, but they were also unable to predict the rise of criminality.

In spite of its weaknesses, the majority of contemporary criminologists now support the multiple-causation hypothesis because it takes both biological and sociological factors into consideration. Even those who have developed hypotheses of their own generally had a multiple-causation orientation. Most, however, tend to support the defensive approach to criminal sociology, although they still belong to the independent members of the parliament of criminology.[79]

The multiple-causation theory is not itself a true theory but is an amalgamation of many theories. It implies that crime is static yet too diverse for specific study. The multiple-causation theory represents, however, one alternative to the extravagances of the more extremist theories. As new causes of crime have been discovered more rapidly, contemporary ability to evaluate their meaning or influence has hardly increased at all. As a result, growing numbers of criminologists appear to lean toward dual or multiple explanations of criminal or delinquent behavior resulting from their attempts to isolate the subdivisions of criminal behavior.

Although Sutherland was not the first to claim that "efforts should be made to explain particular criminal behaviors," he was also not the last to urge that "conclusions from the studies of particular areas of criminal behaviors should lead to revisions of the generalizations regarding criminal behavior as a whole."[80] His colleague Cressey, for example, proposed to face the problem by specifying the causes of particular kinds of crime.[81] George B. Vold, however, believed that students of causation must approach the question with greater concentration and clearer thought.[82] The problem of causation is vast, however. Stephen Schafer has suggested that the guide in the future must be the old political principle of *divide et impera* (divide and rule). Only when types of crime and criminality are clearly defined can situations and personalities that produce crime be controlled.

No criminal typology is without error, for all such schemes are more or less arbitrary definitions of social life and human behavior too complex to define adequately. Studies of criminal typology, investigations of distinguishable characteristics common to certain crimes and criminals, may, however, produce models of criminal types and offer greater insight into problems of delinquency and crime. Such models can, however, be valid only if they are derived from a single general explanation of delinquency and crime that may ultimately have implications for penological or correctional procedures. Although this task is difficult, it promises advances beyond the static explanations inherent in the multiple-causation approach, transforming the latter into a functional and instrumental approach to the problem of causation.

The life-trend explanation of delinquent or criminal behavior that dominates this volume assumes that the free will of the individual is limited by social factors of which he may not be consciously aware or that he may or may not comprehend. The exact relationship between life trend and delinquency, between professional and organized delinquency, and between participation of the victim and the offender's or delinquent's act, for example, have yet to be clarified. Although the theoretical task is monumental, ensuing empirical investigation buttressed by sound theorizing should yield even greater future insights into the problem of crime and criminals, and delinquency and delinquents.

NOTES

1. Donald R. Taft, *Criminology* (3rd ed.; New York: 1956), pp. 336–349.
2. Frank E. Hartung, "Methodological Assumptions in a Social-Psychological Theory of Criminality," *Journal of Criminal Law, Criminology and Police Science*, 45 (March–April 1955), 655.
3. W. I. Thomas and Florian Znaniecki, *The Polish Peasant in Europe and America* (Boston: 1918). See also Oswald Spengler, *The Decline of the West* (New York: 1927); and Pitirim A. Sorokin, *Social and Cultural Dynamics* (New York: 1941).
4. Hartung, *op. cit.*, pp. 654–655.
5. Adolphe Prins, *Criminalité et répression* (Brussels: 1886). See also Prins, *La Criminalité et l'état social* (Brussels: 1890); and Prins, *La Défense sociale et les transformations du droit pénal* (Brussels: 1910).

6. Émile Durkheim, *De la division du travail social: étude sur l'organisation des sociétés supérieures* (Paris: 1893); Durkheim, *Les Règles de la méthode* (Paris: 1895); Durkheim, *Le Suicide* (Paris: 1897); and Durkheim, *Sociology and Philosophy* (New York: 1953). For a more detailed account of Durkheim's life and work, see Walter A. Lunden, "Émile Durkheim," *Journal of Criminal Law, Criminology and Police Science*, 49 (May–June 1958), 2.

7. Ernst Seelig, "Die Gliederung der Verbrecher," in Seelig and Karl Weindler, eds., *Die Typen der Kriminellen* (Berlin: 1949), p. 6.

8. H. A. Frégier, *Des Classes dangéreuses de la population dans les grandes villes et des moyens de les rendre meilleures* (Paris: 1840).

9. H. Mayhew and J. Binney, *The Criminal Prisons of London* (London: 1862).

10. W. E. Wahlberg, *Das Prinzip der Individualisierung* (Vienna: 1869).

11. G. Moreau, *Souvenirs de la petite et de la grande roquette* (Paris: 1888).

12. Edmund Mezger, *Die Straftat als Ganzes, Deutsches Strafrecht: Ein Grundriss* (Berlin: 1938); Mezger, *Kriminalpolitik und Ihre Kriminologischen Grundlagen* (3rd ed.; Stuttgart: 1944); and Mezger, *Kriminologie: Ein Studienbuch* (Berlin: 1951).

13. Seelig, *op. cit.*

14. Seelig, "Das Typenproblem in der Kriminalbiologie," *Journal für Psychologie und Neurologie* (1931).

15. Georg Dahm, *Der Tätertyp im Strafrecht* (Leipzig: 1940), p. 8.

16. Eric Wolf, *Vom Wesen des Täters* (Berlin: 1932).

17. Wolf, *Richtiges Recht im Nationalsozialistichen Staat* (Freiburg: 1934).

18. Dahm, *op. cit.*, and Dahm, "Die Erneuerung der Ehrenstrafe," *Deutsche Juristenzeitung* (1934).

19. Paul Bockelman, *Studien zum Täterstrafrecht*, 2 (Berlin: 1940), 111.

20. Taft, *op. cit.*, p. 204.

21. Gabriel Tarde, *La Criminalité comparée* (Paris: 1886).

22. George B. Vold, *Theoretical Criminology* (New York: 1958), p. 188.

23. A. M. Guerry, *Essai sur la statistique morale de la France* (Paris: 1833).

24. Mayhew, *London Labour and the London Poor* (London: 1851).

25. Adolphe Quetelet, *Physique Sociale, ou essai sur le développment des facultés de l'homme* (Paris: 1869).

26. A. Lacassagne, "Marche de la criminalité en France de 1825 à 1880," *La Revue scientifique* (1881), 674.

27. Alexander von Oettingen, *Die Moralstatistik in Ihrer Bedeutung für eine Sozialethik* (3rd ed.; Erlangen, Ger.: 1882).

28. Georg von Mayr, "Kriminalstatistik und Kriminalaetiologie," *Monatschrift für Kriminalpsychologie und Strafrechtsreform* (1911–1912), p. 333; and Mayr, *Moralstatistik mit Einschluss der Kriminalstatistik: Statistik und Gesellschaftslehre*, Vol. 3 (Tübingen: 1917).

29. Sophonisba P. Breckenridge and Edith Abbott, *The Delinquent Child and the Home* (New York: 1912).

30. Robert E. Park, Ernest W. Burgess, and Roderick D. McKenzie, *The City: The Ecological Approach to the Study of the Human Community* (Chicago: 1925).

31. Clifford R. Shaw, *Delinquency Areas* (Chicago: 1929).

32. Shaw and Henry D. McKay, *Social Factors in Juvenile Delinquency* (Washington, D.C.: 1931).

33. Shaw and McKay, *Juvenile Delinquency and Urban Areas: A Study of Rates of Delinquents in Relation to Different Characteristics of Local Communities in American Cities* (Chicago: 1942). See also summary articles in President's Commission on Law Enforcement and Administration of Justice, *Juvenile Delinquency* (Washington, D.C.: 1967), pp. 107–118.

34. Calvin F. Schmid, *Social Saga of Two Cities: An Ecological Study of the Social Trends in Minneapolis and St. Paul* (Minneapolis: 1937).

35. Stuart Lottier, "Distribution of Criminal Offenses in Metropolitan Regions," *Journal of Criminal Law and Criminology,* 29 (May–June 1938), 37–50.

36. Bernard Lander, *Toward an Understanding of Juvenile Delinquency* (New York: 1954).

37. Thomas and Znaniecki, *op. cit.,* pp. 20–33, 1128–1170.

38. Lunden, *Statistics on Delinquents and Delinquency* (Springfield, Ill.: 1964), p. 73.

39. Thorsten Sellin, *Culture Conflict and Crime* (New York: 1938), p. 130.

40. Tarde, *op. cit.;* Tarde, *La Philosophie pénale* (Paris: 1891); and Tarde, *Études Pénales et sociales* (Lyons: 1900). For a more detailed account of Tarde's life and work see Margaret S. Wilson Vine, "Gabriel Tarde," *Journal of Criminal Law, Criminology and Police Science,* 45 (May–June 1954), 3–11, or Lacassagne, "Gabriel Tarde," *Archives d'anthropologie criminelle,* 19 (1904).

41. Edwin H. Sutherland, *Principles of Criminology* (4th ed., New York: 1947).

42. Donald R. Cressey, "Crime," in Robert K. Merton and Robert A. Nisbet, eds., *Contemporary Social Problems: An Introduction to the Sociology of Deviant Behavior and Social Disorganization* (New York: 1961), pp. 57–58.

43. Harwin L. Voss, "Differential Association and Reported Delinquent Behavior: A Replication," *Social Problems,* 12 (Summer 1964), 78–85, verified James F. Short's 1957 study of differential association and substantiated the hypothesis that youths who associate extensively with delinquent friends will have more reported delinquent behavior.

44. Walter C. Reckless, *The Crime Problem* (4th ed., New York: 1967).

45. Durkheim, *op. cit.*

46. Robert K. Merton, "Social Structure and Anomie," *American Sociological Review,* 3 (October 1938), 677–682; see also Merton, *Social Theory and Social Structure* (rev. ed.; New York: 1957).

47. Lander, *op. cit.*

48. Richard A. Cloward and Lloyd E. Ohlin, *Delinquency and Opportunity* (New York: 1960).

49. Albert K. Cohen, *Delinquent Boys: The Culture of the Gang* (New York: 1955), pp. 50–70.

50. See Paul Lerman, "Symbolic Deviance and Subcultural Delinquency," *American Sociological Review,* 32 (1967), 209–224, for a discussion of the importance of shared values and symbols in delinquency.

51. Cohen, *op. cit.,* p. 89.

52. Gresham Sykes and David Matza, "Techniques of Neutralization: A Theory of Delinquency," *American Sociological Review,* 22 (December 1957), 666–669.

53. Matza, *Delinquency and Drift* (New York: 1964), pp. 27–59.

54. *Ibid.,* pp. 179–183.

55. David M. Downes, *The Delinquent Solution: A Study in Subcultural Theory* (New York: 1966).

56. Pedro R. David, *Sociología Criminal Juvenil* (Buenos Aires: 1967).

57. Gerald Marwell, "Adolescent Powerlessness and Delinquent Behavior," *Social Problems*, 14 (Summer 1966), 35–47.

58. Solomon Kobrin, "The Conflict of Values in Delinquency Areas," *American Sociological Review*, 16 (1951), 656–659.

59. Reckless, *The Crime Problem* (3rd ed.; New York: 1961), pp. 351–359.

60. Joseph van Kan, *Les Causes économiques de la criminalité: étude historique et critique d'étiologie criminelle* (Paris: 1903).

61. Willem Adriaan Bonger, *Criminalité et conditions économiques* (Amsterdam: 1905). For a detailed account of Bonger's life and work see J. M. van Bemmelen, "Willem Adriaan Bonger," *Journal of Criminal Law, Criminology, and Police Science*, 46 (September–October 1955); see also Bonger, *An Introduction to Criminology*, trans. by Emil van Loo (London: 1936).

62. See Landsberg, *Geschichte der Deutschen Rechtswissenschaft*, Part III.

63. J. M. C. Lucas, *Du Système pénal et du système répressif en général de la peine de mort en particulier* (Paris: 1827); and Lucas, *De la réforme des prisons* (Paris: 1838).

64. F. Engels, *Die Lage der Arbeitenden Klasse in England* (Stuttgart: 1892).

65. P. Turati, *Il Delitte e la Questione Sociale* (Milan: 1883).

66. Bruno Battaglia, *La Dinamica del Delitto* (Naples: 1886).

67. Antonio Marro, *I Caratteri dei Delinquenti* (Turin: 1887).

68. Napoleone Colajanni, *La Sociologia Criminale* (Catania: 1887–1889). In support of his explanation, Colajanni cited data on criminality in Italy, Ireland, England, Scotland, and the United States.

69. August Bebel, *Die Frau und der Sozialismus* (Stuttgart: 1899).

70. Enrico Ferri, *Criminal Sociology*, trans. by J. I. Kelly and John Lisle (Boston: 1917).

71. Lunden, *Statistics*, pp. 158–62.

72. *Ibid.*, p. 166.

73. Pál Angyal, *Büntetöjogi Reform és az Egyéni Szabadság* (Budapest: 1912).

74. Harold J. Berman, *Justice in Russia* (Cambridge, Mass.: 1950), p. 258.

75. V. D. Menshagin, A. A. Gertsenzon, M. M. Ishaiev, A. A. Piontkovskii, and B. S. Utevskii, *Soviet Criminal Law: Textbook for Universities* (Budapest: 1951), p. 247, official Hungarian version.

76. *Ibid.*, p. 188.

77. Franz von Liszt, *Das Verbrechen als Sozial-Pathologische Erscheinung* (Dresden: 1899).

78. Liszt, *Strafrechtliche Aufsätze und Vorträge* (Berlin: 1905).

79. See Marc Ancel, *La Défense sociale nouvelle* (Paris: 1954); Bemmelen, *Criminology* (Amsterdam: 1942); Cyril Burt, *The Young Delinquent* (New York: 1944); Ruth Shonle Cavan, *Criminology* (3rd ed.; New York: 1962); Marshal B. Clinard, *Sociology of Deviant Behavior* (rev. ed.; New York: 1963); Cressey, "The Differential Association Theory and Compulsive Crimes," *Journal of Criminal Law, Criminology, and Police Science* (May–June 1954); Sutherland and Cressey, *Principles of Criminology* (6th ed.; New York: 1960); Max Grünhut, *Penal Reform* (Oxford: 1948); Hans von Hentig, *Crime, Causes and Conditions*

(New York: 1947); Jean Pinatel, *La Criminologie* (Paris: 1960); Sellin, *Culture Conflict and Crime* (New York: 1938).

80. Sutherland, *Principles of Criminology* (4th ed.; New York: 1947), pp. 66–67.

81. Cressey, "Criminological Research and the Definition of Crime," *American Journal of Sociology*, 56 (May 1951), 546–551.

82. Vold, *op. cit.*, p. 314.

Part Three

VARIATIONS IN DELINQUENCY

Chapter 6

■ *Occasional Delinquency*

■ *The Problem of the Occasional Delinquent*

Although the occasional delinquent appears to represent the simplest form of delinquency, in fact he presents the most difficult. In contrast to all other delinquent types, he does not display a life trend markedly different from that demanded by social, ethical, moral, and legal norms.[1] Generally uninterested in truancy, shoplifting, automobile theft, and other deviant acts, he avoids gang organizations. No aberrations are apparent in his home behavior, recreational practices, religious involvements and educational career. He reveals no psychotic or psychopathic disturbance or disorder and does not indulge in potentially delinquent habits. As his type is rare, his delinquency is often categorized with other forms, and he is treated as a committed delinquent with totally antisocial attitudes. The occasional delinquent clearly poses a difficult correctional problem. The inconsistency of his delinquency with his life pattern makes it difficult to know what to correct.

The delinquency of the occasional delinquent is only an episode in his life and has no rhythm or pattern.[2] His socioethical personality conforms to developing social demands, and his aspirations and decisions are on the whole in accord with the behavioral expectations of his social group. As his socioethical personality develops, his socioethical resistance works with expected opposing force to resist pressures toward crime and delinquency. Nevertheless, one or more times during his juvenile years, abruptly and unexpectedly, his normal resistance confronts pressure toward delinquency so forcible that he cannot withstand it. The boy who shoots a man attacking his mother, for example, is an occasional delinquent. So is the girl who steals a loaf of bread to ease the hunger of her penniless widowed mother. Even the youth who swindles his way into a football game to see his favorite team may be an occasional delinquent. The concept of occasional delinquency refers not to the gravity of the delinquency but to the delinquent's typological personality type.

Is the occasional delinquent always a properly developing socioethical personality? Is it possible for a professional delinquent whose whole life is oriented toward delinquency for profit to commit an act that really typifies occasional delinquency? Although the girl who shoplifts and the male juvenile-gang leader who directs acts against property may also participate in acts that are common to occasional delinquents, they represent alternative delinquency *forms*. The girl, for example, may be a *professional delinquent*, whereas the latter represents *organized delinquency*. Pressure toward delinquency in response only to strong incidental or immediate factors is alien to these types. The "occasional" delinquency of the professional or organized delinquent is only an episode in his delinquent life trends.

Both the occasional delinquent and the professional or organized delinquent accept the conventional attitude toward crime and delinquency. This attitude, however, operates differently upon their other attitudes. Incidental or immediate pressures toward delinquency operate as independent variables outside the value systems of occasional delinquents and conflict with both their general behavior and their life trends. Although the occasional delinquent is usually opposed to delinquency, the professional or organized delinquent is inclined toward, or at least indifferent to it. Delinquency thus seems inappropriate behavior to the occasional delinquent, but seems appropriate or neutral to the professional or organized delinquent. Nevertheless, the incidental or immediate pressure toward delinquency appears rather negative to the professional or organized delinquent, challenging his delinquent reasoning or socioethical standard. He thinks of himself as a "good delinquent"[3] and acts as if he were a law-abiding member of his group in an occasional-delinquency situation. He does not exhibit any planning, preparation, skill, technique, or daring, and, in his occasional delinquency, resembles the nonprofessional delinquent.

Whereas the "law-abiding" adolescent is dominated by positive social values, the professional or organized delinquent is dominated by negative values. Because episodic pressure toward delinquency is experienced by the "law-abiding" child as a negative value, it forces him to deviate from the norms that are the foundation of his life trend. Such episodic pressure is, however, also experienced by professional or organized delinquents as negative pressure upon their value system (a positive system from their point of view), which stimulates them to disregard the norms by which they ordinarily live. Conformity and occasional delinquency, professional delinquency and occasional delinquency, and gang activity and occasional delinquency can therefore coexist without being correlated.

Characteristics of the Occasional Delinquent

The unusual and unexpected appearance of incidental or immediate pressures toward delinquency often serves the juvenile offender as justification for his deviant behavior. He may argue that the special characteristics of the situation justify the actual violation, assuming a philosophical position that the overwhelming force of the delinquency pressure did not allow him to settle his problem through legitimate or conventional procedures. If the pressure toward deviation from the value system is especially powerful, he may feel that the right to redress the situation is his alone. The occasional delinquent tends therefore to act on the assumption that he and no one else can and must decide right and wrong and execute the decision. The youth who shoots his mother's attacker, for example, cannot wait for the defense of law enforcement or for the retribution of criminal justice. Instead he justifies his crime with the claim that he lacked institutional help to prevent the act. The girl who steals bread to appease hunger also cannot postpone her theft long enough to seek assistance or intervention from welfare agencies; she justifies her delinquency on grounds that no help from society has been available. The boy who enters the ball park without having bought a ticket believes that he cannot delay his attendance to another game, at which legitimate entrance to the stadium might be possible. He justifies his delinquent behavior on the grounds that this particular game will not be repeated.

Occasional delinquents' *justification of delinquency* mainly reveals the immediate pressures in a given situation but not necessarily the absence of alternative ways to achieve the immediate goal. On some occasions the juvenile may simply be unable to conform to the norms of his group successfully. At other times, probably more frequently, his not-yet-mature socioethical personality has little chance to relate his delinquent behavior to social values adequately. In each instance, the pressure toward episodic delinquency prompts the youth to deviate from his conventional reactions and offers him grounds for self-justification. Although such self-justification is a result of the high pressure upon him, it should not be confused with another form of self-justification common among juvenile delinquents who indulge in minor or casual violations of norms because of ineffective transmission of all the positive cultural values or because of faulty socialization.[4]

Thefts of watermelons and souvenirs or underage smoking and drinking are not occasional delinquencies but are forms of casual delinquency. Casual delinquency, in contrast to occasional delinquency, is not episodic but may occur frequently. It is not a symptom of powerful pressures toward delinquency but rather a product of inadequate indoctrination in positive social values. The casual delinquent, however, may justify his delinquency in a manner similar to that of the occasional delinquent. Whereas the occasional delinquent's self-justification is based on claimed absence of legitimate alternatives, the casual delinquent does not understand the illegitimacy of his behavior; the former delinquent is thus more adequately socialized than is the latter. The occasional delinquent is overpowered by *unusual* pressures; the casual delinquent falters before *usual* pressures. Although all other delinquent types tend toward certain kinds of delinquent behavior, occasional delinquents engage in a wide range of delinquencies, ranging from truancy or parking violations to murder, that society cannot adequately prevent, for the situation or opportunity more or less governs the direction of the deviance. For this reason "some situational criminals," Harry Elmer Barnes and Negley K. Teeters have warned, "are executed."[5]

The pressures of need and emotion are underlying motives in all occasional delinquencies, nearly all of which also originate in particular circumstances or unusual situations for which ordinary socialization does not prepare the child. If a powerful need or emotion drives the juvenile to protective behavior and if his socioethical resistance proves to be insufficient, he may seek illegitimate goals that were prohibited in his earlier socialization. Such social and psychological motives nearly always appear as overpowering pressures that push the juvenile toward immediate illegitimate action. Consequently, preventive intervention is difficult, for the action follows the motive pressure rapidly; pressures may not occur at predictable times or, for that matter, more than once.

Although the near-spontaneous response to motivational stimuli in occasional delinquency seems to imply the absence of planned delinquent behavior, an element of planning still exists. The planning inherent in occasional delinquency, however, differs greatly from that of the professional delinquent or the delinquent gang and is closest, though less exacting, to the planning of the casual delinquent. When a boy, for example, decides to kill his mother's attacker, he obviously does not act at random but quickly decides how to defend his mother. When the girl decides to steal a loaf of bread, she too considers how and where the theft should be committed. The boy who cannot resist watching his favorite team seeks the best opportunity to sneak inside the ballpark. Each act reflects an element of planning *frigido pacatoque animo* (by a cold and peaceful mind), under the stress of circumstances and a driving motive. Occasional delinquency is still, however, far from being premeditated conduct. The overpowering pressures of the motive and the immediate context do not leave room for coolly calculated behavioral response.

The occasional delinquent cannot engage in evaluation or rational premeditation. Neither the immediate situation nor the existing pressure level allows him to weigh his behavioral decision in the light of the norms to which he has been socialized. The occasional delinquent lacks the knowledge and experience of a practiced delinquent, and professional or gang delinquency even appears to him as an alien form of behavior. Participation in occasional delinquency involves limited preparation, and planning is characterized by absence of skill, technique, method, and care. A professional juvenile shoplifter represents a different problem from that posed by the occasional delinquent who steals something that he really needs from the counter. It is more difficult to trace and to bring to court a juvenile-gang member who has killed another in a gang fight than it is to arrest and try the same gang member if he has murdered a man attacking his mother. While the decision to defend her and the actual violence do not occur at precisely the same moment, the time lag between them is short enough and the strain sufficient to render the occasional delinquent unable to consider the value difference between delinquency and conformity.

The Complexity of Occasional Delinquency

The second and subsequent delinquent acts of an occasional delinquent are not necessarily symptoms of persistent or professional delinquency but may instead be further isolated delinquent episodes. As delinquency is not a built-in facet of the occasional delinquent's life trend, it occurs irregularly, as occasion and opportunity arise. One cannot therefore safely predict how many times "episodes" may occur or how many times incidental or immediate motives are accompanied by situational pressures toward deviance. The occasional delinquent acts in accordance with the pressure of circumstances at particular moments. As the number of such moments cannot be calculated in advance, they can be neither regulated nor restricted by any hypothesis. An increased resistance through socialization and corrective treatment does not guarantee that further occasional delinquency will not occur. As the first delinquency can be an act of professional delinquency for profit or an occasional delinquent act motivated by random stimuli, the so-called *first offender* should not automatically be equated with either the occasional or the professional delinquent. He may be either one or even a casual or organized delinquent.[6] The term "first offender" or first delinquent can hardly mean anything more than that the juvenile has never before been tried, or he has never before been heard by a juvenile court judge.[7]

The failure to distinguish among the wide variations in juvenile delinquencies and motivations has led to the confusion and partial ineffectiveness of juvenile courts. Where state or Federal legislation has prescribed probation, lenient action, or outright discharge for first offenders, it may actually stimulate the activity that it seeks to control. The juvenile court may judge too leniently, may trust the delinquent excessively, and may permit "understanding" to overshadow application of sanctions in cases of first offense. Comprehension and judgment of delinquency cannot therefore depend only upon the number of delinquent acts but also must depend upon qualitative evaluation of those acts. The first offender may have committed a serious crime or may have participated in undesirable gang activities, whereas the youth committing his fifth delinquent act may be amenable to specific corrective treatment. The type of delinquency and the type of delinquent should not be confused with the mild or serious result of delinquency or with the frequency of delinquent behavior. "We can better define and deal with the problems in · criminology," Nathaniel F. Cantor has written, "if we are clear about what it is we are after."[8]

The popular belief that frequency of delinquent behavior indicates the professionalism of the juvenile delinquent is open to serious question.[9] Although it is possible that an occasional delinquent may turn to professional or organized delinquency, his delinquency is more often over-dramatized. The first truancy, the first shoplifting, and the first swindle are not necessarily the first steps on the road to crime. Too many people without previous delinquency or crime records are serving life sentences to permit this generalization. The myths of public opinion and law enforcement are not necessarily correct, except to the extent that, in response to public opinion, excessive punishment for minor acts produces a social climate that actually serves to drive the child or juvenile to a delinquent or criminal life trend. Shifts from occasional to professional or organized delinquency cannot, however, be understood merely by enumerating the sequence of delinquent acts.

Future delinquency patterns cannot be generalized from initial juvenile violations. If the juvenile participates in professional delinquency or gang delinquency after his first occasional delinquent act, it should be regarded as the first evidence of professional or organized delinquent behavior rather than as a continuation of his earlier deviance. In most instances, however, this distinction is not made. The mere fact that the juvenile has already engaged in two episodes of delinquent behavior, even though dissimilar, generally leads to such errors as application of excessive sanctions and uncertain attempts at treatment. Failure to distinguish between the two different types of delinquencies and the two divergent roots from which these delinquencies grow thus often permits the damage of the punishment to reinforce the damage of the act.[10]

The transition from occasional delinquency to delinquency for profit or to participation in gang activity depends not on the sequence of delinquent acts but upon the weakening of the socialized personality or the weakening of his continuing socialization. Whereas occasional, professional, and organized delinquency are independent phenomena, they may converge in particular cases to transform a delinquent into a criminal. Although occasional delinquency thus may eventuate in professional delinquent behavior or participation in a juvenile gang, this result is neither automatic nor accidental. The transformation process may result from absence of socializing forces and the fortifying presence of pressures toward delinquency, rather than from a sequential development of delinquent activity. The boy who redresses the offense against his mother by killing the offender may participate in gang activities and turn to violence in order to achieve gang goals, but his first act remains a form of occasional delinquency. The girl's theft of a loaf of bread similarly remains an occasional delinquency in the sense that she is acting under the pressure of need. If she notices, however, that stealing is easy and involves little risk, she may subordinate her earlier value system to a profit motive and turn to professional delinquency. Her first theft nevertheless remains an act of occasional deviance.

Under normal circumstances the occasional delinquent eventually develops normal ethical attitudes as a result of his continuing socialization. His inner control, his socioethical resistance to wrong, which is learned through the socialization process, functions according to the value system of his social group. Occasional delinquency, however, is the result not of shortcomings in his socialization but of the specific social situation that neutralizes his learned values and causes him to betray them.[11] Although some youths may be strongly socialized or indoctrinated to socially acceptable aspirations and opportunities and prepared to avoid even occasional delinquency, the average juvenile does not receive a comparably intensive socialization to prepare him for these unexpected occasions or opportunities. As occasional delinquency does not result from conflict between outer pressures and inner controls, in which a choice is made in favor of the delinquent behavior, socialization for the unexpected is largely impossible. Because the inner control system is not prepared to exert the necessary resistance against unusual external pressures, occasional delinquency frequently occurs.[12]

A social situation arising after the original act of occasional delinquency may provide an opportunity for participation in professional delinquency or gang activity. Weakened socioethical attitudes, which may have been encouraged by the frustrating experience of the occasional delinquency, may encourage this tendency. The conflict between the child's or juvenile's image of the world to which he has been socialized and his occasional delinquent behavior, which is alien to this image, may also produce a reassessment of meanings and values. The realization that deviation *is possible* despite the existence of strong values may lead him to reexamine and modify the values themselves. In such an instance, a new opportunity (pressure toward delinquency) coupled with the modified socioethical attitude (weakened socioethical resistance) may direct the child or juvenile toward delinquent behavior in which profit appears as the decisive goal or in which violence appears as a permissible means to the ultimate goal.

■ The Casual Delinquent

Although the occasional delinquent is periodically called a "casual delinquent" and vice versa, the two are different enough to demand separate categories. Both represent forms of delinquency quite distinct from either professional or gang delinquency, but they differ in frequency and in source. The occasional delinquent deviates on occasion; the casual delinquent deviates spontaneously and irregularly, whenever he has the chance. In occasional delinquency "the opportunity uses the child," but in casual delinquency "the child uses the opportunity." The former is unable to resist *unusual* delinquency pressures, but the latter lacks strength to resist even *usual* ones.

Early drinking, sexual aberrations, petty theft, periodic shoplifting, minor fraud, small-scale truancy, and violations of city regulations are typical casual delinquencies. Although the juvenile may aspire to some profit goal and may associate with other children or juveniles in his delinquent acts, his behavior is not professional and does not reveal any of the organizational features of the gang. Casual delinquency is primarily characterized by irregularity, unmethodical performance, and disinterest in normative standards.

Deviant behavior occurs in uneven sequences. The time span between delinquent acts varies unpredictably, and depends primarily on the child's delinquent opportunities and his vulnerability. For example, when he leaves home with his friends he may not plan to drink, but he may drink if someone has a bottle. He may not plan theft but may steal if the opportunity arises. He may not visit department stores in order to shoplift but may do so if no clerk is readily available. Casual delinquency is only partly a product of faulty socialization; it is also a result of random social opportunities.

The unmethodical character of the casual delinquent's performance reflects the absence of premeditation and planning. If the opportunity appears, the casual delinquent decides how to take advantage of it but does not exert special effort to plan procedures. Although his planning is more extensive than that of the occasional delinquent, it is looser and less carefully designed. The patterns that might be observed in his delinquency would therefore be not signs of planning and method but of delinquent habits.

Because the casual delinquent is indifferent to existing values, he is directed toward delinquency under the right circumstances. His delinquency is therefore the result of mistaken but not faulty socialization. As individual behavior is ultimately determined by the interaction of group socialization and individual potential, it differs for each person. The individual's full potential may remain unrealized because of inherent deficiencies in existing socializing agencies, the limitations of the home atmosphere in reinforcing social values, and negative community forces that counterbalance many social values. Socialization may produce a considerable degree of conformity yet be incomplete for a specific individual. As some values are inadequately emphasized or adjusted to individual potential the child or juvenile is vulnerable to social situations involving these values. The specific value may not be missing from his value system, but its necessary reinforcement may not be present. It cannot therefore prompt the socioethical personality to exert socially expected resistance to pressures toward delinquency. The otherwise adequately "inner-controlled" child or juvenile therefore responds carelessly to these particular values. Because the value *does* exist in his value system, however, he does not actually aspire to contrary goals. Nevertheless, if the opportunity arises, he takes advantage of it casually without evaluating the consequences of his action. Such mistakenly socialized children or juveniles are ready recruits for future delinquency and crime.

NOTES

1. Data on the frequency and demographic distribution of occasional juvenile delinquency are not available. Not only are many of these cases handled in an unofficial or informal manner by the police, but also more than half of them never come to the attention of the juvenile courts at all. See Walter A. Lunden, *Statistics on Delinquents and Delinquency* (Springfield, Ill.: 1964), pp. 23–24. For data on arrest trends of people under eighteen years of age, see Federal Bureau of Investigation, *Uniform Crime Reports—1967* (Washington, D.C.: 1968), pp. 118–119.

2. See Jackson Toby, "Affluence and Adolescent Crime," in President's Commission on Law Enforcement and Administration of Justice, *Task Force Report—Juvenile Delinquency and Youth Crime* (Washington, D.C.: 1967), pp. 132–144.

3. See similar assumptions in Ruth Shonle Cavan, *Criminology* (2nd ed.; New York: 1957), p. 181.

4. Marvin E. Wolfgang, "The Culture of Youth," in President's Commission on Law Enforcement and Administration of Justice, *Task Force Report—Juvenile Delinquency and Youth Crime* (Washington, D.C.: 1967), pp. 145–154.

5. Harry Elmer Barnes and Negley K. Teeters, *New Horizons in Criminology* (3rd. ed.; Englewood Cliffs, N.J.: 1959), p. 54.

6. See Nathan Goldman, *Differential Selection of Juvenile Offenders* (New York: 1965).

7. Ernst Heinrich Rosenfeld, "First Offenders," in Alexander Elster and Heinrich Lingemann, eds., *Handwörterbuch der Kriminologie und der anderen strafrechtlichen Hilfswissenschaften*, 1 (Berlin: 1933), 435.

8. Nathaniel F. Cantor, *Crime and Society: An Introduction to Criminology* (New York: 1939), p. 9.

9. Carl Werthman, "The Function of Social Definitions in the Development of Delinquent Careers," in President's Commission on Law Enforcement and Administration of Justice, *Ta k Force Report—Juvenile Delinquency and Youth Crime* (Washington, D.C.: 1967), pp. 155–170.

10. See Martin Gold, *Status Forces in Delinquent Boys* (Ann Arbor: 1963).

11. See Hans J. Eysenck, *Crime and Personality* (Boston: 1964).

12. T. C. N. Gibbens and R. H. Ahrenfeldt, *Cultural Factors in Delinquency* (London: 1966).

Chapter 7

■ *Professional Delinquency*

■ *The Profit Motive*

The *professional delinquent* commits deviant acts for profit. Whereas the *occasional* delinquent acts under the pressure of need or emotion and the *casual* delinquent acts out of carelessness in value considerations, the *professional* delinquent has profit goals. If the occasional delinquent achieves financial gain, it is incidental to some other primary goal. If the casual delinquent achieves economic advantage, it is secondary to his basic aspirations. The professional delinquent, however, seeks financial gain or economic advantage as a primary goal. Profit is not accessory to his delinquency but its direct target. As these deviants are children or juveniles, the profit is rarely related to material needs. A professional delinquent rarely acts to gain what are ordinarily considered necessities. He steals, burgles, or cheats, not to pay for his rent, food, and medical expenses, but to pay for pleasures and conveniences that he cannot achieve legitimately because of his ascribed social position. Desires, rather than needs, are the source of his deviant behavior.

Although profit is the prime factor in professional delinquency, it is conceivable that an occasional or casual delinquent may turn to professional delinquency, just as it is possible for the professional to commit occasional deviance. If, for example, he kills the attacker of his mother, he is committing an occasional delinquency. If afterward, however, he steals the dead man's wallet, he is committing an act of professional delinquency. If he only steals a man's wallet, without any thought of defending his mother, he is engaging in professional delinquency. If he discovers while engaged in theft that his victim has attacked his mother and shoots the man under the pressure of his emotions, he is still an occasional delinquent in that segment of his behavior.

Although profit motives are the main pressure toward professional delinquency, they may also represent pressure in casual and organized delinquency. They are dominant motivators thanks mainly to the tolerance of socioethical resistance to profit goals. As man's expected pattern of behavior is to satisfy his desires (through socially acceptable and legitimate activity), profit motives often encounter levels of socioethical resistance lower than the supposed "average." An "average" inner control in the occasional delinquent is outweighed by pressures toward delinquency. The pressures toward delinquency in the professional delinquent are no more intense, but his socioethical resistance operates at a lower level.

The professional delinquent reveals inadequate transmission and socialization of norms. Consequently he is not equipped with acceptable socioethical attitudes. His personality is thus the product of faulty socialization or of failure of socialization. Although the socialization process may adequately transmit cultural material to the individual, mental disturbance or retardation may undermine his attempts to understand and internalize prescribed norms. This example reveals the failure of socialization, but faulty socialization may take the form of inability to transmit values, that is, of incompetence or incompatibility among the agents of socialization.

■ *The Life Trend of the Professional Delinquent*

The basic profit motive is common to both professional delinquency and professional criminality. The characteristic life trends associated with them, however, do not correspond in all respects, largely because of age differences. The volume and varying direction of desires at different stages of maturation cause differences in life trends. Whereas the professional juvenile delinquent deviates to obtain conveniences and pleasures, the professional adult criminal primarily commits crimes to make a living. The former usually does not and cannot fully break his family ties; the professional criminal is incorporated into a separate caste, popularly called the "criminal world" or the "underworld."

Adult professional criminals function in ways "comparable to the organization of the work and life of the banker, the doctor, the businessman or the skilled craftsman."[1] According to Edwin H. Sutherland and Donald R. Cressey, "the professional criminal argues that the ideal of public service is no more developed in the legal profession than in the criminal profession,"[2] but such a comparison seems bizarre. It is equally strange to compare professional delinquents with conformist children or juveniles on athletic teams, chess clubs, or civic organizations. The absence of a constructive social role strikingly distinguishes the professional delinquent and criminal from the rest of society.

As the professional delinquent is primarily interested in delinquency for profit, his attitude and behavior are generally dominated by this interest. Other motives may also play a part, but they grow proportionally less important as the youth matures. Although the typical professional delinquent still finds some security and gratification within his family, he increasingly seeks pleasure in extrafamilial activities. The scope of such outside activities depends, however, upon the relationship between home opportunities and personal desires. The desire for gratification through the family necessitates continuing ties with the family. Although the professional delinquent seeks material objects and pleasures, his home environment thus remains his operating base. The professional criminal, however, has a "full-time job" and establishes a locus of operations away from his home environment.

The professional delinquent's interests influence the development of his attitudes. Although oriented toward his home for the necessities of life, he becomes oriented toward delinquency to obtain goods and pleasures. He therefore distorts his family role by confining his rights, duties, and functions in the family to those connected with material necessities, so that even faulty socialization cannot be continued within the family setting. Because his delinquent interests divert his attention from maintaining family relationships, he denies the family's function as a medium of social control and as the primary agency of socialization. Negative values stimulated by forces outside the home dominate his socioethical attitudes,[3] and reflect his delinquent achievements.

Although social stratification, social disorganization, class roles, and economic deprivation are important in current explanations of delinquency, no available systematic study has revealed a correlation between the professional delinquent type and desires for higher status or social-class position. The delinquent's desire for particular objects and pleasures does not develop as a consequence of his observation that young people of other social classes readily obtain such fulfillment; instead it represents recognition that his class or economic position blocks him from equal achievement. He desires goods and pleasures simply because they exist.

Albert K. Cohen has suggested that lower-class gang delinquency is a form of protest and rebellion against middle-class culture.[4] The professional delinquent, however, cannot be equated with Cohen's gang member; not only does the professional delinquent fail to operate through a delinquent organization, but also his deviation is not motivated by desire to share in middle-class rewards. The professional delinquent aspires to goods and pleasures for themselves, regardless of their availability to others and only because they are available at all. Consequently, we may hypothesize that any attempt to understand the etiology of professional delinquency must first take into consideration the role of opportunities in the formation of professional delinquency. As no society can provide all the necessary opportunities to fulfill rising aspirations, professional delinquency has its origins in both greater accessibility of opportunities for delinquency and shortcomings of socialization.

Crimes against property committed by children and juveniles in Soviet territories suggest that professional delinquency is not an expression of upward social mobility and that opportunities in themselves may exert pressures toward delinquency even in a theoretically "classless" society. Richard A. Cloward and Lloyd E. Ohlin have come closer to understanding this type of delinquency,[5] although they also alluded to middle-class aspirations as central determinants of lower-class delinquency. The professional delinquent does not, however, make comparisons between his social status and that of members of other social classes, or between his own and other juveniles' economic positions before he decides to commit a delinquent act. His central consideration is fulfillment of his own desires; he considers only his economic position and his own potential for gaining the desired objects or pleasures. Gratification of desire, rather than class status or economic success, seems to be the determining factor in professional delinquency.[6]

The professional delinquent does not necessarily enter into gang relationships. Although gang members may show similar interests in objects and pleasures, they may also share other aspirations that outweigh the profit goal. Professional delinquency may therefore be a feature of the delinquent gang, but the basic goals of the gang are different. Nevertheless, the professional delinquent's attitudes, socioethical value assumptions, delinquent skills, behavior in juvenile court, contacts and friendships with others, and recreational habits are all geared to his primary delinquent goal. Not all professional delinquents have identical attitude patterns; the shape, range, and intensity of such patterns depend on the interests and experiences of the professional delinquent and upon his opportunities.

■ Relationship of Professional Delinquency to Professional Criminality

Although the cliché is that professional delinquency and even juvenile delinquency in general are the first certain steps toward professional crime, the professional delinquent's development is marked by multiple influences that affect his choice of life trend after he has reached maturity. Because later opportunities may mobilize his socioethical attitudes in favor of illegitimate aspirations or aspirations to be achieved by illegitimate means, the normative attitudes instilled by childhood socialization may function only in meeting his personal needs rather than in satisfying his desires. If his family cannot or does not want to provide for his needs, he is forced to do so himself. Although this necessity may not lead him to reevaluate his socioethical attitudes, it may fortify his recognition of reality by causing him to assess his own needs. This reassessment can serve to introduce him to a two-track life trend as the first step toward replacing deviant patterns with new socialization, but such a change is accomplished infrequently.

Retrospective and other investigations of causes of professional crime emphasize the influence of juvenile delinquency in the creation of the professional criminal's life trend.[7] Juvenile delinquency is frequently identified as an antecedent to professional criminality, but no available evidence "proves" that a cause-and-effect relationship is probable. Professional juvenile delinquency, however, *may* or *may not* lead to professional criminal activity. A professional criminal career, however, necessarily begins in amateur crime. Training, practice, and experience are required for graduation to professionalism. Professional criminal accomplishment and identification occur only as the individual develops appropriate skills to reach his profitable goals. Although professional delinquency is directed toward obtaining conveniences and pleasures, professional criminality is oriented toward gaining a living, as well as satisfying hedonistic desires. Socialization of the individual to criminal attitudes, as well as development of illegal skills, profitable contacts with legitimate citizens and politicians, and other varied characteristics reveal that the adult professional criminal is not a newcomer to crime.

Although a man's behavior patterns are subject to change and his thinking, reactions, and behavior are continually modified as he matures, his personality and life style remain fairly consistent throughout the maturation process. Changes in his socioethical attitudes and behavior patterns develop only if new experiences cause him to reconsider his value system. Such a reevaluation of self can occur, however, only as part of a reevaluation of the environment. As the professional delinquent meets frequent opportunities for deviation with inadequate socioethical resistance, a nearly smooth transition from professional delinquency to professional criminality logically occurs, unless the socioethical personality is remobilized. Professional juvenile delinquency is, however, far from always being an inevitable path to adult professional criminality, for multiple social forces operate not only for, but also against, delinquency and direct the individual to self-reevaluation.

■ *The Juvenile Prostitute*

The professional delinquency of females necessarily differs somewhat from that of males.[8] Differences in biology, aspirations, and social control in childhood clearly influence the two sexes. Different sexual natures, which emerge in early infancy, lead to subsequent differences in role and behavior patterns, which in turn influence the aspirations and goals in connection with physical energy and strength. Although social control is tighter upon girls, female deviance is also more easily excused or minimized.

Varying aspirations and congenital differences in physical energy encourage different kinds of behavior. But professional delinquency is not totally dissimilar for the two sexes. Sexual promiscuity is one factor that is strikingly different in the delinquency of girls, although Ruth Shonle Cavan suggests that "boys are fully as prone to this behavior as girls."[9] Juvenile promiscuity differs from juvenile or adult prostitution and appears to be an alternative form of delinquent behavior, but it may lead to later prostitution, a form of female professional crime.

Few social problems have longer histories and inspire greater controversy than does prostitution, usually defined as the common lewdness of a woman for gain.[10] Although the British Wolfenden Committee declared that prostitution is publicly and morally deplorable, it also noted that prostitution has been present in most civilizations.[11] "The failure of attempts to stamp it out by repressive legislation," the Committee noted, "shows that it cannot be eradicated through the agency of the criminal law."[12] Without a demand for prostitution it could not exist. But "there are enough men who avail themselves of prostitutes to keep the trade alive."[13] Although many accept this argument, whether or not prostitution is merely the product of interaction between supply and demand is debatable. Whether demands for prostitution are traditional or are merely responses to specific offers of sexual favors by prostitutes is unclear.

How much more prevalent, if at all, prostitution is today than in the past cannot be answered. The absence of agreement on just what prostitution is makes official statistics questionable. Current data reflect only prosecutions and convictions for certain types of "disorderly conduct" or other broad categories. It is therefore impossible to obtain a realistic view of the problem of prostitution or of how many people are engaged in the trade. Even if existing data were to show an apparent decline in prostitution, they would not necessarily prove that prostitution has in fact decreased. The Wolfenden Report, for example, cites the 1881 testimony of a senior officer of the London Metropolitan Police, who revealed that from 3:00 to 4:00 in the afternoon certain London streets were crowded with prostitutes who openly solicited male customers in broad daylight.[14] He calculated that about 500 prostitutes were practicing their trade in the small area between Piccadilly Circus and the bottom of Waterloo Place at 12:30 A.M. Although public solicitation by prostitutes has diminished in recent years, Walter C. Reckless noted in 1955 that an estimated 600,000 prostitutes and an equal number of part-time prostitutes, including housewives, ply the trade in the United States.[15] Although there has been a general moral decline,[16] criticism of prostitution and of free sexual practices has also become more common. Street prostitution still exists in capitals and large cities, though in smaller numbers than eighty years ago, but sexual emancipation has not been without cost to morals. Conservative attitudes toward premarital and extramarital sexual relations still prevail. Yet, youthful promiscuity and modified socioethical attitudes seem also to reflect change. The disintegration of the family observed mainly since World War II, the relaxed control of sex life, the frequently immature strivings of youth for independence, and

other symptoms have not favored the decrease in prostitution in its broadest sense, that is, promiscuity. The wide-scale use of tricky and artful
methods of selling "camouflaged" prostitution also suggests an immense
increase in the problem.

The magnitude of the problem and its influence on juveniles cannot
be realistically considered without evaluating new forms of prostitution,
which survive under the guise of private "immorality," or, more appropriately, the *sanctity of invisible deviations*. The height of such over-
objective formalism was reached in the Wolfenden Report, which suggested that "it is not illegal to offer her body to indiscriminate lewdness
for hire, provided that she does not, in the course of doing so, commit any
of the specific acts which would bring her within the ambit of the law."[17]
Such a standard would, however, automatically exempt the overwhelming
majority of juvenile prostitutes from what is now regarded as professional delinquency.

Prostitution can no longer be defined as it was 50 to 100 years ago.
Modern prostitution includes the sorry figures who walk the streets and
also girls and women who may be tentatively called "white-collar prostitutes." Whereas the Wolfenden Report referred only to those who
habitually loiter or importune passersby for the purposes of prostitution in
any public place,[18] Sheldon Glueck and Eleanor Glueck criticized this
narrow scope. They suggested alternative types of female sex deviation
and distinguished the professional prostitute, who lives entirely on
prostitution, and the occasional prostitute, who mixes prostitution with
legitimate work, from the one-man prostitute, who serves as a mistress in
return for money.[19] "Prostitution," Reckless suggested, "is the practice of
selling sexual intercourse or other substitute forms of sexual gratification."[20]
Such an elastic definition, with its emphasis on the business element, helps
to clarify the concept of the "white-collar prostitute" and serves to unmask
the real dimensions of prostitution. It also aids our understanding of
female professional delinquency in the form of prostitution. Definition
of the prostitute as an "idle or disorderly person" of some kind inevitably
leads to misinterpretation when applied to the problems of delinquency
and potential criminality. The element of business *(selling)* in sexual
behavior, however, more clearly applies to a poorly defended socioethical
personality that is susceptible to crime or delinquency. Not that crime
and delinquency are synonymous with either vice or sin; rather they reflect value systems and patterns of life.

The so-called *common prostitute* is most typically associated with
delinquency and crime. Not only is the business element stronger in her
case, but also the sale of her favors is publicly arranged, almost without
any selection of the client. The common prostitute, comparable to the
Gluecks' professional prostitute, usually associates with members of the
criminal world in a criminal atmosphere. Juvenile prostitutes, however,
fall into this category of professional delinquency least frequently.
Although the juvenile prostitute may associate with other professional or

gang delinquents, she does not engage in sex for profit, at least at first, despite her ties with organized delinquency. She identifies with the aspirations and goals of the gang and remains unconcerned about gaining economic advantage. She is not a professional delinquent but an associate in organized delinquency.

The *private prostitute* also lives entirely or partly by selling her sexual services, although she is usually more selective in her clients. She differs from the common prostitute only in the actual degree of delinquency or criminality but not in her potential for them. In this form of prostitution the juvenile girl comes closest to becoming a professional delinquent. Not only does she exercise some selection of her male partners, but she also shares in a parallel life trend. The great majority of prostitutes, the Wolfenden Committee believe, "are women whose psychological make-up is such that they choose this life because they find in it a style of living which is to them easier, freer, and more profitable than would be provided by any other occupation."[21]

The assumption that prostitution always results from the free choice of the prostitute is not grounded in fact, however. The appearance of free choice may result from shortcomings in socialization that permit formation of deviant values. Faulty or unsuccessful socialization, however, is not the only cause of prostitution, which, although it is not completely understood, is recognized as the product of many dynamic elements. Sexual deviations arise from such diverse factors as neuroses, emotional disorders, retardation, disturbed family relationships, broken homes, unhappy families, fears, anxieties, emotional frustrations, inadequate training in the formative years, economic deprivation, peer-group influence, status seeking, and learned desires for sexual experience. Although each factor may be enough to stimulate involvement in prostitution, it may also combine with one or more other factors for a similar result. The prostitution of girls does not arise exclusively from desires for convenience and pleasures. Although the ultimate objective is the acquisition of profit in order to gratify these desires, the selection of an illegitimate means to this goal is only partly determined by its ease or economic potential.

Juvenile prostitution is no less commercial than the trade of adult prostitutes. The range of activity, the style of performance, and the scope of financial return may vary, but the process of negotiated exchange and the desire for profit make the difference one of degree only. The juvenile prostitute is selling sexual gratification of others' desires; the return may take the form of money, clothing, jewelry, or gifts that are convertible to cash. Although such delinquency usually begins with non-commercial promiscuous behavior, or at least promiscuity for insignificant returns, the success of these first experiences can easily lead to professional delinquency patterns if it is coupled with faulty socialization. If a girl indulges in prostitution as a form of professional delinquency, her values may undergo further deterioration. The shortcomings of her socialization will grow more acute, and her socioethical personality will be more susceptible to the variety of other pressures toward delinquency. Her professional prostitution may lead to other forms of professional delinquency and may result in her stopping prostitution as she turns to these other forms; or she may combine prostitution and other illegitimate activities to reach profit goals. In this process the female's professional delinquency partly parallels the basic patterns of male professional delinquency.

NOTES

1. Ruth Shonle Cavan, *Criminology* (3rd ed.; New York: 1962), p. 96.

2. Edwin H. Sutherland and Donald R. Cressey, *Principles of Criminology* (6th ed.; New York: 1960), p. 232.

3. For a study that attempts to isolate delinquent subcultures and the opportunities open to individuals as their criminal careers develop, see Irving Spergel, *Racketville, Slumtown, Haulberg* (Chicago: 1964). Racketville, Slumtown, and Haulberg refer to organized racketeering, gang fighting, and professional thievery, respectively.

4. Albert K. Cohen, *Delinquent Boys: The Culture of the Gang* (New York: 1955).

5. Richard A. Cloward and Lloyd E. Ohlin, *Delinquency and Opportunity: A Theory of Delinquent Gangs* (New York: 1960).

6. The current state of the delinquency problem seems tragic, rather than dangerous. Most theories, in fact, explain delinquency in terms of social disorganization or class structure, mostly without comparing American social disorganization with that of other countries and without investigating other class structures.

7. See Clifford R. Shaw, *The Jack-Roller* (Chicago: 1930); and Shaw, *Brothers in Crime* (Chicago: 1938).

8. For an examination of adolescent sex offenses see Albert J. Reiss, Jr., "Sex Offenses: The Marginal Status of the Adolescent," *Law and Contemporary Problems*, 25 (1960), 2.

9. Cavan, *Juvenile Delinquency: Development, Treatment, Control* (New York: 1962), p. 101. See also Norman R. Jackman, Richard O'Toole, and Gilbert Geis, "The Self-Image of the Prostitute," *Sociological Quarterly*, 4 (April 1963), 150–161.

10. *225 SW Reporter 897*. Other definitions include the "act of sexual intercourse for a price" and "the act or practice of a female for sexual intercourse with a male for money or its equivalent." *115 NE 632*.

11. Home Office, *Report of the Committee on Homosexual Offenses and Prostitution* (London: 1957). This report is popularly known as the Wolfenden Report, after Sir John Wolfenden, chairman of the Committee.

12. *Ibid.*, p. 79.

13. *Ibid.*, p. 80. See also Robert K. Merton and Robert A. Nisbet, *Contemporary Social Problems* (New York: 1966), pp. 346–372.

14. Home Office, *op. cit.*, p. 82.

15. Walter C. Reckless, *The Crime Problem* (2nd ed.; New York: 1955), p. 268.

16. Robert L. Sutherland, Julian L. Woodward, and Milton A. Maxwell, *Introductory Sociology* (5th ed.; New York: 1956), p. 449.

17. Home Office, *op. cit.*, p. 79.

18. *Ibid.*, p. 88.

19. Sheldon Glueck and Eleanor Glueck, *Five Hundred Delinquent Women* (New York: 1934), p. 89.

20. Reckless, *op. cit.*, p. 266.

21. Home Office, *op. cit.*, p. 79.

Chapter 8

▪ *Organized Delinquency*

▪ *The Nature of Delinquent Organizations*

Organized delinquency differs markedly from individual professional delinquency. Whereas professional delinquency is primarily the behavior of *one* juvenile, even though it may take place in company with other individuals, organized delinquency is by definition conceived and initiated in a group. Individual professional delinquency by one or more participants during a relatively short period of association involves less intimate, if any, associations and more purely profit-oriented goals and aspirations. These characteristics are qualitatively different from tnose of delinquencies or crimes committed by associates bound together in a more or less permanent organization.

The concept of organized delinquency and crime offers many difficulties. Simple teamwork of juvenile deviants is believed by some people to exemplify organized delinquency, whereas others confuse gang activity with organized rackets. The confusion surrounding the associational types of crime leads interpreters to categorize them differently.[1] Alfred R. Lindesmith, for example, suggests the cooperation of "the several different persons or groups" in the successful execution of a delinquent act as the criterion of this category.[2] Edwin H. Sutherland and Donald R. Cressey, however, find the distinction in the organizational process, which involves the "association of a small group" for the execution of certain types of crime, together with "the development of plans by which detection may be avoided. . . ."[3] Although these theorists pose the dilemma, its solution can best be found perhaps through examination of the commonly recognized major elements and characteristics of organized delinquency. Organized delinquency involves a permanent, although often haphazard and semiorganized, structural and functional association of delinquents. The permanence of this association, the relatively large number of par-

128

ticipants, and the absence of long-range planning for specific delinquent acts are important elements of this delinquency. The vital element, however, is the relations among the members and between the participants and their delinquent acts. The organization itself is the distinctive factor in organized delinquency. As with adult criminals, however, organized crime "must be distinguished from the efforts of a large number of individual operators, petty thieves, drunks, disorderly persons, and others of this type who try their hand at crime, but without much effective accomplishment" and from "partnerships of two or three who work together sharing risks and dividing profits."[4] As pure profit is not one of the major aspirations of most delinquents, the profit motive does not offer a major criterion for organized delinquency. Several assumptions and qualifications should also be noted, however.

First, the permanent nature of organized delinquency does not imply that members permanently agree or that the group's existence is fixed for some formal length of time. It does suggest the "moral" commitment of group members to a comparatively permanent association, which may last even longer than originally intended by specific members. If the interests of the organization (for example, the need for secrecy or for special skills) necessitate continued participation of a member despite his own desires, he may be forced by threats or other methods to continue membership. Although an individual may voluntarily join an organized delinquent group, he may find it extremely difficult to resign from one.

Second, the type of delinquency reflects the goals and aspirations of the organization. Although they may involve profit, economic gain is of secondary importance in most delinquency. Delinquent groups seeking political goals through opposition to dominant political forces should not be regarded as examples of organized delinquency and crime in the ordinary sense.

Third, a large number of participant members is an obvious precondition of organizational existence. Organized delinquency necessarily involves an association of individuals.

Fourth, the group itself, rather than its activities, is the major reason for the existence of the group. Although professional and other individual delinquents may decide and agree in advance upon specific conduct, such behavior is neither necessary nor customary in organized delinquency. Individual professional delinquents may plan their activities well in advance, agreeing, for example, to shoplift specific items from a certain branch of a major department store. Only the general type of delinquent behavior is, however, specified in advance by organized delinquents or criminals. The actual form of behavior is determined by conditions when and where it takes place. They may decide, for example, to physically attack Jews, but not two Jews on Monday and four Jews on Tuesday. These delinquents do not deliberately seek to involve themselves in delinquency and crime but rather reflect conditions of social conflict and tension. When white youths, for example, attacked Negroes at random in the Chicago race riots after World War I, crime itself was not the ultimate aim. Similarly, when youthful groups voluntarily beat or killed Jewish citizens during World War II, their action was not specifically planned, nor was the participation of London youth in the 1958 race disturbances at Notting Hill Gate. In each of these instances, individuals acted in order to have some "fun" and were caught up in the emotional contagion of events. From boredom they turned to emotional acts that brought serious, even tragic, consequences.

Whereas the individual professional delinquent may associate and cooperate with others because of the specific requirements of his planned delinquency, organized delinquency is a by-product of an organization formed for other purposes. The organization is therefore a primary, rather than secondary, group and involves the whole individual. Delinquent organizations are specialized and seek predetermined organizational goals. This effort may include establishing economic or social monopolies, but it is not limited to such goals.[5] Although a delinquent organization frequently controls or monopolizes an entire geographical area or type of delinquency, all delinquent organizations are not completely successful in attaining their objectives. Several delinquent organizations share control in many geographical areas and types of delinquency. Such coexistence is, however, usually fraught with conflict.

Fifth, the structure of the organization is the outstanding feature of organized delinquency. The organization is a functional group, designed to meet the needs of its members, each of whom participates in a variety of activities commonly accepted by group members and generally coordinated through the leadership and discipline of one youth or a small clique of youths. Although girls may fulfill designated roles in predominantly male organizations, the leaders are nearly always boys.

As the efficiency and complexity of the group generally depend on the size of the membership, all delinquent organizations provide for at least two main phases of delinquency—preparation and action—and occasionally for a third, postdelinquency immunity. As the life of the group depends upon the dependable performance of duties and responsibilities, performance is rewarded or punished appropriately. The loyalty of members to the organization is maintained through rigid and ruthless discipline. George B. Vold compares its organizational discipline with that of the armed forces: "As in a military unit in battle, everyone participates in the active combat, but only the commanding officers may give orders or make major decisions about the course of action to be followed."[6] Such formidable discipline requires the leader to administer justice and to inflict punishments upon errant members in the interests and name of the organization, as is common in any special-interest group.

Because of the structure of organized delinquent groups and despite the secondary nature of delinquent activities, organizational planning receives the highest priority. The goals of the group and its interest in survival require the greatest effort on the part of all members. Although planning is recognized as essential to group success, it is characterized by a high degree of flexibility and imagination. Sometimes standardized methods are invoked; at other times new and creative approaches are attempted. In each instance, the goal of the moment governs the decision to use a particular technique.

■ *The Conceptual Development of the Gang*

Most people, assuming that only one type of delinquent organization exists, equate children's or juveniles' delinquent organizations with delinquent gangs, the most common type of delinquent group. Care must, however, be taken not to confuse the juvenile gang with or treat it as the counterpart of the adult criminal syndicate, which exists to provide legal and illegal services, including the confidence game, black-marketeering, or the rackets. Although the term "gang" has been in use for about 300 years, it did not have invidious connotations until the early 1920s, when it became associated in the public mind with organized delinquency and criminality. Although criminal gangs had existed before that time, they were not separately categorized until after World War I. Even now, however, there is much disagreement on what a gang is.[7]

If a gang is defined merely as a group of people banded together for common activities, it can include practically any kind of youth or adult group from conforming to criminal extremes. More than two-thirds of the men and approximately one-third of the women in a study by Sutherland and Cressey of university students, for example, had belonged to harmless "gangs" of children.[8] But there is a basic difference between a group that conforms to the norms of society and represents constructive interest in play, sports, or recreation and a group whose interests are antagonistic to the social order.[9] Whether conforming or delinquent, the gang is, however, a common social form among juveniles. Although it is possible that some juvenile gangs may pass from conforming to criminal, the vast majority do not. Although Frederic M. Thrasher called children's play groups "the real beginning of the gang,"[10] he was unable to show that all or even a few of these groups develop into juvenile delinquent gangs. Hans von Hentig also suggested that small groups of friends may grow into juvenile gangs,[11] but he too was unable to offer sufficient evidence that they often do.

■ *Differences Between Adult and Juvenile Gangs*

The belief that juvenile and adult gangs share characteristic features is probably based upon certain similar group characteristics. The essential differences in their activities make it impossible, however, to correlate juvenile and adult gangs, despite Hentig's suggestion that "there is no clear dividing line between the juvenile and adult gang."[12]

First, the juvenile gang is a more spontaneous association than the planned and deliberately organized adult criminal gang. An adult gang engages in planned activity, based upon reason and pure self-interest. Members of a juvenile gang, friends from the outset, often band together from sentimental motives. Friendships may also emerge among members of adult criminal gangs, but their fundamental goals are pragmatic.

Second, the juvenile gang is, in a sense, counterfeit or "make-believe" when compared to the crudely realistic adult criminal gang. The juveniles' imitation of the "serious" or "famous" gangs may result in unrealistic behavior by members. However tragic the consequences may be, play or adventure motives, even though distorted, are what stimulate their conduct. By contrast, the stakes for adult criminal gangs are so high that no sort of play or adventure can be tolerated.

Third, the delinquent gang prepares and acts, whereas the adult criminal gang prepares, acts, and defends. Defense of gang members, although it occasionally occurs, is not a customary or developed aspect of juvenile-gang activities. Adult criminal gangs, however, make every effort to defend their members, an essential element of the gang's conceptual structure and framework.

Fourth, the juvenile gang is a less complex and a less highly structured organization than the highly institutionalized adult criminal gang. Many roles in the latter, for example, those of doctor, lawyer, and technician, are almost never found in the juvenile gang. Disciplinary procedures also differ. Treachery in delinquent gangs is seldom a matter of life and death. Instead, juvenile gangs maintain order through the use of humiliation or corporal punishment rather than through murder. Adult criminal gangs, however, maintain discipline through the use of organized force or murder.

Fifth, although the juvenile gang generally possesses a variety of interests and objectives, the adult criminal gang limits itself to certain specific types of crimes for profit. Not that the profit motive is never present in juvenile gangs. But it is generally of secondary importance. Conversely, status, one of the most important goals of a delinquent gang, is of less importance to the adult criminal gang.

Sixth, the juvenile gang also differs from the adult gang in geographical mobility, despite the fact that the activities of both generally require participants to "disappear" afterward. Although the adult gang tends to leave town or even the state after committing one or more crimes, the juvenile gang is much more restricted, perhaps even confined to the general area where its activity occurs. This difference arises not only from such greater resources of the adult gang as money, automobiles, and multiple fronts but also from the dependence of juvenile delinquents upon their families.

.   .   .

The major similarity between the two types of organizations is the willingness of each to resort to physical force and violence to accomplish its ends. It may take various forms, ranging from fist fights to armed threats and outright murder. Violent acts by juvenile groups, however, are generally unpremeditated, whereas those of most adult gangs are planned.[13]

■ The "Ganging Process": Some Characteristics of the Delinquent Gang

Any attempt to understand the ganging process rests upon the answer to three central questions: In what geographic areas are gangs found? From what segments of society do they mainly arise? What is the basic cause of their creation? Thrasher suggests that "the beginnings of the gang can best be studied in the slums of the city where an inordinately large number of children are crowded into a limited area."[14] Not only are spontaneous play groups formed there, but the crowded environment also stimulates conflicts that cause youths to join gangs, from which they gain a sense of belonging. The ganging process, Thrasher hypothesized, has its origins in social experience and conflict.

Although "white-collar gangs" are not unknown, the overwhelming majority of gangs known to the police involve the children of families at the lower end of the class scale. Albert K. Cohen states that "the delinquent subculture is mostly to be found in the working class,"[15] and William C. Kvaraceus and Walter B. Miller hypothesize that the juvenile gang is an ordinary product of lower-class culture.[16] These two comments suggest that the terms "working class" and "lower class" are commonly confused by theorists who fail to distinguish between individual delinquents and delinquency in its organized form. Gangs, however, are products of the metropolitan area or the big city, as in New York, Chicago, London, and Paris, but rarely of the village. Their activities are thus primarily an urban problem. Urban conflict seems to stimulate gang organization and activity. Conflict may occur, however, not only between gangs but also between social classes, ideologies, legal norms, enforcement agencies, and personal attitudes.

Although the technical aspects of the *ganging process* are not well understood, preliminary evidence suggests that the juvenile gang probably has its origin in the social clique. Although typically the clique is a small exclusive group whose members are loosely bound together by some common interest, it cannot be regarded as an organization. Thrasher calls it a "spontaneous interest group," "an embryonic gang," usually formed within the structure of another group like a club or a political party.[17] Although the common interest of such a clique can be anything—sports, chess, literature, dancing, or even stamp or coin collecting—it is mainly conforming and noncompetitive and is rarely oriented toward delinquency.

It consists of perhaps only three to five members and has no formally recognized leader, except when the members' interests are threatened.

As outside competition emerges, the conceptual structure of the clique changes, and it becomes an "opposition group" engaged in both offensive and defensive maneuvers. As circumstances necessitate organizational development, an informal but partially disciplined hierarchy, usually dependent on the members' ages, skills, or physical strength, develops. In order to defend its basic interests, the clique recruits additional members or affiliates with other cliques with similar interests. The different cliques, however, may eventually compete for power and leadership in the coalition. As the situation continues to demand even more structured organization, it offers members increased self-esteem and prestige.

As the sizes and structures of the cliques change, the coalition develops multiple interests. Although individual problems and concerns are increasingly supplanted by those of the larger group, the clique still remains basically conforming in nature. The expanded group, like the original separate cliques, is also rather informal and loosely defined, not yet fully involved in delinquency. The competitive situation in which it increasingly finds itself, however, causes it to turn from its conventional approach and directs it to more open, though not necessarily physical, conflict.

A second type of clique is one that Thrasher calls "orgiastic,"[18] keeping its members busy with group activities or expression, usually in the form of inspired and ritualistic singing, dancing, or other emotional behavior, but remaining aloof from competition. Except for the size of the group and its sensual interests, the orgiastic clique is basically similar to the first kind but does not move into delinquent activities.

The *street-corner group* is yet another juvenile group that may be either a further development of the clique or an independent development. In either case it may ultimately become a gang. Although the clique itself may first become a street-corner group, it may also become a gang without passing through the street-corner phase. A simple street-corner group may also develop directly into a gang. The basic difference between the clique and the street-corner group is in its genesis. Although the clique grows out of the common interests of a few individuals, the street-corner group is more an ecological phenomenon, in which individuals band together because of proximity. The "street corner" is the meeting place, not, of course, necessarily a street corner; it can be any part of a street, park, or other location easily accessible to group members. Although the demands of the street-corner group are likely to necessitate more structure than do those of the clique, the fullest development of the former occurs only when it reaches the gang stage. Although leadership roles, rules, and goals are more precisely defined in the street-corner group than in the clique, they are still not as highly developed as in the gang. The street-corner group is very similar to the formless "near-group" that Lewis Yablonsky defined as a "collection of individuals" somewhere between an organized society and the unorganized mob.[19] Both types of group have similar structures with uncertain leadership, vaguely defined goals, and fluctuating membership. Although both may possess permanent membership nuclei, most of their members at any given time are rather loosely and unstably affiliated.

The *gang* is the final stage of development after the common needs, problems, and aspirations of the juveniles have been sufficiently clarified and recognized by themselves and have been transformed into accepted group needs, problems, and aspirations. At this stage group goals, directed primarily at profit or status, which can be achieved only through delinquent activities, are formed.

"The ganging process," Thrasher has noted, "is a continuous flux and flow."[20] Even in its final stage, when the gang proper can be recognized, it seems rather unplanned, in comparison to clubs, business associations, labor unions, and other organizations. Nevertheless, the gang is an organization whose members have a "feeling of distinctness from other groups."[21] Although group consciousness is not an exclusive characteristic of the gang and also typifies the clique, the street-corner group, and other types of groups, it is more developed in the gang. Because the lives of gang members are dominated by organized activities and reflect their membership in a functional division of society, all together they constitute what might be called a distinct "caste," often identified as "the gang world." Not only is the gang a distinct group in such a context, but it also occupies a distinct place in society as a whole. Although each individual gang has its own characteristic symbols, organization, structure, aspirations, goals, and behavior, all gangs share a common design.

The gang world consists of multiple gangs composed of members who are products of very different backgrounds and have a variety of ambitions and goals. Their relative status in the gang world is determined by gang aspirations and relative success in achieving such goals. Experienced gangs with power and prestige thus tend to look down upon the small groups of beginners who possess little power and even less status in the gang world. As the gang world is not a communistic society, profit, status, and orgiastic pleasures are not shared equally. The various attainments of the different gangs represent the distribution of "wealth," and "class struggle" is thus not unknown in the gang world. Lower-status groups make serious efforts to overcome the barriers of prejudice and to gain respected reputations, whereas higher-status groups make every effort to maintain their positions in the power structure.

Acceptance in this gang world requires adequate command of its special language. Knowledge of criminal argot is mandatory both for communication and to indicate one's full-fledged membership.[22] Although argot has traditionally been used to distinguish the "greenhorn" or intruder from the gang member, this tool of gang security and control has gradually lost its effectiveness as gang studies and other investigations into the criminal world have popularized gang terminology to the point at which many expressions have become integrated into normal conversation. Criminal argot or cant, as Eric Partridge has suggested, is remarkably conservative. For example, the term "phony," which many people believe is a modern expression, has been current in American criminal circles since 1890 and in England, where it was originally spelled "fawney," since 1770.[23]

Another symbol of identification and acceptance is the bestowal of nicknames upon gang members according to their individual peculiarities as noted by their colleagues. One boy might be nicknamed Fat, although he might not be particularly heavy, merely because he ate a great deal; another might be called "Nigger" because of his dark complexion, although he was not a Negro. Physical characteristics, ethnic or religious origins, habits, special skills, or lack of skills are generally the sources of such nicknames.

A third identification symbol common in the gang world is the naming of the groups themselves. The name may express the theme of a gang's activities, proudly declaring that crime is cause not for shame but for glory, as in the Murderers, the Adventurers, the Fearless Thieves, the Big Robbers. Gangs may also identify themselves by names that suggest their fighting spirit or courage (Warriors, Lions, Brave Boys, Tigers, Heroes) or their status (Kings, Lords, Aristocrats, Dukes). Even the names of streets, parks, and other geographical areas are occasionally adopted, although meaningless phrases may also be used. One group of "dirty little ragamuffins" was named the Lilies of the Valley, although it probably would have been more accurate, Thrasher believes, to call it the Lilies of the Alley.[24]

The physical appearance of a gang member is also symbolic. As the soldier, the railroad conductor, or the postman wears a uniform both to distinguish himself from others and to strengthen his own pride in belonging to a particular group, the gang member wears characteristic clothes and distinguishing haircuts. Despite the fact that he risks easier identification by law-enforcement authorities, the criminally oriented gang member usually insists upon emphasizing his gang identification.

■ Gang Typology

The gang population is not homogeneous but can be divided into several categories. H. A. Frégier was probably the earliest "criminologist" to suggest a typology worthy of attention,[25] although he felt many gaps, as did his successors over the next hundred or more years. His typology was an arbitrary classification applied to a wide variety of social phenomena. Although he initiated this approach to description of crime and criminal types, later typologists shared and even accentuated the initial weaknesses.

An effective general typology should meet three essential conditions:

1. It should be derived from a single hypothesis or general explanation of the delinquency problem (*explainability*).

2. It should be based upon characteristics common to many delinquents and delinquencies, even though its divisions are not precise but simply offer a model to which actual examples are referable (*reality*).

3. It should allow for the systematic arrangement of the different types of delinquents and delinquencies into groups so that proper correctional procedures can be adopted (*instrumentality*).

Obviously, if there is to be any meaningful typology of delinquent gangs, the general explanation of delinquency must be related to the problem of correction, offering a delinquent "profile of the mass."[26]

Of the different typologies that have been attempted, Thrasher's is one of the best known.[27] In his classic study of 1,313 Chicago gangs, he distinguished four types: the diffuse, the solidified, the conventionalized, and the criminal. As he attempted to classify gangs according to participants' ages, he found that the gangs were usually divided into "midgets," "juniors," and "seniors," or often only into juniors and seniors. Although his classification was confined to the mere description of different gang structures or activities and lacked sophisticated analysis, it served a useful purpose.

The *diffuse gang*, Thrasher believed, is the most rudimentary form of gang. Marked by weak solidarity and loyalty and limited leadership, it resembles a mere agglomeration of individuals and exhibits little delinquent behavior. The *solidified gang* is the antithesis of the diffuse gang. It is characterized by high degrees of loyalty and is a "well-integrated fighting machine," presenting a "solid front against its foes." This type of gang is not "inherently evil" and does not necessarily engage in delinquent behavior. The *conventionalized gang* is often an "athletic club," although its members may engage in dancing, billiards, and other social activities as well. Although it may function as a "destructive and demoralizing agency," it apparently achieves a level of social status among the general public through its legitimate activities. The *criminal gang*, however, engages in illegal and violent activities.

A second attempt at construction of a gang typology deserving of attention is that of Cohen,[28] in his somewhat psychoanalytical approach to the delinquency problem; he suggested that gang delinquency is at least partly dependent on the problems of individual delinquents. Departing from Thrasher's purely descriptive approach, Cohen suggested that three types of juvenile delinquents develop as a result of different etiological or causal processes: the *predominantly subcultural*, the *predominantly psychogenic*, and the *integrated combination* of the two. In the last category the subcultural and psychogenic factors supposedly work "simultaneously but independently" to provide separate "pushes" toward delinquency.

Richard A. Cloward and Lloyd E. Ohlin distinguish three general types of delinquent gangs as expressions of the "varieties of delinquent subculture." They are gangs whose criminal, conflict, or retreatist patterns of behavior are "the principle orientations of each form of adaptation as seen from the perspective of the dominant social order."[29] They describe the *criminal gang* as a group of youths whose frame of reference is one of the lower-class traditions and who seek success goals through delinquent and criminal behavior. A member of such a gang admires and respects the older criminal, adopts him as a role model, and attempts to win acceptance in criminal circles. In contrast the *conflict gang* seeks status through competition with other gangs and compels deference from the conforming segment of society. Unpredictable destruction and violence are its major means to its goals. The *retreatist gang*, however, is characterized by orgiastic characteristics, primarily based on drug addiction. The "kick," an ecstatic experience, is the dominant goal of the retreatist subculture.

Although many other typologies have offered further variations, most have simply been refinements of their predecessors. Can any new typology shed new light on delinquency? An examination of the relationship between effectiveness of socialization and pressures toward delinquency or crime suggests a simple new direction. This typology, tentatively formulated by Stephen Schafer, includes three types of gangs: the social, the antisocial, and the asocial. The *social gang* accepts and abides by social norms; its members are oriented toward conforming activities. Although both antisocial and asocial gangs may also originally have been organized around nondelinquent interests, the social gang does not deviate from its original purpose. That gang members' behavior conforms to society's normative standards does not, however, imply that the social gang never faces competitive situations or conflicts with other groups or that its members have unlimited resistance to pressures toward delinquency; rather, gang members' socialization appears to be sufficient to enable them to resist the pressures toward delinquency that they encounter in certain situations. Chess, stamp collecting, and similar interests provide typical outlets for this norm-accepting gang.

The *antisocial gang*, on the other hand, engages in various forms of nonconformist and delinquent activity that threaten and challenge social norms. Desire for status, profit, or both, is the leitmotif of this group, which is similar to the criminal gang described by Thrasher or the criminal and conflict gangs defined by Cloward and Ohlin. Failure to achieve an adequate balance between gang members' socioethical personalities and pressures toward delinquency leads participants into situations in which they actively respond to these pressures. Criminal offenses, hooliganism, vandalism, and gang wars are typical activities of a norm-attacking gang.

The *asocial gang* is midway between the social and antisocial types; it consists of socially indifferent youths, who indulge in only certain kinds of nonconforming and delinquent behavior. The asocial gang is characterized by passive delinquency. Failure to achieve a balance between members' socioethical personalities and pressures toward delinquency leads to passive accession to these pressures and to further failure to live up to the norms of the social order. As in Thrasher's conventionalized and Cloward and Ohlin's retreatist gangs, members typically engage in disorderly sexual behavior, drinking, drug addiction, truancy, vagabondism, and participation in the hippie movement. The asocial gang is, in effect, a norm-denying group.

■ *Understanding the Gang*

Available statistical data suggest that gang delinquencies accounted for increasingly higher percentages of juvenile delinquency from the end of World War II through the 1950s. Ruth Shonle Cavan, for example, has noted that in recent years "from 70 to 85 percent of boy delinquencies are committed by two or more boys, only 15 to 30 percent by one boy alone."[30] The impressive increase in this type of delinquent conduct undoubtedly prompted the many studies of gang activity.[31] The more prominent studies may be divided into six categories, according to approach.

The Ecological Approach

Thrasher's study of Chicago gangs,[32] which David J. Bordua rightly called "the classical view,"[33] initiated the ecological approach to delinquent gangs. In brief, Thrasher found that gangs originate in the physical environment to which juveniles' activities are confined, in attractive opportunities that encourage them to participate in deviant behavior, and in the absence of adequate controls that would normally restrict them to socially acceptable behavior. Using the sector-analysis concept of Robert E. Park and Ernest W. Burgess,[34] Thrasher suggested that "gangs, like most other social groups, originate under conditions that are typical for all groups of the same species; they develop in definite and predictable ways."[35] He seemed to be hypothesizing that individual choices and free will count for little when weighed against predetermined and innate delinquency factors.[36] If so, then an understanding of gang behavior depends upon acquaintance with the characteristic features of the gang and more or less descriptive information about its development and behavior. Gangs may arise spontaneously but only if conditions and milieu favor their development.[37]

The gang area, Thrasher hypothesized, is a "geographically and socially interstitial area in the city."[38] Because such gangs are composed of members who live in deteriorating slum neighborhoods with shifting populations, lower-class children almost automatically find themselves in the focus of gang activities. The formation of a gang occurs as a group of children attempt to break "the humdrum of routine existence" and seek new experience.[39] Conforming children and delinquent-gang members,

Thrasher believed, can be differentiated by the ways in which they satisfy their normal wishes for security, experience, recognition, and mastery; these wishes were defined and described by William I. Thomas.[40] Although the four wishes are characteristic of all children, certain groups cannot fulfill them in socially approved ways because of ecological conditions, limited opportunities for expression, and lax social and parental controls. Then they find satisfaction in delinquent relationships and conduct.

Thrasher, however, also believed that the ganging process involves other than social factors. Among the more important are failure of the family to meet the needs of its children and to end the anomic condition of its younger male members, the inability of religion to make its wisdom seem real and vital, the powerlessness of the schools to catch and to hold the interest of children or to provide satisfactory organizations, and the failure of the community to offer adequate guidance in leisure activities. Although society fails to treat the delinquent "as a person," the delinquent gang, Thrasher found, is able to fill this need. American delinquency is thus a product of social disorganization largely resulting from the nation's rapid economic development and the unequal acculturation and assimilation of vast numbers of alien workers.[41]

For nearly three decades after the publication of Thrasher's pioneering work in 1927, no important specific study of gangs appeared, except in the sense that general studies of delinquency and crime applied to them. The postwar increase in gang delinquency did not stimulate new attempts to understand gangs until the latter half of the 1950s. Since then, however, several studies of organized delinquency have been undertaken.[42] All have agreed that the lower class produces proportionately more delinquents than does any other social class. Each has suggested that the lower class has elements of a delinquent subculture in which general social norms are redefined in the context of the group. Although lower-class normative group-behavior patterns may be defined as deviant by the rest of society, they differ radically in their level of sophistication and degree of acceptance by lower-class members.[43]

The Delinquent-Subculture Approach

Cohen attacked the "unsolved problem in juvenile delinquency" with the hypothesis of a lower-class delinquent subculture.[44] "If one wants to explain something which has a number of distinct parts, his explanation," Cohen remarked, "must fit all the parts and not just some facet of the thing which happens, for some reason, to intrigue him."[45] He therefore approached the problem of gang delinquency within the network of "the delinquent subculture," though he limited the applicability of his hypothesis by stating that "not all crime, not even all juvenile crime, will fit this description of the delinquent subculture."[46] He argued that the delinquent subculture can be identified from official statistics, that "almost all statistical analyses of juvenile delinquency agree that delinquency in general is predominantly a working-class phenomenon,"[47] a position supported by Kvaraceus,[48] Clifford R. Shaw, and Henry D. McKay.[49]

Cohen suggested that delinquency differs from adult crime in that it is "non-utilitarian, malicious and negativistic."[50] As he believed that a "valuable" has little monetary worth to those who have stolen it and is therefore "non-utilitarian," he did not regard juvenile stealing, whether by individuals or groups, as a means to an end. Stealing, he believed, does not even offer a satisfying way to fulfill the universal desire for status. Delinquency is instead a form of "apparent malice, an enjoyment in the discomfiture of others, a delight in the defiance of taboos. . . ."[51] Although the gang exhibits hostility toward contemporaries who are not members, as well as toward adults, this hostility is gratuitous in that it is not aimed at gain. Delinquency in the delinquent subculture, however, is also characterized by versatility, short-run hedonism, and group autonomy.[52] The theory of the deviant subculture assumes that all human actions are efforts to solve problems or, in William Graham Sumner's terms, are aimed at maximizing pleasure and minimizing pain.[53] As not all such efforts are successful, defense mechanisms are developed in order to cope with failure. Cohen believed that delinquency is a product of social and psychological factors, but it must also be a product of socioeconomic influences, for it is neither randomly nor equally distributed throughout society. Despite these dual frames of reference, Cohen argued that neither sociologists nor psychologists have adequately explored the role of social structure and environment in delinquency causation. Different types of behavior, he noted, cannot be accounted for merely by describing the problems of adjustment, "as long as there are conceivable alternative responses."[54] Any solution to the delinquency problem that "runs counter to the strong interests or moral sentiments of those around us invites punishment or the forfeiture of satisfactions which may be more distressing than the problem with which it was designed to cope."[55]

The delinquent subculture, Cohen asserted, offers a way to deal with problems of adjustment,[56] chiefly those concerned with status. Because many children are excluded from high status by those who enjoy it, the delinquent subculture provides status criteria that the excluded youths can meet. The delinquent subculture enables the delinquent to compete successfully with those in similar social positions, and it also eliminates or mitigates their status inferiority. Children of middle-class families grow up in a different social atmosphere, yet both groups are expected to meet middle-class standards. Noting this paradox, Cohen suggested that the "same value system, impinging upon children differently equipped to meet it, is instrumental in generating both delinquency and respectability."[57]

Status deprivation, he noted, seems to be decisive in leading lower-class children toward delinquency, providing a common core of motivation in the male working class, for which the delinquent subculture provides the outlet. The antagonism of the delinquent subculture to the ruling middle-class system actually represents conformity, for "the hallmark of the delinquent subculture is the explicit and wholesale repudiation of middle-class standards and the adoption of their very antithesis."[58]

Cohen hypothesized that, as delinquent children participate in common activities, they are "governed by a set of common understandings, common sentiments, and common loyalties,"[59] which are the three characteristic elements of the delinquent subculture that challenge the middle-class norm system. Members of this hostile lower-class delinquent subculture are aware of norms set by the middle class, and they violate them, but they are ambivalent, wanting both to participate in the middle-class system and to destroy it.

In brief, then, Cohen interpreted gang delinquency in the context of the American class structure. As our middle class dominates the lower class and deprives it of overall status, members of the lower class must find status within their own class. In such a condition of status deprivation an antagonistic subculture emerges as a lower-class adaptation to middle-class institutions. This subculture, however, is ultimately expressed in pleasure-seeking or status-gaining behavior, rather than through profit seeking.[60]

The Personality-Development Approach

Herbert A. Bloch and Arthur Niederhoffer[61] focused their attention on developmental drives rather than on the antagonistic attitudes of lower-class boys to middle-class institutions. They disagreed with the common assumption that delinquency is an exclusive characteristic of slum areas and presented evidence that delinquency is also found in the middle class, in the form of cliques. As the adolescent period is "a phase of striving for the attainment of adult status,"[62] it produces new experiences together with reactions to these experiences. Bloch and Niederhoffer suggested that this phase is a cultural universal and can be observed among youth in all cultures; the degree to which this phase is socially disruptive, however, depends upon a variety of factors, especially upon the extent to which the society has provided rites of passage to facilitate entrance into adulthood through supportive rituals and emotional and intellectual preparation. Whereas Cohen saw the gang as a product of lower-class protest against the middle class, Bloch and Niederhoffer believed that it is an adolescent revolt against adult society, to be understood only in terms of the emotional and psychological needs of adolescents.

Bloch and Niederhoffer did not place major emphasis upon the class structure of society, but they denied neither the major role of the lower class nor the function of the delinquent subculture in gang delinquency.

In fact, they believed that lower-class youths are excluded from middle-class goals and that the unique delinquent subculture is a natural response of lower-class youth exposed to powerful delinquency-producing forces in their milieu.[63] But the middle class, they asserted, is not exempt from the influence of lower-class delinquency. Although class and cultural differences, primarily in degree rather than in kind, can be clearly distinguished, "middle-class adolescents, singly or in groups, participate in a variety of delinquent episodes."[64]

In their concern with the general characteristics of the adolescent group process, Bloch and Niederhoffer correlated delinquency with obstacles to adult status that restrict personality development before the youth reaches full maturity. Although the lack of the mobility necessary to reach a desired goal causes frustration, the goal itself still remains influential. The result of this impasse is the development of substitute delinquent gratifications in which the adolescent interprets the value system in his own terms, usually in negative attitudes and values "distorted and inverted for uses best suited to a philosophy of youthful dissidence and protest."[65] Rejecting Cohen's "non-utilitarian" concept of juvenile delinquency, Bloch and Niederhoffer declared that money and valuable property are often sought in burglaries and robberies by lower-class gangs.

Conformity to Lower-Class Values

Miller saw the role of the lower class in gang delinquency as an independent variable[66] and attempted to show that "the dominant component of motivation" underlying delinquent acts "consists in a directed attempt by the actor to adhere to forms of behavior, and to achieve standards of value as they are defined within that community."[67] Consequently he disagreed with Bloch and Niederhoffer, who viewed class structure as a secondary factor in delinquency, and with Cohen, who insisted that delinquency is a product of value conflicts between lower and middle classes.[68] Miller argued that the most influential cultural system in gang behavior is the lower-class community, although he maintained that it is not a "subculture" in conflict with middle-class values but "a long-established, distinctively patterned tradition with an integrity of its own."[69] This lower-class way of life is characterized by a set of "focal concerns,"[70] which, together with the whole lower-class culture, become stabilized as the numbers of their adherents increase. Such focal concerns include toughness, smartness, trouble, excitement, fate, autonomy. *Trouble,* the dominant concern in lower-class culture, "represents a situation which results in unwelcome or complicating involvement with official authorities or agencies of middle class society."[71] As law-abiding and law-violating behavior are the only perceived alternatives, personal status in lower-class culture is frequently measured in these terms.

Toughness refers to a combination of qualities, the most important of which are strength and endurance, also known among Mexican-Americans as *machismo*, or masculinity. Lower-class concern with toughness is presumably related to the fact that significant proportions of male children are raised in female-dominated households, or matriarchies, in which male parents' participation in child rearing is minimal or nonexistent and in which the principal responsibility is placed on the mother or another woman from the kinship. As no male figure from whom the child can learn the male role is consistently present, the child expresses his focal concern in a compulsive overreaction to the female-dominated setting. The so-called "tough guy," a hard, fearless, and skilled physical fighter, expresses this focal concern.

Because *smartness* is the capacity to achieve one's objectives with maximum mental agility and minimum physical effort, considerable prestige is attached to it. The ideal lower-class leader is expected to be both tough and smart. *Excitement* is the focal concern of another type, who finds a "thrill" in alcohol, gambling and dice throwing, horse racing, and sexual adventures. Concern with *fate* reflects widespread lower-class fatalistic belief in luck. Although members of the lower class feel that their lives are subject to forces over which they have little control, they are nevertheless concerned with *autonomy*, "the extent and nature of control over the behavior of the individual."[72] On the overt level such concern takes the form of strong and frequently expressed resentment of external controls or restrictions and desire for personal freedom. "No one's gonna push me around" is a common reaction of lower-class members to what they perceive as coercive authority.

Two other focal concerns, *belonging* and *status*,[73] are found only among lower-class adolescent groups. *Belonging*, represented by acceptance into the group, is largely determined by the degree to which one shares the main focal concerns. *Status*, however, is achieved by the juvenile through his proficiency in performing appropriately to these concerns. Miller suggested that the single-sex peer group, which is directly related to the "female-based" household, is a significant structural form in lower-class society. Although the street-corner "society" and the so-called "delinquent gang" represent merely adolescent variations of this type, the focal concerns of both are derived from the general cultural milieu.

These focal concerns, as they are found among adults or adolescents, represent, according to Miller, the *sine qua non* of lower-class culture. Satisfying them automatically involves violation of various legal norms. Even when alternative action is possible, nonlaw-abiding avenues provide greater and more immediate returns. In certain situations, however, illegal action may be mandatory in order to fulfill the norms. Because the desire of lower-class youths to conform to their own class culture inevitably brings them into conflict with the larger society, lower-class practices in and of themselves, Miller suggested, lead to legal violations.

The Differential-Opportunity Approach

In presenting their theory of delinquent gangs Cloward and Ohlin disagreed with the conclusions in all the foregoing studies.[74] In fact the
only point of agreement seems to be the emphasis on delinquency of lower-
class juveniles and on the contrast between their delinquent behavior and
middle-class standards. Cloward and Ohlin offered the hypothesis of
"differential opportunity," which was intended to answer the question of
"how the relative availability of illegitimate opportunities effects the resolution of adjustment problems leading to deviant behavior."[75] Believing
that differential support for one or another type of illegitimate activity is
available at different points in the social structure, they suggested that
the type and strength of this support determine how individuals will
resolve adjustment problems. According to their hypothesis, each individual
is located in both a legitimate and an illegitimate opportunity structure.
When legitimate access to success goals is limited, "the nature of the delinquent response that may result will vary according to the availability
of various illegitimate means."[76] In their theory of juvenile and gang
delinquency they combined elements of Émile Durkheim's[77] and Robert
K. Merton's[78] theories of anomie, the ecological outlook of the "Chicago
school" of Shaw and McKay,[79] and Sutherland's differential-association and
learning theory.[80] Although they accepted the general conception of a
delinquent subculture, they argued that it really consists of three subcultures that form the principal orientations of the urban lower class's
dominant groups.[81] Although the *criminal subculture* stimulates crimes for
profit[82] and the *conflict subculture* encourages status aspirations, the *retreatist subculture* produces narcotic addiction. The social milieu in each
subculture, Cloward and Ohlin believed, is the most important factor in
the development of each subcultural pattern, regardless of such factors
as age, sex, and race of participants.[83]

The "socialization of potential criminals" primarily takes place in the
criminal subculture.[84] Although the lower class has its successful role
models, as does the middle class, they are often criminals, rather than
bankers and businessmen. Because delinquents in this subculture are
already oriented toward criminal values arising out of the social structure,
their delinquency is oriented toward crime. In the *conflict* subculture of
the lower class the transience, instability, and weak middle-class social
controls of the slums are expressed in delinquency. The disorganization of
the slums severely limits both legitimate and illegitimate opportunities to
achieve status and recognition; Cloward and Ohlin hypothesized that
"adolescents seize upon the manipulation of violence as a route to status."[85]
Attainment of status through force is the dominant motif of the conflict
subculture.

The use of drugs in the *retreatist* subculture is partly the result of a breakdown in interpersonal relations, as the boy is rejected by the legitimate, criminal, and conflict subcultures. The retreatist subculture develops as failure to attain legitimate or illegitimate goals produces pressures toward retreatist behavior at the same time that the opportunity to use drugs occurs.[86] The drug addict must therefore be understood "not only in terms of his personality and the social structure . . . but also in terms of the new patterns of associations and values to which he is exposed as he seeks access to drugs."[87] Consequently, the retreatist subculture arises from alienation from socially accepted roles based on internalized prohibitions or socially structured barriers, which represents a double failure for the retreatist.

Emphasizing the concept of anomie, Cloward and Ohlin suggested that the breakdown in the regulation of goals encourages unlimited aspirations and creates constant pressure to depart from social norms. As such circumstances obviously do not exist in all societies, Cloward and Ohlin concluded that human nature or the structure of industrial life must lead "members of industrial societies to make a virtue of dissatisfaction."[88] Because industrial societies define success goals as potentially accessible to each citizen, all members of the societies strive to attain them, even though it is impossible for all to succeed. At this period in their development industrial societies have cultural structures that are inconsistent with their social structure.[89] The cultural structure consists of stated goals and norms, and the social structure is composed of patterned relationships of people who are differentiated through stratification. Anomie develops as a result of inconsistencies between these two dimensions not because of a breakdown in the regulation of goals but "rather, because of a breakdown in the relationship between goals and legitimate avenues of access to them."[90] People situated differentially in the social hierarchy have different chances of attaining success goals, and, because the lower-class boy faces obstacles in his quest for status, he is more likely to engage in law-violating behavior. "The disparity between what lower-class youth are led to want and what is actually available to them," theorists have noted, "is the source of a major problem of adjustment."[91]

Most Americans aspire to two major "success values" or goals: membership in the middle class and improvement in economic position. Lower-class adolescent males, however, face greater educational, cultural, and structural barriers in their attempt to achieve success goals than do others more favorably situated in the social structure. Consequently, many juveniles abandon legitimate status systems and turn to illegitimate alternatives to attain their ends. This course, in turn, encourages their alienation from society, a "process of withdrawal of attributions of legitimacy from established social norms."[92] The lower class does not blame itself for this development; rather it blames the social order for not providing opportunities for status improvement while encouraging success striving. As such alienation occurs, it creates the conditions for the development of a delinquent subculture and, to this extent, encourages delinquent conduct.

General Gang Theories and the Socialization Approach

The problem of juvenile gang delinquency, Bordua once remarked, "has led to some of the most exciting and provocative intellectual interchange" in the sociology of deviant behavior, although this interchange "has often been marred by unnecessary polemic and, even more, by a lack of relevant data."[93] Conclusions drawn from research in one geographical area are not necessarily more meaningful than are general theoretical speculations; Thrasher's field study of the gang is probably the most important exception to this statement. Unfortunately, the speculative gang theories, though written in sophisticated terminology, use postulates whose fundamental validity seems questionable and rather equivocal, offering more symptomological explanation than meaningful insight into broader aspects of the problem. Many theories are supported by statistically inadequate data, confuse gang and individual delinquencies, identify the lower class with the working class, attribute anomie exclusively to allegedly disorganized American society, depict the middle class as the only source of social power, and emphasize the regulative function of the law while overlooking its purposeful aspects.

The use of inadequate statistical data in the formation of delinquent gang theories can no longer be ignored. Although statistics may reveal more frequent apprehension of the lower-class child or youth by the police, they do not necessarily reflect social truth. "There are," as Benjamin Disraeli once said, "lies, damn lies and statistics." Juvenile-delinquency statistics are no exception, for they do not generally include statistics on the "white collar" delinquency of middle- and upper-class children and youth. Any gang study that analyzes only one kind of delinquency, for example, deviance that attracts the greatest public disapproval, will necessarily offer different conclusions from those of studies that focus upon general gang behavior or juvenile delinquency.

Similarly, in most gang studies the terms "lower class" and "working class" are used interchangeably, despite quite obvious differences. Whereas the term "working class" reflects the function of certain people who can be in the lower, middle, or upper classes, "lower class" refers to a position in the system of social stratification. The *working class* consists of the vast numbers of those who are engaged in physical labor and who are also members of other *social* classes, but the *lower class* is defined by other factors than function. Income is not the sole determinant of class. "A position," Kingsley Davis and Wilbert Moore have noted, "does not bring power and prestige because it draws a high income. Rather, it draws a high income because it is functionally important. . . ."[94] Obviously, many members of the working class hold functionally important positions and are not of the lower class. Although the lower class, even though it may be distributed among various subsubcultures, may represent only one subculture, the working class may be represented in more than one subculture. Occasionally the terms may coincide.

A proper understanding of the functional nature of the working class is necessary if the social structure is to be understood.[95] Not only are workers dispersed throughout the social strata, but the identification of individual workers with class also depends upon the type of work that they perform. Although theorists have long emphasized the difference between the working and other classes, the distinction has not always been clear. Stratification experts have not even agreed on the proper method by which to place individuals in the various strata of the social structure. No agreement on the meaning of social class as a research tool even exists.[96] Whatever the composition and status of the working and lower classes, they are both confused and complex conceptual groupings that have resulted from the advent of modern industrial society.

Laymen and scholars have erroneously believed that the poor have been disproportionately involved in delinquent or criminal acts, despite lack of evidence to support this belief. Even today popular thinking continues to assume that the economically deprived have greater criminal potential.[97] As a result, contrary evidence from other cultures has been ignored, and unfounded generalizations have become accepted "facts." Studies by Cesare Beccaria,[98] Charles Lucas,[99] Adolphe Quetelet,[100] Napoleone Colajanni,[101] Gabriel Tarde,[102] Joseph van Kan,[103] and W. A. Bonger,[104] for example, generally concluded that there is a connection between economic deprivation and crime. The data upon which they based this assumption, however, cannot be validated. Although some relationships between individual poverty and crime and between economic deprivation and development of a delinquent subculture do exist, they do not guarantee that all members of a poverty subculture are potential delinquents or criminals and that all the poor belong to the same subculture.

Many crime factors are frequently and erroneously confused with Reckless's[105] idea of *categoric risk*, which is the chance that a person in a particular group has of being arrested or imprisoned. Membership in the lower class, which forms a proportionally larger part of the population, increases the categoric risk. Existing evidence like the higher percentage of poor people who are criminals suggests that poverty contributes to the development of delinquency and crime. An investigation of the occupational backgrounds of criminals and parents of delinquent children may, however, reveal clues to enable future theorists to distinguish between the effects of individual economic deprivation and membership in the lower or working class. Although economic deprivation, membership in the lower class, and identification with the working class represent three distinct categories, they are not necessarily interrelated within any one subculture even when it is delinquent.

Gang behavior may continue to be misinterpreted if theorists continue to restrict discussion and analysis of anomic situations to the allegedly disorganized American culture. Anomie is neither the sole explanation for the rise in the American delinquency and crime rates nor the major characteristic of American delinquent subcultures. Some researchers avoid the explicit use of Merton's variation of Durkheim's explanation of suicide in their hypotheses. Instead, they focus on striving for goals, blocked aspirations, and choices of illegitimate means to achieve desired goals as central causes of delinquency and crime. Although they argue that American gang delinquency can be explained by the fact that all success values and aspirations are not attainable, thanks in large part to such handicaps as class barriers, these theorists assume that success goals, aspirations, and barriers to lower-class achievement are largely American phenomena. Ignoring the universal crime problem, they seem to emphasize a distinctively American explanation of crime rather than relating these so-called symptoms to general social structure. But, as Merton has written,[106] "disassociation between culturally defined aspirations and socially structured means" is neither an exclusive or even typical feature of American society nor a necessary characteristic of disorganization. Opportunity and lack of opportunity for attaining goals have always been present in all societies, regardless of their structures. Wealth, income, job, status, and prestige are historic and current goals sought not only by Americans in our affluent, though perhaps disorganized, society but also by most other peoples. Otherwise the world crime problem would appear in different form. If gang behavior is explained by the claim that a significant number of lower-class individuals "aspire beyond their means,"[107] similar conduct is also to be expected in other societies in which similar conditions exist. The idea of illegitimate means for achieving blocked goals is therefore an oversimplified generalization in the study of delinquency and crime causation. It does not provide the answers to these problems. As all human goals cannot be achieved by any one person, then theoretically all frustrated people, rather than only known proportions, can be expected to turn to illegitimate alternatives.

Although the blocked-aspiration explanation seems inadequate to explain the volume of crime and delinquency, it does offer a more adequate explanation of all crime known to the police. From the beginning of human history, crimes have been committed because of blocked economic, intellectual, communal, sexual, or other aspirations. The whole course of human personality development from infancy and early childhood to old age has always been oriented toward striving for specific goals and learning to live with frustrations caused by failure to reach goals; learning to deal with failure has always been a necessary part of group membership. Even in the so-called "primitive era" of private vengeance and kin revenge the "offender" was motivated not by an innate drive to violence but rather by the desire to secure things that he wanted and could not gain as readily through other conduct. Even though the goal may have been only food, an animal skin, a special stone, or social status associated with power and success, the offender has been primarily goal-oriented in his conduct. Today's criminal is not basically different from the offender of any other period. Only his aspirations have changed from time to time and from place to place, determined by social and cultural definitions in any given era.

Although the Soviet Union, for example, may be regarded as an over-organized society in contrast to the apparently disorganized United States, its people are also aware of aspirations, goals, barriers, and illegitimate alternatives. The emphasis upon achievement, upward mobility, competition, and equal rights, common goals of American culture, are also official goals of socialist philosophy. Nikolai Lenin, for example, argued that "only socialism . . . opens the way for competition on a really mass scale."[108] Four decades later Nikita Khrushchev confirmed that "every person who lives in a communist society must make a contribution by his or her labor towards the building and further development of that society."[109] Even the Stakhanovite movement[110] encouraged individuals to produce more than their quotas and thereby to reap both financial rewards and greater status and prestige. The network of physical and intellectual "socialist competitions" also emphasized achievement and offered substantial monetary and prestige awards. Even now the whole Communist Party organization is marked by fierce competition for power and prestige, for higher status and better living conditions are associated with promotion within the party structure. The Soviet Union has therefore encouraged competition by offering a "rising scale of real income for those who work harder or who are prepared to accept more responsible tasks" and an "elaborate graduation of awards and prizes to supplement material incentives with the almost universal desire of men for communal approval." In general the regime, Walt W. Rostow argued, "does not frustrate those ambitions to acquire prestige."[111] Russian status symbols are also similar to their American counterparts: an automobile for private purposes, occasional foreign travel, a paid vacation in a domestic resort, and a bigger apartment. But, although similarities do exist, Soviet-type societies impose greater restraints upon their citizens. They employ positive propaganda and more highly organized and pervasive control procedures to persuade their citizens to accept available rewards, but dissatisfaction nevertheless occurs when individuals or social groups cannot achieve desired goals. The proletariat, or working class, composed predominantly of industrial workers and peasants, serves, for example, as the basic source of the new "middle class," blocking the aspirations of the old middle class perhaps even more sharply than the aspirations of the American lower class are blocked. "It appears," Rostow continued, "to be the case that important conflicts exist between the aspirations and expectations which are generated by life in Soviet Russia and the realities which are confronted."[112]

Encouragement to compete is not balanced by unlimited opportunities to succeed in the United States; the problem is no less acute in Soviet territories. The extreme American emphasis on success and role models is also found in the Soviet Union, where goals are apparently equally uncoordinated with opportunities. The basic distinctions between the two societies seem to be greater state compulsion under the Soviet system, specific aspirations, and the composition of the privileged and unprivileged groups. Problems arising from social stratification seem to be a dysfunctional characteristic of all societies that have evolved beyond the simplest level.

The blocked-aspirations explanation of gang delinquency resembles the theory of the individual drive for "power and superiority" developed by Alfred Adler. The delinquent's freedom of action, according to Adler, is severely inhibited by his life style. As he becomes obsessed with himself, he loses his ability to relate properly to other people.[113] The status seeking of immature individuals, learned from and supported by their respective subcultures, can therefore be understood only as a rejection of socially approved ways of achieving ambitions. Most modern gang studies, however, assume that the adolescent gang delinquent simply desires upward mobility in the normal middle-class fashion, and falls victim to a class-conscious gang delinquency theory that vainly attempts to measure delinquencies in adolescence in terms of what these researchers think should be as opposed to what actually is. The imaginary working-class boy "standing alone to face humiliation at the hands of middle-class agents," as John I. Kitsuse and Daird C. Dietrick have suggested, "is difficult to comprehend."[114] This whole approach is comprehensible only if the delinquent's ambition to challenge the middle-class system can be interpreted as a substitute social gratification for his lack of constructive ambition, which in turn presumes that he has an accurate picture of himself, his social environment, and the social class system. To make this assumption, however, is to contradict what is already known about such adolescents. The ability to perceive, learn, think, and reason in mature fashion cannot be effectively taught to most people who live and function exclusively in an isolated subculture.

Under these circumstances, the inadequate socialization of delinquent-gang adolescents results in complete lack of constructive ambition or positive values, ultimately expressed in destructive tendencies. Because of his inadequate socialization, a youth cannot determine what are his rights and duties and so cannot identify the constructive roles that he would otherwise play. *Rolelessness* rather than *roleness* may therefore develop. Given this roleless state, the adolescent's nonrecognition of positive values prohibits formation of positive aspirations. The youth who turns to destructive ambitions is therefore choosing not among illegitimate alternatives but the only option available to him in the absence of a positive value system. Although some delinquents who have been adequately socialized to positive and constructive aspirations are blocked in the acquisition of higher status and upward mobility and then turn to delinquent behavior, they rarely become gang members. Most gang delinquents are recruited from the inadequately socialized youths whose lack of understanding of positive social values results in lack of direction in their activities. The rolelessness hypothesis therefore seems to offer a meaningful explanation of the utterly destructive and nonutilitarian character of many delinquent acts, even though delinquents are occasionally used by criminals to further their own interests. Although a youthful search for belonging may explain why juveniles form groups or join gangs that accept or even welcome the absence of constructive ambitions and in which rolelessness ceases to operate as a source of frustration, the lack of socially approved roles may also eliminate their "need to be loved."

Given the sort of personality development common to these youths, gang delinquency is difficult to understand in terms of class struggle or status seeking within a middle-class system. It is better explained in terms of inadequate socialization and immature personality development. The question, posed by Cloward and Ohlin, of how society "persuades the poor man to accept his station in life as just,"[115] though recognizing the problem of the distribution of wealth, misses the central issue. As delinquency is a product of achieved rather than ascribed criteria, the relationship between poverty and gang delinquency is better sought in the concept of adequate socialization. Even then, the differentiation between lower- and middle-class delinquency and the predominant identification of the lower class with gang delinquency make sense only if the middle class is also identified with the social power that establishes norms. Because privileges and prohibitions are never evenly distributed in any human society or organized group, the question of "whose ox is gored" depends for the most part on the ruling social power, that is, the law. Disadvantaged individuals and groups may feel frustrated, whereas the privileged enjoy their own positions and justify the encumbrances placed upon their social competitors. Although the privileged ruling social power has already internalized and legitimated its own value system, disadvantaged people find it restrictive and not relevant to their experience. If the system could be internalized, it would lose many of its frustrating characteristics. As the hopes and goals of many citizens will continue to remain unsatisfied, however, societies will continue to offer only limited opportunities to some of its more marginal members in the foreseeable future. Whether the barriers in American society against the lower class or those in Soviet society against the old middle class are "right" or "wrong" is impossible to judge. The values of the social power are neither "good" nor "bad" in any absolute sense. Rather they must be accepted as long as the power is supreme. George Bernard Shaw recognized this fact when he replied to a young lady who told him that she had learned to accept life, "Gad, Ma'am, you'd better."

The existence and operation of any power structure may well lead to the development of an opposing structure that may ultimately overwhelm the existing structure and partially or wholly change its value system. The dynamics of such change depend largely upon the degree of discomfort caused by the disagreement in values. If such an upheaval is successful, a new value system may be formed and new norms created as previously accepted values are rejected or reversed. As long as the existing social power prevails, however, it will satisfy or block aspirations and goals, accept or reject roles, and oversee socialization according to its defined values. Socialization in this sense, then, teaches the individual not what he *needs* to know but what he *has* to know in order to participate in his group. Only as men are conditioned to acknowledge and to accept these basic values as their own do culturally approved aspirations and goals seem constructive and legitimate, barriers to them justifiable, and socialization adequate.

Because the gang delinquent has not been socialized to accept the value system of the ruling social power, he suffers from destructive ambitions, rolelessness, and tendencies to violate legal norms. The approved roles and legal norms have not "come through" to him. His delinquency is not a deliberate act of opposition against the social power because he does not know and therefore cannot judge the values of the latter. Rather, the law, in its deepest sense, appears as alien, its rationale incomprehensible. Conceptualization of gang delinquency in terms of revolt against the social power (that is, the middle class) makes sense only if the delinquent understands the values upon which these norms are based. Although he may know the norms in terms of what can and cannot be done, he is not and cannot be acquainted with the values underlying them because of his inadequate socialization. The delinquent, for example, may know that murder, rape, and shoplifting are prohibited, but he may not understand why. Although he knows that many of his aspirations for improved opportunities and personal advancement are blocked and those of others are satisfied, he does not understand the value criteria that justify existing barriers and opportunity structures. Without such understanding he can form only a phenomenalistic attitude in which the world appears to operate without rhyme or reason and he is at its arbitrary mercy. Although most prohibitions are expressed by the ruling social power in the form of laws, their effectiveness is increased when they are reinforced by what might be called the "informal extralegal armament of the power structure" in the form of norms, biases, prejudices, or other means of social control. Most studies of gangs, however, ignore this aspect and stress the regulative structure of only the law. The law, as the formal expression of the prevailing value system, is always with the individual; it surrounds him and pursues him in all circumstances to the end of his life, and it is therefore not only coercive and negative in nature. It is also positive, in that it affirms the values of the ruling social power. Its central ideal is not only what "is" but also what "should be," for law is not always or exclusively concerned with the realities of life.[116] Civil rights legislation, for example, is concerned with what "should be."

All laws are assumed to be just, although they do not appear equally just to all members of society; particularly those who feel that they are at a disadvantage and enjoy fewer opportunities are likely to regard some laws as unjust. If one asks, however, "which human interests are worthy of being satisfied and . . . what is their proper order of rank?" he is likely to find that "the answer to those questions is a judgment of value."[117] The law depends upon the value system of the existing social power that enacts its interpretation of justice. No more can be claimed. "Were it possible," Hans Kelsen noted, "to answer the question of justice as we are able to solve problems of the technique of natural science or medicine, we would as little think of regulating the relations among men by positive law, i.e., by authoritative measure of coercion."[118]

Although the law consists of norms or rules of human behavior, it is more than a regulatory tool. It serves as a purposive instrument in the service of the existing social power. It is unconcerned about the reasons why particular types of behavior are required or prohibited, but it attempts to achieve certain ends established by and related to the values of the social power. Consequently, whenever the law seeks prescribed ends, it presupposes a certain value that enables members of a society to distinguish between social right and wrong. The values that the legal system supports do not result from the law but instead are the reason for the law's existence. The law, Roscoe Pound wrote, "presupposes that one has a mental picture of what he is doing and of why he is doing it"[119] and thereby propagates the values created by the ruling social power. If the gang delinquent resorts to "illegitimate" alternatives, he is rejecting legal assumptions simply because his inadequate socialization does not permit him to understand their purpose.

Although legal interpretations of rightness or wrongness can easily be argued, they always represent what *should be*. A demand for more or different opportunities for gang delinquents or for reconciliation between the statuses of the middle-class boy and the lower-class delinquent can be regarded as a hedonistic approach; it cannot solve the basic issue of relative values. The existence of barriers for certain individuals or groups, however, does not mean that the law is "wrong," for it is never right or wrong except as it interprets action and conduct. The law makes objective rather than absolute judgments, in the sense that its objective judgments are regarded as "right." Whenever the gang delinquent turns to violation of law his act can therefore be regarded as formal opposition to law only if he understands but disagrees with the value system that underlies the law. The fact that he understands and accepts the norm only as a regulation reveals his inadequate socialization, rather than an antisocial attitude.

NOTES

1. See the list of various typologies in Charles Hamilton, *Men of the Underworld: The Professional Criminal's Own Story* (New York: 1952).
2. Alfred R. Lindesmith, "Organized Crime," *The Annals of the American Academy of Political and Social Science*, 227 (September 1941), 119–127.

3. Edwin H. Sutherland and Donald R. Cressey, *Principles of Criminology* (6th ed.; New York: 1960), p. 229.

4. George B. Vold, *Theoretical Criminology* (New York: 1958), pp. 222–223.

5. Ruth Shonle Cavan, *Criminology* (3rd ed.; New York: 1962), p. 124.

6. Vold, *op. cit.*, p. 224.

7. A study of gang formation among isolated vagrant youths in India is presented in Shankar Sahai Srivastava, *Juvenile Vagrancy: A Socioeconomical Study of Vagrants in the Cities of Kanput and Lucknow* (London: 1964).

8. Sutherland and Cressey, *op. cit.*, pp. 163–164.

9. In 1966 no organized crime-oriented juvenile gangs existed in Geneva, Switzerland. Small groups of three to seven youths, however, organized their leisure around motorcycles, bars, cafés, and amusement centers. See Roland Berger, "Les Gangs d'adolescents à Genève," *Revue Internationale de criminologie et de police technique*, 20 (1966), 273–280.

10. Frederic M. Thrasher, *The Gang* (Chicago: 1927), p. 26.

11. Hans von Hentig, *The Criminal and His Victim: Studies in the Sociobiology of Crime* (New Haven: 1948), p. 192.

12. *Ibid.*, p. 195.

13. Lewis Yablonsky poses the following interrelated propositions to explain the character of the violent gang:

   1. Varied negative sociocultural dislocations exist in the disorganized, rapidly changing urban slum area.

   2. These dislocations produce dysfunctional gaps in the socialization process that would properly train the child for normative social roles.

   3. Inadequately socialized children develop asocial or sociopathic personalities.

   4. The resulting sociopathic personalities are essentially characterized by lack of social conscience; limited ability to relate, identify, or empathize with others, except for egocentric objectives; impulsive, aggressive, and socially destructive violent behavior when immediate needs are not satisfied.

   5. The sociopathic individual, because of his personality deficiencies, cannot relate adequately to more socially demanding groups (including other "delinquent" and "social" gangs).

   6. Individual emotional outbursts are more stigmatized, are considered bizarre, and are to some extent more unrewarding than are group pathological expressions. Such individual expression is considered more socially "legitimate" in the violent gang.

   7. The malleable "near-group" nature of the violent gang makes it a compatible and legitimate vehicle for adjusting the emotional needs of the sociopathic youth, an individual unable to relate adequately in more demanding social groups.

   Lewis Yablonsky, *The Violent Gang* (Baltimore: 1966), pp. 155–156.

14. Thrasher, *op. cit.*, p. 26.

15. Albert K. Cohen, *Delinquent Boys: The Culture of the Gang* (New York: 1955), p. 73.

16. William C. Kvaraceus and Walter B. Miller, *Delinquent Behavior, Culture and the Individual* (Washington, D.C.: 1959).

17. Thrasher, *op. cit.*, p. 320.

18. *Ibid.*, p. 320.

19. Yablonsky, "The Delinquent Gang as a Near-Group," *Social Problems,* 7 (Fall 1959), 108–117.

20. Thrasher, *op. cit.,* p. 35.

21. *Ibid.,* p. 55.

22. *Ibid.,* pp. 266–267.

23. Eric Partridge, *A Dictionary of the Underworld* (London: 1950).

24. Thrasher, *op. cit.,* p. 275.

25. H. A. Frégier, *Des Classes dangéreuses de la population dans les grandes villes et des moyens de les rendre meilleures* (Paris: 1949).

26. Ernst Seelig, "Die Gliederung der Verbrecher," in Seelig and Karl Weindler, eds., *Die Typen der Kriminellen* (Berlin: 1949), p. 1.

27. Thrasher, *op. cit.,* pp. 58–76.

28. Cohen, *op. cit.,* p. 17.

29. Richard A. Cloward and Lloyd E. Ohlin, *Delinquency and Opportunity: A Theory of Delinquent Gangs* (New York: 1960), pp. 20–27.

30. Cavan, *Juvenile Delinquency: Development, Treatment, Control* (New York: 1962), p. 164.

31. Although in the administrative handling of gang delinquencies the problem is frequently reduced to the number of individual delinquents, one cannot identify the gang member with the individual delinquent. Unfortunately, many of these studies have overlooked this fact and have erroneously applied their conclusions on gang delinquency to the interpretation of individual delinquency, despite the differences in etiology.

32. Thrasher, *op. cit.*

33. David J. Bordua, "Delinquent Subcultures: Sociological Interpretations of Gang Delinquency," *The Annals of the American Academy of Political and Social Science,* 338 (November 1961), 120–136.

34. Robert E. Park and Ernest W. Burgess, *Introduction to the Science of Sociology* (Chicago: 1924), p. 873.

35. Thrasher, *op. cit.* For a study of the formation and character of adolescent gangs in France that rejects the ecological theory of the Chicago school see Philippe Robert, *Les Bandes d'adolescents* (Paris: 1966).

36. In this respect Cohen's analysis of almost three decades later is not very different in its reference to "the possibility of subcultural and psychogenic factors." Cohen, *op. cit.*

37. Walter C. Reckless, *The Crime Problem* (2nd ed.; New York: 1955), p. 2, called these conditions "vulnerability components." "In a situation which taxes them, removes the props from under them, puts pressure on them, confronts them with strong temptations, persons with vulnerability components break through and get into difficulty."

38. Thrasher, *op. cit.,* p. 22.

39. *Ibid.,* p. 82.

40. William I. Thomas, *The Unadjusted Girl* (Boston: 1923), pp. 4–5.

41. Thrasher, *op. cit.,* pp. 487–530. Thrasher obviously overlooked the fact that juvenile-delinquent gangs are far from unknown in the "overorganized" Soviet territories and that all generations of Americans have had to cope with large numbers of children of former immigrants.

42. Recent research by the New York City Youth Board suggests the development of

a type of delinquent group that is more sophisticated than the tightly structured aggressive gangs of the 1950s. Intergroup conflict has declined and many large fighting groups have dissolved into smaller cliques. See, for example, Thomas M. Gannon, "Dimensions of Current Gang Delinquency," *Journal of Research in Crime and Delinquency*, 4 (1967), 119–131.

43. See J. Milton Yinger, "Contraculture and Subculture," *American Sociological Review*, 25 (October 1960), 625–635; Yinger suggested that the term "contra-culture" might be more appropriate to distinguish between "normative systems of subsocieties and emergent norms, that appear in conflict situations." It seems apparent that some of the difficulties he discussed arose in many of the studies considered here.

44. Cohen, *op. cit.*

45. *Ibid.*, p. 21. How far Cohen applied this postulate to his analysis will emerge later in this discussion.

46. *Ibid.*, p. 22.

47. *Ibid.*, p. 37.

48. Kvaraceus, *Juvenile Delinquency and the School* (New York: 1945).

49. Clifford R. Shaw and Henry D. McKay, *Social Factors in Juvenile Delinquency* (Washington, D.C.: 1931); and Shaw and McKay, *Juvenile Delinquency in Urban Areas* (Chicago: 1942).

50. Cohen, *op. cit.*, p. 25.

51. *Ibid.*, p. 27.

52. Jean Monod, "Juvenile Gangs in Paris: Toward a Structured Analysis," *Journal of Research in Crime and Delinquency*, 4 (1967), 142–165, notes that juvenile gangs have particular historical significance and offer the Parisian youth cultural diversity in a juvenile subculture.

53. William Graham Sumner, *The Science of Society*, II (New Haven: 1927), 751.

54. Cohen, *op. cit.*, p. 55.

55. *Ibid.*, p. 56.

56. *Ibid.*, p. 121.

57. *Ibid.*, p. 137.

58. *Ibid.*, p. 129.

59. *Ibid.*, p. 178.

60. Sixty-three "hard core" juvenile offenders in Córdoba, Argentina, were members of delinquent gangs that were relatively small, often lacked clear leadership, and offered membership to most boys who were vouched for and who engaged in group activities. The author found that the theoretical formulations developed in the United States do not seem to apply to the Argentine situation. See Lois B. De Fleur, "Delinquent Gangs in Cross-Cultural Perspective: The Case of Córdoba," *Journal of Research in Crime and Delinquency*, 4 (1967), 132–141.

61. Herbert A. Bloch and Arthur Niederhoffer, *The Gang: A Study in Adolescent Behavior* (New York: 1958).

62. *Ibid.*, p. 17.

63. *Ibid.*, p. 15.

64. *Ibid.*, p. 8.

65. *Ibid.*, p. 13.

66. Miller, "Lower Class Culture as a Generating Milieu of Gang Delinquency," *Journal of Social Issues*, 14 (1958), 5. Although he did not quite make himself

clear, it may be that Miller did not believe that juvenile delinquency or gang behavior is monopolized by the lower class. Such an impression arises from his limitation of discussion to lower-class delinquency. It should be noted, however, that he selected "one particular kind of 'delinquency,'" that is, the "law-violating acts committed by members of adolescent street corner groups in lower-class communities."

67. *Ibid.,* p. 5.

68. *Ibid.,* pp. 5–19.

69. *Ibid.,* p. 6.

70. The concept of "focal concern" is used by Miller as a substitute for the concept of "value," because he found it more readily derivable from direct field observation, more flexible in allowing independent consideration of positive and negative valences, and more useful in refined analysis of subcultural differences.

71. *Ibid.,* p. 8.

72. *Ibid.,* p. 10.

73. *Ibid.,* p. 12.

74. Cloward and Ohlin, *op. cit.*

75. *Ibid.,* p. 151.

76. *Ibid.,* p. 152.

77. Émile Durkheim, *Suicide: A Study of Sociology,* trans. by J. A. Spaulding and George Simpson (New York: 1951).

78. Robert K. Merton, "Social Structure and Anomie," *American Sociological Review,* 3 (October 1938), 672–682; and Merton, *Social Theory and Social Structure* (rev. ed.; New York: 1957).

79. Shaw and McKay, *op. cit.*

80. Sutherland and Cressey, *op. cit.*

81. It should be noted that, even before Cloward and Ohlin suggested their three subcultures, Cohen seemed to have abandoned his hypothesis of a single delinquent subculture. With J. F. Short, he described what he saw as the major subdivisions of American culture, in a way similar to that of Cloward and Ohlin. See Cohen and J. F. Short, Jr., "Research in Delinquent Subcultures," *Journal of Social Issues,* 14 (Summer 1958), 3.

82. Cloward and Ohlin referred to profits from criminal activities as "income."

83. Cloward and Ohlin, *op. cit.,* p. 160.

84. *Ibid.*

85. *Ibid.,* p. 175.

86. "Opportunity to use drugs" means the opportunity to meet habitual drug addicts, who traditionally recruit new ones.

87. Cloward and Ohlin, *op. cit.,* p. 179.

88. *Ibid.,* p. 80. Cloward and Ohlin were probably thinking almost exclusively about American society, despite the occurrence of unlimited aspirations and anomie in many human societies in different eras.

89. In essence this statement is Merton's refined theory of anomie. See Merton, *op. cit.*

90. Cloward and Ohlin, *op. cit.,* p. 83.

91. *Ibid.,* p. 86.

92. *Ibid.,* p. 110.

93. Bardua, *op. cit.,* p. 136.

94. Kingsley Davis and Wilbert E. Moore, "Some Principles of Stratification," *American Sociological Review,* 10 (April 1945), 246–247.

95. See Karl Marx, *Das Kapital* (New York), or any of his other works, as well as those of N. Lenin and the other Marxist ideologists. In Marx's theoretical formulation, the proletariat does not yet exist as a class but must be recruited from all segments of the population, as he and F. Engels suggested in their *Manifesto of the Communist Party* (1847–1848), when they remarked that "the proletariat . . . is compelled . . . to organize itself as a class." Marx and Friedrich Engels, *Selected Works,* 1 (1955), 54.

96. Milton Gordon, "Social Class in American Sociology," *American Journal of Sociology,* 55 (November 1949), 262–268.

97. Among the few thinkers who have tried in any meaningful way to investigate the relation between criminality and individual poverty, Ettore Fornasari di Verce was probably the first. He found that in Italy at the end of the last century, although about 60 percent of the population was poorly off, 87 percent of the criminals came from this segment of the population, compared to 13 percent from those in better economic conditions. See Ettore Fornasari di Verce, *La Criminalita e le vicende economiche d'Italia* (Turin: 1894). Despite this comparatively early study, investigation of the relationship of individual poverty and crime has been largely neglected.

98. Cesare Bonesana di Beccaria, *Dei Delitti e delle Pene* (Milan: 1764).

99. Charles Lucas, *Du Système pénal et du système répressif en général, de la peine de mort en particulier* (Paris: 1827).

100. Adolphe Quetelet, *Sur l'homme et le développement de ses facultés ou essai de physique sociale* (1st ed.; Paris: 1835).

101. Napoleone Colajanni, *La Sociologia Criminale* (Catania: 1889).

102. Gabriel Tarde, *La Philosophie pénale* (Paris: 1895).

103. Joseph van Kan, *Les Causes économiques de la criminalité* (Paris: 1903).

104. W. A. Bonger, *Criminalité et conditions économiques* (Amsterdam: 1905).

105. Reckless, *The Crime Problem* (3rd ed.; New York: 1961), pp. 31–37.

106. Merton, "Social Structure and Anomie," p. 673.

107. Cloward and Ohlin, *op. cit.,* p. 88.

108. Lenin, *The Immediate Tasks of the Soviet Government: Selected Works,* 7 (New York: 1943), 333.

109. Nikita Khrushchev, in his speech to the 13th Komsomol Congress, as recorded and broadcast in Moscow, April 18, 1958.

110. In 1935 Alexei Stakhanov cut a record amount of coal and in a few hours earned more than the average coal miner's monthly wage.

111. Walt W. Rostow, *The Dynamics of Soviet Society* (New York: 1960), pp. 164–165.

112. *Ibid.,* p. 189.

113. Alfred Adler, *Understanding Human Nature: A Key to Self-Knowledge,* trans. by W. Beran Wolfe (New York: 1961), p. 155.

114. John I. Kitsuse and Daird C. Dietrick, "Delinquent Boys: A Critique," *American Sociological Review,* 24 (April 1959), 211.

115. Cloward and Ohlin, *op. cit.,* p. 79.

116. This affirmative aspect of the law is very clear in the passage of the 1964 Civil Rights Bill and the remarks of President Lyndon B. Johnson when he signed it.

117. Hans Kelsen, "The Metamorphoses of the Idea of Justice," in Paul Sayre, ed., *Interpretations of Modern Legal Philosophies: Essays in Honor of Roscoe Pound* (New York: 1947), p. 392.

118. *Ibid.*, p. 397.

119. Roscoe Pound, *An Introduction to the Philosophy of Law* (New Haven: 1954), p. 25.

Chapter 9

■ *Collective Delinquency*

The concepts of delinquency and crime are conventionally applied to individuals, to individual acts, or to the totality of such acts in society. Measurement customarily consists of enumerating the increase or decrease of specific known violations. Individual acts are generalized into a composite picture that may be quite different from the nature of the original violations. Both individual and gang delinquency are treated statistically as individual delinquent or criminal acts. A different kind of crime or delinquency can occasionally be found, however, in which the individual is assimilated into a larger unit of criminals or delinquents and appears simply as a member of the temporary criminal or delinquent crowd.

■ *The Concept of the Crowd*

The first comprehensive account of the psychology of the crowd was probably that published by Gustave LeBon.[1] His "discovery," however, had little early impact, although his work has received high praise in recent years. Although LeBon believed that the crowd is a sporadic morphological unit, he also acknowledged that it periodically reflects the nature and character of society. A society and a crowd are not, however, collectivities on a continuum of organizational characteristics.[2] The crowd is not even a component of the society but only one of its social forms. Characteristically, the crowd is an unorganized assemblage of many people who are *temporarily* united by emotional contagion and shared motivation. The idea of the crowd is neither a logical nor an experimental concept, and its definition necessarily lacks measurable accuracy and occasionally reflects an incomplete evaluation of its total characteristics. A person who is not part of the crowd, for example, may be strongly impressed by its behavior, so that he perceives the crowd's collective attitude as if he were part of it.

Although a crowd may be only temporary, around a single event, it may also continue through subsequent occasions. As its nature tends to minimize internal discussion or reflection, the decisions of crowd members are often spontaneous and without rational evaluation. Depending upon circumstances the emotion that has given birth to the crowd may also lead its members into rioting or mob action.

Emotional contagion is a fundamental characteristic of the crowd. As "unity of feeling and behavior"[3] develops, the crowd becomes a psychological unit rather than a mere gathering of people. According to Robert L. Sutherland, Julian L. Woodward, and Milton A. Maxwell, even if its members have some common interest, it is qualitatively different from a group of individuals with common interests. Although a number of people may be looking at a new washing machine displayed in a shop window at the same time, the interest lines of the assemblage in such an instance are only parallel, rather than crossed. Independent individuals stand beside one another, but they are not emotionally related as a crowd would be. As emotional contagion motivates crowd members, however, the parallel interests of individuals are replaced by the interconnecting or interlacing relationships of the crowd.[4]

Robert E. Park and Ernest W. Burgess argue, on the contrary, that even the common presence of people sets up a lively exchange of influences that are expressed in both social and collective behavior.[5] Kingsley Davis, as noted by George A. Lundberg, Clarence C. Schrag, and Otto N. Larsen,[6] distinguished between the "casual crowd" and the crowd represented by a unity of collective motivation.[7] People caught in a traffic jam, fleeing from a burning building, or drawn together to witness a spectacular event share parallel relationships as separate individuals in a crowd. Although they stimulate one another, they continue to represent competitive individual interests. The fact that a thousand people are together at the same time in a public square, as LeBon noted, does not mean that they can be described as a crowd.[8] A crowd should be distinguished from a mere collection or aggregation of individuals.

Crowd Typology

The type and character of the crowd vary according to its basic motivation. The crowd cheering the victory of a prize fighter, for example, is different from the congregation at a religious service, and the crowd helping the police to chase a burglar is different from that welcoming a foreign sovereign. The attitude of the crowd may also vary according to geographical location and cultural "set." English, Italian, and Russian crowds may respond in different ways. Enthusiastic response to an Olympic winner may take different forms in New York City, London, a little town in Kent, or Tallahassee. Even spectators at a football game protest the referee's mistakes with varying intensity, reflecting location in the stadium, cultural diversity, and age.

Herbert Blumer distinguishes four crowd types: the casual crowd (with transitory interest), the conventionalized crowd (based on the excitement in traditional patterns), the active or aggressive crowd (similar to the mob), and the expressive crowd (representing unrestrained emotions).[9] Crowds, however, can also be distinguished by their responses to law and order.

The Aggressive Crowd

Delinquency and crime are frequently products of the active or aggressive crowd, which Davis called the "lawless crowd." Although the aggressive crowd is often called a *mob*, this term generally refers to a pathological aggressive crowd. "As a rule," Leonard Broom and Philip Selznick suggested, "the term 'mob' refers to one crowd that is fairly unified and single-minded in its aggressive intent."[10] This definition, however, tends to minimize the distinctive forms that characterize the aggressive crowd, which is not necessarily motivated to lynching, destruction, or rioting but may intend simply to uphold existing patterns of law and order. The aggressive crowd works toward a goal that it cannot reach with similar efficiency through the dominant enforcement and power structure. For example, a crowd that is reluctant to deal with complex social structures may quickly turn to a simple solution (for example, lynching) if legitimate judicial procedures do not seem likely to guarantee the result it demands (for example, the death penalty). The lawlessness of an aggressive crowd, however, is relative, for the lawless act may be legitimated if the content of the law changes. When individuals participate in criminal acts and then succeed to power, they are rarely prosecuted, for the former definitions of lawlessness are changed, and those who formerly exerted power have been redefined as legal violators. Aggressive behavior in the storming of the Bastille during the French Revolution, for example, led to the punishment of the incumbent politicians rather than of aggressive crowd members.

Aggressive crowds can be classified according to degree of aggression in single static, cumulative dynamic, and totalitarian crowds.[11] The *single static crowd* evinces limited emotional contagion and does not produce other similar units. Because the stimulus is largely confined to a single unorganized aggregation of people, whether a ticket queue or a lynching party, the response remains localized. The stimulus of the *cumulative dynamic crowd,* on the other hand, generates further reactions and successively stimulates additional crowds. The cumulative dynamic crowd may become a *totalitarian crowd* that controls all the activities of its members. Although totalitarian-crowd members may not outnumber other group members, that is, of the society or community, who fail to participate in active crowd behavior, they are able to exert a controlling influence over the rest of the group and define the direction of crowd goals. Although other crowd types may also develop, the exact conditions giving birth to them cannot be predicted or fully defined. Their development depends not only upon the intensity of promotion of ideas and emotional contagion but also upon the disparity between goals and existing law and order. Collective delinquency is that conduct that occurs as people are interstimulated in crowds that lack the ecological or permanent organizational structure typical of organized delinquency.

The delinquency or crime of an individual in an aggressive crowd is committed by a different "phase" of personality from that which prevails in ordinary circumstances. The emotional pressures of the crowd produce a dislocation of his traditional value system and temporarily transform his personality to one whose socioethical resistance to crime and delinquency is considerably lower than normal. The emotional contagion of the crowd captures the individual's personality and "free" will and directs him to the collective crowd goal.

The extent to which personality transformation takes place depends upon the normal level of socioethical resistance. If it is deeply rooted in the traditional value system, the individual may well resist crowd pressure toward delinquency or crime. When it is only partially founded upon a socioethical understanding, however, and depends mainly upon fear of criminal justice, the individual is more easily attracted to the aggressive action of the crowd. The anonymity of the crowd then effectively neutralizes a portion of the resistance capability of the socioethical personality. Just as the irreligious or ungodly man may kneel or bow his head in prayer in a crowd of worshipers, the normally gentle person may attack with a knife when stimulated by the aggressive crowd. The extent of his deviance from his original behavior patterns, however, also depends largely on the strength of his socioethical resistance.

The depersonified leader of an aggressive crowd is hardly a genuine crowd member. Although he is not entirely free of the influences of the crowd, his role and behavior distinguish him from the total collectivity. Although a crowd may exist and function even without a leader, aggressive crowds usually have visible leaders. If a leader appears in the aggressive crowd, however, his presence may influence its character, resulting in reclassification of the group. Crowd leaders, usually representing their own ideas or acting in the service of others, build motivation and emotional tension, suggest and justify alternative actions, encourage flexible crowd emotional and action patterns, and attempt to expand personal or organizational responsibility to the crowd.

Although members of an aggressive crowd who violate the law may be called "occasional delinquents" or "criminals," the leader is more likely to be another delinquent or criminal type. Except for those who deliberately join the aggressive crowd in hopes of expected profit or out of mental derangement, the individual crowd member is generally not one whose life trend coincides with delinquency or crime. On the whole, crowd members lead conventional, nondeviant lives and share conventional antidelinquency and anticriminal attitudes. Their delinquency or crime is a product of the crowd "occasion." The crowd leader, on the other hand, is not a creature of the occasion but is rather the premeditating creator of this "occasion." He may be, for example, a *convictional criminal*, acting under the pressure of his beliefs or a *pseudoconvictional criminal* who participates primarily for prosaic advantages in the guise of a convictional criminal.[12] As repressed emotions are easily released through unconventional forms of crowd behavior,[13] pseudoconvictional criminal leaders may use conditions of social disorganization to their own advantage.[14]

■ The Dilemma of the Convictional Criminal

The concept of the *convictional criminal*,[15] vaguely mentioned in the criminal typologies of Cesare Lombroso and Franz von Liszt, appears to be a distorted product of the English language. Because the *conventional criminal* acts to fulfill his ego or personal interests, his acts often lack an overarching coherence. Although the occasional criminal may steal a loaf of bread when hungry, shoplift a gold ring if overcome by desire, or kill another out of jealousy, he must be stimulated by personal need, desire, or emotion. When the *professional criminal* burgles a bank, he acts for personal gain. The *convictional criminal*, on the other hand, has an altruistic rather than an ego motivation. This motivation may be related to a political, social, moral, or religious ideal; he is acting in order to realize a universalistic or suprauniversalistic ideology that tends to emphasize a concept of justice. Believing unconditionally in his altruistic goal, he acts upon his beliefs, and so his crime is not a strict form of ego fulfillment. From origin to completion, *his crime is a communal, or nonpersonal, experience.* His ideals and convictions dominate his being, giving his delinquency or crime secondary importance in his own view. The legendary hero who robbed the rich to give money to the poor, the suffragette who broke the law in order to fight for a better law, members of the Resistance who injured others to hamper the invader, the counterrevolutionary who killed to preserve his ideology, for example, believed in their causes and attacked established law and order to realize their defined ideals.

Although the ideal stands in the forefront, the convictional criminal does not necessarily discount the implications of crime and punishment. The genuine convictional criminal inevitably faces a catastrophic internal clash between two antagonistic convictions, which creates a major psychic and ethical strain, for it represents a nearly insoluble and tragic contradiction between moral and socioethical demands. Although he struggles to reconcile the two ideals, the convictional criminal ultimately commits the crime out of a sense of obligation. Because of the power of his conviction, he cannot refrain from committing the crime even at the sacrifice of his life or freedom. Although the legendary hero, for example, may have disapproved of robbery, he committed one or more robberies in favor of the poor. Although the Resistance member may have condemned violence, his own conviction overshadowed his condemnation and induced him to commit violent crimes in an effort to expel the invader from his country. Even the counterrevolutionary knew that homicide is a capital crime, yet he killed for the good of his nation.

Implementation and Publicity of the Convictional Crime

The high pressure of his ideal causes the convictional criminal to commit crime. Because he views his delinquency or crime as merely disobedience or disloyalty to the laws of his society, his internal conflict does not result from fear of penal consequences or personal socioethical-resistance factors. Although he may show signs of anxiety and agitation, they are not directly associated with the crime itself. His crime is not his main purpose but merely an act that intervenes between his convictional decisions and his ultimate ideal and may lead eventually to other similar crimes and ultimately to the successful implementation of his ideal. Consequently, it is not self-contained behavior but is *instrumental crime* for ideological purposes. The legendary hero's purpose, for example, was not robbery but aid to the poor. The violence of the Resistance member was a tool to crush the invader. Nevertheless the commission of crime puts a temporary end to the convictional criminal's anxiety. Although he may not yet have realized his ideal, he sees his act as a step toward such realization. His tragic dilemma is resolved, and his psychic balance is restored through the force of his conviction and the commission of the criminal act. His intellectual response to his own crime therefore proceeds in a specific direction.

As the ordinary criminal undergoes little internal struggle before committing his crime, his anxiety is confined mainly to careful planning, maintenance of security, and accomplishing successful deviance. The convictional criminal, on the other hand, is often less concerned with the actual mechanics of his crime. Although his excitement is greater, he seeks a difficult goal. The conventional criminal is often restless after the commission of a crime, possibly because of pangs of conscience, fear of arrest, or other conditions that may upset his psychic equilibrium; the convictional criminal, his conscience satisfied, is relieved by his crime, and his previously upset balance is restored.

Because every breach of secrecy may jeopardize his success and his future, the conventional criminal places great importance upon security. Planning and preparation, method, and the hiding place of plunder are kept confidential. He also does his best to maintain security among his accomplices and, to an extent, even among his victims. Any form of publicity, even by word of mouth, presents a clear danger to the ordinary criminal. In contrast, the convictional criminal, with his altruistic attitudes and ideology, places less emphasis upon secrecy and even seeks publicity for his cause. He hides and disguises his activities only to guarantee their success. His motivation, his antagonism toward the given law and order, and the propagation of his ultimate aim are communal in character and generally serve his final objective, the promotion of a similar communal ideal. Dramatic publicity is therefore almost a necessity for the convictional criminal, in order to maximize understanding of his actions. Tales of the robberies of the legendary hero, the dramatic stories of Resistance members, and the sight of the counterrevolutionaries' reckless deeds, for example, were designed to stimulate attention to the poor, to recruit new fighters, and to stimulate the general population to participation in the uprising.

Publicity about convictional crimes almost inevitably leads to further deviance, for the convictional criminal summarily rejects much of the established political, social, moral, religious, or economic order. As he succeeds in disseminating his ideals to the broader population, the number of convictional crimes increases. His crime thus serves as an example to would-be followers. Although publicity for conventional crimes has little effect on the overall increase in the crime rate, it does encourage further convictional crimes. As the convictional crime may even be supported by public opinion, punishment of the offender may fail to deter later convictional crimes. Punishment may also serve only to interest others in the movement's ideals and to recruit members for other convictional crimes. As the acts of the legendary hero, for example, stimulated and encouraged others to overcome their inhibitions, they too joined in robbing the rich. As the violent activity of the Resistance inflamed others, they also acted criminally against occupation forces. As the counterrevolutionaries' fight for freedom touched the consciences of fellow citizens, they also followed the path of blood.

The Pseudoconvictional Crime

Some conventional criminals may be attracted by the publicity stimulated by convictional crime. Many simply use the convictional ideal as an excuse for their own deviant acts. Moved by love of adventure, psychopathic deviation, or hope for gain, the pseudoconvictional criminal may join forces with the true convictional criminal. Friends of the legendary hero, for example, joined him because of their thirst for adventure. Some followers of the Resistance took the opportunity to satisfy their criminal inclinations. Some participants in counterrevolution sought future or immediate rewards. These participants were not true convictional criminals but rather individuals attracted to convictional violations by other motives. Their target was crime, not the service of an ideal. Their motivation was neither altruistic nor universalistic but selfish. Any aggressive idealistic movement is likely to have both convictional and pseudoconvictional criminal participants. The pseudoconvictional criminal, however, reveals several typical characteristics, including absence of any moral basis for his crime and of altruism in his "conviction." Dominated by his personal aims, he simply takes advantage of convictional crime to steal, rob, or murder.

Juvenile Convictional Delinquents

Juveniles also engage in convictional crime as they are recruited to service of ideals. As adolescents are often highly idealistic, they may act upon their commitment without clearly understanding the issues. Just as adults may either serve or use the ideal, juveniles may seek ideals or adventure and delinquency. If the juvenile participates in any form of convictional crime, he can do so in one of several ways:

First, he may engage in convictional delinquency as a result of his acquaintance with convictional crime. As he identifies himself with the genuine convictional criminal, he accepts the latter's aspirations and actions and enters into the tragic dilemma between service of the ideal and commitment to law and order.

Second, his desire for thrills and adventure may lead him to participate in convictional delinquency after the occurrence of a publicized convictional crime. As he does not identify himself with the convictional criminal, he does not confront any tragic dilemma.

Third, the new opportunity created by convictional crime encourages the juvenile to commit ordinary delinquency. Although he may not share the conviction, he may simply use it as an excuse for his own activity.

Fourth, he may accept the pseudoconvictional criminal as a genuine convictional criminal and may follow his lead by participating in convictional delinquency.

Fifth, he may participate in pseudoconvictional delinquency as a result of the influence of pseudoconvictional crime. The quest for thrills and adventure may offer the dominant motivation.

Sixth, he may engage in ordinary juvenile delinquency as a consequence of the new opportunities provided by the occurrence of pseudoconvictional crime. Although the juvenile may not understand or is disinterested in pseudoconvictional crime, he may use it to participate in ordinary delinquent acts.

Each of these forms of juvenile delinquency is a distinct category to be differentiated according to participants' attitudes toward the "conviction" and toward social values; only the first and fourth categories represent real "convictional" delinquencies, however. Although the delinquency is not strictly "convictional" in the second case, it is closely aligned with genuine convictional crime. The third, fifth, and sixth categories, on the other hand, represent ordinary delinquencies in which the basic convictional crimes serve only as opportunities for ordinary delinquent or criminal behavior. The exact relationship between general delinquency and "convictional" social values and delinquency, however, remains a controversial question.

■ *War, Revolution, and Delinquency*

Convictional or political crimes and delinquencies frequently appear in time of war or revolution. War and revolution also, however, stimulate increases in number and seriousness of ordinary "peacetime" crimes and delinquencies. This increase, conventionally called "war criminality" of "war delinquency," is also known as "criminality of necessity" (*Notkriminalität*).[16] Losses through war and revolution include not only deaths and ruins but shattered moral and socioethical values.[17] Although war and revolution appear to be causes of crimes of necessity, such crimes are more logically a product of the particular economic conditions that appear during war or revolution to undermine socioethical values, thus encouraging widespread delinquency and crime for survival.

The Austro-Prussian War of 1866 was probably the first conflict ever to be analyzed from a criminological point of view.[18] Relative Prussian statistical data revealed that the crime ratio had decreased during the war period, although a considerable increase occurred during the postwar years. Whereas the postwar crime increase was attributed to governmental weaknesses and lenient handling of offenders, the wartime decrease in crime seemed inexplicable, as economic conditions were poor, crops failed, and cholera took its toll. Nevertheless theft, cheating, and assaults had declined during the war period.[19] Similar features emerged during the Franco-Prussian War of 1870–1871 and were also confirmed by French statistics.[20] As no distinction between acts of juveniles and adults or even of males and females was made in these early observations, the data must be approached with caution. Whereas a significant increase in crime was noticed in France after the Revolution of 1884 and in the United States after the Civil War,[21] the true meanings of the data remain unclear because of inadequate methodology in assembling them.

During World War I (1914–1918), only sporadic data offered any insight into the effect of war on delinquency and criminality. During and after the war, crime increased mainly in countries that faced disintegration of their social institutions: Germany, Austria, and Hungary. Although juvenile delinquency increased during the war period, adult criminality decreased, but the figures were slightly reversed in the immediate postwar years.[22]

Although the work of the police and courts was occasionally frustrated by bombing, World War II (1939–1945) provided more detailed information on the relationship between war and crime. Because this war was stimulated by an international territorial dispute, as well as by desire for power and ideological fulfillment, it had a marked effect upon delinquency and crime. Since World War II came close to the noncombatant populations of most countries involved, an extraordinarily sharp increase in crime occurred. In some areas juveniles were not only authorized but also incited to commit grave and brutal crimes that were subsequently ignored by the courts. In Germany, Italy, Austria, Czechoslovakia, and Hungary young people committed more crimes during 1944–1945 than had been committed by all known criminals during all the preceding years of World War II.

The coincident increase of crime and military action may be superficially explained by the assumption that war, which is little more than large-scale murder, pillage, arson, and destruction, is bound to have a major influence upon youth. False romanticism about war encourages a sense of adventure and participation in violence. The former belief that "violent criminals (in general) do not seem to come from any highly characteristic social class, group, or family background"[23] was modified as the violence of the battlefield touched friends and home communities. Consequently, the moral and socioethical resistance of youths, as yet largely undeveloped, was unable to counteract the force that might restrain them from violence and slaughter. Wartime ethics, which emphasized the need for and value of killing, took firm and deep root in receptive young minds and outlasted the war itself.[24] Socioethical and moral dislocation appeared among juveniles,[25] especially at the beginning of the war. The conflict not only dislocated their value system but also undermined the socioethical and moral quality of penal sanctions. The militaristic spirit of totalitarian countries especially revealed its full character in violence and aggression.

Under the stress of rushing political events and war, parents and teachers became more irritable, impatient, and careless. Children were ineffectively and sometimes negatively socialized, by default. Recognizing a power that exceeded the authority of their parents or teachers, they were reluctant to accept the socioethical standards of adults. Owing to father's absence in military service, youths often went to work for their families' livelihood at comparatively high wages at an early age. In some totalitarian countries antidemocratic and antihumanist education had already prepared the ground for crime. Youths began to preach the apotheosis of brute force, hatred, and outlawry instead of peace, humanity, and justice. With easy opportunity at hand, many youths continued in violence. They became not just uncritical onlookers but also emotional and active participants in the criminal process. Whereas Edwin H. Sutherland and Donald R. Cressey believed that "arrests and convictions of juveniles are not only an indication of delinquent behavior of juveniles but are also an indication of reactions of officials and other adults towards that delinquent behavior,"[26] this observation is largely true only of countries rather distant from the wartime conflict. In conflict-torn countries, however, the delinquency and crime situation was quite different.

Adult crime ratios varied in relation to the participants' distance from actual combat. Whereas some increase in female crime was observed in the United States during the war,[27] the American male crime ratio remained rather constant. World-wide, however, the criminality of women revealed a wartime increase, which continued as women assumed active participation in increasing numbers in economic positions that placed them in closer contact with criminal pressures. As youths matured at earlier ages, they too became increasingly involved in delinquency and crime. The increase in juvenile and female delinquency and crime in the war period, however, appeared as a gross increase in absolute numbers. When the absence of some male population, however, is taken into account, the significance of this increase diminishes. A decreased male presence necessarily results in a decrease in the total number of male crimes.

Although the public commonly believes that postwar criminality and delinquency are related to the accustomed violence of the battlefield, no convincing data support this belief. Among criminals who had previously served in World War II, robbery, homicide, and other violent crimes, for example, were much less common than were fraud, forgery, and embezzlement.[28] Although this preference may have arisen partly from disorganized postwar economic conditions, it was also related to the difficulties that ex-servicemen faced in resuming civilian life.

Although revolutions generally involve shorter periods of conflict than do wars, much similarity exists between their respective delinquency and crime patterns.[29] Children and juveniles may engage in convictional crime in both. The wartime increase in female criminality, related to the greater economic opportunities available to women during wartime, seems, however, to be absent in periods of revolution. But male criminality follows a pattern similar to, though less pronounced than, the wartime pattern, Political crimes are typically prevalent in postrevolutionary periods as means of retribution.

Leslie T. Wilkins found that children born in wartime or within four or five years before evinced high delinquency rates in their later lives.[30] Undoubtedly the evacuations and hardships of the years between 1939 and 1945 had lasting effects upon them. Children born between 1935 and 1942, Wilkins found, were more delinquent during the postwar period than were those born in any other seven-year period. The highest delinquency rates occurred among those children who were four or five years old during some part of the war. Eight-year-old English boys in 1948 evinced the worst crime rate for that age of any of the years studied; seventeen-year-old boys in 1957, essentially the same group, revealed the highest crime rate for that age group. Their delinquency and crime, however, may have been the result of unexpected factors. People with large families after the war, for example, may have differed in social and economic status, factors often associated with delinquency, from those who had large families before the war. Continuing investigations will undoubtedly offer greater insight into the problem of the "delinquent generations."

■ Organized Delinquency in Disasters

Conventional organized delinquencies and crimes most frequently appear in organized societies. Elements of social organization, including rules, roles, functions, and institutional machinery, aid the development of criminal associations. As social organization encourages the formation of both supporting and opposing associations, it gives substance to all aspects of planning, preparation, and performance within conforming or deviant social systems. Organized delinquency and crime are thus aspects of social organization, and any disorganization in the total social system tends to frustrate their normal development and function as well. A disruption of the normal flow of the social order, however, does not necessarily lead to a *decline* in organized delinquency or crime; it may actually help to create distinctive deviance patterns adapted to social disorganization.

Because the change from social organization to social disorganization may deprive them of their original goals and methods, some delinquent or criminal organizations, structured around the regularities of organized society, may not prosper in the changing context. Others may be able to adjust their activities to the changing situation and to continue their functioning. New criminal or delinquent organizations may also develop, born out of the very processes of disorganization and dislocation of the traditional value system, which may offer new opportunities for crime. Disaster, which can cause partial or major disintegration of the traditional social order, may thus serve to disorganize and eventually to reorganize conventional organized crime.

As the concept of disaster is not absolute, its meaning is open to argument. Ultimately, it depends upon the volume of its effects, the degree of existing community organization, and the subjective interpretations of its victims. A boxing champion who loses his title, an industrial tycoon who goes bankrupt, a professional criminal who is caught, a resident whose house burns down, or a lover whose loved one is killed experiences individual disaster. When an earthquake renders thousands of people homeless, a fire deprives many families of shelter, or an air raid ruins parts of a city, the *group* faces disaster. Whereas some theorists view disaster as a sudden expected or unexpected occurrence,[31] others identify it with crises[32] or added catastrophes.[33] Several definitions of disaster include extensive injury to, or deaths of, persons.[34] Others emphasize the loss of material possessions,[35] the disruption or breakdown of the social system,[36] or a combination of these elements.[37] The distinction between disasters arising from natural and from social forces, the variations in the impact of the threat of danger, and alternative descriptions of panic have resulted in other, somewhat dissonant definitions of disaster.

Although the disaster concept is complex and multifaceted, its social implications cannot be avoided. In a literal sense a disaster is an abnormal destructive condition that is caused by natural or social forces, subverts the established social order, causes panic abruptly or expectedly, and results in human injury and death, material losses, threats to persons or groups, or similar effects. Disaster kills, demolishes, makes useless, neutralizes, or threatens men, objects, or values. Because it is abnormal and subversive, it causes panic, a form of infectious fright leading to irregular behavior and extraordinary measures. Disaster may therefore stimulate a wide variety of social responses, including defective functioning of institutional machinery and individual adaptation to the threat of repetition.

Institutional machinery may lose productivity or cease functioning because of disaster-imposed burdens upon normal administration. Shortage of supplies, scarcity of food and other consumer goods, housing difficulties, increased disorders or deviations, and the necessity for vastly expanded medical services demand extraordinary capabilities and efforts. Inadequate communications, transportation, and control facilities during the disaster are often complicated by shortages of competent administrative and law-enforcement personnel.

Such complexity of administrative deficiencies offers opportunities for a variety of uncontrolled behavior, including deviant conduct. Individual aspirations, normally gratified through social channels, are often redirected to illegitimate goals if legitimate channels are blocked. Legitimate achievement may also be redefined in the context of extraordinary illegitimate opportunities. A person's unwillingness to surrender or revise his own aspirations may lead him to participate in illegitimate conduct, in order to reach goals that can no longer be reached through normal channels.

Panic develops from awareness of the danger inherent in a specific situation. It is thus an anticipation of the future, based on an understanding of the past. The fright that infects the individual is not necessarily the product of an existing disaster but may be fear of the consequences if it is repeated. Panic, for example, does not usually develop if individuals susceptible to it can be convinced after the actual destruction that the disaster process has been completed. Panic is thus a response to the event and may cause upset of existing social values and dislocation of the traditional value system.[38] Disaster-stricken individuals not only are unable to fulfill their predisaster aspirations, but also they fear repetition and even more drastic and intolerable events. Although they attempt to maintain their predisaster aspiration level their efforts are ultimately governed by their adherence to traditional values.

The values attached to persons and properties are embodied in social norms and defended by criminal law. At the time of disaster the value system is neither forsaken nor restructured but only temporarily dislocated. Neither a surrender or alteration of traditional values nor a breakdown of meanings occurs. Murder, robbery, theft, and black-marketeering remain crimes, despite the disaster. Panic-stricken or distressed group members still respect life and property. They continue to perceive and accept moral, ethical, social, and legal definitions of procedures and goals. The value system does not seem to change in a disaster; the individual's aspiration crisis does not automatically result in change of values. Even in disaster situations, participants are not normally permitted to engage in general theft or murder.

The threat of prolonged or repeated disaster, however, may encourage a shift in the value system. Some social and legal norms attached to persons and properties may suffer dislocation. As only certain value items are modified, however, the dislocation may be neither total nor very profound. Only particular persons or specific properties may lose their traditional values. Not all human beings lose the recognized right to life; only certain ones may be murdered. Not all items or commodities are desired; many items that have lost their value are no longer stolen. The threat of repeated disaster and the individual's predisaster aspirations, rather than criminal law, deprive the specific person or property of value. Whereas people and property can lose their values in the eyes of the disaster participant, the structure of traditional values is not altered or surrendered but is instead reordered as the disaster participant adapts to the crisis. As he tends "to particularize and personalize the disaster,"[39] former impersonal social distinctions become more personal.

The events of World War II in the east European countries, first experienced in Hungary, proved that the overwhelming majority of violators of the law were former law-abiding citizens whose basic behavior patterns seemed still to correspond to traditional standards of law and order. At first, they regarded themselves as morally, socially, and legally guilty for killing, robbing, stealing, black-market operations, and certain other crimes, depending upon the occasions and their own aspirations. The implications of legal norms and cultural values were not always clear to these people. They were, however, able to adapt to each situation and to modify traditional values to meet the requirements of the disaster occasion as necessary. Whereas some participants in disaster demonstrated their conforming attitudes at first by disapproval of a theft of a pack of cigarettes, condemnation of the ransacking of ruins, or shock at ordinary murder, the same people demonstrated dislocated value patterns in their own subsequent attempts to satisfy their aspirations through illegitimate means.

Although some victims of theft sought only the aid of the police, others made every effort to establish claims directly against those who had robbed them. Several expressed loud indignation or anger over existing disorganization and the shortage of commodities. Although many people demonstrated their conforming attitudes and desires for stable law and order, they also joined the crowd robbing a store, committed individual thefts, or sold food or other commodities on the black market. The threat of repeated disaster encouraged behavior guided by rational self-interest.

Some people, for example, stole not only loaves of bread or a few eggs but also dozens of typewriters, hundreds of plates, many alarm clocks, and packages of carbon paper in order to guarantee security in the face of possible insecurity. Although these people generally disapproved of robbery or black-marketeering, they had modified their views to adapt to the crisis, temporarily abandoning their former valuations of persons and properties, and juveniles proved to be "valuable" help to adult looters.

As the selective dislocation of traditional values in war disaster is an individual response designed to reconcile predisaster aspirations with opportunities presented by the disaster situation, any shift in the value system, even if expressed in some form of criminal behavior, takes on defensive overtones. Although survival becomes the major postdisaster goal, other aspirations, including predisaster aspirations, are reevaluated according to the defensive attitudes of participants in the disaster. As the participant functions under the threat of repeated disaster, he attempts to defend against the loss of his aspirations rather than merely to repair or replace lost aspirations or goals. His anxiety to maintain his predisaster aspiration level, precipitated by disaster-caused insecurity and accentuated by the loss of legitimate opportunities, leads him to such a dislocation in his value system that he may generate *defensive disaster crime.*

Such defensive dislocation of the value system may, however, also generate *offensive disaster crime*, which may provide opportunities for new types of criminal organization. The threat of repetition not only conditions participants in disaster to dislocation of their value systems but also stimulates new criminal opportunities. Whereas some of the basically law-abiding participants deviate from standards of law and order as they struggle to maintain their predisaster aspiration level within their dislocated value system, others take advantage of their unsatisfied aspirations, dislocated values, and fears for the future. The defensive disaster crime often appears as an independent individual effort but it may also be coupled with a form of offensive disaster crime, in which the criminal defense of aspirations is aided by a criminal misuse of other people's aspirations.

During World War II, the European *defensive* disaster criminal was usually a single person, whereas the *offensive* disaster criminal was more frequently a member of a criminal organization. The latter often took advantage of the defensive disaster criminal's unsatisfied aspirations, converting him into a "victimized criminal" or a "criminalized victim." The offensive disaster criminal exploits the blocked aspirations of other people for his own profit. In effect, he is an opportunist.

The confidence game, adapted by criminal organizations to specific situations, was a common organized war crime. Taking advantage of its victims' desire to survive, its practitioners promised help to those who feared deportation, torture, murder, or other losses. In the atmosphere of terror inspired by continued bombing and likelihood of personal suffering, organized operatives quickly developed new ways to enhance their profits.

Whereas peacetime confidence games are aimed at persuading victims to participate in dubious business propositions, these wartime versions centered strictly on promises of survival. The conman, for example, offered hope of successful escape from the war zone in exchange for payment, the amount and form of which were adjusted to the given circumstances; usually jewelry, fur coats, or food were required, as most victims were short of cash and money would in any case decline in value as the war progressed. The confidence man's price and proposed "solution" were adjusted to the victim's wealth and apparent fear. An apartment in a lonely place in the country with a bombproof shelter, a permit to buy extra food rations, a passport with a visa to a neutral country, exemption from military or other eventually dangerous service, a certificate of baptism for a Jew were only a few of the enticements offered to those whose dislocated value systems allowed them to follow illegitimate defensive alternatives.

Simply by accepting the proposition, the victim violated the law, and he was prevented from reporting the swindle by fear of his own prosecution. Participants in organized crime were defended by negative use of the law, and the victims were skillfully led into the trap; confidence operatives were even able to explain self-confidently why the propositions ultimately failed, as, of course, they did, and why the victims had lost their investment. In other cases they simply disappeared, leaving the victims to "cool off" on their own.

The public's need for commodities and intellectual satisfaction encouraged the rise of black-marketeering. The illegal sale of food and drugs satisfied the human desire for survival. Consumer goods were also sold by organized black-marketeers to those who sought to satisfy ordinary predisaster tastes. The need for intellectual satisfaction led to the sale of politically banned newspapers, magazines, and books. Juveniles participated in this blackmarketeering at a high rate.

Peacetime criminal gangs, which had primarily used force, extortion, or other kinds of coercion found little opportunity for activity during the war. Deprived of their normal targets, these criminal organizations found robbery, burglary, and other crimes of violence increasingly less productive. Many such organizations had therefore to suspend or at least to restrict their activities or to adjust their goals and methods to the situation. The criminal syndicates that dominated the world of organized crime and were more accustomed to selling illegal services were, however, able to adjust more easily. Temporary new associations of deviant or conforming people also emerged in order to profit from the disaster.

The emergence of defensive and offensive crimes in some European countries during World War II seems to support the hypothesis that the disaster and its threatened repetition may cause temporary dislocation in the traditional value system as the individual personality adapts to the need for survival. The balance between the conditioning threat of repetition and the individual's socioethical resistance capability is crucial in determining his conduct in the disaster situation. In war stress some people, who perceive only the motivation underlying each specific action and the absence or weakness of social control, justify the dislocation of their value systems in their painful adjustment to the extraordinary insecurity of the circumstances. This adjustment involves selective and individual value dislocation, rather than the development of some communal or universalistic change of values. If it leads to new forms of organized crime, it may be because blocked legitimate opportunities for one person may open up illegitimate opportunities for another.

NOTES

1. Gustave LeBon, *The Crowd* (London: 1895).

2. This suggestion was made in Lewis Yablonsky, "The Delinquent Gang as a Near-Group," *Social Forces*, 7 (Fall 1959), 108–117.

3. Leonard Broom and Philip Selznick, *Sociology* (3rd ed.; New York: 1963), p. 259.

4. Robert L. Sutherland, Julian L. Woodward, and Milton A. Maxwell, *Introductory Sociology* (6th ed.; New York: 1961), p. 149.

5. Robert E. Park and Ernest W. Burgess, *Introduction to the Science of Sociology* (Chicago: 1921), p. 865.

6. George A. Lundberg, Clarence C. Schrag, and Otto N. Larsen, *Sociology* (rev. ed.; New York: 1958), pp. 412–415.

7. Kingsley Davis, *Human Society* (New York: 1949).

8. LeBon, *op. cit.*

9. Herbert Blumer, "Collective Behavior," in Alfred McClung Lee, ed., *New Outline of the Principles of Sociology* (New York: 1946), pp. 178–179.

10. Broom and Selznick, *op. cit.*, p. 262.

11. Stephen Schafer, "The Crowd in Crime," paper presented to the American Sociological Association, Los Angeles, August 1963.

12. Schafer, "Juvenile Delinquents in 'Convictional Crime,'" *International Annals of Criminology*, I (Paris: 1963), 45–51.

13. Sutherland, Woodward, and Maxwell, *op. cit.*, pp. 151–152.

14. Lundberg, Schrag, and Larsen, *op. cit.*, p. 415.

15. Although this expression may be open to some criticism, it was used in the original formulation of the concept (see Schafer, *op. cit.*) as a tentative name for this type of criminal.

16. Franz Exner, "Kriminalsoziologie," in Alexander Elster and Heinrich Lingemann, eds., *Handwörterbuch der Kriminologie und der Anderen Strafrechtlichen Hilfswissenschaften*, 2 (Berlin: 1933), 25.

17. Schafer, "The World War and Child Delinquency in Hungary," *The Howard Journal*, 7 (London: 1948–49), 247–250.

18. Wolfgang Starke, *Verbrechen und Verbrecher in Preussen 1854–1878* (Berlin: 1884).

19. Alexander von Oettingen, *Moralstatistik in Ihrer Bedeutung für eine Sozialethik*

(3rd ed.; Erlangen, Ger.: 1882); and H. Mischler, "Hauptergebnisse in Moralischer Hinsicht," *Handbuch des Gefängniswesens* (Hamburg: 1888).

20. Franz von Liszt, *Das Verbrechen als Sozial-Pathologische Erscheinung* (Berlin: 1899).

21. Edith Abbott, "The Civil War and the Crime Wave of 1860–1870," *Social Service Review,* 1 (June 1927).

22. See Albert Hellwig, *Der Krieg und die Kriminalität der Jugendlichen* (Halle, Ger.: 1916); Liszt, "Der Krieg und die Kriminalität der Jugendlichen," *Zeitschrift für die gesamte Strafrechtswissenschaft* (1916); F. Zahn, "Kriegskriminalität," *Schmollers Jahrbuch der Gesetzgebung, Verwaltung, Volkswirtschaft im deutschen Reich* (Munich: 1924); P. Yocas, *L'Influence de la guerre Europénne sur la criminalité* (Paris: 1926); Franz Exner, *Krieg und Kriminalität in Österreich* (Wien, Ger.: 1927); Exner, *op. cit.;* M. Liepmann, *Krieg und Kriminalität in Deutschland* (Berlin: 1930); Abbott, "Juvenile Delinquency during the First World War: Notes on the British Experience 1914–1918," *Social Service Review,* 17 (June 1943); and Schafer, "The World War."

23. Herschel A. Prins, "Social and Family Aspects of Violent and Aggressive Crime," *The Criminal Law* (October 1960), 672.

24. Schafer, "The World War"; see also Hermann Mannheim, "Some Reflections on Crime in Wartime," *Fortnightly* (January 1942).

25. Victor H. Evjen, "Delinquency and Crime in Wartime," *Journal of Criminal Law and Criminology,* 33 (July–August 1942), 136–146. See also S. W. Slater, J. A. Ritchie, and Wendy Lynne, "Delinquent Generations in New Zealand," *Journal of Research in Crime and Delinquency,* 3 (1966), 140–146.

26. Edwin H. Sutherland and Donald R. Cressey, *Principles of Criminology* (6th ed.; New York: 1960), p. 206.

27. Edwin H. Sutherland, "Crime," in William F. Ogburn, ed., *American Society in Wartime* (Chicago: 1943), pp. 185–206.

28. James V. Bennett, "The Ex-GI in Federal Prisons," *Proceedings of the American Correctional Association* (1953); and Bennett, "The Criminality of Veterans," *Federal Probation* (June 1954), 40–42.

29. Exner, *Kriminalbiologie in Ihren Grundzügen* (Hamburg: 1939).

30. Leslie T. Wilkins, *Delinquent Generations* (London: 1960).

31. Allen H. Barton, "The Emergency Social System," in George W. Baker and Dwight Chapman, eds., *Man and Society in Disaster* (New York: 1962), p. 222; James D. Thompson and Robert W. Hawkes, "Disaster, Community Organization, and Administrative Process," in Baker and Chapman, *op. cit.,* p. 268; and Gideon Sjoberg, "Disasters and Social Change," in Baker and Chapman, *op. cit.,* p. 357.

32. Robert N. Wilson, "Disaster and Mental Health," in George W. Baker and Dwight Chapman, eds., *Man and Society in Disaster* (New York: 1962), p. 124.

33. Sjoberg, *op. cit.,* p. 357.

34. William H. Form, Sigmund Nosow, Gregory P. Stone, and Charles M. Westie, *Community in Disaster* (New York: 1958), p. 11.

35. Reuben Hill and Donald A. Hansen, "Families in Disaster," in George W. Baker and Dwight Chapman, eds., *Man and Society in Disaster* (New York: 1962), p. 185.

36. Ralph H. Turner and Lewis M. Killian, *Collective Behavior* (New York: 1957), p. 521.

37. E. S. Marks and C. E. Fritz, "Human Reactions in Disaster Situations," George

W. Baker and Dwight Chapman, eds., *Man and Society in Disaster* (New York: 1962), p. 30.

38. Turner, "Value-Conflict in Social Disorganization," *Sociology and Social Research,* 38 (1954), 301–308.

39. Charles E. Fritz, "Disaster," in Robert K. Merton and Robert A. Nisbet, eds., *Contemporary Social Problems* (New York: 1961), p. 675.

Chapter 10

■ *The Youthful Offender*

■ *The Concept of the Youthful Offender*

The term "young adult" or "youthful offender" refers most commonly to those between the ages of eighteen and twenty-one, although these arbitrary age limits may differ from country to country. In one nation they may apply to the offender at the time of his offense or at the time of his trial, whereas in another they may apply at the point of commitment or termination of the sentence. In Lebanon, for example, the upper age limit is between fifteen and seventeen years, a range quite common in the Middle East and neighboring areas. The Federal Republic of Germany, on the other hand, proposes to include everyone under twenty-one in the juvenile-court jurisdiction. Few countries have so far shown any willingness to accept the recommendation of many authorities that the upper age limit be raised to twenty-five years, thus allowing greater flexibility in dealing with the often immature young adult offender.[1]

No consensus on the treatment of the young adult offender as a separate and distinct problem exists, even though many countries are continuing to examine the nature and scope of the problem. In Belgium members of the judiciary and present administration, criminologists, sociologists, psychiatrists, and psychologists agree to some extent on recognition of the special needs and status of the young adult offender. The possibility of legally defining such a group has been discussed with increasing frequency in France, India, and the Federal Republic of Germany, and similar efforts will no doubt increase in the future. Nevertheless, the young adult offender as a concept remains largely new and undefined. The European Consultative Group on the Prevention of Crime and the Treatment of Offenders, at its meeting in Geneva in 1956, stressed the need to enact special legislation to ensure young adult offenders treatment appropriate to their ages and conditions.[2] A meeting of the Section on Young Adult Offenders of the United Nations' Strasbourg Working Group and a later session of the European Consultative Group reiterated support for this position. The Sixth International Congress of Social Defense at Belgrade in 1961 also declared that "young adult offenders raise a special problem because of the difficulties inherent in their age, difficulties which are accentuated by certain present-day ways of living," and recommended special legal status for those who have attained their majority but were still below the age of twenty-five.[3]

■ *Characteristics of Youthful Offenders*

Young adult offenders have many special characteristics related to the maturation process. They reveal a disproportionate tendency toward unrestrained pleasure seeking, inability to defer gratification of immediate desires, and distorted perceptions of self, society, and their roles in society. Proposals to treat postdelinquents as a separate category are based on their specific problems. The maturation process involves physical, mental, emotional, and social dimensions, which may mature at different times in each young adult. Such unbalanced development is especially common among offenders. Precocious youths who have been unduly restricted in the use of their talents within their immediate social environment may suffer emotional maladjustment, and delinquency may result from such a maturational imbalance.

Young adult offenders come disproportionately from broken homes or homes characterized by unsatisfactory family relationships. They frequently lack the necessary training for successful participation in technologically advanced economies. In Ceylon between 1956 and 1960, however, no convicted offender was actually homeless, although 83 percent lived in inadequate housing.[4]

The majority of young adult offenders are male. In India and Ceylon, women account for less than 3 percent of the young adult offenders. But 15 percent of those between the ages of eighteen and twenty-five convicted in Italy in 1959 were women.[5] Although the marital status of young adult offenders varies with each country, male offenders in Indian rural areas tend to be married. On the other hand, more young adult offenders are unmarried in technologically developed countries.[6]

■ *Political Response: United States*

The first specialized institution for youthful offenders in the United States was the Detroit House of Correction, established in 1861; the New York

State reformatory at Elmira, for offenders between sixteen and thirty, opened in 1876.[7] Widespread concern for the problems of these offenders has, however, emerged only since the late 1930s, when the world-wide rise in delinquency and crime among youths sixteen to twenty-three led to continuing demands for training and treatment methods, in place of punishment, to correct and prevent antisocial tendencies. Although this approach appears to be new, it is in fact simply an attempt to relate the best in penal and correctional philosophy to a largely neglected age group.

The sharpening focus upon postwar social problems and the major realignment of socioethical values among members of this age group (from about sixteen to about twenty-four years) have created an emphatic recognition of the importance of this dimension of crime.[8] The idea of separate sentencing and punishment, known to criminology and criminal law for decades, has, however, gained broader influence only in recent years. "The proceedings that determine the guilt or innocence of a defendant," Nathaniel F. Cantor has written, "must be differentiated from the disposition proceedings; the question of conviction, too, is independent of any particular penal philosophy."[9] It was predictable that this point of view would gain widespread support in connection with youthful offenders.

The American Law Institute drafted the first Model Youth Correction Authority Act in 1940; it provided that the treatment of youthful offenders of both sexes between the juvenile upper age limit (usually sixteen to eighteen) and twenty-one should be directed and supervised by a state administrative panel, to be called the Youth Correction Authority, empowered to decide the correctional method and the content of the rehabilitation program. The Model Act recommended appointment by the governor of each state of a three-member authority over sentencing and assignment and transfer among institutions and establishment of central diagnostic facilities.[10] In order to allow the authority the opportunity to use every possible method of correction or treatment, the act proposed that youthful offenders remain under its jurisdiction for an indeterminate period not to extend past the twenty-first birthday. Using the full potential of training schools, medical care, and other facilities at their disposal, youth correction authorities, aided by teams of psychiatrists, psychologists, teachers, supervisors, social workers, and other experts, would be empowered to create and enact successful treatment programs.

California first established its youth-correction authority, now the California Youth Authority, in 1941, several years before the creation of the Federal program. Minnesota, Texas, and Illinois have since established similar youth authorities, generally under modified titles like Youth Commission or Youth Council and with varying organizational powers. Although a few other states have created only such organizations as community needs dictate, each has adopted in its program many of the essential provisions of the Model Act.

The Committee of the Judicial Conference of the United States, which studied the general subject of punishment, several times made similar recommendations for dealing with youthful offenders, which were embodied in a legislative proposal following its September 1949 meeting.[11] Relying on data from the Federal Bureau of Investigation's *Uniform Crime Reports,* which showed a continuing increase in criminal offenses, proponents of this bill argued that development of new treatment methods for youthful offenders was urgently needed because established correctional programs did not lead to correction. Instead, a large percentage of youthful offenders "released from our reformatories and penal institutions, returned to antisocial conduct and ultimately became hardened criminals."[12] Experimentation therefore seemed justified, in order to find some solution to the problem. The successes of the long-standing English borstal system, these adherents believed, were evidence that change does not have to be blindly experimental but can be designed to ensure predictable results.

The passage on September 30, 1950, of Public Law 865 (the Federal Youth Corrections Act) by the Eighty-First Congress redefined the treatment program for youthful offenders, a program that was finally put into operation on January 24, 1954, when suitable facilities became available. The act defined the age of the youthful offender as between the upper limit for juveniles and twenty-two years, thus establishing a new category between juvenile delinquent and adult criminal.

Although the exact value of the Federal Youth Corrections Act is still unclear, the continuing controversy over its provisions reveals that the premises of the English Borstal system have not been adequately developed in implementation of the act. Whereas the Borstal system emphasizes extensive treatment and training, the youth-correction authority operates primarily as an administrative organization empowered only to encourage development of treatment programs. Yet, according to Edwin H. Sutherland and Donald R. Cressey, "in some states, it is doubtful whether the practices under the Youth Authority are any less punitive than they were before the Authority was established."[13] Framers of the Federal Youth Corrections Act took a conservative approach to the delinquency and crime problem and focused upon the deviance of the youthful offender without sufficient concern for the total configuration of social problems specific to this age group. Its unqualified reference to the numerical volume of major crimes, continuing use of the outdated term "antisociality" without clarification, and lack of guidance on relative treatment methods placed the burden of program development upon the state youth authorities.

Consequently, the Commonwealth of Puerto Rico and forty-four of the fifty states today have no separate protection for or procedures for processing or handling offending minors above the juvenile-court age limit, usually fifteen to nineteen in the United States. Most youthful offenders therefore bear the same stigma, face the same restrictions, and receive the same legal judgments and treatment as are accorded to convicted adult criminals. Among these restrictions are legal prohibitions on voting, limitations upon licenses to enter certain businesses and most licensed professions, exclusion from public office, restrictions upon civil-service employment, and required registration of a criminal record when seeking employment.[14] Because of the harshness of these requirements, many people convicted of criminal acts while under the age of twenty-one often seek executive clemency through pardons, certificates of good conduct, and other forms of legal dismissal that allow the convicted offender to resume his suspended rights.

■ *Other Procedures in the United States*

A variety of other plans has also been put forward in the United States in order to create more flexible court procedures for dealing with youthful offenders. The Federal courts have *deferred prosecution* pending satisfactory adjustment of behavior through informal probation, special placement, or other designated treatment. If this approach is accepted by defendant and counsel, the court may dismiss the complaint. Under *deferred disposition*, a variation used in Chicago's Boy's Court, which has jurisdiction over those between seventeen and twenty-one years old who have committed misdemeanors, selected youths are placed under supervision with their own consent. If the arrangement is successful, conviction can be avoided.[15] Similar arrangements are in operation in the Baltimore City Court, where preliminary fact finding is required. Upon successful completion of probation this fact finding is confirmed in a formal hearing but without entering a verdict against the youthful offender. Violation of probation results in trial, however. Youth fifteen to twenty-two convicted in Detroit Recorder's Court may receive probation that allows placement for up to one year in the Michigan Department of Correction's probation camp. The youthful offender in this jurisdiction may, however, apply for a new trial upon successful completion of probation and may seek acquittal "under the rubric of a claim of newly discovered evidence."[16] In New York City the Youth Counsel Bureau interviews youths between sixteen and twenty-one before arraignment. Its findings serve the district attorney and judge in disposing of particular cases and often encourage substitution of "wayward minor" for adult procedures, deferment of official action during good behavior with subsequent privilege of requesting dismissal of charges, release on bail or recognizance, transfer to an adolescent court, or vacation of the charge.

   Wayward-minor procedures, often applied to minors between sixteen and twenty-one, legally extend the definition of misbehavior, incorrigibility, and disobedience for those below sixteen to older minors. Designed for application to a legal status rather than to a type of offense, the wayward-minor provisions allow older minors greater personal consideration for less serious offenses, including truancy; running away from home; failure to obey lawful commands of parents or guardians; habitual association with thieves, pimps, procurers, or dissolute persons; presence in a house of prostitution; willful injury to or endangering of personal morals or health; or moral depravity or danger of becoming so.[17] Although wayward minors in New York are tried in adult courts and given special correctional treatment, those (between the ages of seventeen and nineteen) in Michigan usually appear before juvenile courts. In New York wayward-minor proceedings are available to youths who have no prior record and do not deny the criminal charges. Judgment in these instances is not, however, equal to criminal conviction and does not result in disqualification for public office or licensing or in forfeit of any legal right or privilege. Although probation for up to two years is a preferred remedy in such cases, the court has the authority to commit a wayward youth to a charitable or reform institution for up to three years. Michigan juvenile courts have concurrent jurisdiction over wayward minors and juveniles; if judged a wayward minor, the Michigan juvenile can be either placed on probation or committed to the adult corrections department.

Although they originated as a means by which to reinforce parental control and to correct the shortcomings of older minors, wayward-minor proceedings have only limited value. They have done little to ameliorate problems arising from slow maturation of the individual. Because they offer an alternative to the direct sentencing of older minors to criminal institutions, however, they have some value in altering the conditions and situations of young delinquents and often of potentially criminal young adults.

■ *Political Response: Great Britain*

The problem of the child, the family, and the young offender has received major government attention in Great Britain since World War II. The increase in crime in the British Isles has stimulated the publication of numerous reports and proposals by official and unofficial government bodies, including the report by Lord Ingleby for the Committee on a Probation Service, the report of the Royal Commission on Police, and the report of the Home Secretary's Advisory Council on the Treatment of Offenders. In Scotland Lord Kilbrandon's Committee on Children and Young Persons also submitted a report.[18] Although the scope of these reports differed, a common concern with more effective means of sustaining the family and preventing and treating delinquency dominated each.

British law divides youths under the age of twenty-one into two broad categories. First, there are children and young people under the age of seventeen who are thought to be in need of care, protection, or control, including those over the age of ten who are alleged to have committed offenses and have been brought before the juvenile court. Second, there are youths between the ages of seventeen and twenty-one, who have normally been processed in the ordinary courts. More recently, however, the government has proposed that offenders under the age of twenty-one should be placed in two modified categories: those under the age of sixteen and those between the ages of sixteen and twenty-one. Because sixteen is usually the terminal age for compulsory school attendance, it marks a significant point in the lives of many young people, who leave home, begin to earn, and often marry immediately upon completion of school. Children under sixteen, who are currently under the jurisdiction of the juvenile court, the government concluded, should be processed by procedures clearly different from those of the criminal court, from which the early juvenile court was derived. Consequently, current juvenile-court practices in Great Britain should be radically changed:

1. Children should be spared the stigma of criminality.
2. In the majority of cases involving offenders brought before the juvenile court the facts are not in dispute; central emphasis should be placed upon appropriate testing, treatment, and social services required for the child or his parents.
3. Present arrangements do not encourage the parents to assume more personal responsibility for the behavior of their children.
4. The current practice of issuing a court order instead of a sentence does not allow sufficient flexibility for effective response to the child's changing needs for treatment.[19]

The government further proposed that family councils, consisting of social workers experienced in children's services and other adults selected for their understanding of, and experience with, children, should be appointed by the local authorities in each county, county borough, and borough of greater London. Such councils would include at least one man and one woman who would conduct discussions with parents in an unhurried manner at meeting places convenient to the parents and their children. If the facts presented before the juvenile court were to coincide with those discovered by the family council, treatment might be undertaken immediately. If the facts of the case remain in dispute, however, the search for a proper judicial decision then takes precedence over speedy treatment. The cooperative interaction of the family council, the family court, the child or youth, and his parents, according to the government, can best meet the needs of the delinquent.

On the other hand, the government argued, special magistrates' courts, selected from panels of justices according to capacity for work with young people, should be created to deal with the problems of young adults. They would assume responsibility as a family court for matters involving children under the age of sixteen and as a youthful offenders' court for those between sixteen and twenty-one. In the latter capacity they would bind over to trial in the appropriate superior court youthful violators charged with offenses that cannot be tried summarily for adults and are punishable with fourteen or more years' imprisonment (murder, rape, or robbery, for example). All other cases, however, would be processed in the young offenders' court. Not only would it have the power to impose noncustodial sentences in the form of absolute and conditional discharge, binding over, probation, fines, and required presence at attendance centers if such were available, but it would also have the authority to impose a sentence of detention for up to three years under specifically defined circumstances.[20]

■ Into the Future

The major differences in procedures and results between the American and British approaches to problems of the youthful offender suggest the need for continuing modifications in the current American system of justice. Because treatment for the young adult offender clashes sharply with the "get tough" attitude of the public, it remains unlikely that the goals of the English Borstal system will be immediately realized in the United States. Nevertheless, their value remains clear. The existing approach is grossly inefficient in most states. For as long as the characteristic immaturity of youthful offenders is ignored, the present problem of the young adult violator will be compounded rather than treated.

NOTES

1. U.N. Department of Economic and Social Affairs, *The Young Adult Offender* (New York: 1965), p. 9.
2. U.N. European Consultative Group on the Prevention of Crime and the Treatment of Offenders, *Report of the Third Session* (New York: 1956).
3. *Le Statut légal et le traitement des jeunes adultes délinquants: actes du VIe Congrès International de Défense Social* (Belgrade: 1962), p. 182.
4. U.N. Department of Economic and Social Affairs, *op. cit.*, p. 21.
5. *Ibid.*
6. *Ibid.*, p. 22.
7. *Ibid.*, p. 2.
8. *Correctional Systems for Youth Offenders*, pp. 2–4.
9. Nathaniel F. Cantor, *Crime and Society: An Introduction to Criminology* (New York: 1939), pp. 254–299.
10. President's Commission on Law Enforcement and Administration of Justice, *Task Force Report: Juvenile Delinquency and Youth Crime* (Washington, D.C.: 1967), p. 124.
11. *Correctional Systems for Youth Offenders*, pp. 2–4.

12. *Ibid.,* p. 2.

13. Edwin H. Sutherland and Donald R. Cressey, *Principles of Criminology* (6th ed.; New York: 1960), p. 418.

14. President's Commission, *op. cit.,* p. 121.

15. *Ibid.,* p. 123.

16. *Ibid.*

17. *Ibid.*

18. Committee on Children and Young Persons, *The Child, the Family and the Young Offender* (London: 1965), p. 3.

19. *Ibid.,* p. 5.

20. *Ibid.,* p. 10.

Part Four

SOCIOCULTURAL INFLUENCES IN DELINQUENCY

Chapter 11

■ *The Family and the Home*

■ *Personality Development in the Family*

Criminologists share a consensus that certain functions and characteristics of the family are among the primary causes of juvenile delinquency. Although the family normally assumes the task of constructing and integrating social life, not all families are able to fulfill this function. Delinquency problems in the developing African countries, for example, seem to be closely related to the disintegration of the family as youths move from the interior to the cities in search of greater opportunity and adventure. In Senegal delinquency is at its highest (60 percent) among youths between sixteen and eighteen years old.[1] The destructive and disorganizing impact of delinquency and crime is especially strong when family functioning has been deficient. A deficiency in familial socialization may thus encourage delinquent conduct by failing to develop adequate socioethical personalities.

The exact contribution of families to increases or decreases in delinquency is, however, open to question. In the nineteenth century Napoleone Colajanni expressed his conviction that an integrated family serves as a factor in crime prevention,[2] and H. Joly theorized that mere family participation in fighting crime within the family performs a similar end.[3] Georg von Mayr believed that the family "in its real sense" (traditional sense) is an important socializing force.[4] F. Corre, on the other hand, wrote of the family as if it were a barometer of delinquency and crime,[5] and E. Mischler, after investigating family patterns in European countries, concluded that family life is closely connected with crime.[6] Since the early twentieth century, however, nearly all criminological theorists have maintained that delinquency is a product of family inadequacy or malfunctioning. Although the data do not unconditionally support this belief, it is logical to assume that the family is of central importance in the formation or nonformation of delinquent patterns, as it is the first social group to which the child belongs and remains his basic group during his juvenile years, despite his gradual development of other associations.

Socialization in the family remains of decisive importance in the development of conformity or delinquency. Although the child is normally also influenced by other agencies during his youth, the family provides the foundation from which he either resists or accedes to delinquency pressures. As an agency for transmitting the fundamental value system, the family influences the development of personality from helpless infancy to maturity, maintaining its influence as long as it is the child's primary group. The transmission of values by parents or other adult family members continuously declines in intensity, however, as the child grows to intellectual, emotional, social, and biological maturity; becomes more independent of family influences and controls; and accepts the reinforcing or competing socialization of extrafamilial forces. Although the family is charged with the responsibility for socializing its members to the value system of the prevailing social power, it may not succeed in this task because of its own inability to transmit or even to receive these values, to overcome contrary extrafamilial influences, or to assist the value system of the social power. Aspirations, goals, restraints, allowances, prohibitions, skills, social relations, roles, responsibilities, rights, and duties are stipulated in some form by the controlling social power and are generalized to the varying social groups through cultural norms or legal codes. Whereas the sanctity of private property, for example, is part of Western socialization, group or collective ownership of goods and lands may dominate the socialization system of another culture or cultural area. The first and direct agency to socialize the child to conformity to approved, and resistance to disapproved, values, however, is the family. The parent is expected to acquaint his child intimately with the requisites of the prevailing value system and the need to resist deviant forces or values.

■ The Family and the Home as Factors in Delinquency

Direct parental socialization of the child and the basic condition and quality of family life in large part determine the child's tendency toward delinquency.[7] Edwin H. Sutherland and Donald R. Cressey distinguish six types of homes or family relationships that frequently encourage delinquency: homes in which immoral, alcoholic, or criminal members live; homes in which one or both parents are absent; homes in which parental control is lacking; homes in which favoritism, extreme severity, neglect, crowded conditions, or interference by relatives prevails; homes in which there are racial or religious differences or foster homes; and homes in which economic pressures exist.[8] Family culpability in delinquency formation, Ruth Shonle Cavan believes, involves four dimensions: Children cannot receive adequate personality training because of their parents' personal and emotional difficulties; parents' cultural defects prevent them from countering destructive community forces; parents and children share criminal patterns of behavior; and parents never rear their children in isolation from the community.[9]

For nearly half a century[10] the belief that the "broken home," a term covering a wide variety of familial situations, is a delinquency factor has been popular. Herbert A. Bloch and Frank T. Flynn defined the broken home technically as "one in which a significant adult member, usually a parent, is missing because of death, desertion or divorce."[11] Although the importance of broken homes in delinquency cannot be denied, their effects are highly individual and necessarily vary according to the familial role of the missing person, the child's original emotional attachment to this person, and the age and sex of the child. The loss of the father, for example, may considerably influence the socialization upon which socioethical or deviant choices depend. Clifford R. Shaw and Henry D. McKay, however, demonstrated in their Chicago study that a breakdown in family life or a broken home is not necessarily crucial to the development of delinquency. Many other underlying conditions have to be taken into consideration in evaluating the effects of a broken home.[12] As a result of his Philadelphia study, however, Thomas P. Monahan arrived at a different conclusion, accepting the broken home as a destructive factor that tends to lead to delinquency.[13] Jackson Toby gave only slight significance to broken homes, reserving the right to modify his views after cross-checking data for sex, age, and racial factors.[14]

Sheldon Glueck and Eleanor Glueck generalized the sociocultural meaning of home atmosphere as a delinquency factor, mentioning "homes of little understanding, affection, stability or moral fibre," in which children "readily give expression to their untamed impulses and their self-centered desires by means of various forms of delinquent behavior."[15] The influences of the home environment on delinquency, they suggested, operate selectively, according to the juvenile's constitutional traits and his "sociocultural conditioning." Suggesting that delinquency arises from *differential contamination* rather than from *differential association*, the Gluecks hypothesized that such contamination "depends not merely on exposure but also on susceptibility as opposed to immunity."[16]

As do most other crime data, delinquency rates vary from one part of the United States to another. R. E. Watt, S. Lottier, and M. B. Clinard have consistently noted that delinquency rates in big cities are greater than those in the country, a discovery that implies that family mobility and conflict of values within the city have greater effects upon urban than upon rural youth. A. P. Jephcott and M. P. Carter also noted that the high delinquency rates in the slums of an English city are closely related to characteristically "rough" family life. In the areas where delinquency rates are higher, the behavioral standards of these families, they discovered, are clearly different from those found among "respectable" families at the same low economic level. Sexual relations are casual, quarrels are more frequent, language is coarser, and children are left without parental supervision[17] (see also Table 11.1).

Although a long list of family features that may cause delinquency can be readily compiled, one cannot escape the feeling that the family, in general, cannot be detached from other factors conducive to delinquency. Although too severe family discipline and parental laxness are both blamed for adolescent delinquency, even a middle course that results

Table 11.1. Incidence of Broken Homes

		Delinquents		Controls	
Investigator	*Sex*	N	%	N	%
Burt, 1929	both	197	57.9	400	25.7
Shaw and McKay, 1932	boys	1675	42.5	7278	36.1
Hodgkiss, 1933	girls	362	66.8	362	44.8
Weeks and Smith, 1939	boys	330	41.4	2119	26.7
Carr-Saunders *et al.*, 1944	boys	1955	28.5	1970	15.8
Gardner and Goldman, 1945	men	500	58.6	200	32.0
Merrill, 1947	both	300	50.7	300	26.7
Glueck and Glueck, 1950	boys	500	60.4	500	32.4
Oltman *et al.*, 1952	both	90	47.7	230	32.2
Nye, 1958	boys	368	23.6	792	17.6
	girls	231	36.4	931	16.9
Monahan, 1958*	white boys	11236	27.7		7.0
	white girls	1984	52.0		
	Negro boys	8706	53.0		33.0
	Negro girls	2736	73.2		

*Monahan's figures for "controls" are those for nonhusband-wife families in the 1950 census. The broken-home percentages for delinquents are based on the usual definition of broken home, which is not quite the same. If comparability is improved by counting only nonhusband-wife families among delinquents, the adjusted figures for the four groups are 22 percent, 42 percent, 49 percent, and 68 percent, respectively.

Source: Herbert C. Quay, *Juvenile Delinquency* (Princeton, N.J.: 1965), p. 68.

in adolescent indifference to parental socialization may result in delinquency patterns.[18] Nevertheless the family is undoubtedly important in the causation of delinquency, especially when parents deviate from socioethical values or are themselves unable to resist pressures toward delinquency, when disharmony exists in the home, or when the family fails to arm the child with the necessary socioethical resistance through adequate socialization.

Most studies of the relationship of delinquency and broken homes reveal that the latter are 1.5 to 2 times more frequent among delinquents than among nondelinquents. Although this finding may vary from study to study, the gross relationship between delinquency and families that have been disrupted by death, desertion, divorce, separation, or prolonged parental absence remains fairly consistent (see Table 11.1). Whereas Toby and Monahan suggested that the impact of family disruption varies with the age and sex of the child, Herbert C. Quay held that family disruption probably operates indirectly through the neutralization of influences that ordinarily would impede delinquency or through exaggeration of those aspects that promote its development.[19]

Cyril Burt found no difference between delinquent and nondelinquent groups as a result of the father's death but believed that groups differ widely in relation to incidence of divorce, separation, and desertion. The absence of the mother, whatever the reason, is, however, closely related to delinquency and is especially important in delinquency of daughters.[20] G. E. Gardner and N. Goldman found that 27 percent of the inmates of the navy brigs came from homes broken by divorce, separation, or desertion and that only 10 percent of those in the control group came from such homes. [21] Although later studies revealed similar patterns the question of whether delinquency results from the void left by a parent through death, desertion, or divorce or from the lack of an adult male role model necessary for the growth of masculinity has been increasingly raised.

The relationship between delinquency and working mothers is unclear. Most data suggest that the mother's outside work may have negative effects upon the child, but no meaningful correlation has yet been discovered. Relationships between youths and parents, their degree of maturity, and their affectional attitudes toward each other seem to be more important. The parents of delinquents, I. F. Nye believed, do not offer their children the models of socially approved behavior that adolescents require.[22] Children who replied that their parents never lie, are always honest, and exhibit strong moral character tended to be among the least delinquent in Nye's study.[23] The main situation that generates delinquency, according to Quay, is parental behavior in which hostility is generated and no control is demanded from the child when he rebels.[24]

Parental Deviation from Socioethical Values

If the parents themselves deviate from the socioethical value system of the group, they almost necessarily encourage the future deviance of the child. When one or more members of the family are directly involved in such severe forms of deviance as theft or prostitution, children may be heavily influenced toward delinquent behavior. In some families children are deliberately taught the techniques of crime and prostitution, not only because these deviations represent their parental value system, but also because such parents want their children to help in their deviant business. They educate their children *to* crime, but the mere atmosphere *of* crime is alone sufficient to orient juveniles toward delinquent conduct, even without training or socialization in criminal tasks. The atmosphere of crime or prostitution rather than the explicit introduction of children to deviant behavior is sufficient to produce a deviant reponse. When sexual assaults upon a child are initiated by a member of the family, the familial climate is even more damaging.[25] In such an atmosphere the social values approved and adopted by the larger part of society appear alien to the children. Nonconformity to social values becomes in itself a value to family members. Although a few parents, in attempts to compensate for their own weaknesses, make occasional heroic efforts to raise their children according to conforming values, the majority of criminal parents make no such attempt.

A further kind of parental deviation that may stimulate delinquent conduct involves no overt deviant act but simply the absence of positive values. Whereas failure of parents to accept and adapt to socioethical values does not necessarily result in parental criminality, lax morals and negligence in familial socialization to socioethical norms may produce juvenile failure to fulfill normative demands. The Gluecks, for example, found that 80.7 percent of 500 delinquent women had had criminal or deviant parents.[26] Burt, in his English study, also discovered that among delinquents the ratio of deviant homes to nondeviant homes was nearly five to one.[27] Homes in which delinquents are reared, as Sutherland and Cressey eventually concluded, enjoy an extraordinary occurrence of delinquency patterns.[28]

Although systematic information on the extent to which children are affected by imprisonment of their fathers is lacking, two basic factors would determine the extent to which such a child suffers: the type of father-child relationship before imprisonment and the effect of the separation on the mother. When the mother depends upon her own or her husband's parents or siblings for help, the children are best adjusted. Grandparents, uncles, aunts, and cousins fulfill the father's role during his absence. Although the effects of his absence may thus be minimized, they cannot be avoided altogether.[29] Sidney Friedman and T. Conway Esselstyn found, for example, that school performance declines when the father is incarcerated. Girls, they discovered, seem to be affected even more than boys by the loss of their fathers.[30]

Parental Inability to Resist Delinquency Pressures

If the juvenile's delinquency patterns result from parental shortcomings, they are most often products of parental inability to defend their children against external delinquency pressures. Although parents may accept the norms of their society and may be armed with ordinary amounts of socioethical values and resistance to deviation, pressures toward social deviation may prove to be of higher intensity than is parental socioethical resistance. Because most parents are prepared to meet only ordinary or average pressures, they are unable to withstand the intensity of extraordinary or above average delinquency pressures.

Parental inability to resist delinquent forces also assumes a second form, in which parental socioethical resistance is lessened even though delinquency pressures are not increased. The United Nations pointed out, on the basis of reports presented to its agencies, that the lowering of parental moral standards is a contributory cause of delinquency. Although it is difficult at any time to demonstrate a decline in values, the United Nations suggested that increasing corruption in parental guidance, protection, or security functions is symptomatic.[31] Lester D. Jaffe found that value confusion, the degree of experienced powerlessness verbalized, and patterns of parental identification differ significantly between delinquency- and nondelinquency-prone youths. Apparently part of a "family anomie syndrome, their feelings of powerlessness and ambivalent parental identification result from a lack of value consensus in the family." Youths experiencing such anomie are more susceptible to delinquency.[32] The modification or disintegration of former values appears extensive enough to overcome the average socioethical resistance of most families.[33]

The growth of juvenile distrust, rebellion, and protest against former "established" mores and principles has not been without social cost. Although modern youths in highly developed countries enjoy clear material advantages over their predecessors in this age group, these advantages have not brought them closer to their families. On the contrary, the near-hypnotic pleasure hunting characteristic of modern social life seduces juveniles from home and causes them to meet delinquency pressures before their socioethical resistance is fully developed. If average parental control and socialization are insufficient to counter the other forces impinging upon juveniles, the juveniles may move from liberty to libertinism. The higher the living standard and the greater the adolescent freedom, the sharper are the conflicts between generations and adolescent preference for libertinism. Parental inability to overcome threats and pressures of delinquency means that parental values, though often conforming and constructive but sometimes destructive, are unable to compete effectively with deviant forces. As children first develop antagonism toward their families, parental guidance may be increasingly rejected and outside values and deviations offering more frequent and pleasurable experiences may replace home control. There is thus a disparity between average degree of parental control and average intensity of pressures toward delinquency. Although the level and intensity of average delinquency pressures increase and gain strength in direct relation to the standard of living, the level and intensity of average parental control do not reflect a similar increase and therefore remain on a comparatively lower level.

Disharmony in the Home

Divorce, separation, or death of one or both parents, as well as religious or political differences, may—but do not necessarily—lead to family disharmony and open the way to deviant or delinquent juvenile behavior.[34]

Although disharmony at home may resemble the tensions of the broken home, it has an even more deleterious effect. Although the broken home presents gaps in the traditional design of the family that may result in intellectual or emotional shortcomings, the disharmonious home, regardless of the completeness or incompleteness of the family group, is defined by such deficiencies. A harmonious home can be established and normal socialization of children achieved despite the absence of one or both parents, and disharmony may exist even when the family is intact. Unhappy families, as Nye found, produce more juvenile delinquency than do the so-called "broken homes."[35] Family disintegration is among the main factors contributing to the increase in juvenile delinquency.[36] Similarly, the British Ingleby Report expressed the opinion that unsatisfactory family atmosphere seems a possible cause of juvenile crime.[37] In discussing some aspects of borstal training, the English commissioners of prisons noted that the type of boy who is now committed to a borstal is little different from the one committed in previous years, though he is more likely to come from homes marked by divorce, separation, maladjustment, and unhappiness.[38]

After analyzing delinquency and crime reports from many countries, the United Nations found that "the gradual or occasionally rapid disintegration of the family under the impact of a variety of forces is frequently mentioned" and that "the family, especially in large urban areas, is not in a position to fulfill the functions traditionally assigned to it."[39] Toby found a similarity between weak family controls and lack of supervision in disintegrated families,[40] and Sutherland and Cressey quoted a well-known phrase that highlights the essential feature of the problem: "The problem child is a child with problems."[41] One question, however, still must be raised: How do family tensions and emotional disturbances produce delinquency?

Emotionally disintegrated and disharmonious families are too often preoccupied with problems that arise from real or imagined tension and are usually confined to one or more (but not all) members of the family. Parental strain and unhappiness thus become family characteristics that prevent parents from presenting, and children from accepting, socioethical values ordinarily taught within the family setting. As the children gradually and almost necessarily lose their affectionate membership and patterned role in the family, they may resolve feelings of insecurity resulting from family disharmony and unhappiness through avenues outside their primary group.

Children are pulled from the home by outside attractions if parents are not able to resist delinquent pressures, but they are actually *expelled* from unhappy and disharmonious homes by the attitudes and actions of their parents. Not only are children in disharmonious homes exposed to increased risks and more intense delinquent pressures than are other juveniles, but they must also face these risks and pressures with underdeveloped socioethical resistance while handicapped by emotional disturbance caused by lack of primary-group (family) support. If parents are unable to counter outside forces encouraging deviance, the latter may alienate the adolescent from his family. If, on the other hand, unhappiness and disharmony characterize the home atmosphere, parents may alienate their own children from the home and enhance the likelihood of potential surrender to delinquency pressures.[42] On the other hand, even a happy home relationship may not overcome the negative characteristics of the community.

NOTES

1. Jean Vincent, "Problems of Maladjusted Youths in the Developing Countries," *Sauvegarde de l'enfance* (December 1964).

2. Napoleone Colajanni, *La Sociologia Criminale* (Catania: 1889).

3. H. Joly, *La France criminelle* (Paris: 1889).

4. Georg von Mayr, *Bevölkerungsstatistik, Statistik und Gesellschaftslehre*, Vol. 2 (Freiburg: 1897).

5. F. Corre, *Crime et suicide* (Paris: 1891).

6. E. Mischler, *Internationale Statistische Übersichten* (Tübingen: 1893).

7. Martin H. Neumeyer, *Juvenile Delinquency in Modern Society* (3rd ed.; New York: 1961), p. 158.

8. Edwin H. Sutherland and Donald R. Cressey, *Principles of Criminology* (6th ed.; New York: 1960), p. 172.

9. Ruth Shonle Cavan, *Criminology* (2nd ed.; New York: 1957), pp. 107–108.

10. Sophonisba P. Breckenridge and Edith Abbott, *The Delinquent Child and the Home* (New York: 1912).

11. Herbert A. Bloch and Frank T. Flynn, *Delinquency: The Juvenile Offender in America Today* (New York: 1956), p. 184.

12. Clifford R. Shaw and Henry D. McKay, "Social Factors in Juvenile Delinquency," *Report on the Causes of Crime* (Washington, D.C.: 1931), pp. 266–276.

13. Thomas P. Monahan, "The Delinquent Child and the Broken Home." Paper presented to the Eastern Sociological Society, New York, 1956.

14. Jackson Toby, "The Differential Impact of Family Disorganization," *American Sociological Review*, 22 (October 1957), 505–512.

15. Sheldon Glueck and Eleanor Glueck, *Unraveling Juvenile Delinquency* (New York: 1950), pp. 281–282.

16. Glueck and Glueck, "Family Environment and Delinquency in the Perspective of Etiologic Research," *Annales Internationales de criminologie*, 1 (Paris: 1963), 211–218.

17. Herbert C. Quay, *Juvenile Delinquency* (Princeton, N.J.: 1965), p. 65.

18. Theory has influenced common attitudes toward the functioning of the family. In a comment on the suicide of a fifteen-year-old mother-to-be, an English coroner warned the parents of teenage girls against being too tolerant or too strict with their daughters, because both approaches might lead to rebellion. *The* (London) *Evening News and the Star* (February 15, 1961).

19. Quay, *op. cit.*, p. 69.

20. Cyril Burt, *The Young Delinquent* (New York: 1929).

21. G. E. Gardner and N. Goldman, "Childhood and Adolescent Adjustment of Naval Successes and Failures,"*American Journal of Orthopsychiatry*, 15 (1945), 584–596.

22. I. F. Nye, "The Rejected Parent and Delinquency," *Marriage and Family Living*, 18 (1956), 291–296.

23. Nye, *Family Relationships and Delinquent Behavior* (New York: 1958).

24. Quay, *op. cit.*, p. 87.

25. Sol Chaneles, "Child Victims of Sexual Offenses," *Federal Probation*, 31 (June 1967), 52–56.

26. Glueck and Glueck, *Five Hundred Delinquent Women* (New York: 1934).

27. Burt, *The Young Delinquent* (4th ed.; London: 1944).

28. Sutherland and Cressey, *op. cit.*, p. 175.

29. Pauline Morris, "Fathers in Prison," *British Journal of Criminology*, 7 (1967), 424–430.

30. Sidney Friedman and T. Conway Esselstyn, "The Adjustment of Children of Jail Inmates," *Federal Probation*, 29 (December 1965), 55–59.

31. U.N. Department of Economic and Social Affairs, *New Forms of Juvenile Delinquency: Their Origin, Prevention and Treatment* (New York: 1960), pp. 49–50.

32. Lester D. Jaffe, "Delinquency Proneness and Family Anomie," *Journal of Criminal Law, Criminology and Police Science*, 54 (June 1963), 146–154.

33. One entire issue of *Sauvegarde de l'enfance* (September–October 1966) is devoted to problems of children's and parents' attitudes toward each other.

34. In socialist countries like Hungary, divorce is granted to the complaining party if it is proved that the spouse's political views may hinder the claimant's political development through Communist studies.

35. Nye, *Family Relationships*.

36. U.N. Department of Economic and Social Affairs, *op. cit.*, p. 49.

37. Home Office, *Report of the Committee on Children and Young Persons* (London: 1960), pp. 7–8.

38. *Report of the Commissioners of Prisons for the Year 1958* (London: 1959), p. 75.

39. U.N. Department of Economic and Social Affairs, *op. cit.*, p. 49.

40. Toby, *op. cit.*

41. Sutherland and Cressey, *op. cit.*, p. 183.

42. Hyman Rodman and Paul Grams, "Juvenile Delinquency and the Family: A Review and Discussion," in President's Commission on Law Enforcement and Administration of Justice, *Task Force Report—Juvenile Delinquency and Youth Crime* (Washington, D.C.: 1967), pp. 188–221, presents a useful overview of recorded data on relationships between the family and delinquency.

Chapter 12

■ *Immigration and Culture Conflict*

The old saying that emigration is the last recourse of those afflicted by misery still seems valid. In fact its meaning has been greatly enhanced by the tragic events of the early 1930s, when emigration also became the last recourse of those afflicted by political oppression. To the desire to escape from want was added the desire to escape from fear. Emigration has become therefore "a weapon of survival."[1]

Economic, political, and social pressures are, of course, not the only factors in emigration; the number and kinds of situations from which people attempt to escape are almost unlimited. Sad memories, public disapproval, unrecognized abilities, dim or uncertain future prospects, or cultural, racial, or religious hostility are only a few examples. Migration may also result from crime, as an attempt on the part of the criminal to escape the consequences of his act.

The relationship between migration and crime is therefore important. It is usually discussed only from the point of view of immigration, however; and emigration is largely overlooked. Immigration has long been cited as a major cause of delinquency and crime on grounds that delinquency and crime rates can be attributed to culture conflict arising from introduction of various ethnic, religious, and racial groups into the United States at various periods in history. "When the members of one cultural group," Donald R. Cressey has remarked, "immigrate to another culture, they may take with them values which condone ways of behaving that clash with the codes of the receiving culture and are, therefore, illegal."[2] The truth of this statement, however, can be considered fully only if the entire migration process, including both emigration and immigration, is examined. As the source of immigration is emigration, any attempt to explain the relationships between immigration and crime is doomed unless questions of culture conflict and reasons for or circumstances surrounding decisions to emigrate are taken into consideration. The process of accultur- ation for the immigrant who is escaping from poverty is quite different from the same process for the immigrant who abandons a fairly settled livelihood in hopes of a higher living standard. The economic emigrant differs from the political refugee. Those who flee racial prejudice are dissimilar from those who seek to escape distressing personal memories.

The circumstances in which the decision to emigrate is made are also important. Traditionally most emigrants have taken their time in making such decisions, weighing the possible advantages and disadvantages as best they have been able. Since the 1930s, however, this group has de- creased and now seems to be a minority of the world's migrating popu- lation. Its primary place has been taken by another group of emigrants, those who have little alternative to emigration if they wish to survive. German, Austrian, and other Central European refugees escaping from Nazi rule before and during World War II are examples of this type. Al- though many such emigrants did have some time to prepare for their emigration, others had little opportunity to consider alternatives and left their homes and families abruptly with no clearly defined goal other than survival. On the occasion of the Hungarian revolution in 1956, for example, nearly 1 percent of the population left the country within seven weeks.

Scattered references to alleged criminality of immigrants are found in the nineteenth-century literature. Nearly three times as many immigrants as natives committed crimes in Geneva during several years of the period between 1829 and 1885,[3] and approximately one-fifth of the criminals in Zürich between 1853 and 1891 were foreigners or immigrants.[4] Criminality in France in 1885 was four times as high among the foreign-born popula- tion as among the natives.[5] At the end of the nineteenth century the rate of convicted persons in Algeria per 10,000 members of the population was 111 for non-French Europeans, 71 for the French, and 34 for the Arabs.[6]

The figures for the United States reveal a similar pattern. Although 71.75 percent of those arrested among the white population in 1890 were natives and 28.25 percent were foreign-born, the proportions of the two groups in the total population were 83.44 and 16.56 percent respectively.[7] Many immigrants to the United States at the turn of the century were single men who sent for their wives or families later. Already at an age when they were highly vulnerable to crime, many were impelled into the criminal process because of their lower class standing, ignorance of American laws and customs, and poor living conditions forced upon them by the events of entry. In the new country they were often concentrated in areas with high delinquency and crime rates, to which they had usually not—at least not to the same degree—been accustomed in their native lands. Donald R. Taft found, for example, that immigrants from northern and western Europe were less often committed to penal institutions than were their brothers from southern and eastern Europe. Although this difference may have reflected variations in class, marital status, cultural experiences, and the restricted residential areas available to immigrants,[8] Taft discovered that the commitment rate of southern and eastern European immigrants, even when corrected for differences in age distribution, was 87 percent higher than that of the northern and western group. Similarly, the commitment rate of second-generation members of southern and eastern European parental groups, when similarly corrected, was more than twice that of their northern and western counterparts.[9] Although exact data on juvenile delinquency before and after immigration are lacking, students might hypothesize that culture clashes brought about by immigration are no less difficult for adolescents than for adults.[10]

The mid-twentieth century yielded no further evidence of higher crime rates among immigrants, however. Nearly every study indicates that the recorded crime rates of the foreign-born are markedly lower than those of the native-born as a whole. In fact, the rate of the native-born appears to be roughly double that of the foreign-born.[11] When compared to population, arrests and imprisonments among native whites in the United States are approximately twice those of foreign-born whites.[12] Even the crime rate among the immigrants who arrived in Australia after World War II is about one-half that recorded for native-born Australians.[13]

Sporadic studies of the relationship between immigration and crime also reveal other social dimensions. The criminality of immigrants, for example, appears higher among people under thirty, comparable to that of the native-born population between the ages of thirty to thirty-five, and lower among those over thirty-five.[14] Although some studies suggest that immigrants have a higher crime rate upon their first arrival in the new country,[15] others conclude that the so-called *second generation* (native-born children of immigrants) evinces a higher crime rate than that of the original immigrants; they explain that the child of immigrants is peculiarly subject to culture conflict as he is both socialized to "Old World" mores and parental values on one hand and educated to "New World" patterns by school, church, peers, neighbors, and media of mass communication on the other.[16]

The process of migration affects not only the criminality of immigrants but probably also that of the host population. Although it has received little attention, this problem is particularly important because the foreign-born immigrant brings not only disappointment in his old life and hope for his new one but also his own ethical, moral, and social ideas. Whether he will exert a favorable or unfavorable influence on the population of the country that admits him largely depends upon his ability to communicate his attitudes and values.[17] Some evidence, however, suggests that the emigrant group may include many people who will participate in future crimes under either normal or abnormal circumstances. Sicilian crimes, especially those committed as part of vendettas in Palermo, decreased before World War I because of major emigration from the area. Organized crime in the United States, on the other hand, grew in the years immediately following the war. Even the assassination of Democratic Presidential hopeful Robert F. Kennedy in 1968 by a Jordanian emigrant who had left his home country at the age of thirteen may reflect the problems of immigrant adjustment and assimilation.

As new attitudes and cultural values are introduced into foreign areas, culture conflicts may actually affect the general social orientation and adjustment processes of the new immigrant. For example, theories of anarchism and communism, originally foreign to English and American social thought, were disseminated by the immigrant population in the United States.[18] Interaction and interrelations between the native-born and immigrant population may therefore influence the basic character of the delinquency and crime problem.

Whether the adult and juvenile immigrants will engage in delinquency and crime depends largely upon their proposed solutions to their basic difficulties. Although some emigrants are able to prepare financially for their changes of residence and to arrive at their destinations with some sense of security, others are unable to regularize their financial situation. Some are able to overcome early anxieties through help from previously emigrated relatives, but first family arrivals are largely on their own. Most families, however, immigrate to the receiving country with empty pockets and little immediate hope of aid. Half a century ago Hungarian emigrants, for example, in their search for a new life and better standard of living, entered the United States with average cash equivalents as shown in the table.[19]

Table 12.1

Year	Average Sum per Immigrant (in dollars)
1894–1895	13.1
1895–1896	12.0
1896–1897	11.2
1897–1898	12.4
1898–1899	12.7
1899–1900	11.6
1900–1901	11.9
1901–1902	11.3
1905–1908	15.8
1908–1910	17.9
1910–1913	26.1

Changes in currency regulations and the political situation have guaranteed that emigrants of the last quarter-century have left their native countries with even less cash than that shown in the table.

Too little money is not, however, the immigrant's only problem. Loneliness may stimulate delinquent or criminal activity. Although those who arrive with their families have immediate advantages in establishing a new life, the building of a real home takes a long time. Nevertheless, the presence of the family lessens some anxieties, stimulates necessary efforts, regulates daily life, and prevents deviations motivated by loneliness. Because the majority of ordinary immigrants are unmarried, the value of family stability is largely unrealized.

Further difficulties may arise from the immigrant's age and physical condition. Whereas earlier immigrants were younger, commonly within *crime-committing age* limits (above juvenile but below thirty-five), the forced emigration of political exiles and displaced persons has resulted in the migration of older people with children in the *delinquency-committing age range*. Coincident with their arrival, however, has been the failure of older and less vigorous people to endure hardship and to build a new life. Immigrants older than the crime-committing age are socioethically mature and more able to resist crime pressures; juvenile immigrants at the delinquency-committing age are often less prepared psychologically to adjust to the new culture.

The greatest difficulty for the immigrant is his ability to make a socioethical readjustment in his new surroundings. Whereas the juvenile or adult immigrant wants to adapt himself in nearly all cases to his contemporary environment, he is often hesitant, cautious, timid, and bewildered in his new circumstances.[20] The immigrant in conflict, unless aided in overcoming his conflict, may turn to delinquency or crime. His conflict is, however, frequently misinterpreted, for the receiving population may believe that an entrance permit, preliminary assistance with charity dollars, and formal suggestions on work opportunities and procedures will solve the immigrant's basic problems. Mere emigration alone stimulates many conflicts that are neither easily classified nor easily resolved. Variations in cultural and socioethical values hinder adjustment and make the immigrant suspectible to hostile forces. Although people of different cultures may live together and contribute jointly to the general human welfare,[21] the immigrant's successful adjustment depends upon the solution of his individual conflicts.

The history of human migration is filled with disaster, but rarely as the single products of the immigrants' unrealistic hopes. Because immigration is not unilateral, it calls for mutual understanding. The receiving country rightly expects the immigrant to become acculturated but little success is achieved until his original conflicts are resolved. Some immigrants, not content with the hospitality of their new country, seek to gain unfair advantage through challenges to law and order.[22] These "failures" among the general mass of immigrants, however, have not proved to be more frequent than those among the native-born population. Although obvious socioeconomic difficulties suggest the high probability of immigrant delinquency and crime, the inhibiting force of physical relocation and new cultural orientation may actually limit such deviance. Although nineteenth-century studies revealed a close relationship between immigration on one hand and delinquency and crime on the other, their conclusions may have resulted from less detailed criminological investigation methods or from differences in the migration processes. It is also possible that the decline in immigrant participation in delinquency and crime during the last forty years has resulted from the different nature of the prevailing emigration pressures.

Most studies of immigration in relation to delinquency and crime neglect to evaluate emigration pressures and negative attitudes in the host countries, focusing instead on ethnic relationships, birthplace, and immigration patterns in relation to delinquency and crime. Although many studies have suggested that the highest incidence of delinquency appears among immigrant children, exploratory studies of Chinese and Japanese children in the United States have suggested that as long as foreign-born children or native-born children of foreigners follow traditional rules of conduct within their families, their delinquency is consistently below the average American rate. Their rate commonly increases, however, as they come into greater contact with American culture.[23] Delinquency among Puerto Rican immigrants, for example, is usually rated rather high, a result of the marginal social roles that they play owing to dual ethnic commitment. Delinquency and crime among new immigrants to Israel, on the other hand, are higher than those of earlier immigrants and the native-born. Oriental Jews have higher delinquency patterns than those found among their European counterparts.[24] As these studies have emphasized the function of culture conflict and risk of arrest among the foreign-born, the applicability of the data is not completely clear.

In addition, the implications of internal migration have not been adequately examined in relation to immigration and culture conflict. In a study of boys who migrated to Philadelphia and who were born between 1939 and 1945, were pupils in the city public schools in 1957, and who had resided for at least part of that year in the area bounded by Broad, Sixth, Poplar, and Susquehanna Streets, Leonard Savitz discovered that the racial composition of the total population was 10 percent white (109), 84 percent Negro (890), 5 percent Puerto Rican (58), and 1 percent "other" (5). Although 56 percent of the subjects had been born in Philadelphia (66 percent of the whites, 58 percent of the Negroes, and fewer than 4 percent of the Puerto Ricans), most of the migrants had been born in the southern states.[25] Fifty-two percent of the Negro migrants and only 19 percent of the "non-Negro" migrants had arrived by age six and 90 and 76 percent respectively by age thirteen. Savitz found that migration does not have the criminogenic effects attributed to it and that the Philadelphia-born population was more frequently delinquent than was the migrant group, though to an insignificant degree. Whereas 39 percent of the natives and 31 percent of those who had migrated before they were seven were classified as delinquent by Savitz, 46 percent of the former and 38 percent of the latter had had only one contact each with the juvenile court.[26] The average native Negro delinquent had committed his first delinquency at an earlier age than had the average migrant delinquent. Savitz found, however, no evidence to support the view that internal migration is a disorganizing force in modern urban life. The migrants are not only less likely to come from broken homes, have illegitimate siblings, or engage in extensive intracity mobility, but they also tend to engage in less frequent and less serious delinquencies.[27] Other studies of migration and delinquency have revealed similar findings.

NOTES

1. Hans von Hentig, *The Criminal and His Victim: Studies in the Sociobiology of Crime* (New Haven: 1948), p. 259.

2. Donald R. Cressey, "Crime and Delinquency," in Leonard Broom and Philip Selznick, *Sociology* (3rd ed.; New York: 1963), p. 549.

3. J. Cuenoud, "Statistique Générale des crimes et des delits divers accomplis à Genève depuis 1817 à 1885," *Zeitschrift für Schweizerische Statistik*, 26 (1890), 97–120.

4. Albert Mayer, *Die Verbrechen in Ihrem Zusammenhang mit den Wirtschaftlichen und Sozialen Verhältnissen im Kanton Zürich* (Jena: 1895), pp. 62–64; and Mayer, "Ergebnisse der Rechtsstatistik in der Siebenjahrigen Periode 1885–1891 and Vergleichung mit der Zehnjahrigen Periode 1875–1884," *Statistische Mitteilungen Betreffend den Kanton Zürich,* (Wintertur, Switz.: 1892).

5. *Compte Général de l'administration de la justice criminelle en France et en Algérie pendant l'année 1885* (Paris: 1887).

6. Gabriel Tarde, *La Criminalité comparée* (8th ed.; Paris: 1924), p. 14.

7. *Report on Crime, Pauperism and Benevolence in the United States at the Eleventh Census: 1890* (Washington, D.C.: 1896), p. 129.

8. Donald R. Taft, "Nationality and Crime," *American Sociological Review*, 1 (1936), 732.

9. Taft, *Criminology* (New York: 1942), pp. 113–115.

10. Walter C. Reckless, *The Crime Problem* (4th ed.; New York: 1967), p. 109.

11. Taft, *Criminology* (3rd ed.; New York: 1956), p. 154; and Taft and Richard Robbins, *International Migrations: The Immigrant in the Modern World* (New York: 1955).

12. Edwin H. Sutherland and Cressey, *Principles of Criminology* (6th ed.; New York: 1960), p. 144.

13. Commonwealth Immigration Advisory Council, *Third Report of the Committee Established to Investigate the Conduct of Migrants* (Canberra: 1957).

14. C. C. Van Vechten, "The Criminality of the Foreign-Born," *Journal of Criminal Law, Criminology and Police Science*, 32 (July–August 1941), 139–147.

15. W. I. Thomas and Florian Znaniecki, *The Polish Peasant in Europe and America*, 4 (Boston: 1918); and Pauline Young, *The Pilgrims of Russian Town* (Chicago: 1932).

16. Taft, *op. cit.*

17. Ervin Hacker, *Kriminalitás és Bevándorlás* (Pécs, 1929), p. 58.

18. Mayo-Smith, *Emigration and Immigration* (New York: 1898), quoted in Hacker, *op. cit.*

19. A. Thirring, *A Magyarországi Kivándorlás És a Külföldi Magyarság* (Budapest: 1904); and Thirring, *Magyarország Kivándorlás És Vissávándorlás 1899–1913* (Budapest: 1918).

20. Hentig, *op. cit.*, pp. 274–275.

21. Taft, *Criminology*, 3rd ed., p. 163.

22. N. Garraud, *Traité Théorique et pratique du droit pénal français*, 1 (3rd ed.; Paris: 1913), p. 440.

23. Norman S. Hayner and Charles N. Reynolds, "Chinese Family Life in America," *American Sociological Review*, 2 (October 1937), 630–637.

24. Shlomo Shoham, "The Application of the 'Culture-Conflict' Hypothesis to the Criminality of Immigrants in Israel," *Journal of Criminal Law, Criminology and Police Science*, 53 (June 1962), 207–214.

25. Leonard Savitz, "Delinquency and Migration," in Marvin E. Wolfgang, Leonard Savitz and Norman Johnston, eds., *The Sociology of Crime and Delinquency* (New York: 1962), p. 200.

26. *Ibid.*, p. 203.

27. *Ibid.*, p. 205.

Chapter 13

■ *Ecological Patterns*

■ *The Study of Environment*

Ecology, a branch of biology, deals with the habits and modes of life of organisms in relation to their environment. There is also *human,* or *social,* ecology, which deals with the environmental relations of human beings, especially their social and institutional distribution in geographical areas. Although human ecology, as Donald R. Taft has written, "deals with spatial relations,"[1] the concept of the community has both social and geographical significance. Robert Sutherland, Julian L. Woodward, and Milton A. Maxwell believed, however, that if people "have a common interest but live in different localities, they do not constitute a community, but rather a special interest group."[2]

The social group is not only an association of individuals and subgroups but also a *local area* having marked influence upon the characteristics of both individuals and subgroups. The geographical influence on human life is not simply fact but is also an element in social functioning. The crime and delinquency problem is therefore not exempt from the influence of geography in social variations. Ecological factors, however, are neither decisive nor exclusive regulators of deviant behavior. Any analogy between the plant world and human society has obvious limitations. The "free will" of the delinquent and the criminal and their ability to resist pressures toward delinquency and crime through the guidance of their socioethical personalities are dynamic concepts, interrelated in most complex fashion with various biological and social factors in which ecological aspects may play only a minimal part.

Because delinquency and crime statistics are necessarily incomplete, thanks to the hidden character of much deviance, criminal ecologists are unable to guarantee the reliability of their crime-distribution maps.[3] Minimal emphasis upon comparative criminological findings has actually hindered the growth of universal theories of delinquent and criminal behavior.[4] As each national and, in some degree, cultural area is apt to have its own criminology,[5] most general hypotheses must be modified to meet the exigencies of particular situations. Not only do delinquency and crime have different meanings in different cultures, but they also differ in type and volume in a single society during the course of its history. Then, too, political and other boundaries have little ecological significance, for causes of delinquency and crime are not restricted by them. Small areas like the district, downtown, a suburb, and the like, whether rural or urban, cannot be delimited accurately. Although similar geographical locales in different societies may present dissimilar social processes, similar ecological processes in different cultures may result in different etiologies of delinquency. Existing, though insufficient, data suggest that crime is only learned behavior. And, even though an investigation of the location of the causes of delinquency and crime—the task of criminal ecology—may help to clarify the dimensions of delinquency and crime, many problems are still involved.[6]

Criminological interest in ecology is not new. Early attempts sought to connect delinquency and crime with the social distribution of human beings and with the geographical characteristics of their surroundings. Gabriel Tarde's Law of Imitation[7] offered the original theoretical foundation for criminal-ecological studies.[8] The cartographic method, pioneered by A. M. Guerry in the first half of the nineteenth century and subsequently applied to the analysis of the physical environment and the crime problem, served as a theoretical pillar.[9] The discovery by Henry Mayhew that crime in England and Wales was higher in industrial centers and below average near the borders buttressed Guerry's work.[10] The investigations of Adolphe Quetelet,[11] A. Lacassagne,[12] and Alexander von Oettingen[13] served to lend further substance to the ecological approach to causation of delinquency and crime. Even Georg von Mayr emphasized that the "condition of accumulation of the population must have a special importance" in any attempt to consider criminality, an important sociopathological product.[14]

■ *Delinquency in Metropolitan Regions*

In nearly all metropolitan areas professional delinquency, crime, and vice are centered in well-known districts. New York, Chicago, London, Paris, and Berlin have their "badlands," where crime prospers. Walter C. Reckless attributed the existence of such criminal districts to the "moral isolation" of pariahs from modern society and the establishment of an area of survival by parasitic social elements.[15] Criminal syndicates, racketeers, gamblers, prostitutes, drug addicts, and hardened juvenile delinquents prefer to visit, meet, and "work" in these districts. In their moral isolation, they view ordinary citizens as aliens. Although it is questionable whether the pariahs and parasitic elements created the "badlands" or whether these areas were developed for them by those who profited from assisting them, the areas do serve as criminal or "underworld" meeting and market places.

Most studies of metropolitan delinquency and crime areas before World War II were conducted in Chicago. Although they focused upon such factors as population change, age differentials, economic status, family structure, criminal records, risk of arrest, and other variables, these studies nevertheless were subject to considerable error. The characteristics of one city, for example, do not hold true for other metropolitan communities. Methodological flaws also negated much of the original discovery.[16] Even inconclusive or questionable data revealed, however, that a delinquent or criminal climate may exist in the well-known "badlands" or even in other areas of the metropolis. That is, criminogenic forces are more common in these city areas.

The pioneer criminal ecologists of this century were social workers Sophonisba P. Breckenridge and Edith Abbott, who investigated increasing juvenile delinquency in Chicago during the ten-year period from 1899 to 1909.[17] In attempting to locate the concentrations of such delinquency in Chicago, they marked the residence of each delinquent juvenile on a map and noted his age, sex, race, and arrest and court records. The heavily populated West Side of Chicago along the river and canals, between railroad tracks, and among industrial plants, they discovered, had the highest concentration of delinquency. What changes occurred in delinquency rates in these "delinquent neighborhoods" during the ten-year period were primarily results of changes in the law or in public attitudes.

Between the two world wars further ecological studies continued, largely in Chicago. Robert E. Park, E. W. Burgess, R. D. McKenzie, and Louis Wirth found that city development could be analyzed in terms of concentric zones.[18] The center zone of Chicago, popularly known as "the Loop," is the business district, composed mostly of a transient commuting population. In a concentric circle around the Loop is the zone of light manufacturing. As this area is vulnerable to expansion of the central business district, it remains neglected and has high delinquency and crime patterns. The third zone is composed of lower-class and immigrant workingmen's homes. Though able to avoid residence in the second zone, such workingmen are unable to move easily into the more favored housing areas of the fourth (residential) and fifth (apartment) zones. The last zone, on the periphery of the city, is comparable to the modern suburb, where growth is related to population needs. The social characteristics of the city, Park and his associates found, are distributed in relation to these zones. Whereas the outer zones enjoy more community stability, the highest volume of juvenile delinquency appears in the central areas.

Probation officer Clifford R. Shaw undertook a similar ecological investigation of delinquency and crime, first by himself in Chicago[19] and subsequently with Henry D. McKay in Birmingham, Ala.; Cleveland; Denver;

Philadelphia; Richmond, Va.; and Seattle.[20] Using a map-plotting technique in order to discover existing "delinquency areas," Shaw and McKay studied Chicago in three juvenile-court investigations from 1900 to 1906, 1917 to 1923, and 1927 to 1933. In spite of the twenty- to thirty-year time lapse between the beginning and end of these series of investigations, the high-delinquency areas of 1900 were still high-delinquency areas in later decades, a discovery that seemed to support Shaw and McKay's hypothesis of ecological consistency. As they divided Chicago into five zones of two-mile widths, designating the central business area as the focal zone from which the others radiated concentrically, Shaw and McKay calculated the number of juvenile delinquents in the male population between the ages of ten and sixteen. They concluded from the Chicago studies that delinquency and crime are functional to an area itself and do not result merely from the interaction of its inhabitants. They reasoned that

1. The specific features of delinquency vary in different areas of the city and that some areas have minimal delinquency and crime, whereas others have extensive delinquency.
2. Higher rates of crime and delinquency are generally found in the center of the city and in industrial areas (adjacent to the Loop, in the stockyards district, and in South Chicago).
3. Delinquency and crime are more frequent in areas of physical deterioration.
4. Criminals and delinquents living in delinquent areas tend to become recidivists.
5. In areas with higher rates of delinquency and crime these rates remained constant throughout the investigated period, although both the populations and their ethnic compositions had changed considerably in the meantime (for example, Polish and Italian immigrants had replaced Germans and Swedes in some districts).

Although these discoveries by Shaw and McKay were significant, their conclusions were open to criticism. Sophia M. Robison, for example, argued that they had failed to consider the 30 to 40 percent of delinquency cases that are dismissed by the courts in their formulation of delinquency rates, to pay attention to the differential distribution of police in the various zones of the city, to recognize the work of many unofficial and nonreporting agencies in handling deviant or delinquent juveniles, to consider ethnic differences within the community, to recognize geographical irregularities in their application of the concentric-zone theory, to comprehend that all immigrant groups do not disintegrate in their first area of settlement, and to perceive that their Chicago data did not support their theory either quantitatively or qualitatively, as the only mathematically significant variation in rates occurred at the two extremes—the Loop and the area farthest from the central city.[21] The English Terence Morris also presented a detailed critique of Shaw and McKay's work. He questioned, for example, whether or not their basic postulates would be applicable to cities and urban areas outside North America. He also noted that they had failed to give adequate consideration to the location of the specific crime vis-à-vis to the offender's home. Additionally, he questioned whether environment tends to precipitate delinquency among those who live and grow up in it or whether it constitutes a complex of selective forces attracting those individuals who are prone to delinquency for a variety of other reasons. Shaw and McKay could not develop conclusions to overcome the problem of anomie and social disorganization.[22]

Another such study was conducted in Baltimore between 1939 and 1942 by Bernard Lander; its conclusions challenged Shaw and McKay's hypothesis. Using anomic and socioeconomic factors as independent variables, Lander discovered that in each of 155 of 157 Baltimore census tracts the distribution of delinquency did not decline from the central business zone outward to the periphery of the city; that the presence of business and industry was not decisive in the delinquency rate; that the delinquency rate is correlated with the percentage of Negroes in the tract; that home ownership is a significant negative variable and that rental areas have higher delinquency rates; and that differences in delinquency rates among areas arise from anomic factors.[23] Limitations in the physical environment and cramped living quarters, Lander believed, can cause tensions and make it likelier that children will witness taboo behavior. Deteriorating residences dissuade children from entertaining friends at home, thus reducing parents' knowledge of their children's activities. Because inadequate housing produces undesirable social costs, it may be influential in and symptomatic of irresponsible attitudes common among adults and characteristic of disorganized families.[24]

Lander's conclusions were also not without critics. Robison, for example, maintained that his use of inadequate official delinquency statistics led him to overlook the fact that the volume of delinquent acts in any census tract is considerably higher than that officially recorded, that home ownership has very different implications in different communities, and that Negroes' risk of arrest in white communities is relatively high.[25] What Lander meant by "anomic or socioeconomic factors" also remained obscure.[26] David J. Bordua, however, did a replication study of Lander's hypotheses in Detroit that supported the claim of the significance of home ownership as a socioeconomic factor, placed less emphasis upon the importance of the nonwhite delinquency problem, and accepted the statistical significance of education and overcrowdedness.[27] Roland J. Chilton, who attempted to reevaluate both the Baltimore and Detroit studies, concluded, as a result of an investigation in Indianapolis that "delinquency still appears to be related to transiency, poor housing and economic indices" and suggested that delinquency in urban areas is a lower-class male phenomenon.[28] Lawrence Rosen and Stanley H. Turner, however, questioned the "fundamental" relationship between anomie and delinquency that Lander had claimed. His methodological approach, they argued, had not been designed to reveal unsuspected interaction effects, a limitation that could have been avoided by the use of their multivariate predictive attribute-analysis technique.[29] Later studies, including most of those done in England, passed beyond the scope of these original ecological efforts and examined the *criminogenic* forces of a given geographical environment in place of the delinquency of a designated area.[30]

■ *Variations Between Rural and Urban Delinquency*

Contributions to criminal ecology were for more than a century almost entirely directed to the comparative study of rural and urban delinquency and crime.[31] At that time the population was sharply divided between rural and urban communities. Increasing exchange of goods, extensive development of commerce and trade, and the growth of industrialization were important factors in the urbanization of rural areas and the migration of rural dwellers to towns, making the differences less distinctive. The effect of industrialization in increasing urbanization is apparent in the changing distribution of population in the United States. The shift from country to town, however, is a world-wide process, and it has implications of major importance for delinquency and crime control.

The U.N. crime congress in 1960 found it difficult to support the thesis that "urban growth and industrialization may be central determinants of the delinquency and crime increase." The lack of coordination between economic and industrial development on one hand and social development on the other may, however, contribute to increased crime. Because social development has in many countries continued to lag behind economic and industrial growth, the necessary social institutions to aid in the solution of delinquency and crime problems have not yet been developed. In Morocco, for example, delinquency is a purely urban phenomenon, largely resulting from family and social disintegration caused by the rapid increase in the population, the migration of many people to urban centers, and the culture conflict brought about by the Westernization of the country.[32] Urban delinquency appears to be a more serious problem than does rural delinquency, not because of urban growth but because of the ways in which people live and are governed in cities.[33] "Political corruption, poor living conditions, discriminatory policies and other factors," the United Nations noted, "may cause a disproportionate increase in the rate of crime in any kind of urban and rural area."[34] Although all age groups are represented among migrants to towns from rural areas, the young are especially vulnerable to the challenges of the new community. If they cannot find immediate and steady employment, pressures toward crime may easily involve them in occasional delinquency, which may in turn lead to professional criminality. Mass-communications media, which seem to stimulate juveniles in rural areas to imitate urban "models," are not without delinquent influence. Although juvenile imitation may not have the impact of full socialization on particular types of behavior, it may nonetheless result in reduction of differences between urban and rural delinquency patterns.

Whereas delinquency and crime in rural areas have traditionally been believed to involve crimes against persons, urban regions have been described as having disproportionately higher crime rates against property. Although in Cesare Lombroso's opinion rural criminality is "barbarous," characterized by desire for revenge and by brutality, specifically city crimes like forgery are "lazy" and intellectual in character.[35] Even now the Federal Bureau of Investigation's *Uniform Crime Reports* continue to note the differences in volume of urban and rural crime. Although city life may be more impersonal, the intimacy of rural life allows less secrecy and often leads to more violent criminal expression. Urban crime is characterized by intellectuality and refinements in the criminal process and economic goals. Rural crimes are, however, marked by crude violence and fulfillment of personal motives. Even the types of crimes vary according to environmental potentials. Whereas urban criminality is periodically expressed in the theft of art treasures, rural crime may take the form of setting fire to neighbors' crops, an act impossible in modern urban areas. Although the distinctions are not as sharp, rural and urban delinquency patterns are similarly differentiated.

Franz Exner, who compared urban delinquency and crime in Munich with rural delinquency and crime in upper Bavaria, reached similar conclusions. He found that assaults were three times as common (in proportion to the population) in the latter as in Munich. Open defiance of legal authority and crimes against property occurred twice as frequently in the rural community as in Munich. Although Exner was reluctant to compare cases of murder because of their various motivations, he did find more sex crimes in the city. Although he pointed out the prevalence of recidivism in urban areas and the smaller volume in the country, he questioned the significance of this finding. Do many criminals repeat because of the influence of urban conditions, or do they become urban inhabitants because they are recidivists?[36]

Emphasizing the obvious fact that the urban population is not biologically different from the rural population and that behavior differences must have their genesis in the social setting, Reckless attributed these variables to situational factors.[37] Although the urban population is more exposed—and adjusted—to materialism, the rural man is comparatively isolated and has not developed "a tolerance toward nuisances and interferences" of materialism. Marshall B. Clinard, however, has suggested that the rural criminal is less sophisticated in techniques of property violation, which would explain the relative absence of this kind of crime in the country.[38] The limited technical proficiency visible in these crimes, on the other hand, may result from lack of necessity for greater skill. Confirming his hypothesis in Sweden, Clinard found that "the greater the degree of urbanism in a community, the greater the rate of property offenses" and that the relationship between the incidence of property crime and urbanization was "an observed regularity."[39]

Although it is generally assumed that delinquency and crime are on the whole more frequent in cities than in rural areas, Mayr noted that, if this assumption is valid at all, it has been so only since the turn of the century.[40] French statistical data buttress this belief. Between 1841 and 1911 the residences of French offenders per 100 convicts took the distribution shown in Table 13.1. These data, however, include only the place of residence and not the location of the crime. It is theoretically possible therefore that rural and urban residents may migrate to other areas to commit crimes. The higher crime ratio of the city has been frequently confirmed, but observed increases in crime in suburban areas have been largely the result of increasing tendencies among residents of more marginal urban areas to engage in theft in communities of greater wealth.

Table 13.1

Period	Residence in Villages	Residence in Cities (population 2,000 or more)	Without Permanent Residence
1841–1845	58	38	4
1846–1850	59	37	4
1851–1855	56	39	5
1856–1860	56	39	5
1861–1865	54	41	5
1866–1870	49	44	7
1871–1875	48	46	6
1876–1880	47	45	8
1910	33	56	11
1911	34	55	11

Source: Georg von Mayr, *Moralstatistik mit Einschluss der Kriminalstatistik, Statistik und Gesellschaftslehre*, vol. 3 (Tübingen: 1917).

Hans Burchardt reached similar conclusions as a result of his study of male, female, juvenile, and recidivist groups in Germany and other European countries.[41] Thomas P. Monahan's study in Iowa also revealed that rural crime in that state was "permanently" lower between 1865 and 1925.[42] Although Reckless did not deny that the crime ratio is higher in urban than in rural areas, he did call attention to the fact that the comparison can no longer be very meaningful because rural and urban crimes are of totally different types.[43] Howard Jones found in a study of English crimes that the differences in life patterns between rural and urban communities are still very real and have effects "in causing differences in both the distribution and the form of criminal activity."[44] Although Jones found in his study of Leicestershire (excluding the city of Leicester itself) that a general tendency to higher juvenile-delinquency rates exists in more urbanized areas, he also discovered that crimes against persons are less common in city areas, whereas crimes against property are more likely to be committed there. Jones noted that the ratio of males to females was much higher in rural than in urban districts. On the whole, girls from rural areas formed a smaller proportion of the total number of offenders in comparison to their urban counterparts. Rather surprisingly, however, Jones found that gang offenses were more prevalent in rural areas. Ganging was, however, slightly more prevalent among less serious offenders.[45]

Comparisons between rural and urban delinquency and crime are inaccurate and unreliable. Variations in law enforcement and court data hinder such comparisons. But internal migration, encouraged by population mobility and social change, undoubtedly is a factor of major importance in rural-urban variations in crime rates.

NOTES

1. Donald R. Taft, *Criminology* (3rd ed.; New York: 1956), p. 204.

2. Robert L. Sutherland, Julian L. Woodward, and Milton A. Maxwell, *Introductory Sociology* (6th ed.; New York: 1961), p. 188.

3. Taft, *op. cit.*, p. 204.

4. Marshall B. Clinard, "A Cross-Cultural Replication of the Relation of Urbanism to Criminal Behavior," *American Sociological Review,* 25 (April 1960), 253.

5. *Ibid.*

6. George B. Vold, *Theoretical Criminology* (New York: 1958), p. 190; see also Vold, "Crime and City and Country Areas," *Annals of the American Academy of Political and Social Science,* 217 (September 1941), 38–45.

7. Gabriel Tarde, *La Criminalité comparée* (Paris: 1886).

8. Vold, *op. cit.*, p. 188.

9. A. M. Guerry, *Essai sur la statistique morale de la France* (Paris: 1833).

10. Henry Mayhew, *London Labour and the London Poor* (London: 1851).

11. Adolphe Quetelet, *Physique Sociale, ou essai sur le développement des facultés de l'homme* (Paris: 1869).

12. A. Lacassagne, "Marche de la criminalité en France de 1825 à 1880," *La Revue scientifique* (1881), 674.

13. Alexander von Oettingen, *Die Moralstatistik in Ihrer Bedeutung für eine Sozialethik* (3rd ed.; Erlangen, Ger.: 1882).

14. Georg von Mayr, "Kriminalstatistik und Kriminalaetiologie," *Monatschrift für Kriminalpsychologie und Strafrechtsreform* (1911–1912), p. 333; and Mayr, *Moralstatistik mit Einschluss der Kriminalstatistik: Statistik und Gesellschaftslehre*, Vol. 3 (Tübingen: 1917).

15. Walter C. Reckless, *The Crime Problem* (3rd ed.; New York: 1961), pp. 53–54.

16. Roland J. Chilton, "Continuity in Delinquency Area Research: A Comparison of Studies for Baltimore, Detroit, and Indianapolis," *American Sociological Review,* 29 (February 1964), 71–83.

17. Sophonisba P. Breckenridge and Edith Abbott, *The Delinquent Child and the Home* (New York: 1912). Supporting the claimed relationship between the ecological distribution of delinquency and the economic characteristics of urban areas, Kenneth Polk showed the necessity for theories to account for the observable differences among the various social areas of the city. He suggested a typological rather than a correlational analysis of the distribution of delinquency. See Kenneth Polk, "Urban Social Areas and Delinquency," *Social Problems,* 14 (Winter 1967), 320–325.

18. Robert E. Park, E. W. Burgess, R. D. McKenzie, and Louis Wirth, *The City: The Ecological Approach to the Study of the Human Community* (Chicago: 1925).

19. Clifford R. Shaw, *Delinquency Areas* (Chicago: 1929).

20. Shaw and Henry D. McKay, "Social Factors in Juvenile Delinquency," *Report on the Causes of Crime,* 2 (Washington, D.C.: 1931); and Shaw and McKay, *Juvenile Delinquency and Urban Areas* (Chicago: 1942).

21. Sophia M. Robison, *Can Delinquency Be Measured?* (New York: 1936); and Robison, *Juvenile Delinquency: Its Nature and Control* (New York: 1960), pp. 93–95.

22. Terence Morris, *The Criminal Area* (London: 1958), pp. 92–105.

23. Bernard Lander, *Towards an Understanding of Juvenile Delinquency* (New York: 1954).

24. Elmer H. Johnson, *Crime, Correction and Society* (Homewood, Ill.: 1968), p. 102.

25. Robison, *Juvenile Delinquency,* p. 98.

26. Morris, *op. cit.,* pp. 100–109.

27. David J. Bordua, "Juvenile Delinquency and 'Anomie': An Attempt at Replication," *Social Problems,* 6 (Winter 1958–1959), 230–238.

28. Chilton, *op. cit.,* pp. 82–83.

29. Lawrence Rosen and Stanley H. Turner, "An Evaluation of the Lander Approach to Ecology and Delinquency," *Social Problems,* 15 (Fall 1967), 189–200. See also Robert A. Gordon, "Issues in the Ecological Study of Delinquency," *American Sociological Review,* 32 (December 1967), 927–944.

30. J. H. Bagot, *Juvenile Delinquency: A Comparative Study of the Position in Liverpool and England and Wales* (London: 1941); A. M. Carr-Saunders, Hermann Mannheim, and E. C. Rhodes, *Young Offenders* (London: 1942); Mannheim, *Juvenile Delinquency in an English Middletown* (London: 1948); J. B. Mays, *Growing Up in the City* (Liverpool: 1954); and Morris, *op. cit.*

31. See Herman Adler, Frances Cahn, and Johannes Stuart, *The Incidence of Delinquency in Berkeley* (Berkeley: 1934); F. S. Bodenheimer, "Bemerkungen eines Biologen über den Begriff der Verstädterung," *Zeitschrift für Geopolitik* (1933); Ettore Botti, *La Delinquenza Femminile a Napoli* (Naples: 1904); Hans Hermann Burchardt, *Kriminalität in Stadt und Land* (Berlin: 1935); Clinard, "The Process of Urbanization and Criminal Behavior: A Study of Culture Conflicts," *American Journal of Sociology,* 50 (July 1944), 38–45; Clinard, "A Cross-Cultural Replication," pp. 253–257; Hans von Hentig, "Der Kriminelle Aspekt von Stadt und Land," *Monatschrift für Kriminalpsychologie und Strafrechtsreform,* 23 (July 1932), 435–436; Hugo Hoegel, "Vergleichende Übersicht der österreichischen Straffälligkeitstatistik," *Statistische Monatschrift* (1898); C. Jacquart, *Essais de statistique morale: la criminalité Belge* (Brussels: 1909); H. Joly, *La Belgique criminelle* (Paris: 1907); Otto Kinberg, "On So-Called Vagrancy," *Journal of Criminal Law and Criminology,* 24 (September 1933), 313–332; Solomon Kob-

rin, "The Conflict of Values in Delinquency Areas," *American Sociological Review,* 16 (October 1951), 653–661; A. Meyer, *Die Verbrechen in Ihren Zusammenhang mit den Wirtschaftlichen und Sozialen Verhältnissen im Kanton Zürich* (Jena: 1895); Thomas P. Monahan, *The Trend in Rural and Urban Crime* (1937); J. R. B. Roos, "La Criminalité des grandes villes et l'influence du principe d'opportunité sur la géographie de la criminalité," *Bulletin de l'institut international de statistique,* 19; Bruce Smith, *Rural Crime Control* (New York: 1933); P. A. Sorokin, C. C. Zimmerman, and C. J. Galpin, *Systematic Source Book in Rural Sociology* (Minneapolis: 1931); Denis Szabò, *Crimes et villes* (Paris: 1960); Taft, "Testing the Selective Influence of Areas of Delinquency," *American Journal of Sociology,* 38 (March 1933), 699–712; M. Thienemann, *Untersuchungen über die Kriminalität in der Provinz Ostpreussen* (Halle, Ger.: 1912); Pauline V. Young, "Urbanization as a Factor in Juvenile Delinquency," *American Sociological Society* (1930); and Young, *The Pilgrims of Russian Town* (Chicago: 1932).

32. U.N. Department of Economic and Social Affairs, *New Forms of Juvenile Delinquency: Their Origin, Prevention and Treatment* (New York: 1960), pp. 44–45.

33. Abdellatif El Bacha, "Some Special Aspects of Juvenile Delinquency in Certain Towns in the Kingdom of Morocco," *International Review of Criminal Policy* (December 1962).

34. U.N. Department of Economic and Social Affairs, *op. cit.,* p. 45.

35. Cesare Lombroso, *Crime, Its Causes and Remedies,* trans. by H. P. Horton (Boston: 1918).

36. Franz Exner, *Kriminalbiologie in Ihren Grundzügen* (Hamburg: 1939).

37. Reckless, *op. cit.,* pp. 64–66.

38. Clinard, Rural Criminal Offenders, *op. cit.*

39. Clinard, "A Cross-Cultural Replication," pp. 354–355.

40. Mayr, *Moralstatistik, op. cit.*

41. Burchardt, *op. cit.*

42. Monahan, *op. cit.*

43. Reckless, *op. cit.*

44. Howard Jones, "The Rural Offender in England," *Bulletin, Société internationale de criminologie,* 1 (1959), 23–32.

45. Jones, *op. cit.*

Chapter 14

■ *Economic Conditions*

■ *Approaches to Economic Conditions as a Delinquency Factor*

Although many people interested in delinquency problems believe the banal statement that economic conditions exert a decisive effect on the formation of delinquency, this assumption cannot be supported with empirical evidence that clearly correlates deviant behavior and economic conditions.[1] But economic factors clearly do have some criminogenic importance. No other delinquency factor is as strongly interwoven with other causal factors as are economic conditions. Culture conflict, class mobility, role constellations, poor living conditions, community organization, poverty, white-collar delinquency, black-marketeering, immigration, prostitution, and many other factors that are often held to be independent variables in delinquency are ultimately related to economic conditions.

The quest for causal understanding of economic conditions is not new but is in fact one of the oldest goals of criminology. The Greeks Xenophon, Plato, and Aristotle and the Roman Vergil wrote on this subject.[2] Because the production, distribution, consumption, and exchange of goods and services have been common to every society,[3] the problem of delinquency and crime cannot be detached from their influence. Even Thomas More, the first "sociologist" to comment directly upon economic conditions and crime in contemporary England, focused upon the relationship between socioeconomic life and existing crime in presenting his Utopia.[4]

In the nineteenth century E. Ducpétiaux, writing about general poverty and its effects, suggested the existence of *economic criminality*, a product of common poverty.[5] Similarly, Adolphe Quetelet, often called the "founder of scientific criminal statistics," noted the effects of sudden economic shocks upon criminality and suggested that statistically measurable relationships between economic conditions and crime exist. Inequities in economic assets, he believed, encourage temptation and increase actual delinquency and crime. The greater volume of crime in large cities, he hypothesized, results from financial stratification and exposure of the proletariat to deviant temptations. Cyclical economic crises, largely in industrial areas, also stimulate increased criminality.[6]

Whitworth Russel found a correlation between the number of offenders and the general English economic distress in 1842.[7] Joseph Fletcher noted the connection between the price of wheat and the number of crimes during the period 1810 to 1847.[8] In the years between 1835 and 1854 John Clay found that "hard times" were responsible for crime, especially among "the young and thoughtless."[9] Richard Hussey Walsh suggested that the increase in crime in the years 1844 to 1854 resulted from bad economic conditions.[10] Subsequently Georg von Mayr, in a comparison between the fluctuating price of rye and criminal offenses,[11] discovered that each half-penny (*sechser*) increase in price "developed" one more theft per 100,000 Bavarian inhabitants between 1835 and 1861. A similar drop in price caused a corresponding decrease in the number of thefts. This conclusion created a long-lasting international stir, and Mayr's approach was not only discussed but also applied to the economic conditions of several other countries.[12] W. Woytinsky, for example, applied it more generally in his investigation of delinquency and food prices.[13] Although W. D. Morrison,[14] Raffaele Garofalo,[15] and Alexander von Oettingen[16] seemed to follow this path, they had some reservations, believing that economic conditions cannot be accepted as a general cause.

The milestone in the study of the causal force of economic conditions was reached in the prize-winning works of Joseph van Kan[17] and Willem Adriaan Bonger[18] of the University of Amsterdam. Although their works included major collections of references to the world literature on economic conditions and crime, both directed their study to the total economic system rather than to particular aspects of it. Each assumed that only adherents of nondeterminism can doubt the importance of economic conditions in criminal causation. In the preface to Kan's work, G. A. van Hamel emphasized that the economic needs of people, the means by which they gain satisfaction, and their wealth or poverty strongly influence them to conform to the demands of law and order or to participate in deviant activities.[19]

■ Grouping of Orientations

Kan, Bonger, and Hamel categorized the authors who had described the relationship between economic conditions and crime according to theoretical schools. Kan, for example, distinguished nine groups:

> 1. The *Italian school* (Cesare Lombroso, Enrico Ferri, Sergi, Ettore Fornasari di Verce, Antonio Marro), which stressed the importance

of biological factors and attributed only secondary importance to economic conditions.

2. The *French school* (A. Lacassagne, Léonce Manouvrier, F. Corre, Gabriel Tarde), also known as the "Milieu school," which accepted economic conditions as one of several causal factors.

3. The *third school* (Terza Scuola of Alimena and Vaccaro), which sought a compromise between the biological and sociological trends, although placing major emphasis upon economic factors.

4. The *socialist school* (P. Turati, Bruno Battaglia, Napoleone Colajanni, Lafargue), which explained crime almost totally in economic terms.

5. The *pathological school*, which recognized the influence of economic factors only insofar as they contribute to the pathology of the individual.

6. The *eclectic school*, which included economic factors among many factors that influence development of crime.

7. The *spiritualist school* (H. Joly, Lejeune, Thiry, and Cuylits), which resisted or minimized the hypothesis of economic causation and emphasized freedom of the will.

8. The *statistical school* (Quetelet, Oettingen, and Mayr), which focused on the numerical relationships between economic factors and crime.

9. Those who did not commit themselves to any of these schools.

Bonger, on the other hand, differentiated seven schools:

1. The *"early contributors"* (Morns, Jean Jacques Rousseau, William Godwin, Robert Owen, Cesare Bonesandi Beccaria, and Friedrich Engels), who "treated the subject before the birth of modern criminal science."[20]

2. The *statisticians* (Quetelet, Oettingen, Mayr, Valentini, Tugan-Baranowsky, and Fuld), who reduced the relationship between economic conditions and crime to quantitative levels.

3. The *"Italian" authors* (Lomborso, Raffaele Garofalo, Ferri, Hans Kurella, and Niceforo), not necessarily Italian nationals, who viewed economic conditions as secondary causes and emphasized the importance of biological or anthropological factors.

4. The *"French" authors* (Lacassagne, Tarde, Corre, and Manouvrier), not necessarily French, who accepted economic conditions as one of many causal crime factors.

5. The *biosociologists* (Adolphe Prins, Franz von Liszt, and Havelock Ellis), who viewed economic conditions in relation to crime from a compromissary approach.

6. The *spiritualist contributors* (Joly, Proal, and de Baets), who believed in the decisive role of the free will and relegated economic factors to positions of secondary importance.

7. The *socialist authors* of the "third school" (Battaglia, Colajanni, August Bebel, Turati, and Lafargue), who regarded the economic system as the determining factor in crime.

It fell to Hamel, however, to offer a simpler categorization:

> 1. The many authors who argued that the nature and number of crimes are determined by economic conditions and thus shared the socialist orientation.
> 2. The fewer authors who maintained that economic conditions had no, or at least insignificant, influence on crime and who supported the influence of biological factors (the Lombrosians) or nondeterministic free will (classical school).
> 3. Those who recognized the importance of economic factors in criminality though holding different beliefs about their influence in criminal causation. As this group offered a wide range of explanations and methods, it was necessarily numerous. Some members used the casework method, some analyzed statistical data or investigated criminal types, others focused upon individual economic backgrounds, and still others compared market prices (most frequently variations in the price of rye) with fluctuating economic conditions.

The Contributions of Lombroso, Ferri, and Garofalo

Lombroso,[21] Ferri,[22] and Garofalo,[23] the "Holy Three of Criminology," focused on the relations of delinquency and crime to economic conditions. After Lombroso seemed to reveal his inability to defend his overwhelmingly anthropological views against the sociological hypothesis of some French and German criminologists, he modified his conception to a limited extent. Admitting the causal influence of changes in the price of rye, he also recognized the deviant influence of poor crops on crimes against property but not on those against persons. Lombroso also recognized the causal influence of hunger or want on theft. Even alcohol, "used by so many poor against hunger," may lead to violent crimes. Poverty, he believed, may also serve as a cause of sex crimes.

Lombroso finally pioneered the concept of "white-collar criminality" in his belief that "wealth" may cause more crimes than poverty does. He mentioned those who suddenly achieve wealthy positions without possessing good character, but he based his observations upon comparative data on taxes, death duties, post-office accounts, and daily wages of laborers. His hasty and incomplete conclusions about the relationship between economic conditions and crime caused him to revise his earlier statements, but his inconsistency was apparent in later editions of his works.

Ferri, influenced by radical political beliefs, viewed the causal connection between economic conditions and delinquency and crime from a different perspective. Originally he had granted only limited economic influence. As he became an economic determinist, however, he revised his earlier conclusions. First, he shifted his emphasis to the importance of poverty, claiming that people are stunted in their development primarily because of it. Not only does poverty lead to illness and madness, but it also encourages crime. The elimination of misery, Ferri admitted, would not result in elimination of all crime. Yet the problem can best be solved, he argued, by a socialist economic system under which the misery of the working class, the main cause of human degeneracy, would cease and crime would largely disappear. Until this reorganization is accomplished, even members of the higher social classes, engaged as they are in fierce competitive struggle with those who want to acquire wealth, cannot avoid involvement in mental illness, suicide, and crime. All these people, Ferri suggested, could live more peaceable and law-abiding lives in a collectivist social organization. Only in such a society will the overwhelming majority of crimes disappear. As selfishness will not prevail in socialist society, crimes committed under the pressure of passion, Ferri came to believe later in his life, would also cease to exist. Although the problem of abnormal and born criminals would decrease with improvement of social conditions, they would not disappear.

Garofalo, famous for his application of methods of sober logic, agreed that biological factors dominate causation of crime, although he differed with the other views of Lombroso and Ferri. He did not deny the influence of economic conditions, but he refuted claims that they are decisive. In his view the poverty of the proletariat is not a factor in the increase of crime, an assumption that led him to doubt the contemporary and still-prevailing view that more crimes are committed against property by the lower classes than by the rich.

Economic Depressions and Business Cycles

The other extreme views rested on the belief that the capitalistic economic system is the major and perhaps the only cause of crime, a socialist point of view essentially embodied in theories of economic determinism and social materialism. As adherents of these approaches argued that crime is a product of existing capitalist organization and economic structure, they were also convinced that the crime rate would decrease if private property and the tools of production were socialized. The primary themes of these analysts differed, however. Some emphasized the injustice of the economic structure and the economic uncertainty of people; others stressed crime as a natural reaction to the capitalist system. Nearly all, including Turati,[24] Battaglia,[25] Marro,[26] Colajanni,[27] and Bebel[28] accepted the doctrine of Marxism, which continues to serve as the central reference point of Soviet criminology.[29] Although this theoretical orientation is less satisfactory in application, the relationship between capitalism and crime is flexibly interpreted according to the political needs of the time.

Much attention was also paid to the effects of the business cycle upon crime rates. Whereas early investigators had studied the effects of economic depressions upon criminality,[30] Franz Exner noted that needs may stimulate criminal conduct in times of either depression or prosperity (*Wie es Notverbrecher gibt, so gibt es auch Wohlstandverbrecher*).[31] These early research attempts were marred, however, by inadequate methodology. Poorly devised indexes varied widely, and offered little foundation for definite and valid generalizations.[32] Although early studies suggested that business cycles were central determinants of criminality, later, more sophisticated methodological works were much less definitive. Fornasari di Verce, for example, found that crimes against property, largely theft and receiving stolen goods, had increased as a consequence of the Italian economic depression during the period 1875–1885, whereas no particular trend was noticeable in frauds and embezzlements.[33] Béla Földes, who studied the Hungarian business crises of 1873, 1876, and 1879, concluded that all three had been instrumental in the increase of general crime.[34] A. Löwe arrived at similar conclusions about the 1858 Prussian economic crisis.[35] Dorothy Swaine Thomas investigated English economic cycles between 1857 and 1913, but she was unable to establish a close relationship between economic conditions and either general crime or crimes against property and found even less evidence of an increase in crimes against persons. She found only that violent crimes against property might show slight increases in times of economic distress.[36]

Studying the effect of the German inflation of 1921–1925, which reached its peak in 1923, Exner found a rise in crimes against property, again largely in thefts and receiving of stolen goods, and observed a decrease in assaults and sex crimes, which he attributed to insufficient nourishment, lack of alcohol, and general psychic depression. Continuing his investigation between 1925 and 1935, he attempted to correlate thefts and economic indexes as a result of his discovery that, as economic indexes showed an increase from 1926 to 1928, the number of thefts decreased, whereas, conversely, as the indexes decreased and costs of living went down, the ratio of crimes against property rose. Crimes with violence appeared to be independent of the business cycle. The only change observed was a slight decrease during the period of the higher indexes, which Exner explained in terms of the higher price of alcohol.[37] Albert C. Wagner, on the other hand, was unable to find a significant correlation between economic depression and crime,[38] nor did W. F. Ogburn find more than a slight increase in New York State criminality during the years 1870 to 1920.[39]

The limited results of studies of the business cycle eventually led other researchers to study the relationships between unemployment and delinquency and criminality. Löwe, for example, found a high correlation between unemployment and crime in Germany in 1895. Of the unemployed workers who committed property crimes seven-eighths had been in desperate need for more than a week beforehand. Theft by females did not show the same increase as did male theft, probably because, Löwe reasoned, female labor is cheaper and in greater demand during periods of unemployment and women thus feel the effects of unemployment less and are less disposed toward crime.[40] Studies of the period between 1893 and 1929 concluded that unemployment results in large increases in the crime rate.[41] As the unemployed lose their accustomed security, they show less ability to resist pressures toward crime.[42] Donald Clemmer's study of unemployment and economic depression in the United States between 1931 and 1943, however, yielded contrasting findings. Only 11 percent of 800 imprisoned offenders had been unemployed during this period.[43] Leon Radzinowicz, however, reported an increase in crime against property in Poland during the business depression of the early 1930s.[44]

Except in instances of sudden economic collapse, the "normal" economic depression exerts its effects only slowly, gradually infecting the total social life. Because economic crises necessarily involve many other factors as well, the effects of depression upon delinquency and crime are difficult to define. Although economic prosperity usually includes general improvement in public morale, stagnant or depressed economic conditions may lead to general deterioration in morale. This decline tends to occur only at the inception of the depression when economic reserves are exhausted, however. The increase in delinquency and crime therefore usually occurs at the beginnings of periods of widespread unemployment brought about by business crises. Such appearance of delinquency and crime does not, however, mean that a correlation between crime and depression can be established. Although political crimes seem to increase during economic depressions, they may be occasioned only by the social atmosphere accompanying the depression rather than by actual economic conditions.

Economic depression, a form of social disorganization, is marked by conflicts in mores and institutions and a decrease in the influence of existing social rules.[45] As such conflicts limit the ability of society to meet the needs of its members, more people turn uneasily to delinquency and crime. Although the general crime picture does not change during periods of economic depression,[46] crime is perceived as a greater threat to the social order. Still, the increase in general delinquency and crime in a society during a depression is not a direct product of the economic situation; other factors are ultimately involved. Official and public attitudes toward delinquency and crime, for example, vary in relation to existing social fears. Public officials usually become preoccupied with those crimes that are related to the increasing depression. Law enforcement becomes more repressive, punishment more severe, and even legislation stricter. Consequently, higher crime rates may not represent an increase in delinquency and crime as much as an increase in the number of convictions, which makes crime rates appear higher. The real, rather than the purely statistical, effects of economic depressions on delinquency and crime cannot be denied, however. Although economic crises create greater needs and opportunities for deviance, the vast majority of the members of most societies does not engage in delinquency or crime despite crises. Only limited numbers of those who suffer in economic depressions, live in poverty, are deprived of opportunities to achieve financial goals, or are unemployed commit delinquencies or crimes. Those who profit from an economic depression, are wealthy, or find new financial opportunities are, however, most likely to avoid delinquent and criminal conduct. But affluence is not without a major effect on crime. Delegates to the 1960 U.N. Congress on the Prevention of Crime and the Treatment of Offenders in London reported an increase in adolescent crime in nearly all countries, whether rich or poor.[47] A congress in Stockholm in 1965 reported that affluence in itself does not reduce crime rates but may even be a causal factor in delinquency. Jackson Toby suggests that people steal because they are envious, not because they are starving. Naturally, they are most likely to be envious in countries that have rising standards of living.[48] The materialistic concern for acquisition of goods, stimulated by advertising in the mass media, can actually make the "sting of socioeconomic depriva-tion" greater for the poor in rich societies than for the poor in poor so-cieties.[49] The extension of formal education has created serious problems in choosing life goals for those unwilling or unable to learn, as well as for those who benefit from the affluent society in the highest degree. The orientation toward consumption characteristic of affluent societies per-meates most strata and enhances the possibility of delinquency.[50]

Although economic conditions are a factor in crime, they are neither the only nor even an independent factor. Wars and revolutions also exact their tolls. For example, as mentioned earlier, a rise in criminality occurred at the time of the Napoleonic wars.[51] A series of studies cited by Ernst Roesner concluded that economic conditions during or after a war cause increased delinquency and criminality.[52] Just as the occurrence of an economic depression cannot be simply correlated with an increase in deviance, however, wartime economic crises may prove to be only one of many factors contributing to the changing crime problem. Even in times of economic prosperity delinquency and crime waves sometimes occur, a fact that undermines the hypothesis that crime is a product of unfa-vorable economic circumstances.[53] Urban disorganization and lack of inte-gration between industrialization and social development, disintegration of the family, decline of moral values, the mass communications media, and many other factors that play dominant roles both in economic depres-sions and in economic prosperity may also wield considerable influence in the formation and fulfillment of delinquency and crime patterns.

■ Economic Conditions as a Contributing Factor

Although many people believe that economic conditions are the only decisive factor in the development of delinquency patterns, there is no valid available evidence correlating delinquency and crime with economic conditions or the economic structure. Nevertheless, economic conditions, if they appear to society's members as "maladjustments" of society, must be considered an important factor in causation of delinquency and crime.

The balance of economic supply and demand depends not only upon the gratification or restraint of aspirations but also upon crude factors that may shape a number of social situations conducive to delinquency. Family, home, labor, status, role, aspiration level, power structure, and other such variables are shaped by variations in economic conditions. George A. Lundberg, Clarence C. Schrag, and Otto N. Larsen suggest that "the dissatisfaction a society feels regarding its distribution of wealth is, of course, determined by the degree to which the existing distribution fails to correspond to the ideals of that society,"[54] but the economic matrix of delinquency rests not so much on the disparities in economic distribution as on the effects of these disparities upon social institutions. The family and home, religious attachment, education, neighborhoods and areas, mass communications, culture conflicts, collective behavior, and health may exert different influences upon the prevailing economic power and the socialization process. Because the economic order is in itself a system of periodic conflicts, other conflicts in the form of delinquency or crime may issue from it. The exact etiological importance and independent effects of economic values on the shape and incidence of delinquency are still unclear, however. Although the specific economic structure, including such dimensions as industrialization and technology, division of labor, organization of work, automation, job control, occupational classification, status, depressions, and business cycles, appears to have marked significance for delinquency and crime, it is not a single causal factor in itself.

NOTES

1. Thorsten Sellin, "Research Memorandum on Crime in the Depression," *Culture Conflict and Crime* (New York: 1937).

2. Ernst Roesner, "Wirtschaftslage und Straffälligkeit," in Alexander Elster and Heinrich Lingemann, eds., *Handwörterbuch der Kriminologie und der Anderen Strafrechtlichen Hilfswissenschaften* (Berlin: 1933), pp. 1079–1116.

3. George B. Vold, *Theoretical Criminology* (New York: 1958), p. 160.

4. Thomas More, *De Optimo Sei Publicae Statu Nova Insula Utopia* (1516).

5. E. Ducpétiaux, *De la justice, de la misère et de l'aisance, de l'ignorance et de l'instruction sur le nombre des crimes* (Brussels: 1827); and Ducpétiaux, *Mémoire sur la pauperisme dans les deux Flandres* (Brussels: 1850).

6. Adolphe Quetelet, *Sur l'homme et le développement de ses facultés, ou essai de physique sociale* (2nd ed.; Brussels: 1869).

7. Whitworth Russel, "Abstract of the Statistics of Crime in England and Wales from 1839 to 1843," *Journal of the Statistical Society of London,* 10 (March 1847), 38–61, cited in Sellin, *op. cit.,* and in Vold, *op. cit.*

8. Joseph Fletcher, "Moral and Educational Statistics of England and Wales," *Journal of the Statistical Society of London*, 18 (March 1855), 74–79, cited in Sellin, *op. cit.*, and in Vold, *op. cit.*

9. John Clay, "On the Effect of Good or Bad Times on Committals to Prison," *Journal of the Statistical Society of London*, 18 (March 1855), 74–79, cited in Sellin, *op. cit.*, and Vold, *op. cit.*

10. Richard Hussey Walsh, "A Deduction from the Statistics of Crime for the Last Ten Years," *Journal of the Statistical Society of London*, 20 (December 1857), 37–38.

11. Georg von Mayr, "Statistik der Gerichtlichen Polizei im Königreiche Bayern und in Einigen Anderen Ländern," *Beitrage zur Statistik in Königreiche Bayern*, 16 (Munich: 1867); Mayr, "Getreidepreise und Kriminalität," *Allgemeine Zeitung*, 93 (Munich: 1895); and Mayr, *Moralstatistik mit Einschluss der Kriminalstatistik* (Tübingen: 1917); see also Mayr's other works.

12. Roesner, *op. cit.*, p. 1081.

13. W. Woytinsky, "Kriminalität und Lebensmittelpreise," *Zeitschrift für die Gesamte Strafrechtswissenschaft* (1929).

14. W. D. Morrison, *Crime and Its Causes* (London: 1891).

15. Raffaele Garofalo, *La Criminologie* (Paris: 1895).

16. Alexander von Oettingen, *Die Moralstatistik in Ihrer Bedeutung für eine Sozialethik* (3rd ed.; Erlangen, Ger.: 1882).

17. Joseph van Kan, *Les Causes économiques de la criminalité: étude historique et critique d'étiologie criminelle* (Paris: 1903).

18. Willem Adriaan Bonger, *Criminalité et conditions économiques* (Amsterdam: 1905).

19. Cited in Roesner, *op. cit.*, pp. 1082–1083.

20. Bonger, *op. cit.*, translated here from the French.

21. Cesare Lombroso, *L'Uomo Delinquente in Rapporto all' Antropologia, Giurisprudenza ad Alle Discipline Carcerarie* (Turin: 1876); Lombroso, *Il Delinquente Politico* (Milan: 1892); and Lombroso, *Le Crime, causes et remèdes* (Paris: 1899).

22. Enrico Ferri, *Sociologia Criminale* (Turin: 1884); revised editions published under the title *I Nuovi Orizzonti del Diritto Penale* (Turin).

23. Garofalo, *Criminologia* (Naples: 1885).

24. P. Turati, *Il Delitto e la Questione Sociale* (Milan: 1883).

25. Bruno Battaglia, *La Dinamica del Delitto* (Naples: 1886).

26. Antonio Marro, *I Caratteri dei Delinquenti* (Turin: 1887).

27. Napoleone Colajanni, *La Sociologia Criminale* (Catania: 1887–1889).

28. August Bebel, *Die Frau und der Sozialismus* (Stuttgart: 1899).

29. A. A. Gertsenzon, "The Ways of Development of Soviet Criminal Science," *Soviet State and Law* (1947), in Russian.

30. See the summary of the most relevant studies in Roesner, *op. cit.*, and in Sellin, *op. cit.*

31. Franz Exner, *Kriminalbiologie in Ihren Grundzügen* (Hamburg: 1939).

32. Edwin H. Sutherland and Donald R. Cressey, *Principles of Criminology* (6th ed.; New York: 1960), p. 192.

33. E. Fornasari di Verce, *La Criminalita e le Vicende Economiche d'Italia, dal 1873 al 1890* (Turin: 1894).

34. Béla Földes, A Bünügy Statisztikája (Budapest: 1889).

35. A. Löwe, "Arbeitslosigkeit und Kriminalität," Abhandlungen des Kriminalistischen Instituts an der Universität, 3 (1914), 4.

36. Dorothy Swaine Thomas, Social Aspects of the Business Cycle (London: 1925).

37. Exner, op. cit.

38. Albert C. Wagner, "Crime and Economic Change in Philadelphia 1925–1934," Journal of Criminal Law and Criminology, 27 (November–December 1936), 483–490.

39. W. F. Ogburn and Dorothy S. Thomas, "Influence of Business Cycle on Certain Conditions," American Statistical Association, 10 (September 1922), 324–340.

40. Löwe, op. cit.

41. S. K. Ruck, "The Increase of Crime in England," Political Quarterly, 3 (April–June 1932), 206–225.

42. Edward A. Rundquist and Raymond F. Sletto, Personality in the Depression (Minneapolis: 1936).

43. Donald Clemmer, The Prison Community (New York: 1940).

44. Leon Radzinowicz, "The Influence of Economic Conditions on Crime," Sociological Review, 33 (January–May 1941), 139–153.

45. William I. Thomas and Florian Znaniecki, The Polish Peasant in Europe and America, 4 (Boston: 1918), 2–3.

46. Daniel Glaser and Kent Rice, "Crime, Age and Employment," American Sociological Review, 24 (October 1959), 679–686.

47. U.N. Department of Economic and Social Affairs, Second United Nations Congress on the Prevention of Crime and the Treatment of Offenders (New York: 1961), pp. 8–18.

48. Jackson Toby, "Affluence and Adolescent Crime," in President's Commission on Law Enforcement and Administration of Justice, Task Force Report: Juvenile Delinquency and Youth Crime (Washington, D.C.: 1967), p. 132.

49. Ibid., p. 143. See also Belton M. Fleisher, The Economics of Delinquency (Chicago: 1966).

50. See Ivar Berg, "Economic Factors in Delinquency," in President's Commission on Law Enforcement and Administration of Justice, Task Force Report (Washington, D.C.: 1967), pp. 305–316; and Martin Gold, Status Forces in Delinquent Boys (Ann Arbor: 1963).

51. A. Böthlingk, Friedrich Cesar Laharpe (Bern: 1925).

52. Roesner, op. cit., pp. 1109–1111.

53. U.N. Department of Economic and Social Affairs, New Forms of Juvenile Delinquency: Their Origin, Prevention and Treatment (New York: 1960), pp. 41–46.

54. George A. Lundberg, Clarence C. Schrag, and Otto N. Larsen, Sociology (rev. ed.; New York: 1958), p. 643.

Chapter 15

■ *Education, Religion, Mass Media, and Delinquent Conduct*

Society is constantly engaged in dissemination of norms and values during the lifetime of each individual. The degree to which it is successful in producing behavior and conduct in accordance with these norms and values determines the degree to which delinquency and crime exist. Mass societies are not stabilized by a single series of integrated norms, however; rather they are founded upon a normative pluralism that dilutes or modifies the integrating potential of each normative system. Although schools, churches, and mass communications media are continually disseminating general or specific norms and values, they often reinforce or undermine one another in the youth's daily experience. The relations of education, religion, and mass media to delinquent conduct are therefore constantly being modified by multiple-value systems, subcultural commitments, and practices prevailing in the existing social system.

■ *Education and Delinquent Conduct*

Attendance at the modern school, a major social institution, is required of all members of advanced societies. The American system, based upon a principle of universal education in which all youths have access to educational channels, requires attendance up to a certain point, in order to encourage at least a minimum level of scholastic accomplishment. Although the school is only one of several agencies that aid in the socialization process, it is one of the most important. The content and scope of courses offered may in themselves operate to help prevent delinquency.[1]

Although the school system is responsible for instruction on various subjects, it is also charged with transmitting prevailing cultural norms that may help the child to avoid deviance. The fact that many youths commit crimes and are judged delinquent without having known that their behavior would have such serious consequences suggests, however, the need for a primer on law for youth[2] and exposes the failure of the school and society to delineate and teach basic norms. The school nevertheless generally teaches, directly or indirectly, what is and is not socially acceptable, what is permitted and prohibited, what is rewarded and punished, and what is conforming and criminal behavior. In order to establish the necessary conditions for maximizing the child's receptivity to socializing influences, the state requires a minimum number of years of education in which each person is to receive the basic knowledge necessary to earn his livelihood and instruction in the social norms upon which law and order are based.

Although many schools transmit cultural goals through various processes, all transmit essentially the same cultural norms, which represent the accepted standards of social conduct at a given period. The child, in a sense a newcomer to society, cannot know or adequately understand these norms without help from the school, which is expected to educate him in conforming rather than in delinquent conduct. Mere transmission of normative content, however, is not enough. Walter C. Reckless and Simon Dinitz, for example, found that self-concepts among white sixth-grade boys are one of the factors dictating their tendencies toward or away from crime. Insensitivity to these tendencies by teachers or parents merely enhances the probability of crime, regardless of objective transmission of norms.[3]

The schools are only one channel through which the youths receive normative information, but they are a major and integral part of the whole complex socializing system. As these varied agencies may attempt to introduce the child to different norms and meanings, the socialization process may not be uniform; the schools may meet difficulties in establishing the necessary conditions in which to gain access to children, and conflicts may develop between the schools and other agencies.

One of the most frequent conflicts occurs between the educational approach of the school and parental attitudes. Whereas parents previously dominated socialization and in some cases encouraged differing or nonconforming values and attitudes, often in conflict with those of the schools, such parental socialization has faltered with increasing employment of mothers outside the home, parental disinterest in socialization responsibilities, and disintegration of the family through divorce. Consequently, the socializing tasks of the school have become greater. As traditional parental responsibilities are shifted to the school, the former conflict between parental and school values is replaced by a three-way conflict as parent substitutes, whether grandparents, other relatives, neighbors, or domestic employees, assume the daytime control of juvenile socialization. The patriarchal or matriarchal attitudes of the parent substitutes, the parent-school socialization conflict, and socialization by other social agencies often undermine the overall success of socialization.

Peer-group influences also frequently undermine the socialization goals of the school. The "peer," another child with whom the youth is in association, is "a non-adult, a non-parent, a non-teacher."[4] As the closeness of a peer group cannot extend to large numbers, the student population divides itself into a number of smaller groups, on the basis of common interests or other factors. As the child finds understanding within such a group, "the effective definition that he follows," according to August Hollingshead, "appears to be more closely related to the definitions other children place upon the situation, at least what he thinks the others think, than it is to definitions his parents, teachers, ministers, police and other adults place upon him."[5] Although the peer group may reinforce school socialization, it may also undermine the efforts of the school. Such opposing values may ultimately "isolate the child from constructive adult influences,"[6] and disturb or prevent the full transmission of cultural norms and knowledge. As the child comes under these disruptive influences, he is frequently led to delinquency and then to crime. Even in the absence of such determining influences, however, the contradiction between meanings and confusion of values may prevent the child from acquiring the ability to resist crime. His ability to resist is not undermined only by the antagonistic or disharmonious activity of other agencies. The school itself may, for example, fail to offer an adequate curriculum or to further the development of appropriate values.

Although fewer than 5 percent of school-age children express their deviance in delinquency, approximately 61 percent of this total is in the older age groups (15 to 17).[7] To what extent the school is responsible for in-school and out-of-school student delinquency is not known. The fact that peak delinquency is reached in the last two years of high school or their equivalent suggests that the educational system must bear major responsibility for the part that inadequate socialization plays in the rise of delinquency. Walter E. Schafer and Kenneth Polk found that schools often actually promote delinquency as they offer often irrelevant curriculums, reinforce students' tendencies toward failure, and rely on inappropriate teaching methods. Failure to offer adequate compensatory and remedial education and inferior teachers and facilities in schools in low-income areas often undermine achievement of the schools' goals. Too few non-college-bound students are given occupational preparation; what vocational education does exist is too job-specific. Not enough training is offered for subprofessional jobs. Even occupational-guidance and placement services provide inadequate preparation for effective entry of adolescents into employment. Delinquency is consequently often a product of ineffective involvement of students in the exercise of authority, educational decision making and planning, the teaching and learning process, and the development of understanding of the nature and purpose of law and order. The tendency of schools to label and dismiss those who misbehave only enhances the negative processes already begun.[8]

■ *School Attendance*

Considerable significance is attached to regular school attendance for two basic reasons. First, a minimum degree of socialization is expected of all members of society, in order to prevent delinquency and crime. Second, excessive absence may itself be a symptom of developing delinquency. Although any child who is absent from school without leave is called a "truant," truancy as a problem may take the form of either *prolonged absence* or dropping out of school. Although neither form of truancy is a crime, both contribute to delinquency, as inadequate or no attendance at school may result in limited or ineffective socialization that may allow the child to drift into the delinquency "danger zone" by default. Truancy may, however, be either the first step toward further delinquencies and eventual crimes or a symptom of already developed delinquent attitudes and conduct. *Prolonged truancy* is not uniformly defined and may refer to consecutive or repeated nonconsecutive absences, depending upon the state or nation in question. *Full truancy* is termination of school attendance by the dropout.

The problems of prolonged and full truancy are complex. Even now their causal roles in juvenile delinquency are not fully understood. Yet it is logical to assume that, as gaps in socialization occur and the youths are unable to fulfill the expectations of the school, their socioethical resistance may never reach the desired level. No convincing evidence reveals the extent or degree of this influence, however. Probably as Alvin L. Bertrand has written, "this problem can be understood in terms of the functional requirements of the social systems to which youths belong."[9] Dysfunctional social subsystems may be related to delinquent subcultures in producing truants and dropouts. Delbert S. Elliott hypothesizes, for example, that dropping out of school is a procedure by which members of lower socioeconomic classes may escape the middle-class value system and goal aspirations present in the school setting. Youths from lower socioeconomic classes, he discovered, have greater referral rates for delinquency when in school than when out of school. Delinquents who drop out have higher referral rates while in school than when out of school.[10] Patricia C. Sexton discovered that dropout rates are six times greater in the lowest- than in the highest-income schools.[11] Schafer reported that 35 percent of working-class students in his study were in the bottom quartile in academic achievement of their graduating class, whereas the comparable middle-class figure was 15 percent. Middle-class students, however, dropped out only one-fourth as often as do working-class students.[12] But James B. Conant argued that the dropout problem arises from poor coordination between the ingredients of the high-school career and potentials for late job opportunities.[13]

In a study of San Francisco truants John L. Roberts discovered that the apparent factors associated with truancy fell into the following groups:

> 1. *Situational factors* like insufficient clothing, parental disorder and inability to keep children at home, difficult school curriculum, and non-acceptance by schoolmates (most cases).
> 2. *Mental factors* like withdrawal, depression, and illness (fewer cases).
> 3. *Social factors* like antisocial aggressiveness, fighting, theft, and other crime (fewest cases).[14]

As this classification indicates, a series of variables that are more complex than simple breach of discipline, laziness, idleness, reluctance to study, misconduct, or malice influences the outcome of school attempts at socialization. Most frequently, the truant is not a "problem child," and his truancy is not his problem. Rather it is the problem of the community that has often failed to accept responsibility for socialization of all juveniles and recognition of their abilities and interests.

The fact that the "dropout has never before been considered a problem per se," Daniel Schreiber concluded, "involves a paradox."[15] In the past half-century the school has made substantial gains. Although no more than 6 or 7 of every 100 ninth-grade pupils in 1900 normally were graduated with diplomas within a four-year period, the proportion had increased to one-half by 1930 and two-thirds by 1963. The growth of national concern with social problems, however, also had produced a popular tendency to equate truants with juvenile delinquents and to focus interest upon truancy and the dropout problem. The tendency to correlate truancy and delinquency is not without foundation. William Healy and Augusta F. Bronner, for example, suggested that nearly 60 percent of delinquents are truants.[16] William C. Kvaraceus found that a third of the delinquents that he studied had been truant before their juvenile-court hearings,[17] and Sheldon Glueck and Eleanor Glueck discovered that nearly 95 percent of truants are also delinquent.[18] Other studies have also revealed a marked correlation between absences from school and delinquent behavior. The underlying causes, among them the dysfunctioning of delinquent subcultures, have not yet been thoroughly analyzed, however.[19] Little work, for example, has been done on the relationships among religious values, subcultural norms, and delinquent behavior.

■ *Religion and Delinquent Conduct*

As observations on the influence of religion in the formation and volume of delinquency are scattered and inconclusive, the exact relationship between religion on one hand and delinquency and criminality on the other is unknown. Yet if religious devotion is moral expression and if morality and conforming behavior represent the same social phenomena, religion should have a marked effect upon the delinquency problem. In his five-year study of 761 delinquent cases, Kvaraceus found that 92 percent claimed religious affiliation, 54.2 percent attended church regularly, 20.4 percent reported irregular or occasional attendance, and only 25.4 percent never went to church.[20] Among the male delinquents whom William W. Wattenberg interviewed in Detroit, 69.1 percent attended church regularly or at least occasionally, and 14.2 percent did not, and there were more churchgoers among first offenders than among repeaters.[21] But in a study of a group of delinquent girls M. Dominic found only 2 percent who attended church with some regularity.[22] The Gluecks and Healy and Bronner also found that delinquents are less likely to attend church regularly that are nondelinquents.[23] Hugh Hartshorne and Mark A. May offered an even more important insight into the relationship of religion and delinquent conduct. In their study of a sample of 8,150 public- and private-school pupils they concluded that "deceit" and "honesty" are not unified character traits, definable only in religious terms, but are specific functions of life situations. Most children, they believed, will deceive in certain situations and not in others.[24] These and other similar findings unfortunately do not offer a definitive picture of the direct influence of religion on deviance. The regularity of church attendance and its connections with religious devotion and belief are products of complex home and community factors that are in themselves inconclusive. Although many juvenile courts and treatment institutions place major significance upon religious affiliation and practices, they place little emphasis upon the development and degree of religious life trends. The religious atmosphere of the home, attitude of the school toward religion, religious orientations of peer groups, organizational activities of the church, personal experiences tending to support or undermine religious belief, religious character of the local culture, and peculiar requirements and patterns of different denominations strongly influence attachment to religion and cannot be ignored in any assessment of religion's effect upon delinquency.[25]

Although it is not easy to determine the exact power of religion to prevent delinquency, "its potential role," according to Paul W. Tappan, "is tremendous."[26] Well before Tappan, however, Émile Durkheim had argued that religion is central to social life and has the force to unite people in a single "moral community."[27] Durkheim's analysis of preliterate groups does not, however, have unlimited application to contemporary societies. Different sects and denominations have divided societies rather than uniting them. Furthermore, different beliefs and practices create excuses or opportunities for religious antagonism and even violence. Even in this "modern and humanitarian Twentieth Century" a shocking number of tortures, humiliations, robberies, and murders committed by juvenile delinquents against those who adhere to different beliefs and practices have taken place. As all who believe and practice religion are not united in a single belief system, uniform attendance at religious services does not necessarily indicate shared attitudes or a morally united community.

The potential role of religion rests in the similarities between secular socioethical norms and religious moral rules. Religious institutions and belief systems can effectively reinforce secular norms and can efficiently participate in social control. "By adding a divine sanction to human values, religion," Leonard Broom and Philip Selznick have written, "can effectively win compliance with the norms of society."[28] T. B. Bottomore, however, argued that the process of sanctification of norms is the reverse. From the time of the Ten Commandments, he argues, criminal codes have evolved from religious or moral codes, perhaps part of the reason why "moral disagreements are now very frequently political disagreements, and moral beliefs are largely incorporated in political ideologies."[29] Although all sins are not crimes, most crimes are sins. As the developmental relationships among religious, moral, social, and criminal codes suggest that their central tenets and prohibitions are essentially similar, religion is potentially able to participate in effective socialization of youth against delinquency and to serve as an important agency of social control. The relationships, however, between socioethical values and particular laws are only loosely, if ever, stated. If parents fail to impart these values to their children and if the church stresses the mystical aspects of religion rather than its ethical teachings, the school remains the only institution that can make up for these deficiencies.[30]

The organized church can, however, assume leadership in preventing delinquency both through the home and through the larger community. Sunday schools, religious meetings, preaching and lecturing, summer camps, discussion and study groups, recreational facilities, leisure activities, and other means offer some potential for preventing the rise of juvenile gangs and increases in other delinquencies. Despite differences among denominations and among members of a single denomination, the widespread presence of religious institutions offers a major resource for prevention of delinquency.

Although several American and European studies have attempted to discover whether or not delinquency and criminality are denominationally oriented, their conclusions have been limited. Several have attempted to prove that Roman Catholics tend to become more deviant than do Protestants and that Jews are less likely to become delinquents than are Protestants. Others reverse the order. But most of these studies are based upon analysis of the institutional population, which cannot represent the whole criminal population. Nor can it provide the basis for answers to any questions about the influence of religion in delinquency or analysis of all factors affecting individual religious beliefs. Current data suggest that no denomination stimulates any more or less delinquency or criminality than does any other, that different delinquency rates associated with denominations probably reflect strengths and variations in actual local religious forces, and that the multitude of factors involved in delinquency and criminal causation makes the measurement of religious factors extremely difficult. In recent years, for example, many of the former social functions of religious groups have been assumed by the mass media, and the normative expectations of religious associations have felt the modifying force of multiple value systems that are often in open conflict.

■ Mass Communications Media

The Task

Since the advent of television the debate over the relationship between mass communications media on one hand and delinquency and crime on the other has continued without conclusive results. Newspapers, movies, radio, television, and certain periodicals, particularly the "comics," have all come under attack.[31] The issue is neither new nor even a product of the television age. As early as 1892 Enrico Ferri, for example, called attention to the relationship between popular literature, the daily newspapers, and illustrated journals on one hand and crime on the other.[32] The use of criminal themes in the arts was not under attack, however, but only "sensational" or "popular" presentations. Johann von Schiller, Victor Sardou, Victor Hugo, Émile Zola, Henrik Ibsen, Feodor Dostoevsky, and Lev Tolstoy did not hesitate to describe crimes and criminals. Even William Shakespeare brought to life a splendid roster of criminal characters. Hardly any of his great dramas—*Macbeth, Othello, King Lear, Hamlet,* or *Richard III*— is without some crime or criminal-psychological lesson that has prompted later criminological analysis. Opera too is filled with crime. Ruggiero Leoncavallo's *I Pagliacci,* Pietro Mascagni's *La Cavalleria Rusticana,* Giacomo Puccini's *La Tosca* and Giuseppe Verdi's *Rigoletto, Don Carlo,* and *Il Trovatore* abound in criminals and crime. Yet no dispute over the presentation of criminals in these works emerged.[33] The real debate began with the growing awareness of crime and criminals in the press, on radio, on television, in the movies, and in comic books. Although some people believe that mass media have little effect on the problem of delinquency and crime, others blame them for recent increases in delinquency rates.

Mass media have broadened the scope of modern communications, as they have extended the influence of actions and ideas. Although not an invention of the twentieth century, mass media may serve to disseminate deviant ideas or as dynamic cultural weapons against crime. Theoretically whatever is written, said, or pictured in mass media is either learned or at least unconsciously absorbed by the masses of readers, listeners, and viewers. Knowledge, symbols, ideas, points of view, patterns, and other cultural ingredients influence legible, aural, and visual communication. These media are thus one of the most powerful forces in the learning process. General public education depends heavily but not entirely upon their success or failure in transmitting insights into the nature and scope of cultural patterns.[34] Although Marshall B. Clinard has called these media "secondary community influences," they nevertheless have primary importance and sometimes even prevail over the influences of home and school.

The delinquency and crime problems are closely related to the effects of mass media. The socioethical personality is a prerequisite for any socioethical resistance against delinquency and criminal pressures. The normal cultural evaluation of the "free will" is a crucial factor in man's constant struggle against pressing delinquent and criminal forces. This evaluation is, however, subject to different modifying influences, among them the mass communications media. These media, for example, may either favorably or unfavorably influence the socioethical personality by reinforcing socioethical resistance or by undermining the personality's normal evaluative powers, thus exposing the "free will" to delinquency and criminal pressures. Socioethical resistance levels are certainly not, however, the only determinants of delinquency or crime. Even very high resistance may be outweighed by heavy pressures toward crime. Although a higher cultural standard as presented in the media reinforces the evaluative function of the "free will," a lower standard neutralizes or weakens its effectiveness.

Mass communications media provide culturally important information and raise problems for the masses. The form that information takes and the setting in which problems emerge may also modify public attitudes toward deviance. Because the supply of information and the exposure of problems through mass media aid normal cultural evaluation, such presentation is an integral part of public education and the struggle against delinquency and criminality. Mass media are also business institutions, however, and they exist to make money.[35] Most are therefore responsive to the interests of the advertisers who are their chief revenue sources. In order to attract the largest share of the advertising market, they offer the kind of entertainment that is expected to attract the largest possible audiences. "There is no denying," George Gallup once wrote, "that a constant and ready market exists for anything sensational, whether it be in a newspaper, a magazine, a book, or a motion picture."[36] Donald R. Taft questioned bitterly, "Do we not get the media we deserve?" referring to the fact that "shocking" entertainment is generally attributed to public demand.[37] Although entertainment and profit goals do not necessarily conflict with the social interest in public education, they frequently do in fact. Media should entertain as well as present broader perspectives, knowledge, and insight into the problems of the day. Only in this way can they contribute constructively to the process of social evaluation and help to stabilize the delinquency and crime problems.

Mass media may well, however, offer the cheapest source of nourishment for both culture and crime. Most of them enter almost every home, even in the lowest social strata. Except perhaps for the Bible, which is the world's continuing best seller, newspapers, films, radio, television, and the comics[38] are the media most readily available to the public. Their availability invests them with formidable power to influence the attitudes of their mass audiences toward the problems of delinquency and crime, and the individual's ability to resist criminal and delinquency pressures.

The Function

One basic charge leveled against mass media is that they treat delinquency and crime not as a social problem or from the point of view of informing the public but rather as a form of entertainment. Modern society seems unable to dispense with the experience of adventure, thrills, sexual excitement, shooting, violence, crime, and sensation. Mass media seek to satisfy these demands by presenting information on delinquency and crime. Although they formally preach the slogan "Crime does not pay," they ignore its implications in their own quest for advertising markets.

"There is no doubt," David Abrahamsen has written, "that there is much emphasis on horror stories in all these media."[39] Whether the story is true or fictional is of little consequence. The more dramatic, exciting, sensational, thrilling, or incredible it is, the more it is likely to be accepted. Mere entertainment, which omits consideration of the "problem" and does not stimulate constructive thinking, serves only to arouse emotion and not to create understanding.[40]

Many critics of mass media express anxiety over the moral well-being of children and youth. Arguing that the sight of hanging, flogging, shooting, and throwing acid cannot help but influence the adolescent, they seek control of "televiolence," the "crime in your home."[41] One study revealed that approximately 60 percent of children in Britain between the ages of five and fourteen watched television at 8:30 P.M., when programs in which crime and violence in various forms are normally presented. Some events shown during "family viewing hours" were "death in boiling acid, a hanging enacted in detail even to the placing of the noose round the victim's neck, a man flogged nearly to death, a village looted and burnt to the ground, red Indians preparing to scalp a youthful victim, the writhings of a man kicked in the stomach, men shot willfully in cold blood, a shower of vitriol thrown into the face of a defenseless man."[42] In a study designed to determine the effects upon youth of violence portrayed in mass media (television, movies, and comic books) S. H. Lovibond found that "There is a relationship between exposure to crime and violence in media and endorsement of an ideology which makes the use of force in the interests of egocentric needs the essential content of human relationships."[43] Lovibond, however, was unable to define the exact relationship between ideology and action.

Of all the mass communications media television has the greatest impact. A form of entertainment that can be simultaneously seen and heard, it calls for less effort from the viewer than does simple reading or listening, while simultaneously involving him in the emotional context of crime and violence. Newspapers appeal mainly to an adult audience, although they are available to the young. Films are shared by the adult and younger generations. Comic books are read chiefly by children. But radio and television make contact with all generations from youth to old age. The effect of a newspaper, a radio, or a television set is almost continuous, whereas films and comics are more intermittently experienced. Nevertheless, Jacques Launay found that cheap magazines (though not television) contribute to the negative influence of idleness among French children.[44]

Condemnations of mass media have been based upon objections to the ways in which delinquency and crime are presented to the masses. Some objections that appear to be similar or even identical are debated in different contexts. They include at least four basic arguments.

Mass communications media help children, youths, and adults to acquire criminal techniques. Detailed information about a criminal case, critics argue, may acquaint the audience with methods of preparing and committing crime and of avoiding detection. Through the media the tricks of criminals become known to all those who are prepared to commit crimes but are deterred by not knowing how.[45] These critics allege that many criminals have admitted that they gained their own technical knowledge of crime, including methods for stealing cars, bank robbery, housebreaking, robbery, and spying, from newspapers, films, or television and suggest that crime will diminish if the dissemination of such information ceases.

Mass media make crime appear attractive. This criticism obviously is directed especially at the impact that media can have upon the impressionable minds of children and youths, who may be influenced to delinquent activity. Young people's imitative tendencies, these critics argue, cause them to respond quickly to activities that they can read about, listen to, or see in action and may induce them to reenact fictional roles in real situations. In some instances media appeal may be so great that it leads to "epidemics" of a certain "type of crime currently portrayed sensationally."[46] "Children impersonate actors in their play, and both children and adults," Edwin H. Sutherland and Donald R. Cressey noted, "imitate them in their everyday language and conduct."[47] Children usually adapt the dominant figures of their world, whether engine driver or soldier, to their play. Although the spaceman may represent the future, the gangster and the violent cowboy are the favorite role models offered in all mass media. To what extent they prompt imitative crime, however, is open to question.

Mass media encourage the belief that "crime does pay." Petty shoplifting, small-scale embezzlements, and insignificant theft fail to make headlines and are used in the "big news," films, television plays, or comics only if they include some personal or other sensational aspect. The typical television crime usually involves large profits in jewelry, money, or other objects. In the mass media crime is always on a large scale. Even the news concentrates on crime itself rather than on punishment. Fictional criminals usually make fortunes before they are actually apprehended. The major bank robbery appears on the front page, but the arrest of the robber is reported, if at all, some days later in a tiny news item.

Mass media lend prestige or sympathy to the criminal. Both factual and fictional crime reports, critics argue, advertise crime and glorify criminals. Violence, crime, and other deviations stimulate propaganda rather than reproaches; crime is devalued as an adventure and the criminal is overvalued as a hero. Not only is the fictional criminal often handsome, but he is also invested with a kind heart and pleasing personality characteristics. In any case, his skill at outwitting the police and repeated evasion of the law arouse admiration. As the ordinary police organization cannot cope with his artful intelligence, the extraordinary ability of a master detective, usually an "unofficial enforcement officer," is required to counter his dexterity and ingenuity. Even so, great virtuosity is necessary to bring him to his "deserved" end. As the criminal engages in a heroic struggle with the law, he may serve as a model worthy of sympathy if not of emulation. He seeks prestige and publicity that will bring him respect in the gang and also in the more inclusive "underworld." Critics maintain that, although the reverse should be true, his self-esteem and group status are glorified and sensationalized to the detriment of society.

Other objections are also loosely related to the problem of delinquency and crime. Advocacy of certain types of criminal treatment methods, for example, tend to increase crime. Both American and English newspapers and other media periodically advocate penal methods developed on the assumption that "crime results from the free and deliberately wicked and uncaused choices of bad men."[48] In the United States the indeterminate sentence and parole have been attacked as "prisoner-coddling"; in England news media periodically demanded the reintroduction of corporal punishment (the birch) and the extension of the list of capital crimes. Nevertheless the media, especially newspapers, also periodically undermine potential justice by publishing biased information on criminal cases before trial, thus endangering the right to a fair trial by an unbiased jury.

The Importance

Despite the rather impressive claims about the influence of the mass media in increasing delinquency and crime, there is no specific evidence that conclusively relates crime and mass-communications media. The nature and amount of crime information are not, however, in question; there is rather wide agreement that news media place major emphasis upon criminal themes and crime reporting. Although it is unfair to generalize too far, a considerable number of books,[49] newspapers, films, radio and television programs, and periodicals (including comics) that emphasize crime, terror, violence, and horror are presented merely as entertainment without acceptable sociocultural or educational meanings. The exact relation of such entertainment to delinquency and crime is not clear.

In the past sixty years this question has been frequently examined. In the late 1800s N. Ferriani claimed to know of crimes that had been committed because of ideas published in newspapers.[50] Even at a later date Herbert Blumer and Philip M. Hauser found that motion pictures seemed to have had an important influence on 10 percent of the male and 25 percent of the female offenders studied.[51] Otherwise their influences were indirect. The U.S. Senate Subcommittee headed by Estes Kefauver called television crime programs a "calculated risk" but was unable to find a direct causal relationship between viewing television crime and actual criminal behavior.[52] Hilde T. Himmelweit, A. N. Oppenheim, and Pamela Vince also found that television violence and crime have "potential impact" in producing tensions and anxiety and in aiding the "expression of aggression."[53] Abrahamsen, however, expressed doubt that any mass communications medium in itself is sufficient to produce criminal behavior in a normal person.[54] Although Frederic Wertham emphasized the inviting character of crime as presented in comic books,[55] Frederic M. Thrasher found no data to support this claim.[56] Liliane Decurtins, after a review of selected studies on the effects of motion pictures and television on juvenile behavior, concluded that no existing method can demonstrate a definite causal relationship between motion pictures and juvenile delinquency.[57] "Bad" films potentially can both incite criminal behavior and serve as factors in crime prevention by providing an outlet for baser instincts. Tests that measure the effect of one particular motion picture can measure only its immediate and not its long-range effects on behavior. Although films may have some effects upon human conduct, depending upon the individual's existing personality patterns and character dispositions, they have little negative effect upon those who are mentally healthy and come from stable environments.[58]

Nevertheless, public concern seems to be fully justified, for it is recognized that "the mass media penetrate more layers of society and permeate more layers of consciousness in less time than any other systems of communication."[59] The potential influence of the mass media is almost limitless. Although it may not be possible to gather direct evidence about the actual role of media in criminal causation, it is questionable that such statistical proof is even necessary. The presentation of violence and crime as entertainment without educational emphasis upon their problematic aspects deviates from expected social values. Although further research on this question may eventually yield different conclusions, at present it is clear at least that mass media do little to help in eliminating the problems of delinquency and criminality.

NOTES

1. This statement is in contrast to a remark by B. B. Khleif in "Teachers as Predictors of Juvenile Delinquency and Psychiatric Disturbance," *Social Problems*, 2 (Winter 1964), 270–282, that "Neither low I. Q., poor academic achievement, nor poor reading are associated with . . . delinquency."

2. W. T. McGrath, *Youth and the Law* (Toronto: 1964) is such a volume.

3. Walter C. Reckless and Simon Dinitz, "Pioneering with Self-Concept as a Vulnerability Factor in Delinquency," *Journal of Criminal Law, Criminology and Police Science*, 58 (December 1967), 515–523. The authors concluded that "teacher's prognostications of sixth-grade boys—even the mother's evaluations—plus the Socialization Scale indicate that directionality toward or away from delinquent behavior can be sensed and assessed" (p. 523).

4. James H. S. Bossard, *The Sociology of Child Development* (New York: 1954), pp. 523–524.

5. August B. Hollingshead, *Elmtown's Youth* (New York: 1961), p. 446.

6. Richard A. Cloward and Lloyd E. Ohlin, *Delinquency and Opportunity* (New York: 1960), p. 128.

7. Bernice Milburn Moore, "The Schools and the Problems of Delinquency: Research Studies and Findings," in Ruth Shonle Cavan, ed., *Readings in Juvenile Delinquency: Development, Treatment, Control* (New York: 1962), pp. 183–184.

8. Walter E. Schafer and Kenneth Polk, "Delinquency and the Schools," in *Task Force Report: Juvenile Delinquency and Youth Crime* (Washington, D.C.: President's Commission on Law Enforcement and Administration of Justice, 1967), pp. 222–277.

9. Alvin L. Bertrand, "School Attendance and Attainment, Function and Dysfunction of School and Family Social Systems," *Social Forces*, 40 (March 1962), 228–233.

10. Delbert S. Elliott, "Delinquency, School Attendance and Dropout," *Social Problems*, 13 (Winter 1966), 307–314.

11. Patricia C. Sexton, *Education and Income* (New York: 1966), p. 163.

12. President's Commission on Law Enforcement and Administration of Justice, *Task Force Report: Juvenile Delinquency and Youth Crime* (Washington, D.C.: 1967), p. 229.

13. James B. Conant, *Slums and Suburbs* (New York: 1961), p. 33.

14. John L. Roberts, "Factors Associated with Truancy," *Personnel and Guidance Journal*, 34 (1956), 431–436.

15. Daniel Schreiber, "Juvenile Delinquency and the School Dropout Problem," *Federal Probation*, 27 (September 1963), 15–19.

16. William Healy and Augusta F. Bronner, *New Light on Delinquency and Its Treatment* (New Haven: 1936), p. 76.

17. William C. Kvaraceus, *Juvenile Delinquency and the School* (New York: 1945), p. 155.

18. Sheldon Glueck and Eleanor Glueck, *Unraveling Juvenile Delinquency* (New York: 1950), p. 148.

19. U. S. Office of Education, "Delinquency and the Schools," President's Commission, *op. cit.*, pp. 278–304.

20. Kvaraceus, "Delinquent Behavior and Church Attendance," *Sociology and Social Research*, 28 (March–April 1944), 283–289.

21. William W. Wattenberg, "Church Attendance and Juvenile Misconduct," *Sociology and Social Research*, 34 (January–February 1950), 195–202.

22. M. Dominic, "Religion and the Juvenile Delinquent," *American Catholic Sociological Review*, 15 (October 1954), 256–264.

23. See Glueck and Glueck, *op. cit.*, and Healy and Bronner, *op. cit.*

24. Hugh Hartshorne and Mark A. May, *Studies in the Nature of Character*, Vol. 1. *Studies in Deceit* (New York: 1928).

25. See Joseph D. Fitzpatrick, "The Role of Religion in Programs for the Prevention and Correction of Crime and Delinquency," in President's Commission, *op. cit.*, pp. 317–330, for a discussion of what different religious groups are doing about delinquency.

26. Paul W. Tappan, *Juvenile Delinquency* (New York: 1949), p. 514.

27. Émile Durkheim, *The Elementary Forms of the Religious Life* (New York: 1947), p. 47.

28. Leonard Broom and Philip Selznick, *Sociology* (3rd ed.; New York: 1963), p. 397.

29. T. B. Bottomore, *Sociology: A Guide to Problems and Literature* (London: 1962), p. 232.

30. Mabel A. Elliott, "Trends in Theories Regarding Juvenile Delinquency and Their Implication for Treatment Programs," *Federal Probation*, 31 (September 1967), 3–11.

31. Harry Elmer Barnes and Negley K. Teeters argued that "comics" or "comic books" are obviously misnamed, as with few exceptions they are definitely not humorous. See Barnes and Teeters, *New Horizons in Criminology* (3rd ed.; Englewood Cliffs, N.J.: 1959), p. 194.

32. Enrico Ferri, "Les Microbes du monde criminel et l'art populaire," *Les Criminels dans l'art et la littérature*, trans. by Eugène Laurent (2nd ed.; Paris: 1902).

33. For a contrasting opinion, see S. Sighele, *Littérature et criminalité* (Paris: 1908); many suicide cases have been attributed to the general effect of Johann von Goethe's *Werther*.

34. Marshall B. Clinard, "Secondary Community Influences and Juvenile Delinquency," *The Annals of the American Academy of Political and Social Science*, 261 (January 1949), 42–54.

35. Donald R. Taft, *Criminology* (3rd ed.; New York: 1956), p. 259.

36. George Gallup, "What Is Public Opinion?" *National Probation and Parole Association Journal*, 4 (October 1958), 306.

37. Taft, *op. cit.*, p. 258.

38. Paul H. Mussen and Elred Rutherford, "Effects of Aggressive Cartoons on Children's Play," *Journal of Abnormal and Social Psychology*, 62 (1961), 461–464.

39. David Abrahamsen, *The Psychology of Crime* (New York: 1960), p. 319.

40. Taft, *op. cit.*, p. 262. See also Leonard Berkowitz, "The Effects of Observing Violence," *Scientific American*, 210 (June 1964), 35–41.

41. William Adrian, "Tele-Violence: The Crime in Your Home," *The Readers' Digest*, 78 (April 1961), 31–34.

42. *Ibid*, pp. 31–32.

43. S. H. Lovibond, "The Effect of Media Stressing Crime and Violence upon Children's Attitudes," *Social Problems*, 15 (Summer 1967), 98.

44. Jacques Launay, "The Child and Leisure," *Sauvegarde de l'enfance* (May–June 1965).

45. See Joseph L. Holmes, "Crime and the Press," *Journal of Criminal Law and Criminology*, 20 (July–August 1929), 246.

46. Taft, *op. cit.*, p. 261. The 1968 release of the film *Bonnie and Clyde* was followed by several American bank robberies and gangster-type murders.

47. Edwin H. Sutherland and Donald R. Cressey, *Principles of Criminology* (6th ed.; New York: 1960), p. 215.

48. Taft, *op. cit.*, pp. 264–265.

49. Michael Gordon, "The Sociology of Literature Reconsidered: The American Juvenile Delinquency Novel," *Sociology and Social Research*, 53 (October 1968), 5–20, reviews literature of this type.

50. N. Ferriani, *Delinquenti Scaltri e Fortunati* (Como: 1897).

51. Herbert Blumer and Philip M. Hauser, *Movies, Delinquency and Crime* (New York: 1933).

52. Estes Kefauver, "Television and Juvenile Delinquency," *U.S. Senate Subcommittee Report* (Washington, D.C.: 1956).

53. Hilde T. Himmelweit, A. N. Oppenheim, and Pamela Vince, *Television and the Child* (London: 1958), p. 226.

54. Abrahamsen, *op. cit.*, p. 319.

55. Frederic Wertham, *Seduction of the Innocent* (New York: 1954).

56. Frederic M. Thrasher, "The Comics and Delinquency, Cause or Scapegoat?" *Journal of Educational Sociology*, 23 (December 1949), 195–205.

57. Liliane Decurtins, "Film und Jugendkriminalität," *Kriminalistik*, 21 (1967), 349–355.

58. *Ibid.*, p. 355.

59. Joseph Bensman and Bernard Rosenberg, *Mass, Class, and Bureaucracy* (Englewood Cliffs, N.J.: 1963), p. 337.

Chapter 16

▪ *Physical and Mental Health Factors and Delinquency*

▪ *Disease and Physical Handicaps*

The individual's reaction to diseases and physical handicaps is not merely, as was once believed, factual acceptance of temporary or permanent physical disorder or disability. Because diseases and physical handicaps involve more than physical suffering or defects, it is a misconception "to think of disease in terms of lists of signs and symptoms: of clinical diagnosis as a cut and dried affair."[1] The ancient view that man consists of three parts (head, trunk, and limbs) in which diseases are localized has been discarded. Modern medicine now suggests that physical diseases and handicaps can be interpreted only within a complex psychosomatic framework that includes the totality of the individual. A defect in any part of the organism thus leads to some disorganization of the whole. Because a disease or physical defect to some extent weakens the harmony among the elements of the organism, the nervous system, which serves as a liaison between the brain and the outside world, loses part of its integrating and organizing power and renders the individual more susceptible to deviant forces. Most delinquents and criminals enjoy perfect physical health; only a minority is sick or disabled. Yet, although investigators must therefore be cautious in their assumption that diseases and physical defects are of decisive importance in the etiology of delinquency and crime, the effects of such misfortunes should not be underestimated. Although no existing evidence effectively correlates health conditions with criminality, some conditions consequent to disease or physical handicap may be connected with deviance.

The increase in pressures toward delinquency and crime and the decrease in socioethical resistance to these pressures are both potential products of disease and physical handicaps. The latter, whether temporary or permanent, can undermine social security, social adjustment, efficiency and progress, role fulfillment, and even status. The sick and disabled, for example, must cope with disparities between their present existence and their hoped-for future (if disease or disability endangers progress) or between their past and present (if the disease or disability endangers status). They may become unstable in body or mind. The loss of intellectual and material necessities consequent to disease or defect or of prospects for intellectual and material success stimulates fears, anxieties, and unsatisfied demands that may take the form of pressures toward delinquency or crime. Losses through sickness, unemployment, faded hopes of promotion, anxiety about security, fear of the future, loss of friends, inability to participate in games, rejection by the opposite sex, scholastic deficiencies, role disturbances, fear of loneliness, and uncertainty about the future may demand compensation through delinquency or crime. In a person already weakened by organic upset the ensuing disorganization may further reduce socioethical resistance. The increase in pressures toward delinquency and crime and the reduction in socioethical resistance are proportional to the seriousness of the disease or physical defect and to its effects upon the social environment.

No general criminogenic importance can be attributed to diseases or defects; their effects can be evaluated only individually. Cyril Burt, for example, discovered that 70 percent of a group of offenders had poor physical health and that health factors were connected with delinquency in boys (10 percent) and in girls (7 percent).[2] Sheldon Glueck and Eleanor Glueck, on the other hand, found that 13 percent of the juvenile delinquents in their study had serious diseases (tuberculosis, syphilis, heart disorders, paralysis, or the like) and 30 percent had poor health, although the corresponding percentages for youthful offenders were 7 and 79.[3] If disease or physical handicaps are present before admission to a penal institution, they may be products of the individual's delinquent or criminal life style. They may also, however, develop in the correctional setting.

Because there is only a small body of research data on the relationship of health with delinquency and crime, few investigators agree on whether or not disease has the same effect upon each person, whether personal or environmental qualities are the primary differentiating factors, or whether persistent recidivists have greater tolerance for sickness. Albert Irk discovered that criminals are generally less sensitive than are noncriminals and that they recover more quickly from injuries. Basing his interpretations on the studies of Cesare Lombroso and Antonio Marro, he found that convicted fraud offenders, followed by thieves and murderers, have the highest degrees of sensitivity.[4] His findings were, however, contradicted by Émile Laurent, who argued that some criminals are less sensitive than normal and that most reveal an oversensitive tendency.[5] Although they were unable to prove that delinquency or crime produces either increased or decreased tolerance of disease, Irk and Laurent did suggest that personality characteristics are major factors in eventual delinquent or criminal conduct. Delinquent or criminal sensitivity or insensitivity may, however, be related to the "hard" nature of the professional criminal's life.

Whereas Irk and Laurent related deviance to sensitivity and insensitivity, Hans von Hentig included "ugliness" among his list of physical handicaps that may be important in causation of delinquency and crime. Beauty and ugliness, he believed, are highly influential factors even "in the district attorney's office or in court," where judges and juries are often impressed by physical advantages or handicaps.[6] The social and economic pressures that accompany ugliness, rather than ugliness itself, however, are probably the factors of criminogenic importance. Unattractive or ugly individuals are at a competitive disadvantage and may attempt to compensate for it by acquiring advantages through delinquency or crime.[7] Although an unattractive appearance may also lead to expressions of social conflict, such consequences are not automatic. Not all ugly people commit delinquent or criminal acts nor are handsome boys and pretty girls exempt from delinquency. Sometimes ugliness itself restrains potential delinquents because very unattractive criminals are more easily recognized. Conversely, attractiveness may be a useful tool in crime, especially in such "intellectual" crimes as fraud, smuggling, confidence games, gambling, and illicit drug traffic. The layman's stereotype of the ugly and horrible appearance of murderers is especially disproved by the good looks of some of the Nazi officials who committed war atrocities.

Because they cause variations in normal social relations, blindness and deafness[8] have also been regarded as having major importance in delinquency and crime.[9] The 1905 Massachusetts Census, for example, revealed a larger proportion of deaf and lame people in the prison population than among the general population, but the blind were represented in the same proportions in both populations. The actual meanings of these data were, however, obscured by imprecision in the study and failure to measure the severity of the defects.[10]

Deaf people, Hentig discovered, are forced into a degree of isolation and often divorced from normal social functions, a factor that may help to explain criminality among them. Inability to hear reduces their contacts with social phenomena and often causes them excessive suspicion and anxiety.[11] Their less frequent marriages may be attributed primarily to this physical and emotional limitation, rather than to lack of interest in potential mates. Criminality among the blind is of minor importance because it is harder for them to participate in deviance; they have less contact than do the deaf with operational reality.

Endocrinological Aspects

Ever since A. A. Berthold of Göttingen successfully transplanted an organ from one part of the body of a cock to another in 1894 and ever since Claude Bernard first used the term "internal secretion," in 1855, to describe the process by which the composition of blood is determined, many "miracles" have been attributed to the functioning of the endocrine or ductless glands.[12] The existence of giants, dwarfs, bearded women, and other strange human types and features has been attributed to the functioning of these particular glands, which secrete endocrine or hormone substances into the blood, in order to stimulate and regulate the human biological system. Whereas early theorists believed that the endocrine glands are potential threats to the governing nervous system, later researchers discovered that ductless glands influence personality disorders, which may be expressed in delinquency or crime.

The first attempt to explain delinquent and criminal causation in endocrinological terms occurred approximately seventy-five years ago. Max G. Schlapp, perhaps the first exponent of the extreme endocrinological explanation of delinquent and criminal conduct, declared that crime should be attributed to glandular malfunctioning and suggested that a large percentage of the prison inmates who revealed emotional disturbances were products of such malfunctioning.[13] With Edward H. Smith, Schlapp proposed a "new criminology," in which the thief and the murderer would be described as criminal types within the framework of glandular malfunctioning.[14] Eventually the European criminologist Adolf Lenz advocated the advantages of the endocrine theory in explanation of delinquent and criminal behavior.[15] Even Louis Berman based his investigation of personality characteristics on the functioning relations of the glandular system. Berman excited readers with his discussion of a "new creature," claiming that abnormal endocrine functioning is two to three times more common in the prison than in the general population.[16]

Although Karl Birnbaum accepted the dominance of the endocrine system, he did not argue that criminal characters should be typed on that basis.[17] Matthew Molitch concluded from his comparative study of a group of delinquents with normal endocrine functioning and a control group of offenders with irregular glandular functioning that known endocrine symptoms do not facilitate diagnostic attempts.[18] Frank Tannenbaum concluded that there is little or no evidence to suggest that glandular dysfunction is more prevalent among criminals than in the general population.[19] Although R. G. Hoskins emphasized the limitations of existing knowledge, noting that many more data must be collected before criminology can be reoriented,[20] M. F. Ashley-Montagu strongly protested the application of endocrinology to the problem of delinquency and crime and raised doubts about the "scientific manner" in which the relevant investigations had been carried out, calling their findings illustrative of "the fallacy of false cause." To explain crime in these terms, he concluded, would be "merely to attempt to explain the known by the unknown."[21]

Because its responsible role in the functioning of the human organism and its effects upon emotional life cannot be ignored, the importance of the endocrine system should not be underestimated. Its dominant role in sexual development and in regulation of the sexual cycle, for example, has important implications for female delinquency and criminality. After the age at which sex-hormone production in the woman ceases, their vestigial masculine sexual glands, several theorists have suggested, often continue further hormone production. Therefore, as masculine hormone production begins to predominate and the natural hormonal balance comes to an end, the woman moves away from her female character and approaches that of man. A similar process may be involved in the eventual manifestation of criminality.[22] Such an assumption cannot, however, stand independently; it must be combined with multiple causes of delinquency and crime, which are primarily social phenomena and not merely biochemical products. Although the glandular system, especially the endocrine glands, influences variations in human emotional behavior, no reliable evidence supports a biochemical explanation of delinquency and crime.

■ Sex Chromosomes

Recent discoveries about the functioning of sex chromosomes in causation of delinquency have offered new insights into biophysiological factors in delinquent conduct. In the last ten years developments in human genetics have led to the recognition that some delinquents and criminals have variant combinations of sex chromosomes.[23] Rather than possessing the normal XX pair characteristic of the female or the XY that is normal for the male, some deviants have had either XXY, XYY, or XXYY combinations. P. Jacobs speculated that the additional chromosomes might predispose such males to delinquent or criminal behavior and would thus occur in unusual numbers among the criminal population. To test this hypothesis Jacobs and colleagues examined 315 men and discovered nine with the XYY characteristics who also were taller than the XY males in the same institution.[24] Stimulated by the work of Jacobs and J. A. Strong, who demonstrated the significance of the extra Y chromosome in sexual underdevelopment,[25] and of S. Muldal and C. H. Ockey, who originally described the "double male" constellation (XXYY) of the tall male with near imbecilic I. Q.,[26] M. D. Casey and his colleagues found a relatively larger number of XXYY males among hard-to-manage male criminals of subnormal intelligence,[27] thus confirming findings in Jacobs' earlier examination of fifty men six feet or more tall at two other institutions. Casey's group also found twelve males with the XYY chromosome complement, which led it to the conclusion that certain features about XYY males predispose them to breaking the law.[28]

A comparative study of nine XYY males and eighteen randomly selected convicted psychopaths by W. H. Price and P. P. Whatmore revealed three important differences between the two groups. Although the average age of the XYY males was thirteen years at the time of the first conviction, members of the control group averaged eighteen years. The variant-chromosome males primarily committed crimes against property; the control group showed greater concentration of crimes against persons (murder, assaults, sexual offenses). Although almost no criminal traces were uncovered in the home backgrounds of XYY males, twelve of the sixty-three siblings of the control group had a total of no fewer than 139 convictions. The XYY males were more frequently unstable and immature, without feeling or remorse, and tended to commit seemingly motiveless property crimes. As a result, Price and Whatmore concluded that "it seems likely that the extra Y chromosome has a deleterious effect primarily on the behavior of these men, predisposing them to criminal acts."[29] Although the exact relationships between delinquency and crime on one hand and sex-chromosome variations on the other are still unclear, that convicted Chicago murderer Richard Speck's attorney considered appealing Speck's conviction on grounds of possible sex-chromosome variations beyond the control of the offender suggests that it will assume greater importance in later court actions. Although tests of Speck's blood chemistry did not support claims of such a condition, the state may find it increasingly difficult in the future to prove that sex-chromosome variants *intended* to commit the particular deviant act for which they are charged.

■ *Abnormality and Normality*

The connection between delinquent or criminal behavior and mental abnormality is also in dispute. Some theorists suggest that all deviant behavior is abnormal behavior and argue that mental illness in some form or another underlies all delinquencies and crimes. Several modern psychologists and psychiatrists still assume that delinquency and crime are products of mental abnormality, an idea proposed by the Lombrosians. Mental degeneration, hereditary insanity, specific mental illnesses, and even psychopathic personality problems are therefore regarded as causes of law violations.

In opposition to this generalizing frame of reference, others have explained the origins of delinquency and crime in terms of mental abnormalities that may be manifest in mental illness or disturbance. Abnormality is, however, difficult to define. Ruth Shonle Cavan, for example, suggests that the motives of abnormal criminals, kleptomaniacs, and spontaneous murderers are hard for laymen to understand. "If we could define the abnormal or deviant crime as a crime emanating from abnormal or deviant motives or needs—which, of course, again should be defined—we could restrict the term abnormal or deviant criminal to persons who had committed one or more crimes from abnormal or deviating motives."[30] K. O. Christiansen, however, noted that such a definition would undoubtedly include many normal criminals.[31]

Edwin H. Sutherland and Donald R. Cressey pointed out that, "although mental disease has been studied for many generations, much disagreement still prevails regarding definitions, classifications, causes, methods of diagnosis, therapy, extent in general population, and frequency in the criminal populations."[32] Because the concept of mental abnormality is so vague, it cannot serve as the foundation for judicial decision, prognosis, and treatment.[33] It is a product of daily life, but there is an inherent difficulty, in that its meaning depends on the definition of normality, an even more confusing concept. Because it is easier to define normality in negative terms, most legislatures are content simply to list the cases in which the element of responsibility does not apply, rather than to attempt to define the exact characteristics of normality. The concept of mental abnormality must not, however, be confused with the idea of nonpathological or "normal" abnormality, which some suggest is a product of adolescence or old age. General functional characteristics of the nervous system can be observed in both age groups. Although "normal" abnormality may be distinguished by characteristics similar to those of a pathological abnormality, it is not identical with the latter.

Franz von Liszt made an early attempt to resolve these difficulties in his suggestion that normality simply means capability of being motivated.[34] A similar approach was also suggested by Gustav Aschaffenburg who perceived free will as the ability to be influenced by motives typical of the same period and environment.[35] Actually, Gabriel Tarde first advanced this explanation in his hypothesis of the Law of Imitation.[36] Normality, he believed, is founded upon personal identity (*l'identité personnelle*) and social similarity (*la similitude sociale*).

Whereas Liszt's definition may distinguish the mental patient from his "normal" counterpart, the capability of being motivated may still be associated with abnormal motivations and with some behavior that is not and cannot be regarded as "normal." The motivation of a murderer diverges sharply from that of the noncriminal. Similarly, the persistent offender's motivation appears to be abnormal because the majority of the population does not engage in repeated crime as a way of life. The murderer or persistent offender, who is abnormally motivated, is thus usually not mentally ill, but it is questionable whether or not he is fully responsible. Despite the confusion surrounding this type of causal explanation, criminologists and psychologists have continued to try to explain crime in terms of mental illness or abnormality. Henry H. Goddard, for example, suggested that feeble-mindedness or low-grade mentality causes criminality.[37] L. D. Zeleny found in 1933 that the ratio of mental deficiency among criminals to that among law-abiding citizens is only 1.2 to 1,[38] but various thinkers even today have nevertheless related mental abnormality to criminal behavior.

If mental abnormality is accepted as a general explanation of crime or if inability to be motivated is recognized as the criterion of abnormality, some rather absurd conclusions may result. The Hungarian uprising in 1956 demonstrated that a mass of people, "unmotivated" according to Communist theories, committed "crimes" in the course of the revolt against the regime. Yet these "crimes" were products of mental anguish and an abnormal quest for freedom. The problem of the persistent offender transcends the limitations of the explanation. Aschaffenburg recognized the defects in his definition and maintained that it does not apply to criminal recidivism. Consequently, he combined the concept of normality with that of responsiveness to punishment.

Paul Boncour, who believed that hereditary or acquired morbid influences result in intellectual or moral *constitutional* defects, suggested the classic definition of infantile abnormality to the Montpellier Congress in 1944.[39] Frequently associated with physical defects, mental defects lead to diminished ability to adapt to the regular environment. Although this approach does not apply to *retarded* children and attempts to relate mental illness to its social symptoms, it also excludes from the concept of abnormality those mental disturbances that are not expressed in social maladjustments.

The concepts of normality and abnormality are products of comparative evaluation. Each day the terms "abnormal" and "normal" are used to describe the behavior of a person, the size of a building, the speed of a car, or the sales of a business. In these instances the comparison is made in relation to some previously established standard. If a situation is abnormal, it may simply be unusual, a deviation from type. Mental abnormality may also involve comparison of the objective reality perceived by the "normal" mind with the subjective unreality perceived by the "sick" mind. If the mind mirrors the realities of the outer world, it is regarded as normal, but, if it seriously distorts them, it is quickly diagnosed as abnormal. If "social similarity" refers to the realities of the social environment and "identity of the person" to their reflection in the mind, Tarde's hypothesis assumes particular importance. Although knowledge of individual normality allows the evaluator to predict probable behavior, a mentally ill person is rarely predictable because his mind has limited or no contact with objective reality. Although a psychiatrist may predict some of the actions and reactions of a mentally ill person, he bases any statements about behavior on the calculated symptoms of the illness. Both the mentally normal and the mentally abnormal person may, however, reveal typical behavior patterns.

Edmund Mezger, following the lead of Tarde, believed that "personal adequacy" is the basic element of normality.[40] In cases of abnormality there is constant tension between the "free" will and both the interior biopsychical organism and the exterior social environment, as a consequence of personal inadequacy. A deficient biopsychical organism with a mental abnormality undermines the free will and paralyzes the evaluative functioning of the socioethical personality, which is charged with the responsibility of guiding the free will to resist pressures toward delinquency and crime. Because the socioethical personality has lost contact with external reality socioethical resistance crumbles before factors encouraging delinquency or crime. The way is thus opened to crime and delinquency pressures both from *without* (because reality cannot be evaluated by the free will) and from *within* (because unreality rules the decisions of the free will). In the absence of a functioning socioethical resistance, internal and external pressures toward delinquency and crime encourage the free will to take delinquent and criminal decisions. In such situations the individual's internal signaling apparatus is either inactive or operating with only limited efficiency.

Many of the shortcomings of present-day criminal justice result from the seventeenth-century philosophy and the eighteenth-century psychology of criminal law.[41] Operating without adequate knowledge of the psychic processes and functioning of the brain, thinkers proposed theories that were subject to modification by later discoveries. A mentally ill person among the barbarous tribes in earlier periods was viewed as a near-saint because people believed that he spoke with the gods. In ancient Egypt and China the mentally ill were believed to have prophetic power; confused and jumbled talk served as a basis for predictions. So common was this point of view that even Immanuel Kant suggested that the faculty of philosophy rather than that of medical science should deal with the problem of abnormality. His point of view did not, however, prevail. As the explanations of psychiatry and neurology replaced those of descriptive psychology, progress became marked. Psychosomatic dualism replaced psychological monism. Actual mental reflection of the external world came more nearly to approximate man's understanding of the function of the mind.

Although much progress toward clarifying some of the earlier unknowns has been made in recent years, modern criminologists, psychologists, and psychiatrists are still somewhat confused about the meaning and significance of abnormality in relation to delinquency and crime and about the most valid diagnostic categories of mental disorder. Sutherland and Cressey included mental defectives, psychotics, postencephalitic personalities, psychopaths, and people with other deviations in their discussion of "psychopathy and crime."[42] Hentig suggested that abnormal criminals suffer from "mental disorders," including insanity, general paresis, paranoia, hysterical conditions, psychopathies, and mental deficiency.[43] M. J. Sethna believed that mental conditions and ailments include feeble-mindedness, dementia praecox, paresis, paranoia, melancholia, hypomania, chorea, cerebral injuries, amnesic fugue, and hysteria.[44] Even Cavan referred to "criminals who are seriously maladjusted"; catalogued such psychoses as schizophrenia, manic-depressive psychosis, involutional melancholia, and paranoia; and cited the criminal implications of psychoneurosis and psychopathy.[45] James C. Coleman,[46] however, noted the scheme developed by the American Psychiatric Association, which established two central groups: *disorders of psychogenic origin,* subgrouped into transient situational disorders, psychoneurotic disorders, psychophysiological disorders, automatic and visceral disorders, functional psychoses, and personality disorders; and *disorders associated with organic brain disturbance,* subgrouped into acute and chronic brain disorders. There is also perhaps a third, independent main category, mental deficiency.[47] The English Mental Health Act of 1959, which essentially embodied the recommendations of the Royal Commission on the Law Relating to Mental Illness and Mental Deficiency, recognized the problem of "mental health" and identified four categories of mental disorder, including mental disorder, subnormality, severe subnormality, and psychopathic disorder. Although the situation remains highly confused, the following division of the remainder of the chapter between discussion of psychotic delinquents and criminals and discussion of psychopathic delinquents and criminals has the merit of simplicity.

Psychotic Delinquents and Criminals

Mental illness and neurological illness are not identical. Although neurological illnesses may cause potential disorder throughout the central nervous system while leaving the brain cortex intact, mental illness primarily affects the cortex while leaving the mechanical functioning of the central nervous system operational.

The classification or even listing of psychoses is not an easy task. Any such grouping may be criticized because of disagreement on the exact dimensions of the problem. In some cases the causes of the psychoses can be quickly diagnosed; in others the illnesses seem without cause. Treatment of psychoses is also difficult and still in an exploratory stage, based more often on experiment than knowledge of causation. Most psychoses are resistant to treatment. If delinquent or criminal trends appear among the general symptoms of psychosis, the problem is complicated further. Schizophrenia, paranoia, manic-depressive psychosis and involutional psychosis, all important functional psychoses, reflect less contact with reality and threaten personality decomposition that may be expressed in delinquency and crime. In all cases, *delusions* (false beliefs without proof) and *hallucinations* (false auditory or visual perceptions without external stimuli) are typical symptoms and may easily lead individuals to delinquent or criminal conduct.

Schizophrenia is not only one of the most frequent functional psychoses; it is also one of the most mysterious.[48] Because of its complex syndrome it may be deceptive and misleading in its early phases or in mild cases. Laymen consequently tend to think that all eccentric, strange, or cranky people are schizophrenic. Generally declining interest, loss of aspiration, withdrawal from the environment, emotional indifference, preoccupation with spiritual or abstract issues, apathy, and dreaminess are typical symptoms that may later develop into delusions and hallucinations. Although these symptoms vary in degree, they are often accompanied by other signs, including stupor or violent excitement.

Although the average ages of hospitalized male and female schizophrenics are thirty and thirty-four respectively, schizophrenia may also appear in childhood. Childhood schizophrenia, usually a female illness, is a product of personality organization, which can be present at any age.

Excessive withdrawal from people, happiness in isolation, unrestrained aggressiveness, and distorted thought processes may signal failure of personality development through schizophrenia. The typical profile of a schizophrenic reveals a division of psychological elements. Although one part seems to be perfectly oriented to existing reality, the other appears out of touch with it and is not controllable. Schizophrenics may therefore be tactful, gentle, affectionate, and apparently normal part of the time yet later reveal extreme delusions, brutal ideas, distorted values, or amazing eccentricities. A schizophrenic may be disoriented, stand outside the world in his thoughts, refuse to allow insight into his sick mind, and appear unpredictable in terms of potential delinquency and crime.

Although *paranoia* rarely appears as an independent psychosis, it is often associated with the other major psychoses, especially schizophrenia.[49] Although it can cause personality disorders independently, paranoiacs are rarely hospitalized. Feelings of persecution or ideas of grandeur often mark their delusions, which may lead to extreme self-involvement and to subsequent conflicts with the social environment. The conflicts may be expressed in deviance. A paranoiac, a show-off, a megalomaniac, and a person actually hunted by others may reveal similar symptoms, making diagnosis of simple cases extremely difficult.

Manic-depressive reaction[50] may take many forms ranging from hypomania to highly irritable, delirious, and violent behavior. Although the manic phase is characterized by degrees of elation and extreme psychomotor activity, the depressive phase ranges from less complex forms to stupor with psychomotor retardation. In the circular form of this psychosis the patient swings from one extreme to another. Complete stability often appears between cycles. Delinquent and criminal potentials are especially enhanced during the manic and depressive periods.

Involutional psychosis rarely, if ever, appears in children or juveniles but is usually found among women between forty-five and fifty-five and among men between fifty-five and sixty-five. Its characteristic symptoms include depression marked by some agitation.

All psychoses involve departures from reality and delusions, including auditory or visual hallucinations in some cases. As disorganization and personality disintegration restrict the person's ability to follow social norms, the delusional elements in his thoughts and values press him toward their violation.

Psychopathic Delinquents and Criminals

Although psychotics generally have lost contact with reality, psychopaths, often called "sociopathic personalities," do not suffer the same loss. The psychopath's contact with reality casts major doubts on classification of this group as "abnormal." Not only is the definition of psychopathy in dispute,[51] but its specific content also includes a wide variety of mental disorders and personality difficulties that cannot be conveniently grouped elsewhere. Therefore the term or classification "psychopath" has become a "diagnostic catch-all."[52] The English Mental Health Act of 1959 defines psychopathic disorder as a persistent disorder or disability of mind, possibly including subnormal intelligence, which results in abnormally aggressive or seriously irresponsible conduct and requires medical treatment. Several definitions of psychopathy identify it with the absence of adequate socialization, rather than with delinquency or crime, and therefore it is worthy of pardon and understanding. Coleman, for example, referred to "disturbed interpersonal relations and social insensitivity," and suggests that they are not classifiable as mentally defective, neurotic, or psychotic because they are *ethically* or *morally* underdeveloped and cannot follow the social code of behavior.[53] Similarly, Donald R. Taft suggests a substitute label like "chronically unsocialized" for the label "psychopath."[54]

The vagueness and uncertainty of the definition of psychopathy may originate in the difficulty of systematizing its symptoms. The inconsistency and absence of objective standards have been well described by Sutherland and Cressey, who suggested that "a person may be a psychopath or not, depending upon the preconceptions of the person making the examination."[55] Robert M. Lindner and Robert V. Seliger were of the opinion that the clinical psychopath "can be readily distinguished from all the other types" and that psychiatrists "learn by experience to recognize the psychopath."[56] Harry Elmer Barnes and Negley K. Teeters suggested that psychopathy cannot be "explained along conventional lines."[57]

Among the commonly accepted symptoms are extremely self-centered general behavior, which may drive the psychopath to almost merciless conduct if his own supposed interest is in question; indifference to others' goals; great impatience in his efforts to reach his own ends; and particularly undisciplined and unrestrained behavior. His inability to accept an ordinary life pattern is not caused, however, by the fact that he is "chronically unsocialized" or a "rebel without a cause."[58] Such interpretations, as Sutherland and Cressey concluded, are no better than the old concept of "moral imbecile," which was only slowly relinquished years ago.[59] Because the general origin and causes of psychoses are not sufficiently known and the causes of psychopathy are almost entirely unknown, the psychopath is "without a cause." Yet psychopathy on one hand and delinquency and crime on the other are two very different problems. The latter are problems of socialization and other social processes, and psychopathy is a pathological deviation from socioethical normality.

Abnormality and Responsibility

Only at the end of the eighteenth century, largely thanks to the efforts of such humanists as Voltaire, Cesare Beccaria, and Filangieri, did definitions of at least obvious mental illness come to exclude concepts of criminal responsibility. Previously criminal law had not distinguished between guilt and responsibility. Furthermore responsibility had been applied not only to the individual perpetrator but also to his family.[60] Even though early legislative and penal thought assumed that crime can originate in mental illness and that mental illness can also produce crime, the basic foundation of law and punishment was individual responsibility for conduct. Once the principle that insane criminals are not liable for their crimes was established, however, the problem of differentiating between criminal responsibility and excusable conduct became critical. After various attempts at definition and clarification, the so-called "M'Naghten rule" established in 1843 an operational principle that still serves as the authoritative English and American guide in deciding the insanity of criminals. First applied in the case of Daniel M'Naghten, a psychotic with delusions who had attempted to murder Sir Robert Peel but had actually murdered Peel's secretary by mistake, it declares that the sanity of the offender is to be presumed in criminal proceedings unless the existence of a mental disorder that precludes the defendant from differentiating between right and wrong is proved. In 1954 the federal court of appeal for the District of Columbia brushed aside the M'Naghten rule, and in the case of Monte Durham shifted the emphasis from "right and wrong" to the existence of "mental disease or defect."

Although most European legal codes had long excused mentally abnormal persons from criminal liability,[61] such exemptions had been granted only if the offender had been insane at the time of the commission of the crime. If he had been sane at the time that he made the criminal decision but had later developed insanity as a consequence of his acts, he was held responsible for them. On the other hand, disorder or an unconscious state was accepted to a lesser extent as a defense in cases involving *actio libera in causa,* in which the criminal used himself as a tool to commit his crime while in an unconscious state. This legal variation represented a basic recognition that the intent of the act might have been sane and deliberate, although the person might have placed himself in an irresponsible state by drinking alcohol, for example, in order to commit the crime.

At the turn of the century a growing recognition of the category of youthful crime, later called "juvenile delinquency," led to development of the concept of *diminished* responsibility. Because the child's mind is not yet developed to the level of an adult mind, attempts were made to take account of this fact in legal procedure. Based upon clinical recognition that many mentally disordered or disturbed people do not suffer complete mental abnormality even though they are outside the limits of normality, the concept of diminished responsibility offered a third alternative to the earlier operational concepts of total insanity and full responsibility. Consequently, pleas of diminished responsibility were increasingly accepted in cases involving neurasthenia, epilepsy, and hysteria.

Actually the principle of diminished responsibility had been embodied in several legal systems long before it achieved general acceptance. The Prussian Landrecht of 1794 mentioned the possibility that responsibility can be both increased and decreased.[62] The 1751 Bavarian Criminal Code[63] similarly mentioned "those whose mind is only half way mad" (*Jene, denen der Verstand nur halb verrückt ist*). The 1840 Criminal Code of Braunschweig prescribed milder punishment for those not totally exempt from responsibility but whose minds were nevertheless "obscured,"[64] and the 1833 Greek Criminal Code clearly provided lighter punishment for those whose mental normality had not been completely lost but only considerably disturbed.[65] The Danish Criminal Code of 1866 recognized mental states in which normality is decreased.[66] Similar recognition was embodied in the Russian Criminal Code of 1885 and the Finnish Criminal Code of 1889.

Perhaps the first forum at which recognition of diminished responsibility was strongly supported was the 1887 German Psychiatric Congress in Frankfurt, at which scholars noted that lighter punishment alone cannot solve the problem of limited mental abnormality. A further significant advance occurred at the 1902 Congress of Lawyers at Dresden, at which the respected criminologists Liszt and van Calker submitted pertinent resolutions. The Seventh International Penitentiary Congress in Budapest (1905) stimulated the greatest debate and led to world-wide acceptance of the concept of diminished responsibility. Acceptance did not, however, mean agreement on its limitations. Although further attempts were made to define the criminal responsibility of abnormal offenders, to match punishment to the criminal by trying to cure him of his abnormality, and to introduce "curative penalties," little was done in practice.

Part of the difficulty rested on the fact that a concept of "diminished" or "incomplete" mental capability involves more than the mere lessening of penalties. Prescription of a five-year prison term for robbery committed by a sane person and two and a half years for robbery by an epileptic, for example, fails even to touch the problem. If deterrence or retribution is the goal of punishment, no concept of diminished mental responsibility can justify a diminished penalty. If reform or correction is the goal, however, *different* measures should be instituted for those who need different reformative, corrective, or curative treatment. Juvenile delinquents probably represent the only category of deviants for whom sanctions and punishments that take into account personality development and state of mind have currently been formulated.

■ *Alcoholism*

Although a disproportionate number of American delinquent and criminal acts occur under the influence of alcohol, it does not specifically create potential or actual delinquency. Its impact depends partly upon the amount and kind of beverage consumed and upon the individual's tolerance for it. Although the Frenchman consumes a glass of wine with his meal and the Hungarian peasant often starts his day with a drink of brandy, French and Hungarian crime rates show little specific relation to alcohol use. If crime is related to alcohol consumption, however, this relationship may take two different causal forms: Alcohol may be a *special originator* of delinquency or crime, as in the case of a particular crime committed after a single acute consumption of alcohol, or it may be a *general originator* of crime, as in the case of crime arising from chronic drinking. A party, a birthday celebration, New Year's Eve, celebration of job success, or any of many similar occasions may lead to acute consumption of alcohol. Distress, loneliness, insecurity, job failure, and lack of social approval may produce patterns of such consumption. Although *positive* situations generally provoke acute alcohol consumption, *negative* situations encourage chronic indulgence patterns.

Acute intoxication may neutralize, suppress, or even paralyze individual socioethical resistance and render the drinker defenseless or unprepared to fight pressures toward delinquency or crime, which thus gain access to the "free" will and dominate ensuing decisions. Although the full effect of alcohol on the functioning brain is not clearly understood, intoxication does cause a temporary personality change and disorientation, which occasionally take the form of considerably lowered apperception and recollection, increased irritability and excitability, and delusions and hallucinations. Loss of self-control, blurring of responsibility, and failure to consider the consequences of the act are typical of acute intoxication and enhance the possibility of delinquency and crime. Crimes like embezzlement, theft, and bank robbery, which require intellectual effort, are infrequently committed under the influence of alcohol. Murder, assault, reckless driving, and public drunkenness itself are the most common forms of alcoholic offense. Although the nonchronic drinker may regret his act and may even deny his intoxicated behavior upon arrest, an offender may decide upon his crime while sober and then place himself in an intoxicated state in order to facilitate its performance.[67]

Although no definite answer can be given to the question of whether chronic alcoholics begin as occasional drinkers or as excessive and persistent drinkers, occasional or even "normal" drinking is more readily accepted in some societies than in others. Albert D. Ullman, for example, found that many societies regard even potentially addictive behavior as a vice and therefore reserve drinking for an age group that presumably is able to be "safely vicious." In other societies and groups, however, children are introduced to alcoholic beverages at an early age and therefore harmful attitudes are not formed before actual experience of drinking. Ethnic and other subcultural groups vary between viewing drinking as a vice and viewing it as a normal habit like eating potatoes or smoking cigarettes. Ullman believed that unsanctioned behavior produces anxiety and guilt. The ambivalence produced by a conflict of values, he hypothesized, ultimately leads to unsanctioned drinking and to higher incidence of alcoholism.[68] Although alcoholism was previously attributed to inherited or constitutional weaknesses, Ullman and other researchers have placed greater emphasis upon social-psychological personality disturbances and prevalent group values in explaining the lower age of alcohol addiction.

■ Drug Addiction

Although drug addiction appears at first to be similar to alcoholism, because of the characteristic dependence of the victim upon drugs or alcohol, it is quite different. Alcohol is sold freely in nearly every society, but traffic in narcotics is everywhere prohibited. Only recently, however, have international agencies begun to cooperate in control of this traffic. And only after serious international disputes over continuing the narcotics trade was action taken to restrict the sale and distribution of drugs at the turn of the century. Earlier competition for the opium markets had unleashed wars between Britain and China in 1839 and again in 1856. Indochina first attempted in 1883 to arouse international public opinion against narcotics addiction and the drug traffic. Although Portugal reached an agreement with China in 1887 and England tried to settle the narcotics problem in the Far East in 1906, it was soon clear that drug addiction and narcotics traffic could not be treated as a domestic problem if any significant control were to be achieved. The need for international collaboration prompted President Theodore Roosevelt to call an international conference under the title of International Opium Commission, which met in Shanghai February 1–26, 1909. Although the enthusiastic American Episcopal Bishop Charles H. Brent pressed for a cooperative agreement to control the narcotics traffic, no decision was reached. President William Howard Taft called a new conference at the Hague on December 1, 1911; it discussed the relevant drug problem for two months. The International Opium Convention, a conference agreement of January 23, 1912, was the first step toward international cooperation in destruction and control of narcotic drugs. The second and third opium conferences, both held at the Hague, furthered this development. After World War I the League of Nations took organizational responsibility for the problem and convened its first conference in Geneva in 1931; since then a continuous international effort has been directed toward the fight against addiction and the narcotics traffic, an effort lately directed by the United Nations.[69]

As a result of such early efforts, international conventions and agreements and national laws (like the American Harrison Narcotic Law of 1914 and its several amendments, including the Narcotic Control Act of 1956) provided punishments for illegal possession of narcotics and consumption for other than medical purposes. Although various international conferences, in efforts to limit the traffic in narcotics to medical and scientific needs, have clarified the concept of "illicit traffic," both international conferences and national legislation have neglected to define the narcotics addict. The United States, for example, forbids the habitual use of habit-forming narcotics that endanger public health and individual responsi-bility.[70] Costa Rica distinguishes between the use of opium and other narcotics with and without medical prescription.[71] Germany cites the in-crease in drug consumption as the cause for its prohibition,[72] and Switzer-land[73] and Turkey[74] simply referred to the habitual use of drugs. Venezuela, however, permits the use of such drugs only in cases of illness.[75]

The problem of drug addiction, as distinguished from alcoholism, is less one of habitual intake and more one of unrestricted drug use which generally leads very quickly to total dependence on ever-increasing amounts. Although some people require larger amounts and more frequent use to become addicted, others may become dependent on the drug after taking a small dose upon a single occasion. Because potential drug addic-tion depends upon the psychological and biological characteristics of the individual, it is largely impossible to define the volume of consumption of a particular drug necessary to cause addiction. Even the medical use of narcotics may involve the patient in addiction if precautions are not taken. Generally speaking, anyone may become a narcotics addict if he starts to use a habit-forming drug. Alfred R. Lindesmith[76] and Sutherland and Cressey[77] noted, for example, that no distinction can be made between psychopathic and normal people in the genesis of drug addiction. Although anyone, regardless of his personality traits, may become a habitual victim of narcotics, most narcotics addicts begin with personality disorganization. Whereas juveniles and young adults may start drug use out of curiosity, they frequently also begin in response to pressures from peers. William H. Haines and John J. McLaughlin, for example, found that young Chi-cago addicts were introduced to narcotics by social groups to which they were seeking to conform.[78] Addiction, Richard A. Cloward and Lloyd E. Ohlin suggested, may promote acceptance and status in the delinquent subculture: "The drug addict wins deference by his mastery of the re-sources and knowledge for maintaining or increasing the esoteric experi-ence of his 'kick.' "[79]

In recent years the habitual use of drugs has been popularly blamed upon the existence of social barriers.[80] Cloward and Ohlin, for example, suggested that drug use by juveniles results from their "double failure" to reach culturally approved goals by legitimate means and to find illegiti-mate alternatives to reach these goals because of their "internalized pro-hibitions" and from their opportunity to use drugs.[81] Although they hypothesized that these members of the lower class and of the Negro population develop a "retreatist subculture" (retreating to narcotic addic-tion), no evidence supports their implied assumption that drug addiction is less prevalent in the upper classes.[82] Retreatism does not necessarily result from frustrations of social aspirations; rather it may result from any negative situation in which the individual dissociates himself from reality and retreats to the illusionistic world of narcotics. Anyone, regardless of class, can indulge in drug addiction. The use of LSD and marijuana by teenagers and young adults in the 1960s is an expression of a similar phenomenon.

Because different drugs have different effects, users' dependence upon habit-forming drugs is their only common factor. *Opium derivatives* lead to relief of tension, extreme relaxation, even euphoria. A decreased sexual desire, drowsiness, and confusion about time and space also appear, largely as aftereffects. The addict may crave a new dose in order to escape extreme discomfort in the aftereffects of the preceding doses. If he undergoes withdrawal, his symptoms may be even more severe, taking the form of deep depression, temperature disturbances, tremors, and even hallucinations. *Morphine* produces unrealistic ambitions, unusual self-confidence, and extreme irresponsibility. *Cocaine* may also lead to euphoria, although headaches and dizziness are often the initial reactions. Increased vitality is followed by physical decline. Although cocaine causes sexual tension in females, it decreases male sexual potential. Loss of self-respect and participation in immoral acts are typical results of addiction. The craving for the next dose may prompt the addict to obtain it through socially disapproved means. Although the use of *marijuana* may lead to the use of other narcotics, in itself it is said to be nonaddictive. As it produces extreme self-confidence, a pleasant sensation of detachment from social norms, and a lessening of moral inhibitions, marijuana or its stronger counterpart *hashish* has been variously prohibited or accepted in international society. In addition to these main forms of narcotics, a number of other *barbiturates, hallucinogens,* and other habit-forming drugs that influence human behavior receive differential acceptance throughout the world. Most habit-forming narcotics, however, lead to temporary, periodic, or continued mental incapacity; loss of intellectual and physical energy; disorientation; decline in self-control; deterioration of character; morbid impulses; and other similar symptoms of abnormal or disintegrated personality. Because maintenance of physical equilibrium generally requires constant doses, only medical intervention can bring the habit to an end.

The connection between drug addiction on one hand and delinquency and crime on the other is open to debate. Delinquencies and crimes committed *for* narcotics are fully understood, but delinquency and criminality *as a result* of narcotics have not been thoroughly investigated. Like alcoholics, drug addicts also commit criminal offenses (forgery of medical prescriptions and theft) in order to satisfy their craving and consequently may follow socially disapproved life styles. There is some doubt that addicts commit delinquencies or crimes independent of their craving for drugs, but they are more susceptible to delinquency and criminal pressures than are nonaddicts. The addict, Meyer H. Diskind argued, is no problem in a drug-free environment such as a hospital or prison, but "the addict must fight his battle in the community."[83] As this battle must be fought with incomplete awareness of the full capability of the socioethical personality, weakened socioethical resistance, and lessened sense of social responsibility, sometimes complicated by delusions and hallucinations, the addict is handicapped in facing delinquency and crime pressures. In this context he may be a potential delinquent or criminal. Although the exact degree of adolescent participation in drug and marijuana usage is still undocumented, the ready availability of narcotics in urban and near-urban areas indicates that the problem will continue into the future.[84]

NOTES

1. A. E. Clark-Kennedy, *Human Disease* (London: 1957), p. 7.

2. Cyril Burt, *The Young Delinquent* (London: 1938).

3. Sheldon Glueck and Eleanor T. Glueck, *After-Conduct of Discharged Offenders* (London: 1945).

4. Albert Irk, *Kriminologia*, Vol. 1. *Kriminalaetiologia* (Budapest: 1912).

5. Emile Laurent, *Le Criminel* (Paris: 1908).

6. Hans von Hentig, *The Criminal and His Victim: Studies in the Sociobiology of Crime* (New Haven: 1948), pp. 64–67.

7. Victor Nelson, *Prison Days and Nights* (Boston: 1933).

8. Hentig, *op. cit.*, pp. 79–94; and Edwin H. Sutherland and Donald R. Cressey, *Principles of Criminology* (6th ed.; New York: 1960), p. 106.

9. Hentig, "Die Kriminelle Tendenzen der Blinden," *Schweitz. Zeitschrift für Strafrecht*, 40 (1927).

10. *Census of the Commonwealth of Massachusetts, 1905* (Boston: 1909).

11. Hentig, *The Criminal and His Victim*, p. 84.

12. "Endocrine" is of Greek origin; *endo* means "within" or "internal," and *krinein* means "to separate."

13. Max G. Schlapp, "Behavior and Gland Disease," *Journal of Heredity*, 15 (1924).

14. Schlapp and Edward H. Smith, *The New Criminology* (New York: 1928).

15. Adolf Lenz, *Grundriss der Kriminalbiologie* (Berlin: 1927).

16. Louis Berman, *The Glands Regulating Personality* (New York: 1921); and Berman, *New Creations in Human Beings* (New York: 1938).

17. Karl Birnbaum, *Kriminalpsychopathologie und Psychobiologische Verbrecherkunde* (2nd ed.; Berlin: 1931), pp. 203–204; and Birnbaum, "Persönlichkeitsforschung," in Alexander Elster and Heinrich Lingemann, eds., *Handwörterbuch der Kriminologie und der Anderen Strafrechtlichen Hilfswissenschaften*, 2 (Berlin: 1934), p. 270.

18. Matthew Molitch, "Endocrine Disturbances in Behavior Problems," *American Journal of Psychiatry* (March 1937).

19. Frank Tannenbaum, *Crime and the Community* (New York: 1938).

20. R. G. Hoskins, *Endocrinology* (New York: 1941).

21. M. F. Ashley-Montagu, "The Biologist Looks at Crime," *The Annals of the American Academy of Political and Social Science*, 217 (September 1941), 46–57.

22. Ludwig Seitz, *Wachstum, Geschlecht und Fortpflanzung* (Berlin: 1939); Franz

Exner, *Kriminalbiologie in ihren Grundzügen* (Hamburg: 1939); and Stephen Schafer, *A Nök Kriminalitásánck Arányairól* (Budapest: 1947).

23. W. M. Court Brown, "Genetics and Crime: The Problem of XXY, XY/XXY, XXYY AND XYY Males," unpublished paper (Edinburgh: 1967), p. 3; and *Medical Research Council Annual Report: April 1966–March 1967* (London: 1967), pp. 38–42.

24. P. A. Jacobs, M. Brunton, M. M. Melville, R. P. Brittain, and W. F. McClement, "Aggressive Behavior, Mental Subnormality, and the XYY Male," *Nature*, 208 (1965), 1351. It should be noted that it is not yet known how frequent XYY males are at birth among the general population.

25. Jacobs and J. A. Strong, "A Case of Human Intersexuality Having a Possible XXY Sex Determining Mechanism," *Nature*, 183 (1959), 302.

26. S. Muldal and C. H. Ockey, "The 'Double' Male: A New Chromosome Constitution in Klinefelter's Syndrome," *Lancet*, 2 (1960), 492.

27. M. D. Casey, L. J. Segall, D. R. K. Street, and C. E. Blank, "Sex Chromosome Abnormalities in Two State Hospitals for Patients Requiring Special Security," *Nature*, 209 (1966), 641.

28. Casey, Blank, Street, Segall, J. H. McDougall, P. J. McCrath, and J. L. Skinner, "YY Chromosomes and Anti-Social Behavior," *Lancet*, 2 (1966), 859.

29. W. H. Price and P. P. Whatmore, "Behaviour Disorders and Patterns of Crime Among XYY Males Identified at a Maximum Security Hospital," *British Medical Journal*, 1 (1967), 533.

30. Ruth Shonle Cavan, *Criminology* (2nd ed.; New York: 1957), p. 229.

31. K. O. Christiansen, *The Social Approach to Prognosis and Treatment of Abnormal and Deviant Offenders* (The Hague: 1960), p. 15.

32. Edwin H. Sutherland and Donald R. Cressey, *Principles of Criminology* (6th ed.; New York: 1960), p. 120. The term "insanity" was used instead of "mental disease" in the fourth edition (New York: 1947), p. 106.

33. Fourth International Criminological Congress, September 10, 1960, The Hague.

34. Franz von Liszt, *Lehrbuch des Deutschen Strafrechts* (Berlin: 1905).

35. A. Hoche, Gustav Aschaffenburg, H. W. Gruhle, and J. Lange, *Handbuch der Gerichtlichen Psychiatrie* (3rd ed.; Berlin: 1934).

36. Gabriel Tarde, *La Philosophie pénale* (Paris: 1892).

37. Henry H. Goddard, *Human Efficiency and Levels of Intelligence* (Princeton, N.J.: 1920); Goddard, *Juvenile Delinquency* (New York: 1921).

38. L. D. Zeleny, "Feeble-Mindedness and Criminal Conduct, *American Journal of Sociology* (January 1933).

39. Paul Boncour, *Annales Internationales de criminologie*, 1 (Paris: 1962), 65.

40. Edmund Mezger, *Deutsches Strafrecht: Ein Grundriss* (Berlin: 1938).

41. Peter Brett, *An Inquiry Into Criminal Guilt* (London: 1963).

42. Sutherland and Cressey, *op. cit.*, pp. 117–137.

43. Hentig, *op. cit.*, pp. 123–187.

44. M. J. Sethna, *Society and the Criminal* (Bombay: 1952), pp. 134–137.

45. Cavan, *op. cit.*, pp. 229–250.

46. James C. Coleman, *Abnormal Psychology and Modern Life* (2nd ed.; Chicago: 1956), pp. 17–19.

47. American Psychiatric Association, *Diagnostic and Statistical Manual: Mental Disorders* (Washington, D.C.: 1952).

48. The term "schizophrenia" (meaning "split mind," or splitting of the personality) was first used in 1911 by the Swiss psychiatrist Eugène Bleuler, who substituted it for Emil Kraepelin's original term "dementia praecox" (mental disturbance); in fact, in this illness the personality is not split but disintegrated.

49. "Paranoia" is one of the oldest psychiatric terms, used even by the Greeks and Romans to label practically all mental disturbances.

50. Manic-depressive reactions were originally classified by Hippocrates; Kraepelin, however, first used this term to describe the type.

51. P. W. Prew, "The Concept of Psychopathic Personality," in J. M. Hunt, ed., *Personality and the Behavior Disorders* (New York: 1944).

52. Walter C. Reckless, *The Crime Problem* (2nd ed.; New York: 1955), p. 71.

53. Coleman, *op. cit.*, p. 337.

54. Donald R. Taft, *Criminology* (3rd ed., New York: 1956), p. 128.

55. Sutherland and Cressey, *op. cit.*, p. 125.

56. Robert M. Lindner and Robert V. Seliger, *Handbook of Correctional Psychology* (New York: 1947), pp. 395–396.

57. Harry Elmer Barnes and Negley K. Teeters, *New Horizons in Criminology* (3rd ed.; Englewood Cliffs, N.J.: 1959), p. 105.

58. Lindner, *Rebel Without a Cause* (New York: 1944).

59. Sutherland and Cressey, *op. cit.*, p. 126.

60. Such collective responsibility, in an even more extended form, is also present in the twentieth century in some totalitarian social systems.

61. In 1843, the year of the M'Naghten case, the Hungarian Draft Criminal Code defined insanity as an illness that excludes ability to comprehend culpability.

62. Landrecht, Part II, Chapter 20, paragraph 18.

63. Section I, paragraph 17.

64. Paragraph 60.

65. Paragraph 47.

66. Paragraph 39.

67. *Actio libera in causa*. See also President's Commission on Law Enforcement and Administration of Justice, *Task Force Report: Drunkenness* (Washington, D.C.: 1967).

68. Albert D. Ullman, "Ethnic Differences in the First Drinking Experience," *Social Problems,* 8 (Summer 1960), 45.

69. Schafer, *Narcotic Addiction and the Task of International Criminology* (Budapest: 1946), in Hungarian.

70. No. 672 (January 19, 1929). For a discussion of the problems of narcotics and drug abuse in the United States, see President's Commission, *Task Force Report: Narcotics and Drug Abuse* (Washington, D.C.: 1967).

71. No. 3 (September 29, 1930).

72. Law of May 31, 1870, amended in November 24, 1933.

73. Criminal Code of December 21, 1937.

74. Criminal Code, No. 765 (March 1, 1926).

75. Law of July 9, 1934.

76. Alfred R. Lindesmith, *Opiate Addiction* (Bloomington, Indiana: 1947).

77. Sutherland and Cressey, *op. cit.*, p. 132.

78. William H. Haines and John J. McLaughlin, "Narcotic Addicts in Chicago," *American Journal of Psychiatry*, 108 (1952), 755–757.

79. Richard A. Cloward and Lloyd E. Ohlin, *Delinquency and Opportunity: A Theory of Delinquent Gangs* (New York: 1960), p. 10.

80. See Herold Finestone, "Cats, Kicks, and Color," *Social Problems*, 5 (July 1957), 3–13; D. M. Wilner, Eva Rosenfeld, R. S. Lee, D. L. Gerard, and Isidor Chein, "Heroin Use and Street Gangs," *Journal of Criminal Law, Criminology and Police Science*, 48 (November–December 1957), 399–409; and Cloward and Ohlin, *op. cit.*, pp. 178–186.

81. Cloward and Ohlin, *op. cit.*, pp. 178–181. See also Ernest Harms, *Drug Addiction in Youth* (Oxford: 1965).

82. See the discussion of the delinquent gang. See also Chein, *The Road to H* (New York: 1964).

83. Meyer H. Diskind, "New Horizons in the Treatment of Narcotic Addiction," *Federal Probation*, 24 (December 1960), 62.

84. The problems involved in formulating a future policy on this question are recorded in Richard H. Blum, "Drugs, Dangerous Behavior and Social Policy," President's Commission, *Task Force Report: Narcotics and Drug Abuse*, pp. 64–79.

Part Five

LAW ENFORCEMENT AND DELINQUENCY CONTROL

Chapter 17

■ *The Role and Structure of the Police*

■ *The Role of the Police*

The traditional police system, long outmoded, has been held by many people, especially minority groups, to threaten their existence. Because the public and members of law-enforcement agencies have held each other in mutual distrust and suspicion, the security of the community has often suffered.[1] Parents have frequently attempted to halt their children's disobedience, mischief, or naughtiness by threatening them with strict punishment or the police. As the policeman's role has largely been one of enforcement, adults have viewed him with discomfort and fear rather than with respect. Although police-community relations have improved, antagonism is still common throughout the country today.[2]

The policeman is the front-line defense of law and order, but how he conducts this defense, carries out his duties, and behaves toward all people largely depends upon his own interpretation of his function.[3] The policeman does not represent final justice, but because he is the first and most crucial judge of delinquency or crime he may use or abuse his power, according to his understanding of his own role and that of modern law enforcement in general. The police have a delegated power to safeguard the security of group members, and the prevention of delinquency and the rehabilitation of delinquents generally, though not entirely, depend upon the use of this power.

Although the nature of police function will always lead to fear among the public, it is possible to confine such fear to those who have violated social laws or against whom police sanctions seem justified. The police cannot avoid administrative and suppressive duties, which will necessarily arouse antagonism and even hostility among those whose illegitimate behavior provokes suppression. Coercion can, however, easily encompass broader circles if police authority is misused to suppress the delinquent and the criminal rather than delinquency and crime. *Suppression of action or behavior* serves to protect society, prevent delinquency and crime, win respect for the police, and encourage the public to assist in law enforcement. *Suppression of the person,* on the other hand, leads to disrespect and public distrust of the police. Unfortunately, emphasis upon suppression of the person rather than of his conduct may "constitute one of the chief sources of indoctrination in attitudes of disrespect for law."[4]

The prevention of juvenile delinquency and the rehabilitation of delinquents require the flexible application of social rules and appropriate use of police authority. The police officer has a wide variety of choices at his disposal, including simply warning a delinquent, visiting his home, offering to aid the child and his family, referral to an agency other than the juvenile court, and petitioning the juvenile court for judicial procedures. The right choice cannot be made by following rigid rules. If, however, the police officer adequately understands his preventive, protective, and helping role and is well integrated into the community he serves, his choice can be a positive contribution to the struggle against juvenile delinquency. In this context the appropriate use of police authority extends the functions of detection, investigation, and suppression to social treatment and of social control to social participation. Although social participation will not replace social control as a function of the police and detection of delinquency or crime will not be neglected, different attitudes toward the use of authority in questions of delinquency and crime and of the delinquent and the criminal are likely. The growing complexity of culture, however, continually compounds the difficulties of the police as juveniles are increasingly affected by the discoveries and innovations of modern civilization and technology.

Targets of legitimate striving are also targets of delinquency and crime. If technology develops some new convenience, it soon becomes an object of crime. Edwin H. Sutherland and Donald R. Cressey suggest that, "when the police develop an invention for the detection or identification of criminals, the criminals utilize a device to protect themselves."[5] In many instances, however, the product is first used by the delinquent or criminal as a tool or object of delinquency and crime and only later by the police as a device to protect society. As Catherin noted at the turn of the century, the highly praised advantages of civilization may well be actual stimulants to delinquency and crime.[6]

Although civilization and technology are essential to social progress, their fruits are available for either the improvement or the hindrance of the quality of human life, thus increasing the difficulties of the police. The negotiable check, an indispensable tool of commercial life, has become the object of many recent crimes. New crimes involve the misuse of credit cards, a relatively recent commercial innovation. Although the radio has become a basic unit of home entertainment, an invaluable aid to communication, and a tool of law enforcement, it is also an instrument by which potential violators gain information, coordinate complex criminal acts, and ease escape. Even a pair of gloves, which ordinarily serves to protect the wearer against dust or cold weather, can be used by criminals as protection against fingerprinting techniques.[7] The delinquent or criminal use of electricity, the automobile, the airplane, the telephone, automatic services, self-service stores, computers, and an almost endless list of other inventions, devices, and ideas suggests that the fruits of progress quickly become the instruments or objects of delinquency or crime. Pál Angyal notes that even the umbrella has been used for criminal purposes.[8] A burglar who wanted to enter a jewelry shop rented the apartment above it and broke through the floor. In order to avoid unnecessary noise, he first made a little hole, through which he thrust an umbrella, which he then opened to catch the additional debris without the noise it would make falling to the floor. Advances in both modern technology and delinquent and criminal techniques have, however, made even the umbrella obsolete.

As delinquent and criminal have become more skillful, superior police work has become more difficult. Cultural change, technological improvement, and the development of a complex civilization have not resulted in abolition of violence. But, although delinquency continues, it is quite different in kind from previous such violence. Robbery, a form of theft accompanied by threat or violence, was being committed 500 years ago and is still being committed today. Much of the violence of the past, however, makes modern violence seem petty in comparison. Although "fashions in crime"[9] have not changed, the method of commission has been refined. Old delinquent or criminal forms have been replaced by new ones, and techniques have been modified and polished, necessitating similar modifications in enforcement. The police have, however, generally been unable to keep pace with these changes.

Although the processes of culture and technology transform brutality into less savage violence, the relative ease of violence opens the way for more delinquent and criminal acts and increases the task of the law enforcement. "It would seem," the United Nations reported, "that in a general way violence is becoming more and more a feature of juvenile delinquency."[10] Although the improvement of material living conditions cannot be presumed to be a cause of crime, developments in technology have broadened public access to the tools and attitudes of violence. The "know-how" is not only disseminated through television, newspapers, comic books, and paperback thrillers, but the instruments and means of delinquency and crime are also available in increasing quantities to potential offenders. The bow and arrow and the fast horse of the forest brigands of past generations hardly compare with the modern hand gun and automobile. Modern delinquency is so easy that the police are faced with a near-impossible task, and they have only highly limited resources for delinquency and crime control.

■ The Structure of the Police

Special Branches for Delinquency Control

The recognition of juvenile delinquency as a special area of crime provided new impetus for development of specialized juvenile branches in many law-enforcement agencies. The majority of police forces have come to realize that law and order are most effectively furthered by placing prime professional emphasis on the delinquent child, rather than on general violation of laws. "Since there are separate laws for juveniles, there should be," one police document noted, "separate police forces to deal with those who may offend against these laws."[11] Special branches, units, or departments with such names as Crime Prevention Bureau, Juvenile Bureau, Juvenile Division, and Youth Aid Bureau have been developed in order to separate the problem of juvenile delinquency from that of crime. Because the organization of these enforcement branches has been determined by local needs and resources, they differ in size, staff, and administrative structure. Some are fully independent from other branches of the police; others are fully subordinate to the general administration of the law-enforcement agency. Still others have partial administrative freedom in dealing with delinquents. Although officers in these branches are often known as "juvenile counselors," "youth officers" or other similar titles, some have no special designation. In some police jurisdictions the juvenile branch consists of a single police officer who specializes in delinquent cases.

When a "complete" department is responsible for delinquency problems, further division and specialization may occur. It can be divided into investigation and prevention branches. The *investigation branch* processes delinquencies that have already been committed; the *prevention division* works closely with community groups and agencies to restrict the development of local delinquency. Sometimes the prevention section is even divided between general and individual prevention groups. Overall, the investigation section generally resembles the traditional law-enforcement organization, whereas the prevention section is more closely involved with social-work practices.

Participation of Women

The first women were attached to police forces in the United States in 1900, at a time "when large numbers of young women were entering the business life of the community."[12] Many years elapsed, however, between recognition of the special problem of juvenile delinquency and use of policewomen to handle youth problems. In recent years policewomen in many jurisdictions have been assigned to work with boys and girls under the age of puberty. Although the reasons why women seem to be better than men at this work are not clear—perhaps they have some maternal instinct or natural aptitude—both their superior officers and the general public are "unanimous in praising their devotion to duty."[13] Both investigative and preventive enforcement tasks have been successfully accomplished by policewomen, originally among girl delinquents and later among young boys as well. The Fourth Congress of the International Association of Children's Judges (Brussels, 1954), impressed by the record of policewomen, recommended that they should be assigned to cases in which effective surveillance and detection are required, especially when children are victims or witnesses of sexual crimes. Because juvenile treatment philosophy assumes that police work in delinquency cases should incorporate a social-work approach, the use of policewomen has been preferred. Although juvenile law enforcement is presumed to be different from the police work required in adult cases, however, it is a mistake to define this function as merely a form of social welfare.

The International Criminal Police Organization (Interpol), at the twenty-sixth session of its general assembly in Lisbon in 1957 distinguished between normal and special duties performed by female police. The duties of the policewoman or of the autonomous female police units are *normal* when they fulfill tasks comparable to those of their male counterparts. In all other cases their duties are *special*, particularly when male and female police officers perform different functions in a mixed unit or when the tasks allotted to an autonomous female unit are different from those of a comparable mixed or male unit.

The Training of Police Officers

Because work with juvenile delinquency is almost unanimously accepted as a special field of police work, special qualifications and training should be required of officers responsible for prevention and investigation of delinquency. These officers should also possess special aptitudes and attitudes necessary to deal with children's cases. In most jurisdictions they do not, however. Although police departments with special juvenile branches or divisions are able to develop juvenile specialists among their officers, most departments demand no greater qualifications for juvenile officers than for any other police officer. Although certain minimum educational (high school), intelligence (sound), health (good), and physical (height and weight) standards are basic requirements, an understanding of social problems, interest in children and youth, a constructive personality, patience in dealing with juveniles, and expert acquaintance with delinquency and crime problems are also desirable for such police workers. Only a few universities offer special training and diplomas in police work with juvenile delinquency and corrections; (they include the University of California, the University of Southern California, Florida State University,

Michigan State University, Northeastern University, and Southern Illinois University).[14] Current trends suggest more widespread development of such programs in the future, however.

The twenty-fifth session of the general assembly of Interpol in Vienna in 1956 strongly urged special training for police officers whose work is connected with juvenile delinquency and submitted suggestions to the Second U.N. Congress for Crime Prevention. These recommendations called for standardized training for delinquency specialists, with a distinction between those who give and coordinate orders and those who carry them out. Preliminary selection of delinquency officers should be based upon several principles:

> 1. *Officers should be volunteers.* Only those interested in children's problems will be able to devote themselves to the "often thankless tasks" of this specialized branch of the police.
>
> 2. *Officers should be young and in good physical condition.* Age differences and variations in mental capacity make it unwise to employ elderly or inactive officers in law-enforcement branches that handle the delinquency problems.
>
> 3. *Potential officers should be mentally and morally well balanced.* Officers with some form of mental instability or sexual abnormality (like homosexuals or pederasts) should be excluded from service with juveniles. Psychological testing is suggested to screen misfits from such employment and duty.[15]

Officers selected should attend, as a minimum requirement, "beginners' courses" in child psychology, in the causes and forms of juvenile delinquency, in the legal position of the minor, in cooperation with parents and social workers, and in contacts between police and children. Interpol recommended, however, even more thorough training, involving a detailed program of theoretical and practical study in such subjects as pedagogics, general psychology, child psychology, sociology, physiology, criminal law, civil and public law, criminology, physical training, and public relations, for those who want to devote their careers to police work on juvenile delinquency. This curriculum should be offered by specialists who are not necessarily police officers, preferably near a large town where access to the practical dimensions of the problem is available. Supplementary training is also recommended in the form of ten days with a social-welfare department, ten days with a school, ten days with a juvenile court, and two months with a specialized juvenile police unit.

The Contribution of Interpol

The problems of police work in the field of juvenile delinquency have always been of central concern to the International Criminal Police Organization (Interpol), whose goals include general improvement in the efficiency and specialization of law-enforcement agencies and development of international cooperation.[16] The work of women in police forces, for example, was first debated at the third session of the Interpol general assembly in Berlin in 1926. At the fourth general assembly session (1928) a definite stand recommending participation of women in law-enforcement agencies that handle juvenile delinquency problems was taken. Although it was agreed that women can assume responsibility for protection of children and girls who are in danger, this resolution of the Interpol general assembly did not refer to instances in which children are the offenders, rather than the victims.

The seventeenth general assembly meeting at Prague (1948) authorized a study of repressive law enforcement in cases of juvenile delinquency and commissioned a committee of experts from nine countries, including Australia, Austria, Belgium, Czechoslovakia, Egypt, France, Italy, Norway, and Venezuela, to report on the problem. The unanimously accepted report to the 1949 Bern general assembly recommended that law-enforcement agencies create specialized departments in order to deal efficiently with the delinquency problem, and that preventive delinquency work be emphasized. The Interpol study of police social functions also led to further recommendations at the twenty-first session of the general assembly (1952) for additional crime-prevention work, a theme reiterated at the twenty-second general-assembly session (1953) in Oslo and at the twenty-third session (1954) in Rome. The twenty-fourth general-assembly session in Vienna (1955) designed a model program for training police officers in work with juvenile delinquency and suggested a centralized organization to maximize the impact of advances in this field.

The First U.N. Congress on the Prevention of Crime and Treatment of Delinquents in Geneva in 1955 approved Interpol recommendations for the development of special juvenile services in law-enforcement agencies and special training of police officers in work with juvenile violations. A renewed emphasis upon the use of policewomen, however, dominated the twenty-sixth session of the Interpol general assembly (1957) in Lisbon. It recommended that policewomen should be used regularly in those police units dealing with the task of reducing juvenile delinquency.

Interpol's Technical Advice

Technical law-enforcement rules and patterns related to juvenile delinquency have emerged through trial, error, and general experience. Influenced by location and circumstance, these patterns and rules serve as guides to police attitudes and conduct. Cases of juvenile delinquency, however, demand from the officer greater flexibility and adjustment to particular situations, in contrast to what is expected in adult cases. Consequently, Interpol attempted to establish a basic set of rules that could be applied in all police departments and countries. Considering the general requirements of police work and the particular care with which violations by children and juveniles should be both investigated and prevented, Interpol submitted the following recommendations to the United Nations as "some advice for police officers dealing with juveniles":[17]

Be discreet. In order to avoid dramatic forms of intervention, plainclothes operations are recommended. A child or juvenile should not be allowed to become the center of attention or to make an exhibition of himself. The police officer should recognize tense situations and should ignore insults or abuse. Summoning or taking children to the police station for questioning should be avoided if possible. If children are victims or witnesses, they can be contacted discreetly at home or at school.

Never be brutal. Although juveniles may in some instances resist arrest, police must be firm but never brutal. They should never hurt, pull, or handcuff children.

Never appear ridiculous. As children observe adults closely, representatives of law and order should be especially careful in their deportment. A policeman who runs after a child will only lose respect.

Prepare the ground. A police officer should take no action unless he is certain of its result.

Separate juveniles from adults. Juveniles should be separated from adults during arrest, transfer, and detention.

Vary your attitude. Adjust to the given situation. Questioning should be conducted differently according to the procedural status of the child (whether offender, victim, or witness). The police officer should never, however, be brutal to the child or make him undress under any circumstances.

See to his physical needs. The juvenile arriving at the police station may be hungry or thirsty or have some other physical need that should be met. If he feels "mental unhappiness," it should not be aggravated by physical discomfort.

Arrange the premises. Avoid creating a bad impression in the juvenile interrogation room. A few photographs, a vase of flowers, and similar objects can make the police station or detention room appear more cheerful.

Be neatly dressed. The police officer should be properly, though not ostentatiously, dressed. Because the child tends to notice the officer's outward appearance and is ready to criticize, the officer should be clean and tidy.

Interrogators should work in pairs. Not only should interrogation be conducted by a pair of interrogators, but they should refrain from discussing the offense too bluntly. As extensive note-taking may distract the child's attention and create an ominous atmosphere, the police officer questioning the child should not take too many notes.

Keep the same people on the case. The same police officers who arrest the juvenile should if possible question him as well. The fewer officers whom the child must see, the better.

Be kind but firm. Whatever situation or circumstances may develop, the police officer should not be vulgar, scornful, pathetic, or pompous. He should respect the child and not treat him as an outcast, sinner, or criminal. The police officer should not attempt to harm the child physically or mentally in any way.

Vary behavior to suit the child's age and sex. Because age and sex have major bearing upon the child's behavior and needs, police officers should vary their treatment according to whether or not the child has reached or passed the age of puberty and whether or not the child is male or female. The officer should remember that a boy of nine differs from a girl of seventeen.

Do not be overfamiliar. The police officer should not behave in a way that might be misinterpreted, especially in cases involving adolescent girls.

Be honest. The officer should not trick the juvenile, especially if the latter is undergoing his first confrontation with a law-enforcement agency. Although the police officer should not overdramatize the case, he should also not minimize it. In keeping with the need for truth, the officer should neither make promises that cannot be kept nor take sides in any conflict that arises.

Do not be obstinate. If the child refuses to answer, the police officer should stop the interrogation process.

Do not embarrass the child. As many cases involve delicate sexual matters, policewomen should process them even if the *victim* is the only girl in the case.

Do not make matters worse. Police officers should avoid references to traumatic experiences, especially those of a sexual nature. Repeated questioning or confrontation may be more harmful than the experience itself.

Always verify. Because the child's imagination can alter the truth "to an alarming extent," his statements should always be checked.

Question the child alone. Children should be questioned in the absence of their parents, teachers, companions, and any other witnesses who might influence them. In questioning a child the police officer should attempt to create an atmosphere of trust, should look the child in the eyes, and should not raise embarrassing questions about his family.

Always approach the head of a gang. As the help of the gang chief is necessary before the police officer can approach other gang members for questioning, attention should be concentrated on him. "In order to obtain his help, play on his wish to remain the chief."

Never be sentimental. Being unsentimental does not mean being inhuman. Interpol quotes a French proverb to the effect that total forgiveness may imply lack of understanding. However important the rehabilitation of the juvenile delinquent or young offender may be, the police officer should remember that someone has been victimized by the delinquent's conduct.

Use special departments. Law enforcement in juvenile-delinquency cases should be carried out by special juvenile police departments to which other police departments should turn for assistance whenever children or adolescents are involved.

Isolate the department responsible for juveniles. This special department should be separate from other departments in the law-enforcement agency, preferably even in a different building.

Keep records. As the task of the police is to protect society, it is important to keep detailed records about each case of juvenile delinquency. If the juvenile moves to another locality, the police officer should inform the law-enforcement agency at the new residence of the child or juvenile.

Take fingerprints. Not only are fingerprints valuable in order to develop permanent identification files, but the process of fingerprinting itself may also cause a "beneficial shock" that may be useful later on.

Do not try to avoid responsibility. The police officer should carefully consider whether or not he should take each case to court. Often a firm warning from the police officer is more useful than a slow and solemn legal procedure. As the decision is often left entirely to the police officer, he must be prepared to accept the responsibility for it.

Follow up cases. The police officer should do all that he can to reintegrate the juvenile into society. Welfare, social, and other agency services should be used. The police officer should not be content with closing the case itself; he should make every effort to prevent further episodes of delinquency or crime.

Cooperate with other departments. Close contact with all law-enforcement bodies, juvenile courts, schools, and social services should be maintained.

Be seen. The police officer should let himself be seen in public places. Because his official presence may have a salutary effect on law and order, he should be correctly dressed in uniform.

Patrol in pairs. Male and female police officers should regularly patrol in pairs and check places where children may come under harmful influences during the day and nighttime.

Check on places open to the public. Swimming pools and public baths; betting shops; public meetings; inside and outside theaters and cinemas, cabarets, and nightclubs; dance halls, cafés, and bars; entertainment and gambling establishments; brothels and districts where prostitutes congregate; railway stations and waiting rooms; hotels; public toilets; parks and public gardens; exhibitions; fairs; race tracks; and major roads, highways, and camping grounds should be regularly patrolled.

Take names and addresses. The police officer should ask politely for the names and addresses of young people found at night "in dangerous areas" or who seem to have no regular occupation.

Pass on information. Officers should pass on information to parents, teachers, welfare officers, social workers, and other juvenile police departments.

Do not shock children. Any police action against adults should not be carried out in the presence of children or adolescents. Children should be sent away, if possible, before a house is searched or an adult arrested.

Protect children. Children should be kept out of large-scale political or sporting events that may cause them potential harm.

Educate them for safety. Children should be taught traffic safety through school lessons on traffic problems. Competitions and awards for road safety and patrol organizations should be made part of the school program.

Make contacts with schools. Because schools may readily identify existing gangs, hooligans, neglected children, persistent truants, and bad parents who are often responsible for the delinquency of their children, their aid should be solicited.

Organize leisure activities. The officer can play a direct role by forming youth clubs or an indirect role by serving as a youth-club leader.

Combat harmful influences. The police officer should see that children are not led astray by undesirable publications, toys, or games.

Educate. Police officers should ensure, if possible, that children receive education and training in ethics, good citizenship, and crime prevention.

Give rewards. Courses in good citizenship should lead to distribution of certificates, prizes, or awards for honesty and good behavior—and bad marks for the reverse.

Because these Interpol recommendations are only tentative guides, their actual application must necessarily be adjusted to local conditions. Because police-juvenile relations vary considerably, some of these recommendations may even arouse heavy criticism.[18] But Interpol argued that police officers should at least be ready to learn and to persevere; only through experience and practice, acquaintance with local conditions and awareness of the general delinquency and crime problem can the juvenile officer gain the skill necessary to handle delinquency cases properly, safeguarding both law and order and the interests of children and juveniles.

The Structural Achievements of the Police in Some Foreign Countries and the United States

Although Interpol has continued to encourage improvement in the quality of law enforcement and special attention to the problem of juvenile delinquency in its various forms, international responses to these goals have been varied and uneven. Some of these responses are described here.[19]

Argentina

No independent department deals with the problems of juvenile delinquency; regular police officers handle all juvenile cases. The creation of a special juvenile department was a political issue in 1947, but it failed because of fear that a special police department would only restrict existing law-enforcement agencies. Although the police cooperate with the Consejo Nacional de Minores (National Juvenile Council), a public body established with the support of the police to handle the problems of children in danger, the Council is in fact responsible for delinquency prevention.

Australia

No special police force for juvenile delinquency exists in Canberra, although law-enforcement agencies are in close contact with the Territorial Child Welfare Officer, whose duties include delinquency prevention. A Canberra Police Citizens Boys Club has been organized, however.

In South Australia, as in Canberra, the ordinary police forces handle juvenile cases, including such special tasks as combatting the hooliganism of juvenile gangs. The Anti-Larrikin Squad, begun in 1958, keeps records of all young people who might be connected with gang activities, associations, and clubs, for future reference. A unit of policewomen was created within the criminal-investigation branch to help prevent female delinquency. Although the South Australian police have not formed youth clubs, they do support and encourage such activities. Members of law-enforcement agencies lecture to clubs, parents, schools, and other community groups and cooperate with the press, radio, the Children's Welfare Department, and other welfare agencies.

The Criminal Investigation Branch and policewomen are responsible for problems of juvenile delinquency in Western Australia. The Federation of Police and Citizens' Youth Clubs continues to work throughout the state to set up numerous youth organizations. Law-enforcement agencies organize lectures on prevention and good citizenship, educate the public through broadcasts, and initiate constructive competitions among children. The police organized a significant seminar on delinquency problems in 1958.

Since 1957 a special police unit, in addition to the squad of policewomen who deal with juvenile prostitution, has handled juvenile cases in Queensland. The Citizens' Youth Welfare Association also sponsors numerous youth clubs. In Tasmania, on the other hand, the general police handle juvenile cases in the course of their ordinary duties. Such departments deal with prevention problems, but police and citizen youth clubs have been organized.

Although no independent police force deals with juvenile delinquency in Victoria, a youth-organization committee, composed of representatives from law-enforcement agencies, the Education Department, the National Fitness Council, and other youth organizations, made efforts in 1957 to coordinate the different activities dealing with juvenile delinquency. Consequently, a Youth Advisory Committee and a youth liaison officer were appointed by the police to help coordinate existing prevention activity. Not only were a number of youth clubs organized, but lectures were also given to parents, schools, and welfare organizations. From time to time the Melbourne police have organized "guest nights" for young people, at which suitable films are shown.

Austria

In 1947 a special department of the juvenile police (Jugendpolizei) was formed in Vienna, where a specially trained police officer, the juvenile referee (Jugendreferent), presides in juvenile cases. The juvenile police force is largely though not entirely composed of women. The Jugendpolizei is responsible for the investigation of delinquencies, the centralization of information on delinquent juveniles or children who are in danger, liaison work with various official and private welfare agencies, and training the general public in handling juveniles.

Since 1958 the Association of Juvenile Courts and Aftercare (Verein für Soziale Jugendarbeit—und Arbeitsgemeinschaft Bewährungshilfe) has kept the police informed about juvenile court orders to help in the surveillance and protection of children. The general public is informed about and trained in coping with delinquency problems through police-sponsored communications in the press and on the radio. Special lectures are delivered to a variety of organizations by expert officers. In 1950 the Vienna police created youth hostels (*Jugendheim*), in which children under the age of sixteen (and in some instances between sixteen and eighteen) are placed for short periods while awaiting final judgments. Many of the children placed in these hostels are in immediate physical or moral danger.

Belgium

Although responsibility for juvenile law enforcement is generally assumed by the gendarmerie brigades, the police in larger cities have recently started to organize specialized branches. As their work is primarily preventive in nature, they are often staffed by women. Lectures and seminars on delinquency and maladjustment help to orient the general public and private organizations to the problem. Youth clubs have been formed with the sponsorship or support of law-enforcement agencies. The police also participate in the work of the Center for the Study of Juvenile Delinquency (Centre d'Étude de la Délinquence Juvénile).

Brazil

A special criminal code (Codigo de Memores) is applied in cases of delinquency in Brazil. Each state, however, maintains its own system of juvenile law-enforcement. Some women are employed in the police force, which works in cooperation with juvenile courts and the welfare agencies. Wherever special juvenile departments (Delegacia de Memores) are established within the police forces, they are responsible for delinquency problems.

Burma

Since 1958 a special juvenile police unit has been operating in Rangoon. Not only do the police sponsor a boys' club, but police officers also serve on children's hostel committees. The police participated in the preparation of the Children Act of 1955.

Canada

In the larger cities special squads, composed of both male and female police officers, emphasize prevention. These squads maintain close contact with the juvenile courts, probation departments, schools, churches, youth clubs, and other welfare agencies. Montreal law-enforcement agencies have organized entertainment and sport activities.

Chile

In Santiago a special juvenile police unit was formed in 1940. In the provinces both male and female police officers of the criminal-investigation department work with juvenile courts, welfare organizations, and individual police specialists in delinquency problems. In the early years investigative law enforcement was emphasized. Since 1958, however, prevention has assumed new importance.

Denmark

No independent juvenile police branch exists in Denmark, although police officers participate in the solution of delinquency problems. In 1952 a Copenhagen police-force youth club was established, an example since followed in other cities. Police officers deliver lectures at schools, churches, and organizations on various aspects of juvenile delinquency and emphasize the need to organize young people's leisure.

France

The Sûreté Nationale, the Gendarmerie Nationale, and the Paris prefecture of police cooperate with juvenile courts and welfare agencies. Whereas the Gendarmerie has specialized juvenile squads or police officers, the Sûreté has more than thirty such units. The Paris prefecture has maintained a juvenile bureau since 1943; it now has more than twenty-five male and fifty female officers.

The Sûreté also operates a mobile juvenile squad, composed of thirty carefully selected police officers with radio cars who function on the Riviera from June to September. They are responsible for order at resort areas and also engage in research on youth behavior. Sûreté officers also lecture on juvenile delinquency to various welfare organizations and disseminate information to the general public through all mass communications media. The creation of an independent central police force designed especially for delinquency problems is currently under consideration.

The Federal German Republic

The Woman's Criminal Police (Weibliche Kriminal Polizei), established in 1930, deals with juvenile delinquency and children's problems. Responsible for all complaints against children of either sex under the age of legal responsibility and against girls regardless of age, members of this force investigate such complaints and intervene when the upbringing and future of children are in danger, as in cases of neglect, abandonment, ill treatment, and kidnapping. The Woman's Criminal Police has branches in all larger cities and its own high-ranking officers and is under the direct supervision of the head of the criminal-investigation department. Specially trained youth experts (Jugendsachbearbeiter) attached to law-enforcement agencies also deal with adolescents between fourteen and eighteen years and with delinquency problems. In some German states or larger cities they are augmented by juvenile defense squads (Jugendschutztrupps), with responsibility for investigation and prevention. Law-enforcement agencies cooperate with existing welfare organizations, private groups, and church bodies to sponsor annual "child-protection weeks" in all larger cities. From time to time seminars are held for police officers. Juvenile officers may use the West German Jugendarrest, detention of young offenders between the ages of fourteen and eighteen in the form of leisure detention (one to four weeks when not in school or not working), brief detention (two to six continuous days), or continuous detention (one to four weeks).[20]

Ghana

The Social Welfare Department and the police responsible for the delinquency problem in Ghana cooperate with the schools in delinquency prevention.

Greece

Not only does an official association for the protection of juveniles cooperate with law-enforcement agencies, but the latter also remain in contact with the juvenile courts.

India

Special police units have been formed from carefully selected officers in Bombay, Calcutta, and Hyderabad. The first, established in Bombay in 1952, consisted of six men and seven women and was commanded by a woman inspector. These units work in close contact with all departments and organizations that have anything to do with the delinquency problem. The Bombay branch formed a police boys' club in one densely populated area.

The passage of the Children Act for the Union Territories by Parliament in 1960 changed the emphasis of police activity in India from arrest, detention, custody, punishment, and discharge to protection and correction. Consequently, many of the Interpol recommendations have become general operating procedures among the Indian police.[21]

Israel

There are juvenile bureaus within the criminal-investigation branch; they were first created in Jerusalem, Tel Aviv, and Haifa. Because great care is taken to avoid a standard police atmosphere in these bureaus, policewomen are preferred. Members of the juvenile bureau maintain contact with all agencies dealing with children and juveniles, organize field trips for school children to laboratories and other parts of the criminal-investigation department, deliver talks and lectures on delinquency problems, offer education in road safety, take part in sporting events and games in local youth clubs, and offer holidays to children whose parents cannot afford them.

Italy

In 1947 juvenile police bureaus with specialized personnel were established at all provincial headquarters. In 1958 it was decided to form a national corps of policewomen in order to oversee and control juvenile delinquency and prostitution. Both police units have cooperated with existing welfare agencies, especially with the National Association for the Moral Protection of Children (Ente Nazionale per la Protezione Morale del Fanciullo).

Japan

The Tokyo agency of the national police operates a juvenile section and other regional divisions operate juvenile bureaus. Under a system inaugurated in 1949 each local police station has at least one specialized juvenile officer. A number of organizations cooperate with these juvenile sections and conduct annual month-long campaigns against juvenile delinquency. Press, radio, and television share in these efforts. Aid-and-guidance centers have been established with the support of the law-enforcement agencies. Delinquency-prevention area programs were introduced by the police in 1955 and have assumed increasing responsibility for prevention.

Libya

Although no special police departments deal with delinquency, law-enforcement agencies broadcast weekly radio programs in a campaign to prevent delinquency.

Monaco

Since 1959 a small team of two policewomen who are qualified social workers has assumed responsibility for delinquency problems, although three male police officers also help, largely with investigation, when necessary.

Morocco

In Casablanca the brigade for surveillance of juveniles is composed of eight carefully selected police officers, including one woman; it has existed since 1956. This brigade is responsible for both investigation and prevention and aids in development of youth activities.

The Netherlands

The Dutch state police is responsible for law enforcement among juveniles. The country is divided into five jurisdictions, each with a headquarters and a policewoman in charge of juvenile cases. In a few larger towns the children's police (Kinderpolitie), staffed by both male and female police officers, has been formed to deal with juvenile criminal cases, enforcement of school attendance, surveillance and control of public places where children are not to be admitted, prevention of gang vandalism, problems of physical or moral danger to children, families dominated by criminal patterns, and the search for juveniles who have run away.

The Netherlands Antilles

A combined vice and juvenile squad, composed entirely of males, was established in Willemstad (Curaçao) in 1944. Although it was charged with the responsibility of handling complaints and problems of the behavior of children, it also assumed responsibility for investigating delinquent offenses of children under eighteen and the control of public places in which juveniles are exposed to danger. Through the Reclassification and Child Protection Institute, the police work in close contact with the Youth Care Department of the Ministry of Justice, the Department of Social Affairs, and the government's Education Institution.

New Zealand

Although no specially trained juvenile police branch has been formed, existing law-enforcement agencies cooperate with official and private welfare organizations. Following the outlines of England's Liverpool Police Project, the police attempted in 1957 to process juvenile delinquents in an informal fashion, avoiding court action as far as possible. Many police officers participate in youth activities in their spare time.

The Philippines

In 1945 the Manila police department established the Juvenile Control Bureau, composed mainly of men and a small number of female officers. Working in cooperation with the Council for the Prevention of Juvenile Delinquency, the Bureau is responsible for all juvenile cases. The police and the Council founded in 1948 a boys' town in the most neglected area of Manila. Since then they have organized discussions, film shows, and lectures, particularly in schools. In 1955 a series of special courses was devised to improve the expertise of police officers assigned to juvenile cases.

Spain

Although a few police officers are specially trained in delinquency problems, juvenile cases are largely handled by ordinary police officers as part of normal duty.

Switzerland

Although no special juvenile police exist, each canton appoints an official to deal with the problems of juvenile delinquency.

Thailand

In 1953 the Bangkok police formed a youth-control section, composed of male police officers and a few policewomen and charged with prevention of delinquency through control, patrol, and supervision. In collaboration with other government and child-welfare agencies, the police have since 1954 sponsored crime-prevention weeks focused upon delinquency problems.

United Arab Republic (Egypt)

A department in the Ministry of the Interior was established in 1938 "for the protection of morals and juveniles," a branch that has since assumed responsibility for crime prevention and law enforcement among juveniles. With divisions in most provinces, its members are predominantly trained officers of both sexes, who work in close cooperation with the police. Members of these law-enforcement branches maintain close contact with the General Union to Protect Juveniles, an official organization responsible for the coordination of the various welfare agencies.

United Kingdom

Policewomen in independent units or combined with male police officers work for the prevention of delinquency within the normal enforcement agency. The police avoid bringing children to court unless they have been engaged in very serious delinquency, and a large percentage of cases is processed through warnings and supervision. In their Liverpool project the police divided the city into sections and placed a responsible juvenile liaison officer in each section. In addition to police youth clubs, mainly organized in London, the police operate attendance centers in which short term punishment of offenders between the ages of twelve and twenty-one is administered in the form of work assignments during their leisure hours, determined by court order. Police officers also present lectures on good citizenship and social responsibility as part of the center's program.

The United States

The police commonly provide a wide variety of official and unofficial delinquency control, prevention, and treatment services through the ordinary police officer. Because most American cities and counties make no provision for special juvenile details, squads, or divisions, almost any police officer may detain juveniles as authorized by law. Although the police officer's primary duty is detention and control in order to secure the youth's observance of existing laws, his activities are also designed to protect the child or teenager from persons who might take advantage of his youth. Consequently, the police possess the authority to intervene in juvenile cases which include participation in delinquent or criminal acts (for example, drunkenness, loitering late at night, fighting, or associating with undesirable persons). The policeman many utilize any of his many alternatives, including the release of the child with a warning, the return of the youth to his parents with or without referral of the case to a social agency, the temporary detention of the juvenile in some lockup facility (a juvenile hall or a local jail), or longer detention of the youth pending investigation of the case by a probation officer and the appearance of the adolescent in juvenile court.

In most jurisdictions approximately one-half of all delinquents taken into custody with a record of consistent and serious offenses come to the attention of the juvenile court through police referral. Common reasons for police referral of juvenile cases to the juvenile court, as defined by the Conference of the Chiefs of Police, include:

1. The particular offense committed by the child is of a serious nature.
2. The child is known or has in the past been known to the juvenile court.
3. The child has a record of repeated delinquency extending over a period of time.
4. The child or his parents have shown themselves unwilling or unable to cooperate with agencies of a nonauthoritative (social) character.

5. Casework with the child by a nonauthoritative agent has failed in the past.

6. Treatment services needed by the child can be obtained only through the court and its probation department.

7. The child denies the offense, the officer believes judicial determination is called for, and there is insufficient evidence to warrant referral, or the officer believes that the child and his family are in need of aid.

8. There is apparent need for treatment.[22]

Because the police officer possesses wide discretionary powers, the bulk of all juvenile cases probably are never brought to the attention of the court or even the central police office.

Some larger American cities maintain special youth police or a youth division, often attached to the investigative branch of the police department, within the regular force. Having been trained in effective juvenile-police procedures, it actually supplements the regular force and assumes responsibility for the apprehension and investigation of juvenile cases. Such special juvenile delinquency control units, juvenile bureaus, and youth or juvenile divisions make use of investigative data provided by other police units, arrange disposition of cases, supervise juvenile gathering places, maintain juvenile case records, and plan or coordinate delinquency-prevention programs. Common case investigations include illegal employment of minors, participation in vice, family abuse or neglect, bicycle thefts, offenses committed on school property, gang activities, and sex offenses. In some cities even more specialized units have been created to deal with particular conditions of the community. The Chicago Gang Intelligence Unit (GIU), for example, has recently been expanded in an attempt to restrict gang activities, especially in black neighborhoods. In New York and Los Angeles, on the other hand, officers of the juvenile division supervise athletic and drama programs, police bands, and public relations work with schools. No single program or outlook dominates the American police approach to juveniles.[23]

Yugoslavia

Although the police handle delinquency cases as part of their broader function, those officers who are assigned to work with children and juveniles receive special instruction and work in close contact with existing welfare agencies.

Because the problem of delinquency is different in each country surveyed, the function and responsibility of the police vary accordingly. The fact that delinquency is a legal category rather than a special form of behavior makes the policeman's task all the more difficult. Although the juvenile offender may commit a violation identical to that of an adult, the policeman's relationship to the juvenile is determined by age and by special laws and is consequently continually changing as legal definitions, administrative practices, and superior-court interpretations change. The police nevertheless do have extensive discretionary powers and can in large part determine through their own action or inaction who the future criminals will be.

NOTES

1. Southwestern Law Enforcement Institute, *Law Enforcement and the Juvenile Offender* (Springfield, Ill.: 1963).

2. Thomas J. Cahill, "A New Concept in Community Relations," *FBI Law Enforcement Bulletin*, 32 (December 1963), 6. Robert L. Derbyshire found that children exposed to "Policeman Bill" in the Los Angeles elementary grades exhibited significantly less antipathy toward the police. Police officers of the same ethnic backgrounds as the students (Mexican-American, Negro, or Caucasian) presented the program. Derbyshire also found that the lower the socioeconomic background of the child, the higher his antipathy toward the police. See Robert L. Derbyshire, "Children's Perceptions of the Police," *Journal of Criminal Law, Criminology and Police Science*, 59 (June 1968), 183–190.

3. Sophia M. Robison, *Juvenile Delinquency: Its Nature and Control* (New York: 1960), p. 207.

4. Marshall B. Clinard, *Sociology of Deviant Behavior* (rev. ed.; New York: 1963), p. 174. The problems and structure of the police in the United States are discussed in President's Commission on Law Enforcement and Administration of Justice, *Task Force Report: The Police* (Washington, D.C.: 1967).

5. Edwin H. Sutherland and Donald R. Cressey, *Principles of Criminology* (6th ed.; New York: 1960), p. 225. The acquisition and use of Chemical Mace by delinquents or criminals will undoubtedly occur in the near future. See also John Kenney and Dan G. Pursuit, *Police Work with Juveniles* (Springfield, Ill.: 1967).

6. Victor Cathrein, *Die Grundbegriffe des Strafrechts* (Freiburg: 1905).

7. Sutherland and Cressey, *op. cit.*, p. 225.

8. Pál Angyal, *A Kultura Kriminál-Aetiologiai Jelentösége* (Budapest: 1914).

9. Sutherland and Cressey, *op. cit.*, p. 226.

10. U.N. Department of Economic and Social Affairs, *New Forms of Juvenile Delinquency: Their Origin, Prevention and Treatment* (New York: 1960), p. 34.

11. International Criminal Police Organization, *Special Police Departments for the Prevention of Juvenile Delinquency* (Paris: 1960), p. 9.

12. Robison, *op. cit.*, p. 213.

13. International Criminal Police Organization, *op. cit.*, p. 60.

14. For discussion of the relevant problems, see U.S. Children's Bureau, *Police Services for Juveniles* (Washington, D.C.: 1954); John P. Kenney and Dan. G. Pursuit, *op. cit.*, and James J. Brennan, *The Prevention and Control of Juvenile Delinquency by Police Departments* (New York: 1952).

15. International Criminal Police Organization, *op. cit.*, pp. 44–56.

16. *Ibid.*, pp. 5–7.

17. International Criminal Police Organization, *op. cit.*, pp. 63–71. This document was submitted to the second U.N. Congress for the Prevention of Crime and the Treatment of Delinquents in London in 1960. Not all these recommendations can be appropriately applied to American juvenile delinquency, especially when the law-enforcement agencies must deal with delinquent gangs.

18. *Ibid.*, p. 71.

19. Abstracted mainly from *Ibid.*, pp. 13–42.

20. Alfred-Johannes Rangol and Walter Peterson, "Aufgabe des Jugendarrestes," *Zeitschrift für Strafvollzug*, 15 (1966), 288–298.

21. Shri G. K. Kasture, "Police and Prevention of Juvenile Delinquency," *Samay-Seva*, 18, No. 1–2 (1967), 24–32.

22. Kenney and Pursuit, *op. cit.*, 1965, p. 20.

23. Ruth Shonle Cavan, *Juvenile Delinquency: Development, Treatment, Control* (2nd ed.; Philadelphia: 1969), p. 374.

Part Six

DELINQUENCY AND THE JUVENILE COURT

Chapter 18

■ *The Juvenile Court*

■ *Development of the Juvenile Courts*

The change in treatment of children and juvenile delinquents represented a revolutionary departure from common-law principles that assume equality of all offenders before the law, regardless of age, and stipulate the public trial of all accused in ordinary courts. Not until the middle of the nineteenth century were juvenile delinquents differentiated from adults in common law. The existing courts therefore applied the same procedures and penal sanctions to all who were charged with wrongdoing. Perhaps the first departure from this practice occurred in England, where a law of 1847 empowered justices to deal summarily with children accused of simple larceny instead of committing them for trial at the so-called "quarter sessions" or "assizes."[1] Provision for such summary trial was, however, extended in 1879 to all child cases to be tried by the magistrates' court, an action that anticipated the creation of juvenile courts. But, as children were still processed in the same courts as adults, "exposed throughout to the danger of contact with hardened criminals and contamination,"[2] the judicial process remained unsatisfactory. Consequently progressive judges in many communities made informal arrangements for special sittings in order to keep children's cases separate. This practice, of course, was not obligatory and depended upon the personal sensibility of each presiding justice. Although this English breakthrough in treatment of juvenile offenders had opened the way to the development of juvenile courts, such courts first developed in South Australia in 1890.[3]

The first totally separate children's court in the United States was created by law on July 1, 1899, in Chicago, as a result of the efforts of the Chicago Women's Club and the Catholic Visitation and Aid Society.[4] Also supported by the Chicago Bar Association and Judge Harvey B. Hard, who had drafted the basic bill (which was passed with several modifications), the juvenile court extended the English concept of separate judicial treatment for juvenile delinquents to include separate juvenile courts. Although earlier American efforts had tended to support a move in this direction, none had gone this far. Separate hearings for juveniles had been held in 1870 in Boston and Suffolk County, Massachusetts. New York had followed this example in 1877; Rhode Island had established similar provisions in 1898. Only the Illinois law, however, established a separate court for "dependent, neglected and delinquent children."

As a result of the efforts of Judge Ben Lindsey, a second juvenile court was established in 1903 in Denver, Colorado. In succeeding years the idea gained rapid acceptance not only among the American states but throughout the civilized world. Although most American states established juvenile courts within a few years of the pioneering Illinois effort, it was not until 1945, when Wyoming at last passed an enabling act, that all states had them. Outside the United States, England, Canada, and Hungary were the first countries to treat children in separate juvenile courts (all beginning in 1908). Switzerland followed in 1910. In 1913 Hungary refined its earlier enabling law, and Belgium created its juvenile court. Although Germany had tried to introduce a separate juvenile court system as early as 1879, the bill had not become law. Today most legal systems, with the notable exception of the Soviet Union, operate juvenile courts. In the U.S.S.R. ordinary criminal responsibility is attached to any crime with violence, intentional damage to property, or malicious hooliganism if the offender is over the age of fourteen, or in special cases over sixteen.[5]

The juvenile court, an adaptation of the English legal doctrine of *parens patriae*, developed from state recognition that the juvenile offender is a child in need of care, education, and protection rather than of criminal punishment.[6] In the United States the states are viewed legally as successors to the British king, who could act on behalf of needy children through the chancery court. As the intentions of the court are considered benevolent, the procedural safeguards necessary for criminal courts are deemphasized, and the informality of the chancery courts is stressed.[7] Although these principles were introduced into international jurisprudence through the efforts of English and American court reformers, they have never been fully realized in the three-quarters of a century that juvenile courts have been in operation. The 1966 *Gault* decision (*Gault v. Arizona*) of the U.S. Supreme Court recognized that juveniles have received neither the Constitutional guarantees offered adults nor the solicitous care proposed for children.[8] Not everyone has agreed with the basic philosophy underlying the juvenile courts. Albert W. Silver, for example, criticized them for placing "too much" emphasis upon rehabilitation. He argued that they should instead place more emphasis on prevention.[9]

The Terminology of the Juvenile Courts

Because the essential philosophy of the juvenile court supports a concept of individual justice, special terminology was naturally created in order to avoid the stigma involved in adult court appearances. Juvenile delinquents were not to be identified with adult criminals and were therefore physically separated from adult deviants, to avoid the criminal stigma that might ruin their chances for rehabilitation and reorientation of life patterns. Terms common to the adult criminal court were modified or excluded from juvenile-court terminology in an attempt to help the public distinguish between act and judgment. "Criminal" was replaced by the term *child* or *juvenile;* "guilt" by *judicial adjudication* that the child is dependent or delinquent; "arrest" by *police custody;* "jail" by *detention,* the physical custody of the youth ordered by the judge before his final decision; "accusation," "indictment," and "charge" by *petition,* a document filed in the court claiming that the juvenile is dependent or delinquent; "sentence of imprisonment" by *commitment* to a detention home, a licensed care or placement institution or agency, or an industrial or training school; 'trial" by *hearing* (without a jury), in which the judge listens to the evidence and renders a decision; and "parole" by *after care,* supervised assistance of the child for a predetermined period after his release from commitment. *Probation,* however, remains the same in both systems.

Effects of Public Opinion

Although court reformers had hoped that these distinctions would gain public acceptance, they did not. The public identified the new terms with their adult criminal counterparts and continued to view the juvenile problem in similar terms. Consequently, juvenile delinquents continue in the eyes of the public to commit "crimes," face "trial," be judged "guilty," and be "sentenced" to "reformatories" for their offenses. Any increase in delinquency rates is apt to alarm the public, as if it represented a crime wave, although no one really knows or seems to care how many of these delinquents are dependent children and how many really fit the public's image of criminals. As a result, juvenile-court terminology has been unable to soften the criminal stigma for delinquents. The child therefore receives serious punishment from *public opinion,* in addition to the juvenile-court judge's official "decision"; the former is the "social consequence" of being a delinquent and even of being a dependent child.

Public opinion is less restrained than is the law. Although legal precedents and codes limit the scope of court judgments and sanctions, public opinion knows no such bounds. It is likely to regard any nonconformity, whether by juvenile or by adult, as a violation of dominant social norms or of law and order. Public opinion, however, too often judges without full proof, on the basis of sentiment or an estimate or evaluation of events from its own limited perspective. Although public opinion is a composite of multiple private opinions, it may be totally inaccurate because it is ultimately based upon emotion and sentiments. It can often be manipulated to desired ends, but affects both delinquent and the criminal whether justifiably, unnecessarily, or even harmfully.

Public disapproval of delinquency, a form of punishment in itself, must be clearly distinguished from conventional legal punishment or other measures against delinquency and crime. Whereas punishment by public opinion is irresponsible, in that it emanates from no predetermined and identifiable source and follows no defined or formal procedures, legal measures can be applied only by duly appointed or elected officials who work within the framework of legal procedures. Although legal jurisdiction and judgment are based upon investigation of facts and conscientious application of judicial procedures refined over centuries of trial and error, the "jurisdiction" of public opinion, which almost always assumes guilt, is hardly more than the sentence itself. Public opinion determines guilt and social sentence without any formal trial. Acquittal is almost impossible. The most constructive response of public opinion to discovery that a charge is inaccurate is indifference or "Let bygones be bygones." The revision or modification of public opinion is rare once a judgment has been "rendered." The "judges" of public opinion are quick to punish but reluctant to forgive. Because anyone may be "accused" through this invisible procedure, questions of age, socioethical personality and resistance, and potential responsibility become insignificant. Guidelines and circumstances that influence conventional juvenile adjudication and sentencing have little or no influence upon the "sentencing" of public opinion. Consequently, minor blunders or unimportant mischief can be more strictly punished by public opinion than are serious crimes or mistakes that happen to be beyond the public's comprehension.

The exact goal of public cries for punishment is unclear. Although public opinion may be nothing more than a simple and natural expression devoid of explicit aims, it may also demand revenge, ostensibly to control or reform other potential or actual offenders. In any case, however, it appears and functions as an effective punishment involving a mixture of public consideration, negligence, and passion. Public opinion is considerate in forming an opinion, negligent in interpreting facts, and passionate in its approach to punishment. Although it hopes for general reform and social control, it undoubtedly sacrifices the individual to retribution.

Punishment by public opinion results in devaluation of personality, as in the Roman *capitis diminutio maxima* (it may morally kill). It isolates its victim through a sentence of distrust that may even prove fatal, for such devaluation may ultimately lead to a kind of *capital punishment* in the form of suicide; to *deportation* if the victim's only defense is escape from his district or even from his country; or heavy *fines* or *confiscation* when the "offender" loses his job or expectations of promotion or suffers other financial loss. Informal punishment by public opinion can therefore sharply undermine the intent and philosophy of the juvenile courts. Although the court is supposed to serve the needs of the child, punishment by the public may undermine its efforts, making individualized justice difficult to achieve.

■ *Juvenile Court Procedures*

The Standard Juvenile Court Act

In order to bring the policies and administration of the different juvenile courts throughout the country to a uniform level, the U.S. Children's Bureau and the National Probation Association formulated a set of juvenile-court standards and a Standard Juvenile Court Act, first published in 1925.[10] As later considerations influenced approaches to child care and treatment of juvenile delinquency, the act was reviewed in subsequent years. It still serves, however, as a model for state and local legislation. Because most juvenile jurisdictions use it only as a guide, adjusting and modifying its provisions to fit local conditions, any description of overall American juvenile-court procedures can be framed in only the most general terms without mention of numerous state variations.

Jurisdiction, Definitions, Personnel, and Procedures

Although the court is the *juvenile* court, it functions in the interest of the *child* rather than of the *juvenile*. In some jurisdictional areas the child is defined as under the age of seventeen or eighteen years; other jurisdictions use higher or lower age limits, but the upper limit is eighteen years in two-thirds of the United States.[11] In some European legal systems the term "juvenile" is equivalent to "child" as used here, whereas "child" is anyone *younger* than the lowest limit for delinquency. Because age is the only determinant of whether a youth is a child or a juvenile, his marital status makes no difference to his legal status. The term "adult" therefore refers to anyone above the higher age limit for children or juveniles.

Approximately 2,800 courts hear children's cases, although the jurisdiction, structure, and type vary from state to state.[12] The widespread creation of juvenile courts has been regarded as desirable, but the relative shortage of qualified judges and trained personnel has confined them to large cities and countries. In many American states, however, the qualifications for a juvenile-court judge are minimal or even altogether lacking. Although the juvenile court ideally should be independent and staffed by specially qualified personnel, in many jurisdictions it is only part of the general court system. This problem is world-wide.

Juvenile-court judges are elected (as in Florida and Ohio) or appointed (as in Connecticut, Georgia, and Massachusetts), according to the traditions of each state. They are elected by qualified voters or appointed by the governor, state department, mayor, or other public official. The juvenile-court judge should be more than twenty-five years old; of high moral character; experienced in problems of family and child welfare, juvenile delinquency, and community organization; and licensed to practice law. Many European legal systems require public statements of judges' attitudes toward contemporary problems and even that judges have families of their own. Because juvenile-court judges have awesome responsibilities, everything should be done to ensure that they are qualified. The future of each child who comes before the judge rests in his hands. He therefore must have integrity, patience, and special knowledge and should be willing to learn new ways to protect children from crime.

The *referee*, or *counselor*, is the first assistant to the judge; he organizes, directs, and develops the cases. Although he should possess a professional degree, he does not always have one. As he very nearly substitutes for the judge, his tenure of office should be subject to the latter's discretion. Although the juvenile-court judge usually oversees all appointments of medical, psychological, psychiatric, and other personnel, the referee has special unofficial and offical overseeing powers and usually determines who will be brought to the attention of the juvenile court. This exclusive jurisdiction is mainly reserved, however, for

1. The child whose proper or necessary support or education as required by law is neglected; who is not receiving medical, psychiatric, psychological, or other necessary care; or who has been abandoned by his parents or guardian.
2. The child whose occupation, behavior, condition, environment, or associations are such as to injure or endanger his welfare or that of others.
3. The child who is beyond the control of his parents or guardian.
4. The child who is alleged to have violated or attempted to violate any Federal, state, or local law or ordinance, regardless of where the violation occurred.

Most juvenile courts also have jurisdiction over those above the juvenile age limit whose violations occurred before they passed that limit. Although juvenile courts are fundamentally courts of law and fulfill primarily judicial functions, they also perform certain ministerial (helping) and administrative functions.[13] Questions of custody or guardianship, adoption of minors, termination of parental rights, marriage of children, treatment or commitment of mentally defective or mentally disordered children, and so on also frequently fall within the jurisdiction of juvenile courts. Consequently, responsibilities periodically overlap and often conflict as court and special agency seek differing goals. Most juvenile courts, however, do not have control over child or juvenile cases involving criminal charges that would be felonies if committed by adults. If the child commits such a serious offense after reaching a specified age[14]—usually fourteen, fifteen, or sixteen, depending on state laws—his case may be waived by the juvenile court or automatically transferred to an adult court for disposition. Normally the state assumes partial or full authority over the upbringing of a child in cases of neglect or delinquency through the following procedures.

Investigation of complaint and filing of petition. After assembling the facts on whether or not an act of delinquency was actually committed or on whether or not a condition of neglect exists, the individual or agency who has received the complaint or made the investigation requests court authorization to file a petition, which must then be supported with evidence. Because investigation and filing petitions are not appropriate functions of the court, service personnel from the school, the police, or other administrative agencies perform them.

Determination of the need for and the nature of court action. Because the court's intake service is usually responsible for screening cases coming to its attention on behalf of the child and the community, this function is within the administrative structure of the court.

Establishment of the court's jurisdiction. Age and place and nature of the alleged act must be determined.

Establishment of the facts alleged in the petition.

Completion of the social study. This study aids the court in determining eventual disposition of each case. After a preliminary review has established prima facie jurisdiction and after the child has voluntarily confessed or the court has rendered a decision, the social study brings to the court's attention additional factors in the case. The social study is generally broader in scope than is the petition and may include facts that are not relevant to the decision but are important to a probation officer or agency that works with the child afterward.[15] It may, for example, include data from medical, psychological, or psychiatric reports on the child and his family; records from other social agencies or courts; observations made during detention; opinions of teachers, police, and friends; and other pertinent information.

Determination of action to be taken and limitation if any on the rights of child or parent. Any changes in the legal status of the child or his parents can be accomplished only by judicial decision.

Providing needed care and treatment. Although the actual supervision of the care and treatment of the child away from home is an appropriate function of specified administrative agencies, the court maintains control over intake and release and supervises visits, interviewing, and other procedures affecting him. Although shelter and care of children awaiting hearings should logically be the responsibility of the administrative agencies, the court is also ultimately responsible for placement and for control of intake and release.

The child may, however, be treated in his own home on *probation* or under *protective supervision*. Probation for children is a legal status that follows a finding of delinquency or other misconduct and permits youths to remain in the community subject to supervision by the court through its probation department or through an agency designated by the court. It is usually supervised by administrative personnel attached to the court and allows them to make the social study and to work with the child and his parents during the probation period. Although probation does not involve a change in the guardianship of the child or transfer of legal custody, it does limit some of the powers of the parent or guardian.[16] Only about 1,300 probation departments administratively attached to courts currently serve juveniles.[17]

On the other hand, *protective supervision* involves casework services that the court is obligated to perform if no other agency is willing to accept this responsibility. It is also a legal status, under which a child who has been found by the court to be neglected is allowed to remain in his own home for an allotted period during which aid is offered to the parents by the court's probation department or another court-designated agency.[18] Protective supervision is prescribed for a definite period (usually ninety days for evaluation or for a longer period not to exceed one year) subject to renewal upon a showing cause. No agency is allowed to remove the child from his home.[19]

Release of the child from state control. Limitations upon the rights of the child or parents are removed upon the expiration of the order or a release through an administrative order in compliance with statutory limitations and requirements.

Initiation of a Case

A police officer representing law enforcement,[20] the court's own referee, or any other interested person may initiate a petition in the juvenile court, claiming that a child is delinquent, neglected, or dependent. Some states, however, permit informal action by the juvenile court without petition even when the court receives information that the child has come within the jurisdiction of the law; a preliminary inquiry may seem necessary to determine whether or not the interests of the public and the child require further action.

Petitions filed in juvenile courts (and often in family courts), as well as subsequent documents (often labeled "In the interest of" a child under "18 years of age" normally include such information as

1. The facts alleged to bring the child within the jurisdiction of the court.
2. The name, age, and residence of the child.
3. The names and residences of his parents or guardian.
4. The name and residence of anyone else who has legal custody or physical care and control of the child.
5. The name and residence of the child's spouse, if he is married.
6. The name and residence of the nearest known relative if neither parent nor guardian can be found.[21]

After a petition is filed and the judge has directed the necessary preliminary investigation, the court issues summonses to those who have custody of the child and to other individuals whose presence is necessary in the opinion of the judge. Although the child is not summoned himself, the parent or custodian is required to appear in court with him. In many systems, however, juvenile-court proceedings have been held valid even when no parents or guardian was present, though in most cases only after diligent inquiry and search had failed to uncover his identity or residence. Because juvenile records are confidential, juvenile courts have been encouraged to maintain separate files and to identify children only by initials and case numbers.

Detention

Most states permit a child to be taken into custody only if the juvenile court issues an order or if danger to the child's welfare or his violation of law creates an emergency situation that demands immediate action. The place of detention is entirely subject to the approval and supervision of the court. If the child or juvenile is taken into custody, his parents, guardian, or legal custodian is usually notified as soon as possible. In some jurisdictions the school principal is also informed. Whenever possible, the child is released to the custody of his parents or another responsible adult. When the child is not released he is generally taken without unnecessary delay to the juvenile court or to a place designated by the court for detention. No child or juvenile should be transported in any police or other vehicle that also contains adults under arrest, nor should he be detained in any police lockup, jail, or prison with adults. Although the judge may order an exception to this practice, children and juveniles, as a rule, must be kept entirely separate from adult offenders. Unless the court directs, no detained child should be fingerprinted or photographed. Detention should last no longer than two days, excluding Sundays and official legal holidays, unless it is extended by court order.

Investigation and Examination

The investigation to determine whether or not the child is delinquent, neglected, or dependent is the responsibility of the referee, the juvenile-court counselor, or his assistants. In the course of this investigation or after its completion, the juvenile-court judge may order a medical, psychiatric, or psychological examination of the child. With the consent of the parent or guardian, he can also order treatment and place the child in a suitable treatment center.

Hearing and Decree

The hearing should be held as soon as practicable after the filing of the petition; it is conducted by the judge without a jury in an informal manner. The child or juvenile is encouraged to seek rehabilitation, often through admitting his "guilt." Although the court presumably does not seek to determine guilt or innocence, "guilt" has often been assumed from the mere presence of the youth in court. Depending upon the discretion of the juvenile-court judge, the hearing may take place in the presence or absence of parents, lawyers, and other participants. The hearing generally involves two dimensions that may or may not be interwoven. The *hearing of evidence* leads to the determination of jurisdiction and of the accuracy of the facts alleged in the petition. The *hearing of social evidence,* if the court finds the child within its jurisdiction, is largely based upon the report and recommendations of the probation officer and usually guides the disposition of the case.[22]

The juvenile-court hearing is usually informal, in the sense that technicalities not essential to justice that might tend to confuse or intimidate the child are omitted, rather than in the sense of relaxed interaction among child, parents, and judge. Court proceedings are usually orderly and dignified yet simple. Although such informality is desirable, it has periodically resulted in violation of juvenile and parental rights. The decision by the U.S. Supreme Court in *Gault v. Arizona* called for correction of some abuses.

The exclusion of the general public and the admission only of those judged by the court to have an interest in the case are world-wide characteristics of juvenile courts. Nevertheless, in some states (like Florida) the rule is the reverse. Juvenile-court hearings are open to the public unless the judge deems it in the interests of the public or the child to close them. Some jurisdictions even continue to rely on juries of the offender's peers to try juvenile offenders. Although this system has been lauded by mass media in recent years, the National Council on Crime and Delinquency argued that such juries probably do more harm than good, as mature judgment and broad human knowledge are necessary for jurors to make proper decisions.[23] Because the juvenile court has extremely broad discretion over what is best for the child, the judge may dismiss the petition or otherwise terminate the case at any point. In most such instances he finds that the child is not a delinquent or a dependent child. If the child is found to be delinquent, neglected, or dependent, the court may order one of several alternative actions.

1. It may place the child under the supervision (probation) of the referee or counselor in the child's own home or in a suitable custodial shelter under such reasonable conditions as the judge may prescribe.
2. It may commit the child to the custody or guardianship of a public or private institution or agency authorized to care for children, place him in a home, or commit him to an industrial training school, for a determinate or indeterminate period, in no case to run beyond his twenty-first birthday.
3. It may direct parents, guardian, or legal custodian to pay the institutional maintenance expenses if they have encouraged, caused, or contributed to the acts or conditions that brought the child before the juvenile court.

The judgment of the court is not a conviction and does not impose any civil or legal limitations, although the public often imposes sanctions of its own. Because the child has not been charged with a crime in the juvenile court, he can neither be found guilty nor be judged a criminal. Any evidence, disposition, or later action should not disqualify the child from any future civil-service application or appointment. Although any child, parent, guardian, or legal custodian may appeal the order of a juvenile court (especially if no counsel was employed) to the proper superior court on matters of law or fact, no new evidence may be presented at the appeal hearing, and only the question of legality or severity of the court's order is open to question. The appellate court may dismiss the original petition or return the case to the juvenile court for disposition consistent with its original findings.[24]

Although many people and agencies influence the fate of the child who appears before the court, his ultimate success or failure is largely "dependent on the performance of the juvenile court and, more particularly, of the judge who functions therein."[25] The role of the judge is therefore central to effective protection, correction, rehabilitation, care, guidance, control, and prevention.[26] The full purpose of the juvenile and family courts can be achieved only if their staffs identify with and are capable of accomplishing nonpunitive individual service. Sufficient facilities must be available in the court and in the community to ensure that decisions are based upon the best knowledge of the children's needs, adequate protection for the community, and necessary treatment for children. The statutory and Constitutional rights of children, parents, and community must be considered and protected throughout.[27] Consequently juvenile and family courts should strive for the appointment of qualified judges with enough time to exercise their responsibilities effectively; protection of juvenile and parental rights; development of an integrated court system in place of multiple specialized courts; uniformity of court practices and procedures throughout each state; adequate probation services; uniform legal and social statistical reporting and record keeping; and effective working relationships between courts and agencies that provide necessary auxiliary services.[28]

■ Continuing Problems in the Juvenile Court

Although a juvenile-court act has now been formulated in every state of the United States, significant gaps still exist between ideal and actual court structures, practices, and personnel. The inconsistency in structure and procedures and the inadequate staffing of the courts themselves contribute to two such gaps. As the juvenile court has become increasingly important in the overall system of justice, the need to close these gaps has become more apparent. The discovery that nearly one of every nine children (one of every six boys) will be referred to the juvenile court before his eighteenth birthday indicates the scope of the problem.[29]

Yet relatively few juvenile courts are separately or independently empowered to deal with problems of adolescents and youth. Most are attached to circuit, district, superior, county, family, common pleas, probate, or municipal courts, often as afterthoughts. Even where a separate but integrated juvenile court does exist, the judge often operates independently of the larger system of justice of which he is ostensibly a part. Because the juvenile court may hear cases of violations that would be adult crimes, as well as cases of violations of ordinances that apply only to children (relating to curfew, school attendance, restrictions on the use of alcohol and tobacco, and so on), its responsibility is extremely broad. Most delinquency cases before juvenile courts in the United States involve incorrigibility, runaways, and other problems of child-parent or child-teacher interaction.[30]

Nearly forty states currently provide for the waiver or transfer of certain cases from the juvenile to the adult court. Waiver laws vary greatly, however. Approximately half fail to attach any conditions to the judge's discretionary powers. About one-third of the states authorize waivers for any offense if the youth is over a specified age, the lowest being thirteen years. In one-fifth of the states waivers are permitted only for specific offenses, often with age limits as well. In several states stringent waiver criteria are softened if the youth is already under supervision at the time of his offense. Generally there are few written criteria to guide the judge in deciding whether or not to waive a case to an adult court. Those that do exist are generally extremely broad (for example, "not amenable to treatment in juvenile court" or "not a fit subject" for juvenile-court jurisdiction). Although many states have allowed judges to waive jurisdiction to adult courts without hearings, this practice has been recently challenged by the U.S. Supreme Court in *Kent v. United States* (1966) and *Gault v. Arizona* (1967). An even more difficult problem is the nature of the evidence that the judge is willing to hear in the juvenile court. The informality of the hearing has often allowed relaxation of the rules of evidence and admission of hearsay or unsworn testimony. Consequently the standard of proof has commonly been lower than that required in the adult court. Prosecuting attorneys and defense lawyers have not very often participated in juvenile proceedings, although provision of lawyers for children has been encouraged since the 1966 and 1967 decisions. One-third of the states now provide by statute for notice of the right to counsel, assignment of counsel, or both. Practices still vary in the remaining states, however.

A survey by the National Council of Juvenile Court Judges in 1963 found that, of 1,564 judges (approximately 70 percent of those handling juvenile cases), 71 percent had law degrees, although 48 percent had received no undergraduate degrees. The average age was fifty-three, and the average salary for a full-time judge was $12,493.15. Nearly 75 percent had been elected to office, a third after initial interim appointments. Of the full-time judges, 72 percent spent 25 or less percent of their time on juvenile matters. One-third indicated that no probation officer or social worker was available to their courts; 83 percent lacked regularly available psychiatric or psychological consultants.[31]

Juvenile-court philosophy has never been fully realized. The community has never provided the material and human resources necessary to fulfill the ideals that prompted the creation of juvenile courts. The juvenile-court judge has not enjoyed high status within the bar. The time spent in hearing a juvenile case has often been a fraction of what was necessary for an effective decision. The National Council on Crime and Delinquency, for example, estimated that the average hearing in Cook County (Illinois) Family Court takes slightly more than fifteen minutes, about half the time that the Council believed necessary.[32] Other community resources are equally lacking. Few psychologists or psychiatrists are available; numbers of caseworkers, foster homes, and youth institutions are inadequate. Only 99 of 235 agencies in a sample studied by the President's Commission on Law Enforcement and Administration of Justice, for example, used foster homes, and only 10 percent operated group homes. Most often, the only realistic alternatives open to the juvenile court are outright release, probation, or institutionalization, each of which operates on a less effective level than juvenile-court philosophers desired.[33]

The Kent and Gault Decisions

The first Federal juvenile case to come before the U.S. Supreme Court was *Kent v. United States* (1966). A minor boy, Morris Kent, was accused of housebreaking, robbery, and rape; jurisdiction was waived to the U.S. District Court of the District of Columbia after a "full investigation" of the facts by the local juvenile court. When the latter refused to grant or rule on a motion by Kent's lawyer to hold a hearing or to permit his access to the social records and probation reports on which the judge had based his waiver, Kent filed a motion in the District Court to dismiss the indictment on the grounds that the waiver was invalid; this motion was denied. After Kent had been found guilty and sentenced to thirty to ninety years in prison, the case was appealed to the U.S. Supreme Court, which reversed and remanded the case to the lower court because the judge had failed to grant a hearing, to give counsel access to requested records, or to state the reasons for his waiver of jurisdiction. Justice Abe Fortas, speaking for the majority, wrote, "There is evidence for concern that the child receives the worst of both worlds: that he gets neither the protections accorded to adults nor the solicitous care and regenerative treatment postulated for children."[34] The presiding juvenile-court judge, Orman W. Ketcham, later suggested that juveniles be given the same rights as those granted to adults under Supreme Court guarantees relative to admission or confessions and due process.

The first *state* juvenile-court case appealed to the U.S. Supreme Court, *Gault v. Arizona,* involved that precise issue. Gerald Gault, judged a delinquent and sentenced to a possible six-year term in the Arizona reformatory for making obscene telephone calls with a son of a Globe, Arizona, policeman, was held in custody for twelve hours before his mother was notified. Although a petition was filed against him the next day, it was never served upon his parents. The complainant did not attend the hearing or testify against the youth, but the latter was finally sentenced to the state industrial school until the age of twenty-one or until a state board determined his readiness for release. An adult facing the same charge would have been subject to a maximum fine of $50 or two months in jail; Gerald Gault served six months. After two unproductive appeals in the Arizona courts, Gault successfully appealed to the U.S. Supreme Court, which, on May 15, 1967, reversed his conviction and extended the principles of the earlier *Escobedo v. Illinois* and *Miranda v. Arizona* decisions to juvenile-court practice. Thenceforth juveniles were to be accorded rights to private or court-appointed counsel in cases that might result in incarceration, to confront and cross-examine witnesses, to receive adequate warning of the privilege against self-incrimination, to remain silent, and to receive early notice of the charges. "Under the Constitution, the condition of being a boy," Justice Fortas wrote for the eight-to-one majority, "does not justify a kangaroo court."[35]

The procession of juvenile-court cases to the state appeals and supreme courts and the Federal courts has not ceased. The search for solutions to the problem of juvenile delinquency continues. This disparity between the goals of the juvenile courts and actual practice remains. Whether or not the gap can be closed is still to be seen. But because delinquency is often the beginning of eventual criminality, the problems of the juvenile court must be solved.[36]

NOTES

1. Home Office, *Report of the Committee on Children and Young Persons* (London: 1960), p. 22.
2. Home Office, *Report of the Departmental Committee on the Treatment of Young Offenders* (London: 1927), p. 1.
3. U.S. Children's Bureau, *The Child, the Family and the Court* (Washington, D.C.: 1933), p. 12, quoted in Pauline V. Young, *Social Treatment in Probation and Delinquency* (New York: 1937), p. 173.
4. Charles L. Chute, "The Juvenile Court in Retrospect," *Federal Probation*, 3 (September 1949), 4.
5. Boris S. Nikiforov, "Fundamental Principles of Soviet Criminal Law," *The Modern Law Review* (January 1960), 41.
6. Herbert H. Lou, *Juvenile Courts in the United States* (Chapel Hill, N.C.: 1927), p. 18.
7. Albert G. Hess, "The American Juvenile Court: Then and Now," *Kriminologische Wegzeichen, Festschrift für Hans von Hentig* (Hamburg: 1967), pp. 271–286.
8. Richard D. Knudten, ed., *Criminological Controversies* (New York: 1968), pp. 265–305.
9. Albert W. Silver, "Retooling for Delinquency Prevention and Rehabilitation in Juvenile Courts," *Federal Probation*, 30 (March 1966), 29–32.
10. U.S. Children's Bureau, *Standard Juvenile Court Act* (Washington, D.C.: 1925).
11. William H. Sheridan, *Standards for Juvenile and Family Courts* (Washington, D.C.: 1966), p. 36.
12. *Ibid.*, p. 28.
13. *Ibid.*, p. 9.
14. *Ibid.*, pp. 34–35.
15. *Ibid.*, p. 66.
16. Institutional care for a single child cost approximately $2,760 a year in the early 1960s. Some states that offer better treatment opportunities spend more than $4,000 on each juvenile annually. Yet the average annual cost of probation services per child is less than $200 to $300 a year. See U.S. Children's Bureau, *Statistics on Public Institutions for Delinquent Children* (Washington, D.C.: 1963), and Sheridan, *op. cit.*, p. 82.
17. Sheridan, *op. cit.*, p. 29.
18. *Ibid.*, pp. 21–22.
19. *Ibid.*, p. 22.

20. *Ibid.*, p. 48.

21. *Ibid.*, pp. 63–64. The police ultimately may use their discretionary powers, even in juvenile cases. If they do not believe that court action should be taken, they may warn or admonish, advise the child or his parents about appropriate community resources and welfare or other agencies, or refer the case to a social agency empowered by law to offer services to children for the good of the community.

22. *Ibid.*, pp. 68–69.

23. See National Council on Crime and Delinquency, "Teen-Age Juries," *Crime and Delinquency* (October 1966).

24. Sheridan, *op. cit.*, p. 77.

25. Paul W. Tappan, *Juvenile Delinquency* (New York: 1949), p. 251.

26. Herbert A. Bloch and Frank T. Flynn, *Delinquency: The Juvenile Offender in America Today* (New York: 1956), p. 358.

27. Sheridan, *op. cit.*, p. 2.

28. *Ibid.*, pp. 27–28.

29. U.S. Children's Bureau, *Juvenile Court Statistics* (Washington, D.C.: 1964), p. 1.

30. U.S. Children's Bureau, *Juvenile Court Statistics* (Washington, D.C.: 1965), pp. 1–5.

31. Center for Behavioral Sciences, *Judges Look at Themselves: Profile of the Nation's Court Judges* (Washington, D.C.: 1965).

32. National Council on Crime and Delinquency, *The Cook County Family (Juvenile) Court and Arthur J. Andy Home* (Chicago: 1963), pp. 28–29.

33. Robert W. Winslow, *Juvenile Delinquency in a Free Society* (Belmont, Calif.: 1968), p. 129.

34. *Kent v. United States, U.S. Supreme Court Reports* (1966).

35. *Gault v. Arizona, U.S. Supreme Court Reports* (1967).

36. See Nathan Goldman, *The Differential Selection of Juvenile Offenders for Court Appearance* (New York: 1963).

Part Seven

TREATMENT OF JUVENILE DELINQUENTS AND YOUTHFUL OFFENDERS

Chapter 19

■ *Attempts at Treatment*

■ *The Absence of a Treatment Philosophy*

Although juvenile delinquents are sent to various state institutions for re-habilitation, institutional treatment methods are limited and often non-existent. A visitor can quickly embarrass his staff escort at almost any state institution by inquiring about the treatment methods there. Almost any-where in the world, in fact, he is likely to receive a vague, hesitant de-scription of daily activities, usually sprinkled with terms like "rehabilita-tion," "correction," "reformation," "reeducation," "making the children good citizens," and the like. Although most institutions pride themselves upon the shining cleanliness of their physical plants, well-designed work and education programs, organized and responsible administrations and staffs, disciplined inmate populations, and skill at maneuvering within budget limitations, very few, if any, are able to outline a coherent and de-veloped treatment philosophy and method for redirecting children from delinquency to socially normative conduct. Most institutions pay lip service to this goal, but few are able to conceive or put into operation a meaningful treatment philosophy and method.

Most institutions are unable to delineate their goals clearly or to find the personnel necessary to enact significant treatment programs. In 1964, for example, the U.S. Children's Bureau discovered that only limited im-provement in institutional personnel and practices of institutions for juve-nile delinquents had occurred in the interval since an earlier survey in 1958. The majority of treatment, educational, and administrative staff of these institutions still did not meet the minimum educational standards of the corrections profession. Staff categories that ranked especially low in educational background included cottage personnel, social workers, teach-ers, occupational supervisors, and medical aides. Nor did the majority of these treatment, educational, and administrative staffs have even the recommended background experience for their employment. In fact 81 percent had less than one year of previous institutional service. Such findings suggest that institutions serving delinquent children experience considerable difficulty in recruiting and retaining sufficient well-qualified treatment, educational, and administrative personnel. High turnover among professionals in many institutions appears to be related to low salary scales and even in some instances to failure to implement recommended personnel policies and practices.[1]

The development and implementation of a treatment philosophy are limited by public demand for security from delinquents and criminals and by the confusion surrounding alternative treatment methods. Because the public, despite the philosophy behind the juvenile court, sees the delinquent as a wrongdoer (if not a criminal) who undermines law and order, it tends to demand his institutional segregation. Most institutions are already oriented in this direction but in any case would try to comply with public desires. And the confusion surrounding alternative treatment methods makes changes in institutional procedure difficult.

Proponents of each treatment system claim sole validity and efficiency for it; even a unified treatment program is undermined by conflicting philosophies. This lack of agreement undoubtedly contributes to the public's preference for incarceration. If students of delinquent and criminal behavior could explain the causes of deviance more specifically, an acceptable treatment philosophy and method could be more easily agreed upon. The complexity of the causes and the diversity of approaches, however, only add to the disagreement over treatment philosophy. Charles H. Shireman doubted that enough present knowledge about the human personality has yet been applied in correctional institutions to permit development of an acceptable treatment method.[2] Nor is enough yet known about juvenile delinquency or how to develop adequate treatment settings and techniques.

Although many professionals believe in individual treatment, others prefer institutionalization as a solution to delinquency. Some suggest individual psychological treatment, and others prefer group therapy. Some believe in the power of work, general socialization, or general mobilization of all community forces in a program that could include institutional treatment as necessary. Bernard Russel's suggestion that staffs in institutions for juvenile delinquents should consist of "clinical personnel, psychiatrists, social workers, psychologists, vocational instructors, recreation and athletic instructors, medical personnel, and a large number of nonprofessionals who have tremendous influence on the children in their daily living activities"[3] suggests the extent of the problem. Strangely enough, postinstitutionalization recidivism does not appear to be as great as might be expected, despite the absence of deliberate treatment methods. But an operational treatment philosophy is no less necessary for all that.[4]

Its absence is also partly the result of the many methods of state administration of juvenile services that exist—as many methods as there are states. State administrative structures fit into one or more of the following classifications: no central state agency (seven states), an autonomous central agency (nine states), a central department of correction administratively responsible for both adults and juveniles (six states), a specific organization of juvenile services as part of a larger unit of government with additional services or functions (thirteen states), and a large unit with several functions but no identifiable organization to supervise juvenile services specifically (fifteen states). Current trends are toward statewide consolidation of services for children and youth, including basic programs of protection, prevention, probation, detention, diagnosis, institutionalization, and aftercare. Maurice A. Harmon argued that these trends should be encouraged; he pointed out that treatment-oriented programs for adults have frequently been accepted only after their counterparts in juvenile correctional programs have been established and that increased organizational independence will allow the freedom and flexibility of protective services, delinquency-prevention programs, and diagnostic and treatment facilities necessary to change with the changing needs of children and youth.[5]

■ *Attempts at Treatment*

The Psychological Approach

One of the most popular treatment philosophies is founded upon the assumption that *ego-alien impulses,* expressed in delinquent conduct, should and can be eliminated or regulated. According to Franz Alexander and Louis B. Shapiro, "Ego-alien impulses are often of an aggressively antisocial nature" and "form the major portion of delinquents."[6] They hypothesized that delinquency is a behavioral disturbance caused by unconscious forces, probably fantasies or impulses expressed through the delinquent act. These unconscious forces may develop from the child's relationship with his parents and may function as dynamic determinants of behavior. Because of a weak superego, a child may be incapable of keeping his unconscious repressed and under control and may therefore express its content in delinquent acts. The ego-alien theory assumes that delinquency is a functional result of an inadequate ego, which may be expressed in neurotic reactions, frequently of an obsessive-compulsive type, and in irrational thoughts and impulses that cannot be successfully controlled.

Although the psychological approach requires treatment of individual personality, the importance of the social environment is not neglected. But it is taken into account only insofar as it influences the individual, rather than the group member. Psychological tools are primarily individualistic in nature, but the rules, discipline, and daily program of the institution apply to all. Adherents of this approach may fail to recognize, however, that many of the delinquent's feelings and attitudes may result not from ego-alien impulses but from self-satisfaction. The delinquent youth, for example, may consider himself a success, even though others view him as a failure, if he completes seven grades when his parents had finished only three.[7]

Group Therapy

Although group therapy concentrates on individual treatment of the delinquent within a group context, it differs from the approach that views him primarily as a member of society. The individual is placed in a smaller group for therapy, in an effort to simulate social reality and establish a "group situation with its social give-and-take."[8] The group-therapy approach assumes that the delinquent will reveal and discuss his anxieties and difficulties once he understands that he is not isolated and that other offenders share similar problems. He will thus be stimulated by others to express himself more fully and with fewer inhibitions. Although his therapy may take various forms, group activity of a particular type remains a central feature of the daily program. The rapid growth of group therapy is the result not only of its recognized effectiveness but also of the lower staff costs.

Community therapy, similar to the kind of guided group interaction used in the Highfields treatment program, has been adopted at the Wisconsin School for Girls to encourage girls who are unable to tolerate the anxiety released in individual psychotherapy and are unwilling to relate to older staff members to find tolerable outlets for their personal anxieties.[9] An experiment with group therapy conducted in a Milan, Italy, prison revealed, however, that prisoners selected because they had held criminal ideals in their youth showed strong polemical and vindictive tendencies in behavior at the beginning of the study. They passed into a maniacal stage, which was followed by depression, and the last stage was characterized by lack of confidence in the group and preference for individual treatment. Nevertheless, each prisoner did surrender his ideas of omnipotence and adopted a more realistic attitude. The researchers concluded that there is a need to establish community treatment centers to continue work begun in prison.[10]

Work Therapy

Work therapy has been encouraged in many institutions, in order to capitalize upon an acceptable treatment method and to achieve a level of institutional efficiency and self-reliance. It is based upon the eighteenth-century penal philosophy of John Howard, who suggested that diligent men will become honest men.[11] Proponents of work therapy have argued that acclimatization to hard, disciplined work, especially when coupled with vocational training, will result in eventual individual conformity to basic social norms; constructive work is the essential feature of social life, and deviance will end once traditional work patterns are acquired. Staff members are content to train institutionalized deviants in habits of work and apparently expect them to become attached to social normality in the abnormal social setting of the institution. Whether or not the institutional work pattern is carried over into the "normal" society depends, of course, on each "treated" individual. Work-therapy proponents hope that work habits will wean deviants from deviance even in an institutional subculture.

Treatment Goals

Not all experts have agreed with any of these earlier approaches, however. Jacob Chwast believed that treatment can scarcely move forward if the problem of value conflict is not confronted.[12] Because almost all delinquents have personal problems and difficulties, ego-alien impulses, repressions, and similar personality factors, no treatment method that fails to account for the specific needs of each person can be efficient. Although many individual problems can be successfully solved in institutional group or multiple treatment, others have been faced within a regular work context that is traditionally part of the male role. Diagnosis and explanation of personality disorders and other deviant behavior, Lloyd E. Ohlin believed, "must show concern for the organizational context in which the behavior occurs, as well as for the traits of the actor" if it is to be successful.[13] Although it has been customary, as Donald R. Cressey noted, to assume that expressions of uncooperativeness, loyalty, honesty, aggression, and even paranoia simply reflect personal characteristics,[14] insight into total personality and development of valid treatment goals require further investigation into delinquent relationships and value conflicts. Although the inmate as an individual may respond positively to the program and discipline of the institution, even in a group-therapy context, he may be unable to transfer his institutional success to his postrelease functioning in the larger and less controlled community. If the institution, for example, operates with a strict unified middle-class value system, ignoring lower-class values and status, his institutional response may differ from his response in pluralistic society with its multiple values. For many, the institution therefore offers a security that is unavailable on the outside. If the delinquent is largely a product of value conflicts between lower and middle class, any treatment that ignores such conflicts ignores a major cause of delinquent conduct. If the institution inflexibly promotes only middle-class values, the conflict will continue within its confines, even though submerged. If, on the other hand, the institution adopts the lower-class value system to avoid conflict within the institution, the conflict will be resumed when the delinquent reenters society. A pluralistic value system may avoid or reconcile the conflict, however. In any case, no treatment method can be efficient if delinquency is merely attributed to individual weaknesses, if its real causes are ignored, and if the social relationships that foster it are overlooked. Many experts have viewed foster-home placement as a viable alternative to juvenile institutionalization, though others have questioned its value. Zira de Fries, Shirley Jenkins, and Ethelyn C. Williams, for example, found that group living in an institution is better for the child than living in a foster family, especially in view of the usual quality of foster parents.[15]

■ Institutional Programs

Early Development of Institutions

"Imprisonment as a punishment of first instance," according to Lionel W. Fox, "has developed, as a complete conception, almost within the time of men now living."[16] Although this statement is true of the adult prison system, it is most aptly applied to juvenile-treatment institutions. Until the eighteenth century corporal, pecuniary, or capital punishment predominated, regardless of the criminal's age. Capital punishment in all its forms, the use of the stocks and the pillory, confinement in irons, ducking, chaining, and other brutal corporal punishments were applied to those who would now be treated separately as children, juvenile delinquents, and youthful offenders. Even ancient societies had prisons, dried cisterns, town guardrooms, abandoned stonepits, the Carcer Mammertinus and the Tullianum in Rome, lockups (ergastulum), and places of disciplinary detention (coercitio) for children and adults.[17] Imprisonment, inflicted upon adults but not upon children in ancient Rome, took the form of restriction on place of residence (relegatio), forced deportation to a desert or an island (deportatio), or an order to do public work (opus publicum, opus metalli).

No distinction was made between children and adults in sentencing to the ergastulum claustri (a type of workhouse) used by the Roman Catholic Church after the fourth century for ecclesiastical punishments. Although municipal authorities in the Middle Ages locked up petty criminals in towers, such detention usually lasted for only very short periods. Because longer imprisonment was avoided, in order not to incur expenses for the maintenance of prisoners, any treatment or institutional program was out of the question. A longer deprivation of liberty, up to six months, was first stipulated for children and adults in the fourteenth century by Italian municipal ordinances, but they did not provide for treatment programs. The ideas of deterrence and retribution that prevailed in these periods did not permit the emergence of any penal or treatment system presently defined. Most places of detention, like the Leads of Venice and the *Lochgefängnis* in Nuremberg, were used primarily for executions.

The first attempt to use convicts economically involved forced labor as galley slaves; employers were the ones to benefit. This system was probably first applied in France in the fifteenth century, but its demonstrated advantages led other countries to follow the French example. Landlocked countries, where galley slaves were not needed, sold their prisoners to naval powers. Although the incredible cruelty of galley slavery killed convicts almost as frequently as did the death penalty, the state did have the benefit of their strength before they died. Galley slavery, however, was less a form of institutionalization than of forced public labor (as in public participation in building roads, fortresses, or buildings), a type of penal sanction applied to physically strong juveniles and adults in the sixteenth to eighteenth centuries.[18] In time transportation, a practice originating in Spain but gathering adherents throughout the world, was also introduced to remove harmful individuals from society by deporting them to the colonies, where they could develop new economic outlets for imperialistic powers. Even recently, *deportation*, a refined form of transportation, has been used to satisfy class or racial rage and to exterminate millions. The proportions of children and youth among galley slaves and those who were transported is not known. In "modern" deportation too there has been no distinction according to age.

After deterrence, neutralization, and elimination had proved to be ineffective against the great masses of beggars, rogues, thieves, and robbers who appeared in society as a consequence of frequent wars, the primitive idea of *special prevention* was reintroduced into penal theory. This reintroduction occurred, however, because of practical needs rather than of theoretical considerations. Impressed by Bishop Ridley in 1553,[19] Edward VI of England gave him an old royal palace, the Bridewell (an abbreviation of its original name St. Bride's Well) for a house of correction. By 1576 county justices were required to provide similar institutions in their jurisdictions, each named Bridewell after the original model. A rather mixed group of inmates was housed in these correctional institutions. Criminals, vagabonds, actors without licenses, and students expelled from school all fell under their administrative control. Although the original plan for these institutions had included training in skills through work with necessary tools or equipment, this goal remained unfulfilled. Several sources refer to trade, vocational training, and the practice of many occupations in the Bridewells,[20] but they refer to plans rather than to operational programs.

Special prevention through individual treatment was born in the Netherlands independently of the English plan. When the Dutch courts grew reluctant near the end of the sixteenth century to inflict death penalties upon juvenile thieves, the Council of Amsterdam in 1589 ordered the conversion of a cloister into a prison (*Tuchthuiz* or *Zuchthaus*, "house of correction") and in 1597 created a separate house for girls and women (*Spinhuiz* or *Spinnhaus*, "spinning house") in order to "keep children working" and to guide them toward "better life-conduct"[21] through work. Forced labor was thus used for disciplinary ends. Under the Dutch plan juvenile delinquents, criminals, vagabonds, and incorrigibles or unmanageables were treated in the Amsterdam house of correction if their relatives desired. After engaging in communal work during the day, the inmates were separated at night. Although the intensive work was at first confined to the spinning of velvet and wool, it was later expanded to include clipping and rasping of colored logwood. Because these houses created a near monopoly in this production, the inmates and those of similar institutions were described in eighteenth-century literature as protected by *Sanctus Raspinus*. The success of the Amsterdam house of correction depended, however, upon the high quality of the work, the earnings from which were partly distributed among the inmates; sufficient food; strict discipline; and a rudimentary program of education.

The Amsterdam approach, in effect, stimulated the development of educational and goal-oriented imprisonment. Although far from ideal for juvenile delinquents, it was a starting point that favorably influenced the creation of other goal-oriented institutions. Because it was particularly well equipped and its institutional atmosphere was especially progressive, the Amsterdam correctional institution represented a radical departure from earlier retributive attitudes. Consequently, it became an object of international interest and was visited by many expert and lay observers from other countries. Many towns, including Bremen in 1609, Lübeck in 1613, and Hamburg in 1699, followed this example, best expressed in the words above the gates of the Hamburg *Spinnhaus: labore nutrior, labore plector* ("education through work, punishment through work"). Although the courts generally determined the sentences to be served, the town councils also possessed authority to stipulate indeterminate sentences and to release "prisoners" on condition of good conduct and work after discharge, a forerunner of modern parole.

Whereas these Dutch and German institutions attempted to reform offenders by exposing them to hard work, the Hospice of San Michele in Rome, established by Pope Clement XI in 1703, emphasized the discipline of "bad boys." Probably the world's first juvenile prison, this hospice was intended especially for incorrigible boys whose parents sought their admission and for criminal offenders under the age of twenty. They were assigned to spin textiles for the staff of the Papal State and for the galley crews; they also participated in religious education as part of a treatment process. They worked in groups during the day but were separated at night. Big signs demanding *silentium* warned of the prohibition against talking. Although efficacy of the theological atmosphere as a tool of discipline is unclear, the establishment of this hospice contributed significantly to the development of delinquent and criminal institutions.

Jean Jacques Philippe Vilain, the energetic Burgomaster of Ghent, followed a different tack in 1773, when he opened a reorganized local prison modeled after the Amsterdam house of correction for the purpose of reforming the prisoners to honesty and diligence. Introducing occupations that might offer future livelihoods to discharged inmates, Vilain also adopted an inmate-classification system based upon age and sex and an early form of parole. As beggars, vagrants, juvenile delinquents, and adult criminals were admitted to this *maison de force* (workhouse), the contours of the modern prison began to emerge.

The Influence of John Howard

Institutions of this type, established by individual initiative, were rare phenomena in the eighteenth century. The overwhelming majority of existing prisons and other penal institutions were absolutely inappropriate for the reform or correction of juveniles or criminals. Children and youths were usually imprisoned with adult criminals, vagabonds, prostitutes, and even lunatics under deplorable conditions. Often they lay idle on rotten straw in underground cellars or chained together in dangerous fortresses, exposed to the torture and exploitation of the guards, who starved the poor and blackmailed those with economic assets. Because any potential advantage or privilege was quickly assumed by adult criminals, children and adolescents were absolutely helpless. Elementary hygiene and sanitation and adequate working conditions were nonexistent. Education of the offender was beyond reason. The despotism of the guards made starvation and physical suffering characteristic of institutional life. These institutions were in fact schools for criminals, hotbeds of various illness, and brothels, rather than prisons designed for criminal justice or education.

As the era of enlightenment matured, John Howard (1726–1790), an assiduous and enthusiastic English philanthropist, personally and in writing exhorted European official and public opinion to recognize gloomy and sordid prison conditions.[22] Dedicated to the cause of humanity, Howard had his first experiences of prison near Lisbon, where he studied the effects of the earthquake of 1775 and the public need for relief. He was then taken into custody with his fellow passengers by a French pirate and, as if Howard himself were a criminal, was transported to the prisons of Brest and Morlaix when the pirate was captured. There he became interested in prison conditions. Upon his return home he was elected High Sheriff of Bedfordshire and visited many English prisons, keeping Parliament informed of his shocking observations through one of his friends who was a member.

Two years later Howard left England to broaden his penal knowledge through visits to other European prisons, largely in Holland and Belgium. He returned to England in 1777 and published his famous *The State of the Prisons* at his own expense.[23] His book, the result of some 42,000 miles of traveling at an expense of £ 30,000, reflects the prolixity of an uneducated man, although it is characterized by practical sense, hard-hitting logic, and humanitarian feelings. Arguing that if one could make prisoners diligent, "they will be honest," Howard supported prison reforms to encourage work opportunities, humanitarian treatment, and inmate classification. His work, however, did not end at this point. He continued to visit Spanish, Portuguese, Austrian, and Russian prisons. He died of gaol fever (a form of typhus) in Russia on his last journey and was buried in 1790 in the Crimean village of Kherson. Although Thomas Carlyle called him a "boringly scrupulous person," the truth of his character is best expressed in the inscription on his grave: *Ad sepulchrum stas, quisquis es, amici* ("Whoever stands here at my grave is my friend").

Institutions for Juveniles

The English Philanthropic Society of London, thanks to Howard's work, established in 1788 the beginnings of a cottage system for beggars, vagrants, and other children arrested for petty crimes. Although Howard had urged the strict separation of children from adult prisoners, it had been very rare up to that time. The London Philanthropic Society, however, provided three small cottages for Oliver Twist type boys picked up in the streets and later employed them in agricultural work.[24] As the Society expanded its activities, it organized a home for dependent children in 1806. In 1815 the Society for the Improvement of Prison Discipline and the Reformation of Juvenile Offenders, another association interested in juvenile delinquency classified the multiple causes of delinquency as deviant family atmosphere, drinking, loitering in places that tempt youth to thefts, dislike of work, and others that are still valid today.[25] Its establishment of an asylum for delinquent children brought world recognition and creation of similar societies in other countries.[26] Consequently, English boys' institutions were opened near Birmingham at Sheldon-on-Dunsmore, in London at Hackneywicks, and in other cities. A home for girls was also inaugurated at Chiswick in London. A hospital in the English Parkhurst, now used as a prison for adult offenders, was converted into a detention and correction center for juveniles and young offenders in 1838. The 1857 Industrial School Act finally made provision for training juvenile delinquents in private industrial schools separate from prisons.

European efforts made a swift impression on the American continent, and a handful of devoted men led by John Griscom established the Society for the Reformation of Juvenile Delinquents in 1823 and opened the first American house of refuge in New York City in 1825. Intended for both sexes, its first residents included three girls who had been picked up on the streets. The rather poor building near Madison Square, originally used for military purposes, soon proved to be inadequate, however, and the Society moved its facilities to another location. A similar institution was established in Boston (1826) and another in Philadelphia (1828), as interest in this approach continued to expand. Although their sponsors were concerned with the treatment of young offenders, these establishments were little more than juvenile prisons, both architecturally and administratively. The mere removal of children away from the criminal influences of the streets and confinement in the gloomy darkness of brick buildings were thought to be adequate to prevent delinquency. Although the proponents of these institutions were motivated by charity and an interest in social work, they did not really understand the essence of the delinquency and crime problem when they began the development of institutions specifically designed for juvenile delinquents.

The emergence of the English Borstal system can now be recognized as a decisive turning point in the evolution of institutions for delinquent youth. Emphasizing both *negative prevention* (keeping children away from criminal pressures) and *positive treatment* (helping children to develop the strength to resist criminal pressures), the Borstal system was conceived by the director of English prisons, Sir Evelyn Ruggles-Brise, on a visit to American reformatories for adult criminals and was patterned after many of the good-conduct and educational incentives in operation at the Elmira reformatory in New York.[27] Upon his return to England Ruggles-Brise immediately converted a part of the prison at Borstal (near Rochester, Kent) to a specialized institution for reformative training of youthful offenders between sixteen and twenty-one. Based upon the philosophy that "the good must be developed to beat the bad,"[28] Borstal training was aimed at the overall development of character and capacities. Emphasizing hard work, progressive development of trust, increased personal responsibility for decision making, and growth of self-control,[29] its success prompted the establishment of a number of similar institutions, all called "Borstal," throughout England.

Only with the emergence of the English Borstals at the turn of the century did institutions begin to offer deliberate and positive treatment for young offenders. Devoting attention to the special problems of the age group between sixteen and twenty-one, the Borstal system sought prevention of delinquency and treatment of delinquents in this group, which especially reflected the changes brought about by World War II. Whether the Borstal philosophy is an enlightened innovation by dynamic pioneers in the struggle against delinquency and youth crime or whether it represents only a revision of the narrow philosophy of the house of correction may be answered by rising delinquency statistics.

Detention Today

The temporary detention of a juvenile delinquent for a short period before or after his court hearing usually occurs in a jail or detention center of some kind. He may also be detained there for long-term treatment if his home or any available institution appears inadequate for the purpose. If detention does occur, it is generally in cases in which the child has allegedly violated the law or has been found in conditions dangerous to his own welfare. In essence, he is taken into custody (jail or detention) when such action is judged to be in his best interests or in that of the community. Such action is most frequent when he is living in circumstances dangerous to his physical or intellectual welfare, when a hearing has not yet been held, when the court has not yet reached a decision, when a medical or psychiatric examination is believed necessary before final judgment, or when further investigation is directed.

The child or youth is usually detained in quarters close to or attached to the court building. The best that can be said for the experience of many young people detained in jail, Sophia M. Robison has declared, "is that their keepers . . . are sometimes kindly."[30] Although many jails are run-down buildings well past their prime, newer jails, built and equipped to provide considerable comfort, are sometimes well above the delinquent's home standard of living. In either location, however, the child remains in custody with little or no treatment,[31] which is usually reserved for long-term detention in training or industrial schools. In most states commitment to such schools is for an indeterminate period, usually to a maximum age of twenty-one. Such detention is prescribed by the juvenile court, and it is not a temporary or interim measure.

The practice of holding children of juvenile-court age in custody for court disposition usually takes two different forms. In *normal detention* the child who may have committed a delinquent act is held in a physically restricted facility pending court disposition or his transfer to another jurisdiction or agency. In *shelter care* the child is placed in a home for a longer period. The latter form is generally used in cases involving dependent or neglected rather than delinquent children. Such children are placed in boarding, foster, or group homes; temporary institutions; or even, in some instances, halfway houses. Although these two forms of detention are designed to serve different ends, not all states or jurisdictions have been able to provide them for the ever-expanding juvenile population.[32]

More than 409,000 juveniles, nearly two-thirds of all adolescents arrested, were admitted to special juvenile facilities in 1965. On the average they were detained for twelve days at a cost of $130 per child, a total of $53 million.[33] More than 100,000 of these children were admitted to adult jail and similar facilities because of the absence of juvenile-detention facilities. Only Connecticut, Puerto Rico, and Vermont refused to use adult facilities for juvenile lockups. Although thirteen states have accepted some responsibility for juvenile detention, responsibility is still largely vested in counties. Only nine states have moved to provide regional detention centers for counties with too few youths to justify local facilities.[34] For the most part, jail detention is characterized by enforced idleness, minimal supervision, and personal rejection.

Modern Juvenile Institutions in the United States

Contemporary training-school treatment, although it avoids some of the shortcomings of detention, has its own limitations; it does, however, help the child to overcome many of his problems.[35] Usually providing a diagnosis of the child's deficiencies and a plan for treatment, the training school strives to prepare the child to return to society. Because rehabilitation and attitude change cannot be measured accurately, the child's general conduct and apparent response to institutional treatment determine his release date. "The people in a training school who spend the most time with children and have a great effect on their well-being," according to Russel, "are those responsible for supervising them in their cottages and for moving them through most of the day."[36] Called "cottage" or "house" parents, these people conduct the actual treatment, a combination of social, psychological, medical, and common-sense prescriptions. The more frequent use of institutional psychologists and the creation of meaningful education programs are, however, necessary in the future.[37]

A 1964–1965 survey of 220 state-operated juvenile institutions in the United States and Puerto Rico, constituting 86 percent of the juvenile-training facilities in the United States, revealed a total 1965 capacity of 42,423 juveniles and an average daily population of 42,389, a 10.7 percent increase over the previous year. Although overcrowding of facilities was a common complaint, most overcrowded units were within 10 percent of their optimum limits. New construction, anticipated for 1975 occupancy, will increase present capacity by more than 42 percent.[38] Although six of the larger jurisdictions operated nine or more facilities apiece, eight states had only one juvenile facility each, and fourteen states managed only a boy's school and a girl's school each. The number of juvenile camps has increased in recent years, thanks to low costs of operation and overall success in dealing with juvenile problems.

Although the length of stay at a state training facility may range from four to twenty-four months, the median length is nine months. This figure may be somewhat misleading, however, for the continuous demand by the courts for use of these facilities may cut short the desirable treatment period. The length of stay in diagnostic treatment centers, on the other hand, ranges from twenty-eight to forty-five days.[39] Although diverse services are offered at these diagnostic or treatment facilities, many are of questionable quality. Nevertheless, 96 percent of the facilities in the survey sample reported provisions for medical, 94 percent for dental, 95 percent for recreational, 88 percent for educational, 86 percent for casework, 79 percent for counseling, 75 percent for psychological, and 71 percent for psychiatric services.[40]

Reported per capita operating expenditure in the fifty-two jurisdictions in the 1965 study was $3,411 a year, although costs ranged from a low of $371 in one jurisdiction to a high of $7,890 in another.

Of the 21,247 staff members employed in 1965, only 1,154 were treatment personnel (psychiatrists, psychologists, and social workers). The recommended ratio of 1 psychiatrist to 150 children was seldom achieved, and the average was closer to 1 to 282. Only 46 psychiatrists served the 220 state-operated facilities; more than half of them were employed in only five states. Sixty percent of all psychologists (106) were concentrated in nine states. Only twelve states approached the recommended ratio of one psychiatrist or psychologist to 150 children. In 1965 there was already need for 100 additional psychologists in juvenile institutions. The need for caseworkers was equally acute. Even the teacher-pupil ratio, recommended not to go below 1 to 15 had clearly done so.

Juvenile-training facilities are normal adjuncts to the state correctional system. Theoretically founded as schools to provide specialized programs for juveniles, these institutions are designed to handle the more serious or frequent adolescent offender and to prepare him for reentry into the community. The industrial school, or reformatory, was originally conceived as a place to teach the juvenile right from wrong and to develop the skills necessary for him to eventually do the "right." Discovery that nearly half those institutionalized eventually return has led in recent years to renewed emphasis upon evaluation of individual needs and creation of a personalized treatment program in which the youth looks at himself honestly.

Although training schools were designed for the more hardened delinquent youths, they have too frequently been used as convenient outlets for removing "undesirable" juveniles from communities. Too often they have been used as detention or holding facilities for youths in need of foster homes or other residential treatment and for youths in need of community supervision, as alternative facilities to overcrowded mental hospitals, and as maternity facilities for some female juveniles.[41] These shortcomings were undoubtedly behind the Supreme Court's decisions in *Kent v. United States* and *Gault v. Arizona*.

Corporal Punishment in Juvenile Institutions

Despite all efforts to modernize the architecture and treatment programs of juvenile institutions, they only gradually became free of the past, including official or unofficial corporal punishment to maintain institutional discipline. Although many institutions charged with the custody and control of several hundred delinquent youths found beating or infliction of pain simple and direct ways to prevent rebellion, corporal punishment in any form is a homeopathic method of curing brutality with brutality. Corporal punishment is based upon the principle that excessive pain will overcome the supposed pleasure of delinquency and crime. Included in the Code of Hammurabi, the Roman Law of XII Tabulares, the Carolingian laws, and the practice of ecclesiastic courts, corporal punishment was a social response to delinquency and crime from the era of blood revenge to the eighteenth century. In that time hardly any part of the human body was exempt from punishment.

Although retribution and deterrence were primary punishment goals, as they still are today, punishment also involved secondary goals of shame and limitation of freedom or rights. As an independent punishment for adult offenders, corporal punishment disappeared earlier in England than in the United States. It was virtually abolished as a judicial penalty for adults in Britain in 1861, remaining in force only for incorrigible roguery, certain actions against an ambassador or his servants, irregular slaughter of horses, shooting at the sovereign, and after 1898 living on immoral earnings (males). Because "corporal punishment was regarded as a valuable alternative to imprisonment,"[42] these limitations were not applied to juveniles. Not until the recommendations of the Cadogan Committee were embodied in legislation in 1948 did the English correct this oversight[43] and abandon legal corporal punishment entirely.

The debate over abolition continues, however. Many people still believe that there is an essential difference between legally ordered corporal punishment and physical pain inflicted by others. Although adherents of corporal punishment argue that parents, teachers, and institutional staff are able to anticipate the value of such punishment and each boy's response to its application, experience proves that this belief is not valid in all cases. Corporal punishment offers an immediate sanction against the violator, compared to lengthier court litigation, but its proponents ignore the questions of guilt, innocence, responsibility, intent, and psychological capacity. In most instances corporal punishment is not inflicted to aid the child but only to punish him. If parents or institutional staff waited a short time after their decision before inflicting pain, punishment would not be executed at all in many cases. The chronological unit of decision and infliction of punishment is a product of the punisher's agitated emotional state, in which the pressure of the moment permits no escape from both the "sentence" and its "execution." Although many believe that parental or institutional retribution through infliction of physical pain will lead the child to develop affection or at least respect for the one who inflicts the pain, it more often develops fear and hatred if administered in an impersonal social setting. Far too often proponents of corporal punishment misinterpret personal responses motivated by fear and hatred as signs of affection and respect. When they do, the goals of treatment and correction are not well served.[44]

NOTES

1. U.S. Children's Bureau, *Personnel and Personnel Practices in Public Institutions for Delinquent Children: A Survey* (Washington, D.C.: 1966), pp. 1–29.

2. Charles H. Shireman, "How Can the Correctional School Correct?" *Crime and Delinquency*, 6 (1960), 267–274.

3. Bernard Russel, "Current Training Needs in the Field of Juvenile Delinquency," *Facts-Facets, U.S. Children's Bureau* (Washington, D.C.: 1960), p. 5.

4. During the past twenty years extensive research has been conducted by social scientists to learn more of the factors associated with delinquency. Consequently, changes in theoretical explanations of delinquency causation have affected the basic orientations of treatment philosophers. Mabel A. Elliott has stated that eight areas of research are especially important in current thinking on delinquency: middle-class delinquency, cultural factors and anomie, personality traits and delinquency, attitudes toward authority, emotional factors in delinquency, deprivation among Negro delinquents, delinquent self-image, and street work research. See Mabel A. Elliott, "Trends in Theories Regarding Juvenile Delinquency and their Implication for Treatment Programs," *Federal Probation*, 31 (1967), 3–11.

5. Maurice A. Harmon, "Unraveling Administrative Organization of State Juvenile Services," *Crime and Delinquency*, 13 (1967), 432–438.

6. Franz Alexander and Louis B. Shapiro, "Neuroses, Behavior Disorders and Perversions," in Alexander and Helen Ross, eds., *Dynamic Psychiatry* (Chicago: 1957), p. 132.

7. E. Preston Sharp and Ellis S. Grayson, "How Delinquent Children Think and Feel," *Federal Probation*, 29 (1965), 12–16.

8. James C. Coleman, *Abnormal Psychology and Modern Life* (2nd ed.; Chicago: 1956), p. 559.

9. Marvin Hersko, "Community Therapy in an Institution for Delinquent Girls," *Federal Probation*, 28 (1964), 41–46.

10. Davide Lopez, Mario Morpurgo, and Wanda Maciotta Rolandin, "La Psicoterapia di Gruppo con i Delinquenti," *Quaderni di Criminologia Clinica*, 8 (1966), 405–422.

11. John Howard, *The State of the Prisons in England and Wales with some Preliminary Observations, and an Account of some foreign Prisons* (London: 1777).

12. Jacob Chwast, "Value Conflicts in Treating Delinquents," *Children*, 6 (May 1959), 95–100.

13. Lloyd E. Ohlin, "The Reduction of Role Conflict in Institutional Staff," *Children*, 5 (March 1958), 65–69.

14. Donald R. Cressey, *The Prison: Studies in Institutional Organization and Change* (New York: 1961), p. 7.

15. Zira de Fries, Shirley Jenkins, and Ethelyn C. Williams, "Treatment of Disturbed Children in Foster Care," *American Journal of Orthopsychiatry* (July 1964).

16. Lionel W. Fox, *The English Prison and Borstal Systems* (London: 1952), p. 19.

17. Ulpian, *Digest*, p. 48. Ulpian, however, did not refer to these "prisons" in their capacity as places of punishment.

18. For a detailed account of the history of imprisonment see, Otto Kirchheimer and

George Rusche, *Punishment and Social Structure* (New York: 1939); Harry Elmer Barnes and Negley K. Teeters, *New Horizons in Criminology: The American Crime Problem* (New York: 1943); Thorsten Sellin, *Pioneering in Penology: The Amsterdam House of Correction* (Philadelphia: 1944); and Max Grünhut, *Penal Reform* (London: 1948). For earlier authors, see Henry Mayhew and John Binny, *The Criminal Prisons of London* (London: 1862); Enoch C. Wines, *State of Prisons* (Cambridge: 1880); V. Holtzendorff-Jagemann, *Handbuch der Gefängniswesens* (Hamburg: 1888); K. Krohne, *Lehrbuch der Gefängniskunde unter Berücksichtigung der Kriminalstatistik und Kriminalpolitik* (Stuttgart: 1889); F. H. Wines, *Punishment and Reformation* (New York: 1895); Rusztem Vámbéry, *Büntetöjog* (Budapest: 1913); and George Ives, *History of Penal Methods* (London: 1914).

19. Fox and Walter C. Reckless give this date as 1553, Barnes and Teeters as 1557. Edward VI died in 1553, and in 1557 Mary I reigned.

20. Kirchheimer and Rusche, *op. cit.*, pp. 41–49.

21. Lothar Frede, "Gefängnisgeschichte," in Alexander Elster and Heinrich Lingemann, eds., *Handwörterbuch der Kriminologie und der Anderen Strafrechtlichen Hilfswissenschaften* (Berlin: 1933), p. 539.

22. For a detailed appraisal of Howard's work, see D. C. Howard, *John Howard: Prison Reformer* (London: 1958); and Stephen Schafer, *John Howard* (Budapest: 1940).

23. Howard, *The State of the Prisons, op. cit.*

24. See E. C. Wines, *op. cit.*

25. According to Frede, *op. cit.* (p. 544), this society was not established until 1817.

26. One of the earliest was established by Theodor Fliedner in Germany in 1826 under the name *Rheinsch-Westfälische Gefängnisgesellschaft.* English influence probably encouraged the development of the German *rauhen* houses, designed to stimulate family life; the first one was established in 1830 by Johann Heinrich Wichern.

27. This reformatory was opened in 1876, and Zebulon R. Brockway served as its first superintendent.

28. Prison Commission, *The Principles of the Borstal System* (London: 1932), p. 8.

29. *The Treatment of Offenders in Britain* (London: 1960), pp. 33–34.

30. Sophia M. Robison, *Juvenile Delinquency: Its Nature and Control* (New York: 1960), p. 352.

31. The educational, recreational, diagnostic, and treatment aspects of the detention home must be integrated into a coherent and integrated program. See Kenneth A. Griffiths, "Program is the Essence of Juvenile Detention," *Federal Probation,* 28 (1964), 31–34.

32. See U.S. Children's Bureau, *Halfway House Program for Delinquent Youth* (Washington, D.C.: 1965), for a lengthier discussion of the value of the halfway house.

33. Robert W. Winslow, *Juvenile Delinquency in a Free Society* (Belmont, Calif.: 1968), pp. 157–158.

34. *Ibid.*, p. 159.

35. U.S. Children's Bureau, *Institutions Serving Delinquent Children* (Washington, D.C.: 1957), p. 5.

36. Russel, *op. cit.*, p. 13.

37. Cressey offered a "Social Psychological Theory for Using Delinquents to Rehabilitate Delinquents," paper presented to the Fifth International Criminological Congress (Montreal: 1965).

38. Winslow, *op. cit.*, p. 203.
39. President's Commission on Law Enforcement and Administration of Justice, *Task Force Report: Corrections* (Washington, D.C.: 1967), pp. 141–149.
40. Winslow, *op. cit.*, p. 204.
41. *Ibid.*, p. 202.
42. *Corporal Punishment: Report of the Advisory Council on the Treatment of Offenders* (London: 1960), p. 2.
43. *Departmental Committee on Corporal Punishment* (London: 1952).
44. *Corporal Punishment*, pp. 4–5.

Chapter 20

■ Flexible Sentencing Alternatives

■ General Characteristics

Flexible sentencing alternatives were developed to mitigate the harshness of the traditional system of retribution. In the form of a conditional sentence or order of probation *before* imposition of punishment and of juvenile after care, these alternatives serve as safety valves. The *conditional sentence*, involving a suspension of the sentence as long as good behavior continues and *probation*, a form of release to the community under supervision,[1] were designed to balance the use of retribution. *After-care* systems, on the other hand, are designed to ease the juvenile problem of reentry into the community from the "treatment" institution.

The purposes of such alternatives have not always been understood by the public. Not only the general public but also all active participants in a criminal case view these alternatives as forms of leniency toward the criminal or as gestures of mercy. The criminal lawyer seeks a probation order or conditional sentence. Although the public prosecutor protests the lack of severity, the offender happily accepts the probation order or conditional sentence as equivalent to acquittal. Even the court renders this sentence condescendingly as if it had charitably granted pardon to an obvious offender. Yet the conditional sentence and probation order were not intended as acts of grace or as mere expressions of the court's consideration of mitigating circumstances but rather as institutional alternatives theoretically appropriate to some offenders' potential for correction or reform.

■ The Conditional Sentence and Probation

The *conditional sentence* and *probation* are largely nopunitive procedures for handling offenders that have developed within a basically punitive

331

legal framework.[2] Although other nonpunitive procedures have also emerged within the same system, they have involved attempts to redraft the punitive criminal code. The existing legal system has, in fact, probably hindered the development of additional nonpunitive methods. Nevertheless, the conditional sentence and probation represent successful efforts to modify the classical (Beccarian) legal philosophy that dominated and still dominates criminal law and to offer an alternative to the less effective punishment philosophy of crime control. Because criminal law is essentially dualistic, applying sanctions yet allowing attempts at reform, many interpret the latter as a form of institutional lenience. The offender's happiness in receiving these lesser sentences, however, is caused less by his escape from imprisonment and suffering than by recognition that the punitive system has chosen to apply a lesser sentencing alternative.

■ The Origins of Flexible Sentencing Alternatives

Conditional sentencing was well known in canon law long before it was introduced into the criminal code. The maxim *moneat lex antequam feriat* ("the law warns before it strikes") means that, even though the eventual assimilation into the criminal code of conditional sentencing and probation makes it possible to diminish the punitive nature of sentencing, the power of deterrence through threatened application of full punishment if the offender commits later crimes is retained. Whether the statistical success of probation in lessening recidivism results from fear of punishment, the efforts of the probation officer, or the coincidental lessening of criminal pressures during the probation is, however, unclear. The sheer threat of punishment is insufficient to keep the penniless woman from stealing bread for her children, the professional burglar from robbing a bank, or the jealous psychopath from stabbing his estranged girl friend.

Although the conditional sentence and probation arose from recognition of the inadequacies of prison treatment procedures, they also serve to lessen the stigma and other limitations imposed upon the offender through institutionalization. These flexible sentencing alternatives offer five basic assets:

> 1. In most countries they do not require a criminal record. Recognizing differences in the personalities of offenders, the court can, through these procedures, exempt in effect those whose expected future behavior does not necessitate control through such records. The disadvantages of a criminal record are eliminated in order to enhance the possibility of treatment.
> 2. They do not deprive the individual of his liberty. Because most offenders do not require imprisonment, they can be better reformed or corrected in a normal community setting rather than in an abnormal

society of captives. As the offender's family, work, and personality needs vary, his continued participation in the community may offer greater rehabilitative potential than does the prison.

3. They eliminate the possibility of further contamination through institutionalization. By allowing the offender to remain in a more favorable social setting, these measures enhance his treatment potential and minimize his exposure to negative moral influences.

4. They express moral reproach for the offender's involvement in criminal behavior without intensifying his antisocial attitudes. The conditional sentence and probation are not without punitive meaning or consequences, but the negative effects of prison are avoided while his future moral resistance is reinforced through disapproval of his criminal behavior.

5. They exceed mere emphasis upon security and control or supervision and assistance and offer a constructive foundation for the correction or reform of the criminal.[3]

■ The Early Development of the Conditional Sentence and Probation

The conditional sentence and probation are undoubtedly related to such thirteenth-century devices as *benefit of clergy,* which protected certain ecclesiastics from severe punishment, *sanctuary,* which offered immunity from arrest and prosecution to those in a church or other designated place,[4] and *judicial reprieve,* under which the judge had power to grant at least temporary exemption from punishment.[5] Although Edwin H. Sutherland and Donald R. Cressey[6] and Harry Elmer Barnes and Negley Teeters[7] argued that such practices were direct antecedents of the current conditional or suspended sentence and probation, it is questionable that such devices, which served primarily to mitigate the severity of the criminal law and served no treatment goals, were the original sources of flexible sentencing procedures.[8]

John Augustus, a Boston shoemaker who started to bail out drunken male and female offenders from jail in 1841 and subsequently to offer them a wide range of personal assistance (new jobs and help for their families, for instance), pioneered the use of probation. Concurrently, Matthew Davenport Hill, a Birmingham (England) recorder, selected guardians for juvenile delinquents who seemed likely to behave well in the future. Another Bostonian, Father Rufus Cook in later years also took an interest in juvenile delinquents and discharged prisoners. The first American probation law was not passed until 1878, in Massachusetts. One year later, the English Summary Jurisdiction Act of 1879 empowered the courts to discharge offenders conditionally. Perhaps because of the favorable results of the American experiment, the Probation of First Offenders Act (1887), an English law, provided that first offenders found guilty of larceny, false pretenses, or other offenses punishable by no more than two years' imprisonment might be released on probation for good conduct.[9] Only after the first American and English legislation, however, did René Bérenger propose, in 1884, the differentiated treatment of French first offenders. Although Belgium became the first Continental country to enact the Anglo-American ideal, in 1888, France finally did introduce conditional sentencing in 1891 (Loi sur l'Attenuation et l'Aggravation des Peines, popularly known as *loi de sursis* or *loi Bérenger*). In the same year Massachusetts extended its early form of probation. By 1895 only Switzerland, Germany, and Austria, which later provided for similar measures, had not yet adopted these procedures. The emergence of juvenile courts near the turn of the century prompted other American states to enact similar legislation quickly.[10]

In subsequent years England continued the steady improvement of its probation system. The 1907 Probation of Offenders Act, which first used the term "probation officer," made this alternative available for all offenses punishable in magistrates' (lower) courts and all crimes punishable in superior (higher) courts by imprisonment.[11] For the first time courts were empowered to hire and to pay probation officers at their discretion. The later Criminal Justice Act of 1925 exceeded even these limits, however, and required appointment of probation officers in each probation area. The Criminal Justice Act of 1948 further consolidated the law relating to organization and administration of these services and made probation available to the court for all offenses, with the exception of treason and certain other rare violations.

The Conditional Sentence

Following its creation in the nineteenth century, the conditional sentence developed in two distinctive forms. In the Anglo-American system, the *imposition of sentence* was suspended; the court refrained from imposing punishment upon the offender for criminal behavior that had been proved. In the Belgian-French system, on the other hand, the court proceeded one further step to impose and then suspend the *execution of* punishment. In recent years, however, most countries have mixed these two approaches, following the Anglo-American system when dealing with juveniles and the Belgian-French model when dealing with adults. Nevertheless, in both systems and in probation punishment is postponed in order to give the offender an opportunity to improve his conduct and to adjust himself to the community, usually under the guidance and supervision of an officer of the court.[12]

Although it is often assumed that the conditional sentence is a substitute for imprisonment or some other penalty,[13] this assumption is mistaken. The conditional sentence is an independent sentence in itself. It is not a substitute for a penalty but an alternative penalty. Because probation necessarily incorporates suspension of the sentence, it is often confused with the suspended sentence itself. But the suspended sentence and probation are not the same.[14]

Not every state includes provisions for both in its criminal or penal code. The conditional or suspended sentence is the product of a treatment orientation in which it is assumed that low-intensity moral disapproval or reproach has a reforming effect. Probation, however, implies somewhat more severe sanctions and treatment in an attempt to fortify the effects of the suspended sentence. Although probation is in some countries not a statutory requirement of the conditional sentence, the courts often formally rebuke the offender and express moral disapproval of his criminal behavior without prescribing probation.[15]

Because the conditional sentence is more effective when applied together with probation, it is closely related to the latter. Because pure moral disapproval without supervision is often ineffective, the inadequacies of the conditional sentence can be compensated for through the use of probation.

Juvenile Probation

The probation system is a treatment method rather than a system of total supervision and control. Although the conditional sentence offers offenders the opportunity to readjust to the community without application of sanctions, probation aids and guides their reform and rehabilitation within the community. In each instance, however, the individual's rehabilitation, correction, or reform is largely a personal responsibility; even though he is supervised, the ultimate success of probation depends upon his own resolve to reform with the aid of the probation officer.[16] Because probation is an attempt to "guard against recidivism,"[17] the function of the officer is to assist the offender to comply with the court's order.[18] As antisocial and illegal behavior are complex matters, however, the redirection and reeducation of offenders through probation is not always possible.[19]

Juvenile probation allows the child to remain in the community under the supervision and guidance of a probation officer. As legal status probation usually is based on judicial findings about the child's behavior and involves a limitation upon his freedom of action and movement combined with use of resources to help him meet the conditions of his probation. Ultimately, probation is an offer of positive assistance to the child in adjusting to his own community.[20] The modern probation department serves the juvenile court through its intake and screening efforts, social-study and diagnostic services, and posthearing supervision and treatment provisions. It is responsible for supervision of the child on the court's behalf and for providing the youth or his family with community counseling services designed to prevent repetition of his delinquent conduct or development of long-term deviance or a criminal career.[21]

The success or failure of probation rests upon the cooperation of its three participants: the offender, the probation officer, and the judge. Central legal responsibility rests with the court in the person of the judge, who makes the appropriate penal decision after considering all the given factors. Not only a judgment but also a complete study of all interacting psychosocial forces is central to the decision-making process.[22] Because the selective use of probation implies that some offenders are more amenable to this kind of treatment than are others, careful evaluation of the probation system and its probationers must be made.[23]

As the preprobation investigation is legally required of the courts in most American states, disposition through probation can be accomplished only after this information has been submitted to the court for consideration. An adequate presentence investigation, Walter C. Reckless has noted, not only indicates whether or not the defendant is "probation-able," but also gives clues to the causes of his criminal behavior, his assets and liabilities, and his need for a constructive probation program.[24] The ideal investigation includes information on the offender's attitude toward his crime and his previous criminal record, family circumstances, neighborhood and other group associations, educational and work history, attitudes toward alcohol and drugs, personal habits, physical and mental health, and perspective on life.[25] In England the investigator must inquire into the circumstances or home surroundings of any person "with a view to assisting the court in determining the most suitable method of dealing with his case."[26]

The term of probation is usually fixed by the legislature; it is limited in England to not less than one and not more than three years. Similar limits exist in most other countries. In 1958 24 percent of English probation orders, for example, were for one year, 59 percent for two years, and 17 percent for three years. The court is not limited to mere imposition of probation, however, but usually also possesses the power to prescribe additional *general* requirements (requirements to observe the law, to work regularly, to abstain from drugs and alcohol, to maintain contact with the probation officer, to receive medical treatment, to fulfill particular residence requirements, and so on) and *specific* requirements (to refrain from driving, for example), depending upon the offense and the personality of the offender. Because probation depends upon "agreement" and the willingness of the offender to comply with all its requirements, the court should explain them all in an intelligible way.

Although probation services are authorized in each of the fifty states and in Puerto Rico, they are not uniformly available in all counties or cities. Supervision of juveniles, as noted in a sample of 250 counties, averages from three months to three years, with a median of thirteen months. Only 233 of these counties, however, have probation services. Thirty-one states offer probation staff services for juveniles; theoretically

2,306 counties (74 percent of all American counties) offer such services, although many take only token form. Although in sixteen states probation is not available in every county, similar services are available from volunteers (six states), child-welfare departments (five states), and a combination of sheriff and child-welfare and other departments (five states). Juvenile probation services are unavailable in 165 counties of four states. Even where such services are rendered, however, they are not always or even often effective. Most juvenile-probation services are organized in centralized county or city systems, or combinations of the two in which the larger communities operate their own departments. Although the overall organization and effectiveness of these approaches vary, each finally depends upon the quality of personnel and the nature of the officer-offender relationship. Juvenile probation is administered in fifty-one jurisdictions—in 32 states by courts, in five by state correctional agencies, in seven by state departments of public welfare, in four by other state agencies, and in three by other agencies or combinations of agencies.[27]

The Probation Officer

The major responsibility for the success or failure of probation falls upon the officer who is assigned to a particular case.[28] The most frequent assignment is *territorial*; the probation officer is responsible for all the probationers in a certain district. This approach makes only limited provision for selective distribution of offenders and their problems. A second method involves limited *classification* of offenders; probationers are assigned to officers according to sex, age, and religion, which avoids the random distribution of the territorial approach. In the third system responsibility is decided according to *types of crime* and *basic needs of the delinquent*. Although this approach offers the best prospects for success, its execution depends upon specialists, who are often available only in larger probation departments.

Whatever the assignment process, the administration of probation is attached to the local courts in the United States and most European countries. Cooperation among the multitude of American probation departments in various states has been encouraged by the National Probation and Parole Association. Administration of such services in England remains, however, the responsibility of local probation committees composed of justices from each probation area. Although the English Home Office guides and stimulates the performance of probation officers by statute, the actual quality of service depends upon the active interest of the justices and the work of field officers who are appointed by the probation committee in each of the 104 probation areas.[29] These committees assign officers to particular courts, pay their salaries and expenses, and generally control all administrative matters. Although case committees and supervisory probation officers help to maintain local organizational control, they are subordinate to the final authority of the central Home Office.

American probation offices, supervisors, and other specialized officers largely oversee the work of investigation, which may be divided into adult, juvenile, training, and other sections. Although the close connection between American courts and probation services has often been criticized on the grounds that probation is an administrative rather than a judicial function and that the court has no more reason to supervise prisons than the probation system, the probation service involves more than the mere entering of data or the filing of records. Although the institutionalized offender has little or nothing to do with the courts after the issue of the court's order, the failure of probation automatically brings the delinquent to the attention of the court again.

The activity of the officer is the essence of probation treatment. According to the provision of the English Probation Offenders Act of 1907, the officer has the duty to "advise, assist and befriend" the delinquent or criminal, a charge that is defined by each officer in terms of his own personality and abilities.[30] Because effective probation work must ultimately be related to the needs of the offender,[31] the officer must be concerned about the probationer's immediate material needs (like finding employment or a place to live) while he also attempts to determine the steps necessary for his normal social readjustment. Because the probationer may be physically or mentally ill, living in an unhappy home or no home at all, under the influence of undesirable companions or personally immature, the officer must adjust his aid and supervision to individual needs.

As the officer becomes better acquainted with the probationer, he becomes more aware of the causes central to his delinquent conduct. Such insight may give the probation officer the chance to eradicate or modify the impact of the causes, or, if not, to help the probationer to minimize their influence. The application of remedies to reduce the impact of causes contributing to delinquency even when they are known is extremely difficult, however, because change cannot be imposed externally but must occur within the probationer himself. The probationer is in effect tested within the probation system, in order to ascertain whether or not its procedures are adequate for bringing about his reform. The ultimate success of probation can be judged only in the light of his behavior after the guidance and support of the probation officer have ceased.[32]

In both the American and English systems supervision is inevitable in probation. The real treatment, however, occurs not in the mere fact of supervision itself but in the officer's specific efforts to redirect the probationer from criminal to conforming behavior. This goal is not achieved by the distribution of charity or the simple meeting of material needs. The probationer's socioethical resistance must be strengthened. *How* it is strengthened, of course, depends upon the rapport of the participants, the sensitivity of the officer to the probationer's personality, and the offender's willingness to seek alternative life patterns. Although some advocates of probation suggest that semiprecise instructions be given to probation officers in order to eliminate the "go out there and somehow rehabilitate" frustrations of trial-and-error methods[33] and to enhance the potential of probation as treatment, detailed instructions are not only impossible but may destroy the flexibility necessary for meaningful application of general treatment principles. When a surgeon operates to remove an appendix, he can decide how to complete the operation only after he has opened the abdomen. Although a military commander must issue strategic orders defining the method and procedures of attack, he must ultimately depend upon his subordinates to determine the precise application of his directives. Similarly, probation is not simply treatment but a *highly individualized* treatment that is probably more dependent upon the participants' personal characteristics than is any other treatment method. Treatment, an overworked word,[34] is not and cannot be a simple method of approach to all offenders. Although similarities may lead to the establishment of general principles, each personality is composed of numerous elements blended together in "proportions and relationships which are unique to the individual."[35]

Statistics on the success or failure of probation are filled with shortcomings (including the unsatisfactory classifications), but the overall picture in most countries suggests the value of probation. The Federal Republic of Germany, for example, found in 1964 that, after its probation and parole system had been in operation ten years, the ratio of youths on probation or parole to those incarcerated was three to one.[36] Although opponents see only the lenience of probation, their argument is primarily philosophical. The system needs further refinement, but it has already proved itself a successful penological device. Nearly 84 percent of those on Federal probation in the United States in 1958, for example, fulfilled the requirements of the court without violations.[37] Of the 33,351 English probationers whose terms ended during 1948, 69 percent of the males and 79 percent of the females had completed the full probation period or had had it cut short by the court because of progress. The remainder had failed to complete the probation period and had been returned to the court for further action.[38] No other penal alternative has approached this degree of success. Yet the recommended caseload of fifty units, which allows an average contact of three hours per month per probationer, is rarely achieved in practice in the United States. The median load in the 250 agencies surveyed by the President's Commission ranged between seventy-one and eighty cases. Of all children being served 0.2 percent were in caseloads of fewer than twenty and 10.6 in caseloads of more than 100. The highest average supervision caseload was 281.[39] Even when the ideal is reached, nearly half the officer's time is spent merely in completing investigations and social studies of cases recently assigned.

In 74 percent of the 250 probation organizations in the same survey the bachelor's degree was the recommended educational standard for officers. Only 15 percent of the agencies required the master's degree in social work or an allied social science; 22 percent of the probation officers in the sample did not even have the bachelor's degree.[40] A 1960 report by the U.S. Children's Bureau revealed that only 10 percent of the nearly 2,000 officers surveyed had graduate degrees.[41] The salary of a chief probation officer in the Children's Bureau sample ranged from less than $2,400 to more than $18,000. Although staff supervisors' salaries ranged from less than $3,000 to nearly $11,000, those for probation officers varied from less than $1,500 to approximately $11,000. Median salaries for each of these three positions were, however, $8,000–9,000, $7,000–8,000, and $5,000–6,000.[42]

■ *Juvenile Aftercare*

Although the conditional sentence and probation are alternatives for institutionalization, *aftercare* is applied to delinquents *after* they are released from institutions. It is misleading, however, to interpret it merely as general care of the delinquent after completion of this treatment (or the criminal after his punishment or incarceration). It is more specifically related to the "duty of society" to help the delinquent (or the criminal) to reenter normal society and to resist future criminal pressures.[43] Aftercare has a positive goal and is an "essential stage in the rehabilitation process."[44] The general public does not seem especially interested in the aftercare and reentry problem, however. Because its attitude focuses so heavily on retribution, the child's social rehabilitation is often sacrificed to social revenge. Rehabilitation, the sum of correctional efforts and the elimination of the consequences of the original delinquency or crime, is too often undermined by lack of public concern and understanding. The reinstatement of the delinquent in society is therefore difficult and unevenly accomplished.

Most legal systems try to protect juveniles from the stigma of delinquency through special courts where they may receive immediate, automatic, and statutory rehabilitation without acquiring criminal records. Distinctions must be made between legal and social rehabilitation. Although statutory rehabilitation of the juvenile delinquent is immediate *legal rehabilitation,* in which his lost civil rights are restored, social rehabilitation restores his suspended social status.

The loss of particular civil rights upon conviction is not new. Since early history the criminal member of the community has been excluded from certain privileges of group life because of the community's distrust of his ability to exercise these rights correctly. In Greek and Roman societies people convicted of crimes lost the right to vote, to hold public office, to represent others, and other privileges of status *(caput).* If the death penalty or a sentence of penal servitude in the mines, for example, was inflicted upon a Roman citizen, he suffered maximum loss of political rights (*capitis deminutio maxima*) in the form of deprivation of citizenship. Although the number of civil rights lost as a consequence of crime varied according to the seriousness of the offense and the type of punishment applied, a "medium" loss of civil rights (*capitis deminutio media*), for example, enjoined deportation to an island. A minimum loss of civil rights (*capitis deminutio minima*), of course, was associated with milder forms of punishment.

Both early and modern deprivation of rights should be regarded less as forms of social degradation and more as social defenses against criminal participation in community matters. Most modern states, following the Roman example, apply additional or secondary punishments in the form of loss of particular civil rights. Although it is impossible to list with certainty the civil rights generally forfeited by convicts, loss of the rights to hold public office and to vote appear to be the principal such restrictions in the United States.[45]

In recent years many attempts have been made by reformers to restore these civil rights to people convicted of crimes. Arguing that it is unjust and a denial of enlightened legal and correctional philosophy to refuse reinstatement of civil rights to those who have completed their punishment and have reoriented their lives, they have attempted to influence national and state legislative bodies. Because the convicted offender has fulfilled the requirements of the court and redressed his earlier violation, the mark or brand of his act, they argue, should be obliterated. This goal is not easily reached, however. When one commits a delinquent or criminal act, his presupposed honesty (*praesumptio boni viri*) is replaced by an assumption of bad fame (*praesumptio malae famae*), an assumption that makes social rehabilitation especially difficult.

Legal rehabilitation has taken many forms in various societies. Among the Romans it took the form of pardon, a practice retained in the French Codes of 1791, 1808, 1842, and 1848 and known as *réhabilitation gracieuse*.[46] The French law of 1885, in its section on recidivist criminals, probably offered the first trace of the *réhabilitation judiciaire*, a judicial or legal rehabilitation stipulated in law. The French law of 1899, on criminal records, further improved and expanded this practice, establishing the so-called *réhabilitation de droit* (rehabilitation of the law, or statutory rehabilitation) in which lost civil rights were to be returned after the expiration of a certain period, according to the different types of crime as stipulated by law. The 1905 Congress of the Union Internationale de Droit Pénal, meeting in Hamburg, discussed this problem on an international level and recommended a form of judicial rehabilitation that would allow the courts to consider and to decide the time when suspended civil rights should be restored.

Although legal rehabilitation restores civil rights, reinstatement of suspended social status depends upon effective *social rehabilitation*, which is a central goal of aftercare. Social rehabilitation, both past and present, has been largely identified with charitable activity. The conditionally or finally released prisoner was cared for through the contribution of alms and kindly words, which were believed to be adequate aids in the "transition from artificial, regimented group life to the normal, independent life of the free individual and with the problems which this transition entails."[47] The names of the first American "aftercare" societies, the Philadelphia Society for Assisting Distressed Prisoners and the Philadelphia Society for Alleviating the Miseries of Public Prisons, reflected this approach. Their successor, the Pennsylvania Prison Society, now the oldest functioning prison society in the world, was founded in 1787 to alleviate the miseries of the prisoners.

Although the need for assistance to discharged prisoners was first recognized by the English Parliament in 1792,[48] the later Gaol Act of 1832 made provision for the distribution of some clothing, food, and money, not to exceed 20 shillings (today equivalent to $2.40) to each deserving released prisoner. The Discharged Prisoners' Aid Act of 1862 established Discharged Prisoners' Aid Societies for the purpose of "finding employment for discharged prisoners and enabling them by loans and grants of money to live by honest labour." In the meantime a number of American societies began to offer aid to released prisoners. The first organized relief came from the Prison Association of New York, founded in 1846 and now known as the Correctional Association. Since that time the number of American and English private and semiofficial societies has grown as the general attitude toward discharged prisoners has progressed from one of charity to a more professional relationship between client and practitioner.

■ Aftercare in Operation

In 1963 approximately 48,000 youths were receiving aftercare in forty states, although the number varied from a low of 100 to a high of 13,000. Naturally, state operating costs also varied widely, ranging from $7,000 to more than $4 million a year. The average per capita cost, however, approached $320 a year, a rather low figure compared with the average costs of institutionalization at $3,400 a year per child. These cost differentials may well be misleading because the political economics of a local jurisdiction may make even less money and fewer personnel available to the aftercare program. Only thirty-four of the state departments administering state juvenile institutions provide aftercare for juveniles released from these institutions.

Approximately 59,000 youths, 47,000 boys and 12,000 girls, received aftercare services during 1964–1965. Of the states reporting, twelve kept juveniles under aftercare supervision for an average of less than one year; twenty-five offered such supervision for an average of one year or more. Most states reported a tendency to keep girls on aftercare longer than boys, a practice probably resulting from society's general tendency to protect females. Although the recommended ratio of aftercare counselors to juveniles was 1:50, the actual ratio ranged from 1:30 to 1:125. The median approached the range between 1:61 and 1:70. In 1964–1965, 133 district supervisors, 76 district assistant supervisors, and 1,033 aftercare counselors were employed. Of the forty states that offered statewide aftercare services, eight did not provide in-service training programs for aftercare personnel.[49]

■ *Probation, Parole, and Aftercare*

Although they are quite different, probation and parole are often confused with aftercare, probably because aid is implied in all three approaches. But, whereas parole is early release from incarceration for good behavior under supervision of the court, aftercare is assistance without supervision or sanction after the full term has been served. Probation, of course, is a substitute for the institutionalization of the offender, who is supervised in the community by the court through the probation officer. The terms of the parole condition the assistance given the discharged prisoner. Aftercare is unconditional. Parole is therefore a test of treatment and corrections success and of the reform of the discharged offender, who still remains under legal control of the court. Aftercare, on the other hand, is not a test and operates on the assumption that treatment, correction, and reform have been successfully completed. It aims at social rehabilitation and is directed less toward the discharged prisoner than toward public opinion, which is often reluctant to accept the successful correction of the individual. Because aftercare follows the completion of incarceration stipulated by the court, its effectiveness is greatly dependent upon the discharged prisoner's attitude and cooperation.[50]

As long as juvenile delinquents are under the jurisdiction of juvenile courts they receive more effective help in reintegrating themselves into society than do adult offenders.[51] Because legal rehabilitation is statutory, theoretically they should be socially "accepted" after the completion of their treatment, whether in or through the training school, probation, custody of relatives, or other juvenile-court prescriptions. This acceptance rarely occurs, however. The delinquent frequently feels that he is handicapped in his future social life by his past actions. Because the public tends to stigmatize most delinquents, this demoralization is not without foundation. Although the released delinquent does not receive the same suspicious response from the police as does the adult offender, his social rehabilitation is not easily achieved. Although the juvenile court may prepare the youth for his readmission to society, the community is often reluctant to accept his return. Aftercare is not part of the court's legal- or social-rehabilitation responsibility, but it should be available to aid delinquents in their return to society. It is not a treatment for delinquency but an approach that enables the community to treat the delinquent's needs.[52]

NOTES

1. The supervision of probation and parole, largely of California adults, is examined in Joseph D. Lohman, Albert Wahl, Robert M. Carter, and Arthur E. Elliot, *The Impact of Supervision* (Berkeley: 1967).

2. Edwin H. Sutherland and Donald R. Cressey, *Principles of Criminology* (6th ed.; Chicago: 1960), p. 421.

3. Maynard L. Erickson and LaMar T. Empey found in a study of juveniles that the official court records of delinquency reflect an individual's most serious violation more accurately than they reflect his pattern of offenses, a finding that has serious implications for treatment. Persistent offenders are more likely to appear before the court than are one-time offenders and official nondelinquents. See Erickson and Empey, "Court Records: Undetected Delinquency and Decision-Making," *Journal of Criminal Law, Criminology and Police Science*, 54 (December 1963), 456–469.

4. Frank W. Grinnel, "The Common Law History of Probation," *Journal of Criminal Law and Criminology*, 32 (May–June 1941), 15–34.

5. Sutherland and Cressey, *op. cit.*, p. 423.

6. Harry Elmer Barnes and Negley K. Teeters, *New Horizons in Criminology* (3rd ed.; Englewood Cliffs, N.J.: 1959), p. 552.

7. Barnes and Teeters, *New Horizons in Criminology: The American Crime Problem* 1st ed.; New York: 1944), p. 373.

8. For an account of the history of probation, see N. S. Timasheff, *One Hundred Years of Probation* (New York: 1941).

9. Home Office, *The Probation Service, Its Objects and Its Organization* (London: 1960), p. 3.

10. Gilbert Cosulich, *Adult Probation Laws of the United States* (New York: 1940).

11. Home Office, *op. cit.*, p. 4.

12. *Attorney General's Survey of Release Procedures: Probation*, 2 (Washington, D.C.: 1939), p. 1.

13. Sutherland and Cressey, *op. cit.*, p. 422.

14. Barnes and Teeters, 3rd ed., *op. cit.*, p. 553.

15. Although this approach is not a Soviet invention, its application to both juvenile delinquents and adult offenders is rather popular in socialist legal systems.

16. Home Office, *op. cit.*, p. 8.

17. M. J. Sethna, *Society and the Criminal* (Bombay: 1952), p. 230.

18. Docle J. Hardman, "The Function of the Probation Officer," *Federal Probation*, 24 (September 1960), 4.

19. Charles L. Newman, "Concepts of Treatment in Probation and Parole Supervision," *Federal Probation*, 25 (March 1961), 11.

20. Robert W. Winslow, *Juvenile Delinquency in a Free Society* (Belmont, Calif.: 1968), p. 175.

21. *Ibid.*, pp. 178–180.

22. Max Grünhut, *Penal Reform* (Oxford: 1948), pp. 305–307.

23. H. A. Prins, "Social Enquiries and the Adult Courts," *British Journal of Delinquency,* 8 (January 1958), 227.

24. Walter C. Reckless, *The Crime Problem* (2nd ed.; New York: 1955), p. 511.

25. Sutherland and Cressey, *op. cit.,* pp. 427–428.

26. Home Office, *op. cit.,* p. 18.

27. Winslow, *op. cit.,* p. 185.

28. Sutherland and Cressey, *op. cit.,* pp. 430–431.

29. Home Office, *op. cit.,* p. 18.

30. *Ibid.,* p. 12.

31. *Ibid.,* pp. 12–13.

32. According to Herman Jung attrition among probation officers in West Germany results from a higher incidence of illness, premature retirement, and death than are found in most other professions. Although he is unable to offer proof, he suggests that the incidence of death and illness among probation officers is influenced by their strong personal and emotional commitment to their work. See Herman Jung, "Der Bewährungshilfer—Seine Gesundheit und Seine Krankheit," *Bewährungshilfe,* 14 (1967), 287–291.

33. Richard R. Korn and Lloyd W. McCorkle, *Criminology and Penology* (New York: 1959), p. 593.

34. Newman, *op. cit.,* p. 11.

35. *Ibid.,* p. 18.

36. Alfons Wahl, "Ten Years of Probation in the Federal Republic of Germany," *Bewährungshilfe* (January 1964).

37. *Annual Report of the Director of the Administrative Office of the United States Courts, 1958* (Washington, D.C.: 1959).

38. Home Office, *op. cit.,* p. 6.

39. Winslow, *op. cit.,* p. 195.

40. *Ibid.,* p. 189.

41. U.S. Children's Bureau and National Institutes of Mental Health, *Report to the Congress on Juvenile Delinquency* (Washington, D.C.: 1960), p. 42.

42. Winslow, *op. cit.,* p. 193.

43. Lionel W. Fox, *The English Prison and Borstal Systems* (London: 1952), p. 253.

44. Grünhut, *op. cit.,* p. 219.

45. *Attorney General's Survey of Release Procedures:* 3 (Washington, D.C.: 1939).

46. The word "rehabilitation" is probably of French origin. Such a word does not exist in Latin. *Rehabilitation* appeared first in the French Ordonnance Royal of 1670. Eric Partridge, however, traced the Latin *habilitas* through the medieval Latin *rehabilitare.*

47. U.N. Department of Economic and Social Affairs, *Pre-Release Treatment and After-Care as well as Assistance to Dependents of Prisoners* (New York: 1960), p. 2. This volume was prepared for the second Congress on the Prevention of Crime and the Treatment of Offenders in London in 1960.

48. Fox, *op. cit.,* pp. 257–259.

49. President's Commission on Law Enforcement and Administration of Justice, *Task Force Report: Corrections* (Washington, D.C.: 1967), pp. 141–154.

50. Home Office, *The After-Care and Supervision of Discharged Prisoners: Report of the Advisory Council* (London: 1958), p. 5.

51. William C. Kvaraceus, "Juvenile Delinquency: A Problem for the Modern World," *Federal Probation*, 28 (September 1964), 12–18, suggests that the delinquent should be more involved in his own reeducation. Kvaraceus discovered that dividing a gang into three competing squads enabled squad members to make decisions and to overcome stifling conformity.

52. Barnes and Teeters, *op. cit.*, 3rd ed., p. 804.

Part Eight

PREVENTION, TREATMENT, AND SOCIAL CHANGE

Chapter 21
■ *Research in Delinquency Prevention and Treatment*

■ *Community Participation in Delinquency Control*

Although community forces have historically participated in programs of delinquency prevention and control, they have often merely added to the delinquency problem. The first community attempt to help the unfortunate or potential deviant took the form of aid to orphans and destitute children, a common approach to the poor in the Judeo-Christian tradition. In succeeding generations voluntary organizations, schools, social-service agencies, and individual philanthropists have added their gifts and voices to the rehabilitation of children exposed to delinquency pressures. The contribution of each, however, has been shaped up by the contemporary approach to moral and social problems.[1] Although "criminal" children were treated cruelly until quite recently, the poor and homeless received charity that frequently appeared to be worse than no support and often competed with the worst in the administration of criminal justice.

When juvenile delinquency was recognized as a separate legal problem at the turn of this century, the effort to uncover its causes stimulated a world-wide movement to prevent delinquency and aid delinquents. As interest in delinquency increased, new organizations offered voluntary assistance in the search for solutions. When the professionalization of services made it possible for at least some helping individuals and agencies to receive adequate pay, even more developed an interest in the deviance of children and youth. The general public's interest in juvenile delinquency, however, did not develop until the end of World War II. Before that time the problem had been left almost entirely to the skilled, semiskilled, and unskilled staffs of numerous agencies which worked with little or no cooperation, different and sometimes sharply divergent orientations, and only sympathy from the public.

In the last two decades the public has become increasingly concerned about the growth of delinquency, leading to the hope that coordination of activities will bring order into the somewhat chaotic contemporary approach to juvenile deviance. Any attempt at control is, however, frustrated by doubts among practitioners, researchers, jurists, and lawyers over precisely what should be controlled. Even the preliminary questions of "what assistance communities need in preventing juvenile delinquency"[2] and how potential delinquents may be identified before they commit their antisocial acts cannot be answered with authority.[3] Programs developed to define the particular needs that must be met if delinquency is to be prevented have not yielded encouraging results.[4] "All project directors," Mary B. Novick has reported, "believed that their program was moving toward its goal, but almost none of the programs were being scientifically evaluated."[5] Although many projects were labeled "experimental," few of their methods were new. It is impossible to describe all attempts to evaluate community delinquency-control programs, but the scope of the problem is illustrated in the following examples.[6]

Street-Club Guidance Projects

Based upon the principle of reaching the unreached,[7] street-club projects appeared soon after World War II. They involved a type of social work, in which workers moved into the streets to visit their clients on their home grounds. A *street worker* in effect "sold" himself to both delinquent and nondelinquent juveniles in his assigned district of the city. Like an honest confidence man, the street worker approached his juvenile "victim" and attempted to "secure" or "buy" his confidence. Offering friendliness and entertainment, in order to acquire the trust of the child, the worker expended immense amounts of patience, skill, and time to bring a few boys into constructive but informal *street clubs*, in which cohesion among members, it was theorized, would lead to ordered and constructive relationships, realistic aspirations, and cooperation between street workers and juveniles under the leadership of the former. Because many actual and potential delinquents refused to join such groups, the "unreached" continued to operate outside guidance projects and even to hinder their efforts.

Although its successes suggest that the street-club approach to delinquency holds promise, it also has serious limitations. The few social workers equipped for this job are unable to handle the volume of juveniles who should be treated. Then too the projects themselves lack the necessary theoretical foundation to delineate specific goals and measure effects. Although street-club work has been viewed as a process for structuring situations, some evidence suggests that it is only a more aggressive form of ordinary social work in which the client is pressed to adapt to an unfavorable situation that might have been the cause of his original delinquency. Because of the personal nature of the relationships between worker and juveniles, the continuity of the group may be threatened if the adult leader moves to another position. Although many social workers assume that their influence will remain after their departure, that is questionable, especially when their persuasiveness is limited even while they are present.

Police Preventive Programs

Police preventive programs also emerged as a form of community participation in delinquency control. Somewhat outside the strict scope of law enforcement, the use of police in social-work programs developed as a public-relations effort to minimize public, especially lower-class, distrust of the police. The Englewood area southeast of Chicago's Loop in which police cooperated with social-welfare agencies, was the scene of one of the earliest such attempts.[8] Other scattered attempts have since been made to apply police authority to social-casework techniques, but most police preventive programs have been less ambitious and have emphasized recreational activities. The Police Athletic League (PAL), established in 1932 by the New York City police, is one of the best known of these programs. Although it offered only recreational facilities at first, its scope was expanded in the 1950s to include such varied activities as arts, crafts, games and sports, dances, and the like. In all these programs police officers have functioned as youth leaders and have fulfilled the mixed roles of authority and friend.

Area Projects

Projects based on centers where recreational and educational opportunities are available to neighborhoods come closest to "community participation." Usually the active role is assumed by community members on the staffs. In each project children are exposed to programs reflecting a single community standard, largely determined by the middle class, and their acceptance of these standards is facilitated by their attachment to the center and avoidance of alternative pressures to deviate. Assuming that "the majority of these young people are socially rather than emotionally maladjusted,"[9] area projects attempt to bring juveniles into constructive relationships with conforming adults in order to lessen the former's contacts with delinquents and criminals. At community centers parents are encouraged to discuss common child-parent problems with other community members. In effect, area projects attempt formally or informally to structure social situations rather than to encourage youths simply to adjust to given circumstances.

Clifford R. Shaw established one of the first area projects in Chicago in connection with his ecological studies of the city. A number of similar projects emerged in later years in different districts of Chicago and in Washington, D.C.[10] The Tokyo police also organized area projects in each district of that city. The Austrian Federal Police established youth hostels (*Jugendheim*) in 1950, in order to care for children in immediate moral or physical danger, and the United Kingdom initiated an area program in Liverpool to prevent juvenile delinquency by coordinating district and welfare agencies through the use of police juvenile liaison officers.

■ Control of Delinquency in Some Other Countries[11]

England and Wales

Deterrence of potential lawbreaking and reform of convicted offenders are the chief aims of the English penal system. Deterrence is sought through fear of detection, publicity, and possible punishment rather than of severity of punishment upon conviction.[12] Because the major rise in crime among British males between seventeen and twenty-four years of age represents an economic as well as a human loss, the rehabilitation of offenders has become an English penal goal.

Before the development of a centralized government, criminal offenses were regarded as injuries against individuals or their families. As the king assumed more and more state authority after the Norman conquest in the eleventh century, prosecution and punishment of crime became increasingly a public responsibility.[13] After Tudor times, the normal punishment for serious crimes was death, regardless of the criminal's age. In 1796, for example, William Blackstone noted that the British code stipulated more than 160 capital crimes. Although transportation of offenders to colonies or other countries became more common during and after the seventeenth century, fines, flogging, and other corporal punishments remained customary for minor offenses.

The earliest prisons were developed in the sixteenth century, and the great prison reformers, John Howard (1726–1790) and Elizabeth Fry (1780–1845) later struggled to overcome their deficiencies and to secure humane treatment of inmates. As the decline of transportation as a form of punishment in the mid-nineteenth century stimulated the building of prisons to house the incorrigible population, many of their proposals were adopted. At the same time and probably for the same reasons, police were organized. The number of capital crimes was reduced to four (murder, treason, piracy, and destruction of arsenals or dockyards).[14] As the penal system became more centralized, prison inspectors were appointed, prison commissioners assumed control of penal institutions, and the Home Secretary took charge of the whole system.[15] Despite the earlier work of Howard and Fry, however, the regime remained punitive, favoring the principles of "hard labor, hard fare, and a hard bed."[16]

The turning point in the official attitude toward delinquency and crime occurred in 1895, when a departmental committee under the chairmanship of William Gladstone recommended drastic changes in the English penal system, including reform rather than deterrence as the major goal and greater differentiation in treatment in order to meet the needs of offenders of all ages. A series of prison reforms followed after 1898. Two important acts relative to the treatment of juvenile delinquents and youthful offenders were passed in 1908: The Children Act created the juvenile court and revised the law relating to juvenile offenders and to children in need of care and control, and the Prevention of Crime Act provided for indeterminate sentences and authorized the creation of Borstals.

Between the two world wars an even greater volume of progressive criminal and penal legislation came to buttress new attitudes toward punishment in general and incarceration in particular. The Criminal Justice Act of 1925, which improved the probation service; the Children and Young Persons Act of 1933, which amended juvenile-court procedure and raised the upper limit of juvenile age from sixteen to seventeen; and the Criminal Justice Act, with its new provisions for probation and Borstal sentences, extended the humanitarian scope of the judicial and penal processes. After World War II the Criminal Justice Act of 1948 provided the legislative foundation for treatment of offenders in the present English penal system.[17] This bill abolished corporal punishment, opened up the possibility of psychiatric treatment during probation, established attendance centers for children, provided "corrective training" for youthful offenders twenty-one years of age or under, and improved the aftercare of those released from Borstals or corrective training. In his 1959 White Paper the Home Secretary announced a program of continuing research on delinquency problems and reorientation of prison construction.[18]

Under the present system no child under the age of eight can be judged or held guilty of any offense. Although a child over the age of eight but under fourteen years cannot be regarded as "guilty," he can know whether or not he is doing wrong. Consequently any child between eight and seventeen can be processed in a juvenile court unless he is charged with homicide. Juvenile courts, however, also have jurisdiction in cases involving neglect, incorrigibility, truancy, and even adoption. Offenders over seventeen are adjudicated before adult courts.

Although the available juvenile treatment methods vary, they generally include absolute discharge by the court, discharge conditional on guarantee of good behavior, fine imposed upon the child or his parents, probation, commitment to the care of a suitable person and detention in one of several different types of juvenile institutions, including remand homes, approved schools, attendance centers, detention centers, and Borstals.[19] *Remand homes* guarantee the safe custody of offenders under the age of seventeen who must be detained before their court appearances, have been remanded while their cases are adjourned, or are awaiting admission to their institutions. The remand home offers a temporary detention location for a period not to exceed one month. During his detention there the child may be subject to observation of his character, level of intelligence, and physical and mental conditions.

Approved schools are industrial schools, originally created in the nineteenth century for destitute and delinquent children, which derive their name from the "approval" of the Secretary of State, who must certify certain schools for residential child care and protection. The schools are classified according to the sex and age of the children; they offer "difficult" boys and girls good and appropriate education in controlled residential environments. As they submit to remolding of their characters, the youths theoretically develop social responsibility that prepares them for ordinary life after discharge from the school. Although the children are generally detained at approved schools for three-year periods, actual tenure may be shorter for those under twelve years of age. After discharge these children and youths receive aftercare until they are twenty-one years old.

Attendance centers provide means for disciplining young offenders or delinquents by restricting their liberty of action without sending them to residential corrective institutions. Although the program is different from probation, the center permits the attendance on Saturdays of offenders between eighteen and twenty-four, who, if found guilty of similar offenses as adults, would be sentenced to imprisonment. Although they may be required to attend for periods of three hours on any single occasion, maximum attendance time may not total more than twelve hours. Such treatment, the Home Office has declared, is designed to teach young offenders respect for the law and to give them some instruction in the proper use of leisure.[20] Activities at these attendance centers include hard physical work, instruction in handicrafts, lectures on practical topics, and physical training.

Detention centers, on the other hand, serve another purpose: They provide crude treatment for young male offenders for whom a more extensive residential training seems necessary but for whom other measures (for example, prison or probation) seem inappropriate or insufficient. Although young people are ordinarily sent to detention centers for three months, the period of commitment may be extended to six months. "The regime," according to the Home Office, "is designed to deprive the boy of his liberty and of every aspect of what he thinks of as a 'good time,' and to oblige him to live a brisk, disciplined life, maintaining the highest possible standards at the highest possible tempo—it administers, in other words, 'a short, sharp shock.'"[21] The boys in these centers must be extremely alert, punctual, tidy, obedient, and diligent. Besides a forty-four-hour work week, each youth engages in one hour of daily physical training. Boys of compulsory school age receive regular instruction; evening classes are provided for those beyond this level.

Borstals are part of a system that also includes reception centers and recall institutions; they furnish remedial and educational training for those between sixteen and twenty-one years of age. Borstal training is divided into two parts, stretching over a four-year period. During the first nine months to three years, the boy or girl undergoes residential treatment. The average time spent in phase one is, however, twenty months. In the second phase, which extends to the end of a total of four years, the offender undergoes treatment in a context of controlled and supervised freedom outside the Borstal. During the initial period, the youth is placed in a reception center, where expert personnel select the Borstal best suited to his character and later treatment requirements. At the Borstal itself he is placed in a "house" of about fifty boys or girls, who are supervised by a housemaster or housemistress and staff.

As the Borstal treatment and training system, based upon "progressive trust and demanding increasing personal decision, responsibility and self-control," is designed to develop personal character and individual capacities,[22] daily activities include useful and interesting work, physical training, various evening entertainments, recreation, and reading. Students are taught to respect good craftsmanship and hard work. Although post-discharge supervision is an essential and integral feature of Borstal training, the release from the institution is gradual rather than sudden, in order to acclimate the Borstal youth to the proper use of freedom. Failure to comply with the conditions of controlled freedom leads to *recall* of the youth to one of the Borstals for a period of at least six months, sentenced by contrast to young-prisoner centers, which offer various vocational and educational classes requiring brisk participation and a high level of discipline.

The English penal system for children and youth is not static. On the contrary, it is highly dynamic, despite the supposed traditionalism of the English. Although recognizing that crime has been increasing as standards in material prosperity, education, and social welfare have continued to rise,[23] the English citizen is realistically aware that effective prevention of delinquency demands more knowledge about treatment; a fundamental reexamination of penal methods, the philosophy and practice of punishment, and the procedures of juvenile courts and institutions; and reconsideration of laws relating to children and young adults.[24]

The Soviet Union

A mere study of Soviet law is insufficient foundation to understand the Russian approach to delinquency control. Because the delinquency question is so closely related to the sociopolitical system, any overview would be incomplete without a detailed review of the fundamental values of the whole system. Although the problem of delinquency is a highly integrated part of the theoretical system that emerged from Karl Marx's shabby Paris attic room more than a century ago, an understanding of the contemporary context of Russian delinquency and crime also depends upon more than a reading of the Marxist classics. "One could not deduce," Harold J. Berman has written, "from the most careful study of Marx's writings the actual provisions of the Soviet legal system, any more than one could deduce from a study of the New Testament the nature of the present-day canon law of the Christian churches."[25] The implications of the entire Soviet system of social control, including delinquency control, can be comprehended only by living in such a controlled environment or by acclimatizing oneself to the technical aspects of the Russian system. Because the Soviet system of social control has evolved from the revolutionary ideas of Marx and Nikolai Lenin, changing as the society has progressed in reorganization and in development since the Revolution of 1917, any attempt to comprehend the system necessarily involves adequate knowledge and recognition of Soviet legal pragmatism. Probably no other modern state attempts to correlate and interrelate its social institutions with one central socioeconomic goal to as great an extent as does the Soviet Union. Soviet delinquent and criminal institutions therefore focus on the past and the future as they treat individuals in the present.

Soviet correctional philosophy has passed through phases associated with classical Marxism; Leninism-Stalinism and the Revolution, civil war, New Economic Policy, the Five-Year Plans, World War II and postwar years; post-Stalinism and de-Stalinization and collective leadership and Chinese-Russian antagonism. Although each phase altered the Soviet system of social control, none caused radical revisions in the basic approach to delinquency and crime. The idea that delinquency and crime are products of capitalism, formerly proposed by leaders of the Russian Revolution, still dominates official Soviet political philosophy.[26] They are regarded as temporary social phenomena, mainly representing remnants of bourgeois thought, gaps in socialist education, and occasional subversive activity by foreign agents; Soviet theory assumes that they will wither away as Communist society is fully realized.[27]

During the first weeks of Soviet power in 1918, the government, ruling by decree, suspended the concept of criminal responsibility as it applied to those under the age of seventeen. Judges were instructed to follow their "revolutionary consciousness," and the Cheka (secret police)[28] extended its original function to the imposition of penalties; little is therefore known about the application of this rule in its early years. A general statute of the People's Commissariat of Justice, passed on December 12, 1919, and entitled Leading Principles of Criminal Law,[29] provided some additional rules for the guidance of the judges, including procedural instructions for cases involving insanity, attempt at crime, accessories, and the like, and reestablished the age of criminal responsibility at fourteen years. Although the first Soviet penal code, the Criminal Code of the Russian Federation,[30] was adopted in 1922, it did not expand the minimal Leading Principles relevant to juvenile delinquency and merely continued the fourteen-year age limit for criminal responsibility. Although this code was revised in 1926, it still failed to embody specific consideration of the scope of delinquency problems.[31]

This omission was probably partly the result of Marxist interpretation of crime, in which delinquency was also viewed as an economic product that will cease when the material wants of children are satisfied.[32] Refusal to recognize the problem of juvenile delinquency was, however, undoubtedly tied to the implication of failure assumed in any acknowledgment that Soviet ideology has not adequately answered the needs of youth socialized in the years following the Revolution. Although Soviet youth has been educated to the need for social order, saturated with socialist consciousness, and expected to refrain from delinquency and crime, its behavior has not always reflected these teachings. Nevertheless, early Soviet legal codes omitted reference to delinquency; Soviet courts presumed that education had instilled a knowledge of and respect for, if not a fear of, the law among younger citizens.[33]

When juvenile delinquency eventually came to be recognized in the 1930s a campaign was launched against it by governmental order on May 31, 1935.[34] The early Soviet attempt to liberate family members from conventional legal and economic relationships, however, was not without its cost in delinquency. A nationwide network of nurseries, community kitchens, and other facilities had been planned and built, in order to expand the labor force and maximize the growth of the economic system. Working mothers were encouraged to leave their children in nurseries, where they could be taught the new goals of the state, which included shifting personal commitments from the family to the state. By encouraging some sort of family disorganization during its attempt to consolidate power, the state effectively reduced the danger of nuclear- or extended-family conspiracy. Berman noted that "the brunt of the Bolshevik attack on family law was therefore directed toward the liberalization of divorce, and toward the emancipation of women and children, as first steps in the 'withering away' process."[35]

Although this program, as 1930 Moscow and Leningrad surveys revealed, produced undesirable juvenile use of leisure and a rise in the number of homeless youths, the Soviet government accepted the potential increase of juvenile deviance as a calculated short-range risk. Although the rise in delinquency eventually did prompt official intervention, even then no special organization, court, procedure, or treatment for juvenile delinquents was inaugurated. Only scattered measures were enacted to meet the delinquency problem. The age of criminal responsibility was lowered to twelve years; institutions were established to provide medical care; guardianship agencies were formed, and heavy penalties were stipulated for neglectful guardians; homes were built for homeless children; the police were authorized to fine parents for the "indecent conduct and street hooliganism" of their children; parents were made liable for civil damages caused by their children; attention was paid to harmful reading material; and some harsh ad hoc measures were taken to establish corrective-labor colonies for deviating juveniles.[36] The government did not recognize the validity of the Western concept of the juvenile delinquent, applying it, if at all, only to criminals in younger age groups.[37] Juveniles were occasionally processed by commissions for the cases of minors, but the latter were only special sessions and not special courts. Even they were abolished in the 1930s, in order to eliminate any tendency to render mild sentences.

The harshness of the campaign against juvenile delinquency seemed to decrease in the 1940s, probably because of the government's need for young recruits during the war with Germany. A decree of the Soviet Supreme Council of December 10, 1940, ordered the selective punishment of young criminals and restricted the infliction of harsh punishments upon youth, especially those under fourteen years. Another decree of May 31, 1941, restored the age limit of criminal responsibility to fourteen years, and a second order, of July 7, 1941, directed that the punishment of young criminals be carried out in children's corrective-labor camps.[38]

The official attention of the Soviet Union was again called to the delinquency problem in the 1950s. Increasing numbers of hooligans, known as *khuligany*, or *stilyagi*, similar to the English Teddyboys and American juvenile-gang members, with their malicious and idle behavior and their distinct language, dress, and hair styles, once again aroused government concern. Even Premier Nikita Khrushchev asked: "How are we to eradicate hooliganism? The decisive role in this matter belongs to the public. The public and primarily the Komsomol (Soviet youth organization) should be the first to show up the loafers, hooligans and drunkards, and without waiting for them to commit some offense or other, should take the necessary steps of prevention and education."[39] Subsequently, a renewed campaign against juvenile hooliganism was coupled with yet another revision of the criminal code, New Fundamentals of Criminal Legislation, adopted by the Supreme Soviet on December 25, 1958.

The New Fundamentals changed the age of criminal responsibility, stipulating in Article 10 that responsibility for certain crimes, like those involving violence against people or property, "malicious hooliganism," and intentional damage to property would commence at the age of fourteen, although responsibility for all other crimes would begin at the age of sixteen.[40] If the crime involved an offender under the age of fifteen and was not itself a serious social danger, compulsory education measures might be substituted for legal penalties. The young criminal might therefore be placed under the supervision of his parents, a guardian, or a public agency or be committed to a children's labor or educational institution similar to the American and English training schools. Generally, no one under eighteen could be deprived of his liberty for a term longer than ten years, although such sentences had to be served in special institutions, usually corrective-labor or other colonies established for youths. In cases of good conduct and conscientious attitudes toward work and instruction, a young inmate could be released, in a manner similar to Western parole, before completion of his term, provided that he had already served one-third of his original sentence. Although further revisions were adopted in 1961, they did not essentially affect the delinquency problem.

The popular Western view that the Soviet state is a police state run by professional revolutionaries who desire to extend their own power at the expense of the public is a "dangerous half-truth."[41] Soviet failure to develop Western-type delinquency courts and institutional systems does not mean that the differences between juvenile and adult personality development are ignored. As the Soviet Union has attempted to build a new kind of society, it has sought to create a new kind of youth and man. Because the child is brought up, educated, and guided exclusively by the social values of the Revolution, he is expected to accept and to follow the demands of this value system without exception. Consequently, he is motivated to learn, believe, and trust these values and to engage continually in activities for the good of his community. In this sense, his life is a duty and not merely a privilege. The busy and structured life of the Soviet youth is therefore a form of delinquency control in itself, diverting as it does attention and time from destructive ideas and activities to more constructive ends. Political and educational indoctrination, among the most basic and essential means for developing this new type of man, serve to develop a Soviet form of socioethical resistance to delinquency pressures.

Under current Soviet practice youths between the ages of fourteen and eighteen are treated as juvenile offenders. At eighteen they reach adult status. From fourteen to sixteen they are held responsible only for certain serious crimes, as in the United States. Although Soviet law assumes that a juvenile under fourteen years cannot be held criminally responsible, the state may take educational or disciplinary action against him, through correctional labor colonies, which may vary from mild to strict discipline. The youth is assigned by the penal administration rather than the courts to the appropriate location, where he may engage in a varied work and educational program centering around an eight- to ten-year prepared syllabus. He lives in a dormitory under the direction of a "non-commissioned officer" inmate.

Children in need of immediate care or protection receive it in "children's rooms" in the local district militia (police) offices. They, as well as delinquents, may be taken to *reception-distribution centers,* homes of "first resort," as the need arises. Any applicant from three to eighteen years old must be admitted whether he comes of his own accord or is sent by an institution or state agency. He is normally allowed to stay no more than one month and after processing by the courts may return to his parents, guardians, or foster parents or be sent to some educational, correctional, or medical-educational institution.

In 1961 commissions on juvenile affairs were established as parts of the executive committees of local soviets (councils); their terms coincide with those of the soviets themselves. Members are nominated by the executive committees and may include representatives of the trade unions, Young Communist League, teaching and medical professions, social-security services and Ministry of the Interior. From their number inspectors are chosen to work among juveniles. They are empowered primarily to deal with petty offenses, but they may nevertheless be given other duties by the court. They can refer persistent young offenders between eleven and fourteen years old to special educational institutions, usually boarding schools with special disciplinary powers.[42]

India

Delinquency control in India is almost as old as that in England and the United States. The Apprentices Act of 1850 gave the courts power to make apprentices of children between the ages of ten to eighteen years who had been found guilty of petty offenses or in destitute circumstances. The later Reformatory Schools Act of 1876 and its revision of 1897 established reform schools where children under the age of sixteen in the Bombay presidency and under the age of fifteen in some other presidencies could be detained from two to seven years. Such schools were provided only for boys until 1917, when the Society for Protection of Children in Western India urged treatment of juvenile delinquents of both sexes.[43]

A memorandum submitted to the government on February 28, 1918, finally resulted in the Bombay Children Act of 1924, which went into operation in 1927 and was revised in 1948. In subsequent years, other Indian legislative bodies in Bengal, Madras, and the Central Provinces passed protective and preventive measures. Juvenile courts, certified schools and institutes, homes, aftercare associations, and children's-aid societies were established, the whole development closely following the Anglo-American pattern of delinquency control. In most parts of India the upper age limit of delinquency was set at sixteen years. A Borstal system, similar to that in England, was organized for youths between the ages of sixteen and twenty-one. Although children could not be sentenced to death and transportation, they could be sentenced to imprisonment in exceptional cases. Delinquent children could be detained in certified schools or institutions or released on probation. If they were found to be destitute, homeless, consorting with thieves or prostitutes, or involved in delinquency, they could be brought to juvenile court. The police were also empowered to seize any cigarette, tobacco, or other smoking material or instrument found in the possession of a child in any public place.[44]

The Indian juvenile courts are separate from the ordinary criminal courts, and a stipendiary magistrate, who sits with one or two honorary lady magistrates (usually psychologists or sociologists), presides over each. The judge investigates the child's total circumstances, in an attempt to discover the best solution for his future. The Indian juvenile court works in the interests of the child, in order to help him grow up to be a decent citizen.[45]

Indian probation services, also organized on Anglo-American lines, were first developed for juvenile cases. As the program grew, special courses were introduced at the Institute of Social Sciences in Bombay and at the University of Calcutta, in order to train probation personnel. Alternative programs for youths not placed on probation were developed at such training or certified schools and homes as the David Lassoon Industrial School in Bombay, the Children's Home in Chembure, the Bryamjee Jeejeebhoy Home in Western India, the Yeravada Industrial School in Poona, and the Shri Shahu Chatrapati Boarding House in Satera.[46] Although India was one of the first countries to recognize the need for organized delinquency control, making great efforts to achieve a level of institutional control comparable to those in England and the United States after World War I, some limitations in its treatment programs result from the nature of the Indian social system (including overpopulation and a less structured political system) and the relative backwardness of the Indian economy.

■ Treatment Research in the United States

Guided group-interaction programs for treatment and prevention of delinquency have been based on the premise that juvenile delinquency is usually a group experience and can best be modified by focusing primarily upon the group. By involving the offenders in frequent, prolonged, and intensive discussions of the behavior of individuals within the group, proponents of guided group interaction seek to stimulate the emergence of individual and group responsibility and self-help efforts. The concentration of group members upon the participant's current experience and problems, they believe, encourages the group to develop a meaningful "culture" of mutual participation in self-correction. When this "culture" emerges and the group accepts greater responsibility, the group leader, a staff member, then attempts to encourage broader sharing of authority between staff and the offenders. Consequently, early group decisions, largely restricted to routine issues, are expanded to include more important questions.

The Hawthorne-Cedar Knolls School

Efforts to prevent delinquency have proceeded with collateral efforts to develop treatment programs for delinquency that cannot be prevented. The Hawthorne-Cedar Knolls School in Thornwood, N.Y., established in the early 1900s by the Jewish Board of Guardians of New York, provided the setting for one of the earliest of these research experiments. It was a relatively small institution housing some 200 boys and 50 girls between eight and eighteen years old, ten percent of whom were not Jewish; the children boarded and roomed in cottages of twenty to twenty-five boys or girls. The campus included administrative offices, a guidance center, classrooms, workshops, gymnasiums, an infirmary, and synagogue, in addition to the student cottages.

The first treatment attempt at this school, similar in many ways to the eighteenth-century programs at San Michele in Rome, failed. It was based on military discipline, in which boys and girls were marched to work; ate, slept, attended classes, and worked in silence and directed by bells; and faced severe punishment for personal infractions of the rules. The ineffectual handling of the institutional budget merely compounded the school's failure. In the mid-1920s, however, the institution underwent a radical change and began to carry on a delinquency-treatment program in a freer atmosphere. Vocational training; organized leisure activities in the form of games, dances, and walks; and visits to neighboring villages were added to the regular institutional educational program. During the average two-year stay of the youth, the institutional staff maintained frequent contacts with the parents and adjusted the program to each individual's home circumstance. Because its treatment was rather individualized and strongly based on psychotherapy, it necessarily depended upon the work of professional personnel and the cooperation of parents.

Berkshire Farm

The Berkshire Farm, located in Berkshire, accommodated only boys between twelve and sixteen years old. As at the Hawthorne-Cedar Knolls School, the boys lived in cottages under the supervision and guidance of cottage parents. School classes continued only through the eighth grade, and students also engaged in recreation and agricultural work. Treatment was largely psychological, tailored to individual needs. Psychiatrists, psychologists, and psychologically trained social workers sought to encourage adjustment and to solve individual problems through group living at the farm.[47]

The Cambridge-Somerville Youth Study

The children of the Cambridge and Somerville, Massachusetts, schools provided the universe of the Cambridge-Somerville Youth Study. Initiated by Richard Cabot and financed by the Cabot Foundation, the study was an attempt to demonstrate the beneficial effects of social work in preventing juvenile delinquency. The treatment program largely consisted of concentrated and intensive social-work services, including counseling, psychiatric and medical care, recreation, and other appropriate social-work assistance, facilities, and techniques.

The program was limited to boys selected from several hundred youth for whom delinquent careers were predicted. They were randomly divided into control and treatment groups. The latter received social-work treatment in an attempt to test the hypothesis that potential delinquents may develop into conforming, law-abiding youths if they receive adult friendship and understanding, counseling, guidance, and maximum community assistance. Consequently, the full spectrum of social-work service was made available to every child in the treatment experiment.[48]

Begun in 1936, the study was terminated in 1945 because of rather vague and partly disappointing results, which made evaluation difficult. A follow-up study of the Cambridge-Somerville Project was launched in 1956. Edwin Powers and Helen L. Witmer praised the generosity and ambition of the project, but they argued that it was a "professionally rather naive program" that could not effectively diminish the problem of juvenile delinquency.[49] Although it was more than mere professionalized charity, the experiment, which accepted given conditions but attempted to overcome juvenile difficulties through specialized help, did little to restructure social situations.

The Orthogenic School

The Orthogenic School, located close to the University of Chicago campus, was established in 1944 for the treatment of seriously disturbed juvenile delinquents.[50] It was a small school, with about forty children, designed for group living. New students therefore were admitted only during the Christmas and summer breaks, when entering newcomers would not disturb the program in progress. The Orthogenic School, an unenclosed urban institution, avoided a country atmosphere. Its proponents hypothesized that city delinquents could not be corrected in a rural milieu, despite apparent reform, because "corrected youths would relapse upon their return to the city." Students, largely from the University of Chicago, were used as fresh, energetic, and sympathetic counselors, and staff members engaged in vigorous therapeutic efforts. Although the school was structured for group living, each child received individual treatment.

The Highfields Project

Highfields was founded by Lloyd McCorkle in the old Lindbergh mansion in New Jersey in 1950 as "an experimental, short-term residential treatment center for twenty adjudicated delinquent boys aged sixteen to eighteen."[51] Relying on group interaction in a rather free and informal institution with a minimum of regulations and a rehabilitative atmosphere, the staff encouraged personal development and treatment of the delinquent. High-fields was an open institution, and the delinquent was informed upon admission that escape would not be prevented but would be regarded as a violation of probation. Although the average stay at Highfields was only about three or four months, the staff believed that attitudes can be changed in a short time if the delinquent boy is psychologically and psychiatrically normal. Staff members applied basic principles and techniques to under-mine delinquent attitudes and build favorable self-concept.[52] By day the youths worked at a nearby mental institution; in the evenings they par-ticipated in group-counseling sessions. On Saturday morning they cleaned up the residence; Saturday afternoon and Sunday were set aside for leisure, family visits, and church attendance. Although few effectiveness studies of Highfields have been completed, tentative results suggest that the program is as effective as that of the reformatory but involves less cost and less treatment time.

Pinehills: The Provo Experiment

Treatment during probation was tested in a community experiment called Pinehills, developed at Provo, Utah, in 1956.[53] Created for male recidi-vists for crimes against property, between thirteen and seventeen years of age, the experiment was designed to gather diagnostic information and to treat juveniles simultaneously. By first submitting youths to new experi-ences and then involving them in a group discussion, the double goal was realized. Two hypotheses dominated the experiment: Delinquent behavior is a group phenomenon, a shared deviation resulting from different group experiences in a particular subculture, rather than an individual act, and the lives of slum or lower-class youth are characterized by learning situa-tions that limit their access to success goals.

The experiment was divided into two parts, according to these hy-potheses. In the first phase an attempt was made to create an institutional social system oriented toward changing social situations. By eliminating normal format structures within the institution, it was hoped that the boys would turn to the group through frequent group discussions, visits to community organizations, and even discussions with selected inmates of neighboring penal institutions. In each discussion the goal was to illustrate the consequences to the boys of delinquency and existing alternatives, to provide means for their personal reform, and to enlist their aid in the re-habilitation of others. The second phase of the program involved an effort to maintain reference-group support while turning the boys toward use-ful activities. Having experienced a certain amount of reform in the first phase, they now learned how to work and study in order to advance to new goals. The Provo experiment necessarily involved the cooperation of the juvenile courts, rehabilitation agencies, and parents. As an attempt to find a substitute for imprisonment, it anticipated many of the educational and reform goals of Soviet institutions.

In the Pinehills and the similar Essexfields experiments in New Jersey, both patterned after the Highfields project, the offenders continue to live at home. At Pinehills all boys work for the city whether on the street, on the golf course, in the cemetery, or at other designated sites, at 50 cents an hour. During the late afternoon they meet daily for group sessions and are free to return home after 7:00 P.M. In these sessions all participants are responsible for defining problems and finding solutions. Because the youths remain in the community, they do not have to adjust to artificial institutional life and are helped instead to adjust to their own community. The apparent effectiveness of this approach stimulated the growth of other variations of the Highfields, Essexfields and Pinehills experiments in the Parkland project in Louisville, Kentucky; the Girls Unit for Intensive Daytime Education (GUIDE) in Richmond, California; and another girls' program in San Mateo, California.

Foster-Home Placement

In recent years foster-home placement has been a common alternative to institutionalization. Of the 233 probation departments surveyed in the National Survey of Corrections (reported by the President's Commission in 1967) 42 percent used foster homes in juvenile care or aftercare. Not only does the foster-home approach minimize the stigma of delinquency and keep the youth within the community, but it also lessens the costs of treatment. Foster care is not without other severe costs, however. A decision to sever family ties, for example, is most difficult, especially if the youth might otherwise have been placed on probation at home. Nevertheless, the use of foster homes continues, although several states have begun to develop group homes that offer similar care for youths who need an institutional setting or are unable to adjust to family life. Under an arrangement with the Minnesota Youth Commission, for example, seven group homes received a nominal retaining fee for each licensed bed, an amount that increased when a youth was actually placed in the home. The Wisconsin Division of Corrections, following a similar plan, maintained thirty-three homes for boys and girls, with four to eight adolescents in each. The plan allowed the Division to care for these delinquents at a saving of 25 to 33 percent over the cost for an equivalent institutional population. Since 1965, California has offered subsidies to those county probation departments that are successful in reducing commitments to state institutions through development of improved community-based programs.[54] Although little research on the effectiveness of foster-home placement has been conducted to date, such care remains a favorite of probation personnel.

The California Youth Authority's Community Treatment Project

Combining sound research with creative innovation, the California Youth Authority has proceeded with a project involving both boys and girls committed to the youth authority from Sacramento and San Joaquin Counties. After a screening process designed to eliminate the most serious and mentally abnormal offenders, the remaining youthful offenders are randomly admitted either to the project or to an institution. Those assigned to the project undergo extensive testing designed to measure their delinquent values, as well as their personality characteristics. The program applies the most modern techniques available through individual or group counseling, group and family therapy or both, on an individual basis. With a staff-to-inmate ratio of 1:12, the treatment plan operates at a high level of intensity. The program center includes a recreation area, music room, and classrooms and serves as a form of state settlement house for counseling, tutoring, and recreational activity. Although evaluations of the treatment project continue, a report covering the 1962–1966 period revealed that 28 percent of the experimental group had had their paroles revoked at the end of fifteen months of parole exposure, compared to 52 percent of the control group, which underwent regular institutional and parole processing.[55] Since 1964 this program has been extended to the Watts area of Los Angeles and a west Oakland neighborhood with less striking results.[56]

Reception-Center and Short-Term Treatment Parole

Under the diagnostic-parole approach all commitments from the juvenile court are referred to a state reception center for determination of eligibility for immediate parole or parole after short-term treatment. Developed in the early 1960s in the states of New York, Washington, and California, these programs have diverted large numbers of offenders from training schools to intensive community-treatment programs followed by parole in the community. Once again California has been in the forefront, making the greatest state use of reception-center releases. Approximately 20 percent of the boys and 35 percent of the girls referred in California are released on regular parole or to foster homes at the end of the reception period.[57]

Under the California Youth Authority's Marshall Plan, a program devised to ease population pressures upon juvenile institutions, selected juveniles may be treated intensively for three-month periods at the Norwalk reception center. Youths work in a half-day program in operation and maintenance of institutions, some specialized education classes, and daily group counseling. Active participation is rewarded by progressively longer and more frequent home furloughs. Parents may participate in group-counseling activities at the center when they accompany their sons back from home visits. An early attempt to measure the effectiveness of the Marshall Plan disclosed that 44 percent of its participants had had their paroles revoked within fifteen months, compared to 47 percent of the matched group, despite the fact that their treatment was only three months and the average institutional stay of control-group members was eight to nine months. These early results suggest the value of this program in delinquency treatment and control.[58]

NOTES

1. The history of social work and charity is outlined in most social-work textbooks.

2. Mary B. Novick, "Community Programs and Projects for the Prevention of Juvenile Delinquency,"*Juvenile Delinquency Facts-Facets* (Washington, D.C.: 1960), 2.

3. Gordon Rose, "Early Identification of Delinquents," *The British Journal of Criminology* (January 1967). See Sheldon Glueck, "Identification of Potential Delinquents: Supportive Rationale," paper presented at the Fifth International Criminological Congress at Montreal, 1965.

4. For a comparison of world methods of prevention and incarceration, age limits for delinquent status, and statistical interpretations of data, see Albert G. Hess, *The Young Adult Offender* (New York: 1965).

5. *Op. cit.*, pp. 11–12.

6. Programs designed to try out treatment methods, rather than deliberately to involve community participation in delinquency prevention and control (as in the Provo Experiment), are mentioned in another chapter.

7. Sylvan S. Furman, *Reaching the Unreached* (New York: 1952); see also John M. Gandy, "Preventive Work with Street-Corner Groups, Hyde Park Youth Project, Chicago," *Annals of the American Academy of Political and Social Science,* 322 (March 1959), 107–116; Walter B. Miller, "Preventive Work with Street-Corner Groups, Boston Delinquency Project," *Annals of the American Academy of Political and Social Science,* 322 (March 1959), 97–106; and Ralph W. Whelen, "New York City's Approach to the Delinquency Problem," *Federal Probation,* 17 (December 1953), 19–25.

8. G. Lewis Penner, "An Experiment in Police and Social Agency Cooperation," *Annals of the American Academy of Political and Social Science,* 322 (March 1959), 79–88. For an international evaluation of future police action, see United Nations, *The Role and Future of the Police in the Field of Crime Prevention* (New York: 1965).

9. Sophia M. Robison, *Juvenile Delinquency: Its Nature and Control* (New York: 1960), p. 470.

10. Solomon Kobrin, "The Chicago Area Project: A 25 Year Assessment," *Annals of the American Academy of Political and Social Science,* 322 (March 1959), 19–29.

11. A wealth of material on this topic has been published by the United Nations, including: "Some Aspects of the Prevention of Juvenile Delinquency: Conclusions and Recommendation"; "Community Preventive Action"; "Social Forces and the Prevention of Criminality"; and "The Prevention of Crime and the Treatment of Offenders." For a comparison of delinquency-prevention programs in nine countries, see William C. Kvaraceus, *Anxious Youth: Dynamics of Delinquency* (Columbus, O.: 1966).

12. *The Treatment of Offenders in Britain* (London: 1960), p. 1. See also United Nations, *The Role of Vocational Guidance Training and Employment Opportunity and Work in Youth Adjustment and the Prevention of Juvenile Delinquency* (New York: 1965).

13. *Ibid.,* p. 3.

14. *Ibid.,* p. 4.

15. The Prison Act of 1877.

16. *The Treatment of Offenders in Britain,* p. 4.

17. *Ibid.,* p. 6; see also Stephen Schafer, *Ax Uj Angol Büntetönovella* (Budapest: 1949).

18. Home Office, *Penal Practice in a Changing Society* (London: 1959).

19. *The Treatment of Offenders in Britain,* pp. 29–37.

20. *Ibid.,* p. 32.

21. *Ibid.,* p. 33.

22. *Ibid.,* p. 34.

23. Home Office, *op. cit.,* p. 1.

24. *Ibid.,* pp. 6–11. For a discussion of the Israeli context, see Shlomo Shoham and Meir Hovav, "Some Social Factors, Treatment Aspects and Criminal Career of 'B'nei-Tovim,' Middle and Upperclass Delinquency in Israel," unpublished paper presented to the Fifth International Criminological Congress in Montreal, 1965.

25. Harold J. Berman, *Justice in the U.S.S.R.: An Interpretation of Soviet Law* (rev. ed.; New York: 1963), p. 13.

26. John N. Hazard, *Law and Social Change in the U.S.S.R.* (London: 1953), p. 85.

27. Many persons cannot or do not want to think of the Soviet social revolution in terms of a fully designed program, in which any apparent "change" is only an indeterminate phase in the state of crime and delinquency problems. See Edward Crankshaw, *The Observer* (March 22, 1964), p. 11.

28. The Cheka, originally headed by Feliks Dzerzhinski, was later reorganized several times under different names but has remained a most important permanent part of the Soviet government.

29. "Ugolovnyi Kodiks," *Sobranie Uzakonenii i Rasporiazhenii RSFSR, 1919 (Collection of Laws and Orders),* No. 66, item 590.

30. *Ugolovnyi Kodiks RSFSR,* 1922, No. 15, item 153.

31. *Sob. Uzak.,* 1926, No. 80, item 600.

32. Rudolf Schlesinger, *Soviet Legal Theory: Its Social Background and Development* (New York: 1945), p. 31.

33. Berman, *op. cit.,* p. 229.

34. *Sob. Uzak.,* 1935, No. 32, item 252.

35. Berman, *op. cit.*, p. 332.

36. *Sob. Uzak.*, 1935, No. 32, item 252.

37. Because eighteen is the age under which capital punishment was prohibited, it can mark the limit.

38. M. M. Isajev, "The Minor Age," in V. D. Menisagin, ed., *Soviet Criminal Law: Textbook for Universities* (Budapest: 1951), pp. 254–259, in Hungarian.

39. Nikita Khrushchev's speech to the XIII Komsomol Congress, on April 18, 1958.

40. Boris S. Nikiforov, "Fundamental Principles of Soviet Criminal Law," *The Modern Law Review*, 23 (January 1969), 41–42.

41. Berman, *op. cit.*, p. 383.

42. Institute for the Study and Treatment of Delinquency, *Russia—A New Look at Crime* (London: 1966), p. 10. This report offers valuable insights into Soviet delinquency and the Soviet treatment system.

43. M. J. Sethna, *Society and the Criminal* (Bombay: 1952), pp. 342–343.

44. *Ibid.*, p. 346.

45. D. A. Dhruva, *Annual Report of the Juvenile Branch on the Administration of the Children Act in the Bombay Province, 1939–1940* (Bombay).

46. Sethna, *op. cit.*, pp. 361–370.

47. For a more comprehensive description and evaluation of the Hawthorne-Cedar Knolls School and Berkshire Farm, see Robison, *op. cit.*, Chapters 24 and 26.

48. Edwin Powers and Helen L. Witmer, *An Experiment in the Prevention of Delinquency* (New York: 1959); and Robison, *op. cit.*, pp. 490–496.

49. Powers and Witmer, *op. cit.*, p. 577.

50. For description, evaluation, and case studies, see Bruno Bettelheim, *Love Is Not Enough* (New York: 1950); and Bettelheim, *Truants from Life* (New York: 1955).

51. Richard R. Korn and Lloyd W. McCorkle, *Criminology and Penology* (New York: 1961), p. 575. See U.S. Children's Bureau, *Juvenile Delinquency Prevention in the United States* (Washington, D.C.: 1965).

52. Lloyd W. McCorkle, Albert Elias, and F. Lovell Bixby, *The Highfields Story* (New York: 1957), pp. iv–viii.

53. For description and evaluation see Lamar T. Empey, *The Provo Experiment in Delinquency* (Provo: 1959); see also Empey and Jerome RaBow, "The Provo Experiment in Delinquency Rehabilitation," *American Sociological Review*, 26 (October 1961), 679–695.

54. Robert W. Winslow, *Juvenile Delinquency in a Free Society* (Belmont, Calif.: 1968), pp. 226–227. See also U.S. Children's Bureau, *Halfway House Programs for Delinquent Youth* (Washington, D. C.: 1965).

55. See California Youth Authority, Division of Research, *Community Treatment Reports* (Sacramento: 1962–1966), Nos. 1–7.

56. See also Virginia M. Burns and Leonard W. Stern, "The Prevention of Juvenile Delinquency," in President's Commission on Law Enforcement and Administration of Justice, *Task Force Report: Juvenile Delinquency and Youth Crime* (Washington, D.C.: 1967), pp. 353–408.

57. Winslow, *op. cit.*, p. 320. See also Stanton Wheeler, Leonard S. Cottrell, Jr., and Anne Romasco, "Juvenile Delinquency: Its Prevention and Control," in President's Commission on Law Enforcement and Administration of Justice, *Task Force Report: Juvenile Delinquency and Youth Crime* (Washington, D.C.: 1967), pp. 409–428.

58. Recent volumes on prevention and control include Robert M. MacIver, *The Prevention and Control of Delinquency* (New York: 1966); David M. Downes, *The Delinquent Solution* (New York: 1966); John R. Stratton and Robert M. Terry, *Prevention of Delinquency* (New York: 1968); Otto L. Shaw, *Youth in Crisis* (New York: 1966); David Street, Robert D. Vinter, and Charles Perrow, *Organization for Treatment* (New York: 1966); Don C. Gibbons, *Changing the Law-breaker* (Englewood Cliffs, N.J.: 1965); S. R. Slavson, *Re-Educating the Delinquent* (New York: 1954); H. Ashley Weeks, *Youthful Offenders at Highfields* (Ann Arbor: 1963); and William E. Amos and Charles F. Wellford, *Delinquency Prevention* (Englewood Cliffs, N.J.: 1967).

■ Epilogue: Into the Future

■ Delinquency and the Future

Despite the many continuing attempts to measure and prevent delinquency, control of juvenile deviance is not likely to occur through the enactment of some simple preventative program or the creation of new juvenile training schools. Although such approaches undoubtedly appeal to many traditionalists, the continuing increase in delinquency makes such procedures financially impractical. Even though it is reasonable to forecast that the number of adult criminals likely to be incarcerated within the next ten years will increase only slightly, juvenile confinement projections, if current policies continue, point to a potential 70 percent increase by 1975. If this estimate holds true, the number of Federal, state, and local correctional institutions would have to be increased from 44,000 to 74,000 by that year.

Ultimately, evaluators of the deliquency problem must recognize the need to involve youths in a society that respects them and provides them with meaningful opportunities for responsibility. The major modifications in social relationships brought about by war, changing definitions of traditional sex roles, the sharp increase in teenage affluence, and the mobility available to the modern adolescent have had a profound effect on family living, employment aspirations, attitudes toward police officers, and styles of ghetto life. Racial fears and hostility, too, cannot be neglected as important ingredients in the delinquency process. Growing American urbanization and delay in political response to the needs of the impoverished are also basic delinquency-stimulating factors. Although juvenile delinquency cannot be directly correlated with poverty, inferior education, inadequate housing, poor health conditions, high unemployment, or working mothers, the influence of these factors cannot be discounted in delinquency causation. Even though it is doubtful that new housing, better schools, full employment, and more adequate health care will cause a direct reduction of delinquent activity, there is little chance that any significant decrease will occur in the rate of such conduct until attempts are made to bring about several of these conditions. Consequently, attempts at treatment of juveniles through probation or rehabilitation at training schools are likely to be undermined by the environmental conditions of the offender's home community.

Obviously, delinquency cannot be prevented or controlled simply by adding more police to the local force. It is a product of the modern social structure, which is characterized by commodity acquisitiveness, individual and group anomie, power-group control, and psychological and familial shortcomings. It is related to the failure of the modern urban community to integrate its members into a coherent whole, a failure that is also evident in many families. Consequently, much of delinquency is a product of the juvenile's need for coherence, which adults view as a threat to their own privileged existence. The failure to understand the subculture of youths, most evident in the so-called "generation gap," is only a symptom of the continuing problem. Because the volume of delinquency has become so large, it is no longer possible to ignore its scope by developing small experimental programs for twenty to forty youths. Neither is it possible any longer to define human worth in terms of the traditional middle-class Protestant ethic that correlates one's personal value with economic productivity. The advent of more leisure time, the shorter work-week, and the unavailability of jobs for many unskilled parents and juveniles have made revision and modification of the traditional ethic mandatory. What is ultimately necessary is confrontation with the basic character of the urban complex, the modern industrial system, and the excessive dehumanization of citizens that have emerged as by-products of the mass society. The failure of the educational system to prepare marginal youths to complete economically, the structural dependence of youths upon the decisions of their elders, and the increasing qualifications and skills demanded for future employment are all factors that make an impact upon youths in the changing community.

Delinquency is not limited to any one community or nation. It is part of the human condition and is in many ways a structural response to that condition. Although it is a problem of the government, it cannot be solved by mere governmental action or the creation of state delinquency programs. Delinquency is partially a product of socioethical immaturity, family instability, depersonalization of living arrangements, and ethnic and racial prejudice. An excessive dependence upon law as a means of forcing expected behavior without the adequate socialization of the juvenile to expected roles is centrally involved in the delinquency increase in America, however. Consequently, greater emphasis must be placed upon the identification and treatment of potential delinquents in the early school years and less upon the desire to purge the youthful offender from the community of man. But the many facets involved in the delinquency process suggest that even when this is accomplished, the prevention and control of delinquency will not become even a near-reality unless greater discretion in invoking its judicial power is developed by the community, less serious types of offenses are excluded from delinquency definitions, problems of dependency and neglect are differentiated from antisocial behavior, revisions are made in police decision-making and referral practices, additional judicial alternatives for disposition of juveniles are developed by the community, and the juvenile court renews its earlier attempt to protect and to rehabilitate youths. These are not simple matters, yet the problem of delinquency can be solved only in this manner.

■ Projecting What the Future Holds

Any attempt to predict the parameters of future delinquency problems is open to a high degree of speculation. However, three general areas of interest—legal, social, and biological—seem to hold some potential insight into our understanding of delinquency in later generations.

The Legal Rights of Juveniles in Court: Kent and Gault Decisions

Probably the most important legal decisions concerning delinquency rendered in the last sixty years have been the 1966 Supreme Court decision of *Kent versus United States* and its 1967 counterpart, *Gault versus Arizona*. As legal judgments, they clearly modified the boundaries of earlier juvenile court philosophy, which originally established that court as one of civil procedure, designed to offer children greater opportunities for regeneration,—opportunities not commonly available to the convicted offender in the criminal court—through the judge and his probation staff. While efforts to achieve the goal of effective juvenile treatment and rehabilitation continue, the Kent decision, made by a Federal court, and the Gault decision, made by a state court, have redefined juvenile due process and civil rights and have guaranteed to children the rights accorded to adults in criminal law. Although maintaining the concept that the juvenile court judge is a potential substitute parent empowered to protect the long-term interest of the child, the Kent and Gault decisions have limited the judge's right to intervene in juvenile family affairs without adequate cause.

The 1966 Kent decision expanded the juvenile's rights in Federal juvenile court by permitting or requiring a regular hearing on a complaint, defense counsel access to records pertinent to the case, and a statement of reasons for waiver of case jurisdiction from juvenile to criminal court. Recognizing that the juvenile often receives neither the protection afforded adults nor the solicitous care and regenerative treatment postulated for children, the Supreme Court has noted that the mere fact that someone is a minor does not excuse juvenile court from following Federal due process procedures.

However, it remained for the 1967 Gault decision to define the boundaries of state juvenile court procedures. The first state juvenile court case heard by the Supreme Court since the 1899 creation of the Chicago juvenile court, the Gault decision affirmed that the adolescent in delinquency hearings possesses the right to counsel, whether private or court appointed, if incarceration may result; that counsel has the right to confront and cross-examine witnesses; that the adolescent is entitled to adequate warning of his privilege against self-incrimination; that he has the right to remain silent; and that he must receive early notice of charges. The youth of the defendant, it noted, "does not justify a kangaroo court."

Although the exact implications of these legal decisions are not yet clear, it is already apparent that cases against juveniles will have to be prepared with greater thoroughness in the future. Whether according adult rights of due process to juveniles will hinder the rehabilitation of youth remains to be seen. Whereas it is possible that many juveniles will still be processed unilaterally in the guise of humanitarianism, it is probable that those who are adjudicated formally will receive greater protection in the court hearing, and consequently, there will be a reduction in the proportion of youths sent to training schools for rehabilitation. Adjudication in juvenile court is often a first step to a life of crime; conversely, it is possible that the increased demands of due process and collateral costs for legal services may encourage the delinquent's career toward criminality.

Many critics will undoubtedly blame the previously discussed decisions for any future delinquency increase, but their arguments will remain inconclusive inasmuch as the number of delinquency-age youths will also increase. Although some will argue that these decisions have undermined the whole concept of the regenerative treatment of juveniles, others will contend that nothing has really changed in actual juvenile court practice. Only the future will provide insight into the question of whether these decisions were advances in the history of juvenile rights or whether they were actually a return to the single status concept of adjudication of past centuries, which required that juveniles be subjected to the same procedures and punishments accorded adults. In any case, the Kent and Gault decisions will have a major influence upon the shape of future delinquency.

The Victim in Delinquency: Victimology

The social issue that will be of paramount importance in the future concerns the study of victimology—an examination of the impact of delinquency and crime upon the offender's victim. Although not a new idea, having been considered several centuries ago by Cesare Lombroso,

Raffaele Garofalo and Enrico Ferri, interest in the victim in the delinquency-crime process has increased as juvenile and criminal deviance
has increased. Emphasizing the interactional totality of the delinquent
or criminal act, the study of criminal-victim relationships recognizes the
role and responsibility of the victim in the origin of the offense, the search
for effective justice, the eventual treatment of the juvenile offender, and
the functional solution of the delinquency problem. A unifying concept,
it treats the deviant or criminal event as an integral part of the youth's
life. In addition, victimology examines the delinquent's potential ability
to reimburse his victim and the relationship of reparations to the treatment and prevention process.

Although studies of the delinquent and criminal victim are only now
coming to the forefront, several tendencies are nevertheless apparent. For
example, Stephen Schafer found that although strangers (third persons)
are victims of crime more often than members of any other category in
interpersonal relations, their frequency at victimization is highest within
the under-twenty-one age group and decreases in relation to the age of
the criminal. In general, the older the offender, the more likely he is to
commit a crime against his family, relatives, and friends. Marvin E.
Wolfgang also investigated this point. On the one hand, Evelyn Gibson
and S. Klein report that infants of less than one year of age account for
over 1 percent of all murder victims and children under fourteen represent approximately 6 percent. This proportion is considerably higher in
England, however, where about 7 percent of infants less than one year
of age and more than 26 percent of children under the age of sixteen
are murder victims. Nearly three-fourths of English juvenile victims are
murdered by a parent or older relative. English girls between five and
sixteen are especially likely to be murder victims.

These preliminary findings suggest that even greater success in research is still ahead. Little work has been done, for example, in determining the exact quality of interactional relations between the victim
and the offender, the costs of the delinquent act to the victim during his
lifetime, or even the effects of institutional victimization upon the adjudicated offender. Although victimology is a fairly new field, discoveries
in this social area may well help to define new future directions in prevention and treatment of juvenile delinquency.

Chromosomes and Delinquency: The XYY Factor

Important to the consideration of the biological dimensions of delinquency
is the current investigation of the relationship between sex chromosome
structures and delinquency-crime patterns. Historically, many theorists
have attempted to link deviance to physical characteristics. Yet only in
recent years have Patricia A. Jacobs, J. A. Strong, S. Muldal, C. H. Ockey,

and M. D. Casey found some evidence to suggest that delinquency is related to a hereditary chromosome imbalance. Although Jacobs and Strong were among the first to demonstrate that the XYY chromosome constellation might predispose its possessor to delinquent-criminal behavior, Muldal and Ockey found evidence that the double male constellation of XXYY, although rare, typically produced tall males with a low I.Q. M. D. Casey subsequently discovered that XXYY males were found in large proportion among hard-to-manage male criminals of subnormal intelligence. W. H. Price and P. P. Whatmore concluded as a result of their studies that the extra Y chromosome has a "deleterious effect" on the behavior of men and predisposes them to criminal acts. Their research gained international attention when the defense for Richard Speck proposed the use of their findings as a ground for an appeal of Speck's conviction for the murder of several Chicago nurses.

In recent months, however, the promise of this lead has diminished. Other researchers have questioned the validity of these findings and noted that their own studies disclosed that the average population is composed of a comparable percentage of XYY recipients who evidence no delinquent or criminal tendencies. Although the question remains unanswered at this time, it nevertheless seems to be one aspect of the most promising future biological approaches to the delinquency problem. But with the speed of change in modern times and the unending insights into human behavior, these findings, as well as promising legal and social leads, are only momentary "absolutes" in the history of relative human relations.

INDICES

■ *Name Index*

■ Subject Index

About the Authors

Stephen Schafer is a Professor of Sociology and Criminology at Northeastern University. He has also been affiliated with the University of Budapest, the Polytechnic, in London, Florida State University, and Ohio University. He is the author of *Restitution to Victims of Crime*, *The Victim and His Criminal*, and *Theories in Criminology*, in addition to articles in various journals published in Hungary, England, and the United States.

Richard D. Knudten is Professor and Chairman of the Department of Sociology at Valparaiso University. He was formerly a member of the faculties of the College of Wooster and Newberry College. He has written or edited *The Sociology of Religion*, *The Systematic Thought of Washington Gladden*, *Crime in American Society*, and *Criminological Controversies*.